Tolstoy and His Problems

SRLT

NORTHWESTERN UNIVERSITY PRESS
Studies in Russian Literature and Theory

SERIES EDITORS
Caryl Emerson
Gary Saul Morson
William Mills Todd III
Andrew Wachtel
Justin Weir

Tolstoy and His Problems

Views from the Twenty-First Century

Edited by Inessa Medzhibovskaya

NORTHWESTERN UNIVERSITY PRESS / EVANSTON, ILLINOIS

*In reverent memory of generous human beings and
nonconformist followers of Tolstoy's quest for justice:*

*Galina Galagan (1935–2014), philologist and Tolstoy scholar,
editor of Russkaia Literatura, Institute of Russian Literature
of the Academy of Sciences of Russia, Saint Petersburg*

*Eugene Lang (1919–2017), son of unemployed immigrants from
eastern Europe, born in Harlem, founder of Eugene Lang College of
Liberal Arts and philanthropist, whose favorite writer was Tolstoy*

Northwestern University Press
www.nupress.northwestern.edu

Printed in the United States of America

10 9 8 7 6 5 4 3 2 1

Library of Congress Cataloging-in-Publication Data

Names: Medzhibovskaya, Inessa, 1964– editor.
Title: Tolstoy and his problems : views from the twenty-first century / edited by
    Inessa Medzhibovskaya.
Other titles: Studies in Russian literature and theory.
Description: Evanston, Illinois : Northwestern University Press, 2019. | Series:
    Northwestern University Press studies in Russian literature and theory | Includes
    index.
Identifiers: LCCN 2018026415 | ISBN 9780810138803 (pbk. : alk. paper) | ISBN
    9780810138810 (cloth) | ISBN 9780810138827 (ebook)
Subjects: LCSH: Tolstoy, Leo, graf, 1828–1910—Political and social views. | Tolstoy,
    Leo, graf, 1828–1910—Criticism and interpretation. | Tolstoy, Leo, graf,
    1828–1910—Philosophy.
Classification: LCC PG3415.S6 T65 2019 | DDC 891.733—dc23
LC record available at https://lccn.loc.gov/2018026415

A quiet, simple country life, diversified by the
occasional arrival of friends and relatives, and
sustained and ennobled by a constant sense
of the world-wide magnitude of the great
problems at which the Count was working—
that was what I saw at Yasnaia Poliana. A
healthy, human, natural life, amidst books, and
children, and flowers, and birds, and bees, and
live-stock of all kinds, and simple country folk,
that was not a bad environment for a thinker
who ever hears through the sighing of the trees
the moanings of a troubled world, and yet
presses onward, nothing doubting, to the light
of a clearer and brighter day.
—W. T. Stead, *The Truth about Russia* (1888)

Considering its central theme of eternal problems interrogated from within the confines of one's own time, what could have been a better illustration for the cover of this book than Tolstoy's own diary drawing from November 30, 1903? He writes a reflection about eternal life in the middle of his work "On Shakespeare and On Drama" and just a few months after his having finished the short stories for the relief of the victims of the Kishinev pogrom. In the process, Tolstoy makes a graphic sketch of our way from the present to eternity: "There is just one thing that we know—that the whole realization of perfection for a human being consists in his greatest possible merger with eternal life, which is incomprehensible to him; in the greater and greater merger of his own line of life with those two infinite parallel lines that exert a pull on him toward themselves. The ideal life looks like this" (54: 199).

Tolstoy's drawing of a human's individuality is symbolized by dotted lines in the form of angled brackets. This individuality is enclosed unto itself at birth, but the arms of angled brackets extend in both directions from left to right to reach toward and then merge with the two parallel lines of eternity. Flowing out of the confines of individual space and extending into an empty space of a page is an unfinished phrase closed by a virgule: "and there is no death," [I net smerti,]. Tolstoy adds a little note just beneath the drawing: "It is without sense, but necessary for me" [Beztolkovo, no mne nuzhno] (54: 199).

Contents

Acknowledgments

To commemorate the centennial of Tolstoy's death and to think about the future of his ideas, Eugene Lang College of Liberal Arts at The New School sponsored an international symposium, "Tolstoy in the Twenty-First Century," that took place from October 14 through 17, 2010, in the renowned auditorium in the 66 West 12th Street building of The New School, which was designed by Joseph Urban. This is when the idea of the volume was born. The New School Provost's Office and Eugene Lang College awarded startup and opportunity research funds for this project at its inception and during the final stages of the work.

I would like to thank Provost Tim Marshall and Deans Stefania de Kenessey and Stephanie Browner for their support. Heartfelt thanks to Olga Knizhnik, Joel de Lara, and Joseph Lemelin for their help proofreading and formatting the essays for style and consistency. Special thanks to Laura Frost for her unstinting encouragement and to Yiye Cho for her art and friendship. At Northwestern University Press, Trevor Perri's expert guidance was invaluable for bringing the volume to completion and publication. He was the ideal editor. I am grateful to Gary Saul Morson and Mike Levine for inviting the proposal and its concept to the Studies in Russian Literature and Theory series, and to Maggie Grossman. We have much appreciated external reviewers' comments on this volume, which have helped us to make improvements. With her characteristic kindness and patience, Anne Gendler steered the book throughout the production process. Mike Ashby's queries and his attention to style have been incredible. Marianne Jankowski designed the cover using a drawing from Tolstoy's diary that illustrates his view on the human role in eternity. Over many years, Donna Orwin has supported the volume and has provided careful criticism to support the best effort that would do justice to Tolstoy's art and his ideas, and she wrote a warm and encouraging endorsement when the book was finished. J.D. Wilson, Greta Bennion, Emily Dalton, and Parneshia Jones have all taken care that the book reaches its potential readers.

Deep gratitude to Galina Zlobina and the Russian State Archive of

Literature and Arts for facilitating the preparation of high-resolution images from the Tolstoy collection and for granting permission for reproduction.

I would like to thank two colleagues at The New School who helped conceive the title of this book. Thank you to Ken Wark, professor of culture and media, for sharing the idea that the Tolstoy of the twenty-first century is so attractive because he remains the primordial force of nature as much as the force of restorative diversion from all heavily trodden and trendy paths and the obstructions caused by intellectual debris (what Guy Debord has termed *détournement*). And I thank Agnes Heller, Hannah Arendt Professor Emerita, for her luminous insight that Tolstoy poses undying problems but that as scholars—whether endangered or not, whether solitary or as part of a school—we should develop historically accurate approaches to these problems and express them through committed and well-grounded yet pluralist points of view and through responsible critical perspectives.

Last but not least, I would like to thank my friend and colleague Zishan Ugurlu, actor, director, and master of stagecraft, who put me face to face with the question: What are the elusive meanings of Tolstoy's problems, really? Can they be articulated precisely? Tolstoy often preferred to cache his meanings in uncouth parables and riddles. Take his tongue-tied character Akim from the comedic-didactic drama in five acts *The Power of Darkness, or "If a claw is caught, the whole bird is lost"* (1886; 26: 123–244). (For a list of citations and abbreviations in the book, see page xiii.) Akim conveys his meanings about godly life in an abbreviated form using the words "seems" and "lurks" [*tayeh*], holding on obstinately to the deep-hidden knowledge of his humble truth. Akim's worldly vocation [*otkhòzhii promysel*] is the seasonal cleaning of cesspools—the cleaning of "earth closets," as it used to be put in Shakespeare's time. It is worth noting that the phrase *otkhòzhii promysel* rhymes in Russian with *bòzhii promysel* ("God's providence"). Akim's speech-impediment in Tolstoy's play and his rhyming wordplay—of the basest with the most divine—is juxtaposed with the garrulous bravado of the retired soldier and heavy drinker Mitrich, who is also seeking justice. These two characters express Tolstoy's idea of a collaboration of the base and the lofty. They both release the "claw" of the passive central characters who are caught easily by evil and render them light like the birds of the air. Repentant, illumined by the inner light of truth, the former evil-doers are ready to bear responsibility for their crimes. To Tolstoy, the mix of the base and the lofty signifies nothing in particular; it was a matter of playful theatrical mechanics that is found all too frequently in Shakespeare. Out of the disparate essentials of Tolstoy's art—with which we have struggled in this volume— Ugurlu was able to produce an unforgettable version of Tolstoy's *The Power of Darkness* in March 2010 at La Mama Theater in New York. Ugurlu's interpretation inspired several central ideas of this volume: those of Tolstoy's unpretentious treatment of the riddles of life, his aesthetic rebelliousness, and his principled rejection of Shakespeare. (See Zishan Ugurlu and Inessa Medzhibovskaya, "*The Realm of Darkness* at La Mama, March 4–7, 2010: Interviews," *TSJ* 22 (2010): 85–90, and Caryl Emerson, Review Article: "Tolstoy on Stage: The Power of Darkness at La Mama," *TSJ* 22 (2010): 118–22.)

The unifying orientation of the contributions in this volume has been defined by this desire to release the claws of tired interpretations beholden to the unquestioning and automated acceptance of hypnotic cultural myths and catchphrases. The phrase "rather than" is therefore frequently used in our essays.

I dedicate this volume to the memory of two remarkable individuals: Galina Galagan, who was at the time of her death the world's leading reader and editor of Tolstoy's manuscripts and a brave resister to ideological pressure and coercion, who visited Lang in 2010 to give a talk, "Leo Tolstoy on Moral Perfection and on Perfecting the World," and who found perfect rapport with Lang students; and to Eugene Lang, who founded our seminar college, which bears his name, in 1985, and who lived by Tolstoy's ideas and proved their fruitful practicability.

—Inessa Medzhibovskaya

A Note on the Text

ABBREVIATED CITATIONS

The Jubilee L. N. Tolstoy, *Polnoe sobranie sochinenii v deviansta tomakh, Akademicheskoe Iubileinoe izdanie* [Complete collected works in ninety volumes, Academic Jubilee edition], ed. V. G. Chertkov et al. (Moscow: Khudozhestvennaia Literatura, 1928–58). Unless otherwise noted, all references in the present volume to Tolstoy's texts in Russian are to *The Jubilee* and cite the respective volume and page numbers, separated by a colon.

SS L. N. Tolstoy, *Sobranie sochinenii v dvadtsati dvukh tomakh* [Collected works in twenty-two volumes], ed. M. B. Khrapchenko, L. D. Opulskaia, et al., 22 vols. (Moscow: Khudozhestvennaia literatura, 1978–85). The majority of citations of the Russian text of *War and Peace* are to this edition, which is based on the corrected readings of the manuscripts.

TD *Tolstoy's Diaries*, ed. and trans. R. F. Christian, 2 vols. (New York: Scribner's, 1985).

TL *Tolstoy's Letters*, ed. and trans. R. F. Christian, 2 vols. (London: Athlone, 1978).

TSJ *Tolstoy Studies Journal*.

W&P Leo Tolstoy, *War and Peace*, trans. Richard Pevear and Larissa Volokhonsky (New York: Vintage, 2007).

Tolstoy's epilogues to *War and Peace* are referred to in the following way: "Epilogue I" for the first epilogue, "Epilogue II" for the second epilogue, and "Epilogues" for both epilogues. Parenthetical citations are as follows: EI followed by volume number (if any) and page number from the edition used for citations from the first epilogue, and EII followed by volume number (if any) and page number from the edition used for citations from the second epilogue, respectively.

TRANSLITERATION

We have stayed close to the modified Library of Congress romanization system for transliterating Russian and Cyrillic.

DATES

All dates of events that occurred in Russia before 1918, unless otherwise noted, refer to the Julian calendar then in effect in the territory of the Russian Empire. All dates in the same period covering the writings, publications, and letters of Tolstoy's correspondents, critics, and translators in the West adhere to the Gregorian calendar. On occasion, both calendar dates were necessary to mention in discussion. On these occasions, the first date given is from the Julian calendar, which is followed by the date from the Gregorian calendar in parentheses.

Tolstoy and His Problems

Tolstoy reading mail delivered on the occasion of his eightieth birthday. Courtesy of The Russian State Archives of Literature and Arts (RGALI), 508-8-1-9.

Inessa Medzhibovskaya

Introduction

Tolstoy and His Problems, Choosing a Perspective

> Any cardinal problem is a window through
> which we regard the world. Its tinted windows
> surely do to a certain degree color the world for
> us during the process. What opens up through
> this window—and through various windows in
> general—is immeasurably broader and more
> significant than the windows themselves.
> —S. N. Bulgakov (1912)

IN 2009, A SECRETIVE and immensely popular Russian postmodernist, Victor Pelevin, published his new novel *T*.[1] Released on the eve of the centennial of Tolstoy's death, it centers attention on liberating Tolstoy's problems from the confining matrices and clichés of reception by means of the creation of Tolstoy's double and the title character of the book, Count T. Count T does not know or remember who he is, whence he comes, or where he is headed in his search for the Optina Pustyn shrine, a place of escape to Russian Orthodox spirituality from the simultaneity of the mundane. The director of Count T's marketing team, which receives guidelines and orders from tech experts in the Kremlin and handles the algorithm of his functioning and its span, explains to him, "Marketing gurus are saying that Count Tolstoy is interesting to the public primarily as a count but not as Tolstoy. His ideas are not especially needed by anyone, and his books are in demand only because he had been a true aristocrat and from his infant swaddling to his very death he was swimming in total chocolate glamour. If *Anna Karenina* and *War and Peace* are still being read today it is to find out how the well-to-do lords used to live in Russia, before the times when Rublevka was even around.[2] And to find this out directly from the count's mouth" (94–95). Count T is a hero unraveling the algorithmic code of his own continuum. He is set up as an imitation of Alan Turing's computing machine, a work in progress in the hands of a conglomerate of marketing technologists, secret services, Church apparatuses, and Buddhist and Gnostic spiritual advisers. Count T malfunctions as a gadget on a sacral mission. He summarizes his doubts and frustrations in a conversation with his marketing director: "It turns out that Lev Tolstoy is solely *the source of problems* for you. You cannot even use his name in full. You need only his title" (95; emphasis added). Inspired by Lev Tolstoy, Count T saves himself by talking with his horse and periodically escaping into an eternal realm at the most crucial and improper moments. Once in a while, he slips through into eternity, where everything, much to his relief, is the same.

❋ ❋ ❋

Are escapes into eternity and eternal problems compatible with the problems of our time? And do they need to be? The conventional academic route for answering such questions is to debate the relevance of classics to our century and to its grim realities and promises: economic indeterminacy, financial profligacy, pessimism about politics, ecological irresponsibility, violence both high-tech and primitive. Can the classics suggest good protective and empowering strategies? How much can we make them implicated in resisting the decisionism that plagues our time? Can they render us free to travel, undocumented and unobserved, sanction our actions of protest and defiance, our love and sharing?

The word "problem" comes from the vocabulary of classical Greek, and it originally signified something completely different from the current understanding, even contrary to it: it is the act of "putting forth" (from the verb *proballein*). The verb literally means "throwing before," which anticipates its other ancient meanings, of putting forth a riddle and putting forth a task. Summarizing these ancient meanings in *Topics*, Aristotle creates the manual of the culture of proper problem identification and development, problem cultivation even, rather than of problem-solving.[3] Aristotle supports a dialectical approach that aims to reveal between "choice and avoidance, or truth and knowledge," leaving in their wake a good riddle and, in the aftermath of pondering the latter, we "come to know something else" (104b1–17, 173–74). Good problems (both universal, referring to all cases, and particular, referring to special cases) puzzle for a long time and may not quickly deliver a particular argument or perception—or a punishment for the wrong choice.

Tolstoy, with his many glaring contradictions—as Lenin had stamped them—a feudal lord with a penchant for antiautocratic anarchical exposure, a lover of simplicity and minimalism who lived in and conjured a world of plenitude, is a perfect fit for a puzzling problem that should be subjected, per Lenin's instructions, to a correct political and historical critique.[4] We do not necessarily need a leader of the Bolsheviks to promulgate this truth.[5] Critics are usually divided in their consideration of whether Tolstoy's integral epic complexity suffers or benefits from his crises and his attempts to return to patriarchal simplicity and religion. Take Tolstoy's contemporary Konstantin Leontiev, a religious thinker of a more conservative persuasion who observed in Tolstoy an unmatched "all-embracing totality" (*vsetselost'*) but asked that Tolstoy get rid of characters like Platon Karataev. Karataev is normally interpreted as Tolstoy's genius symbol of timeless Russianness, but to Leontiev he was quite the opposite: a trademark of transient Slavophile ideology.[6]

The question remains open about how to make the eternal and the undying palatable, useful, and instructional for the needs of the twenty-first-century reader counting every second of their earthly time and bristling quickly against the dangers of existential aggressions and social microaggressions. There is no denying that our communication with the classics is strongly influenced by the inherited and inculcated perceptions of them. In this regard, the weight of the twentieth century is still strong. It goes without saying that there has been a fair amount of ideological exploitation of Tolstoy and his problems: despite his patron image during the creation of the socialist-realist canon, Tolstoy resonated very poorly with the domestic and international projection of Stalinism or with developed socialism in the Soviet period with its marked interest in appropriating Tolstoy's genius for its own political gain combined with an ideological denial of Tolstoy's worldview. Let us look at the example of S. M. Breitburg, who is quoted several times in the essays in this volume. A faithful watchdog of Marxist-Leninism, Breitburg offered a lens for reading Tolstoy's problems as examples of a utopian-retrograde, moral-religious worldview and its crumbled past.[7] "His problems are not our problems" was for decades the motto of the Soviet era.

It is especially illuminating to note that the post-Communist kitsch version of Tolstoy described by Pelevin pushes aside as undesirable liabilities the spiritual struggles and humanitarian passions of Tolstoy in much the same way. The defamiliarization of Tolstoy's image from twentieth-century clichés has been the effort of the past thirty years and is reflected in several seminal collections of essays. The task of Hugh McLean's *In The Shade of the Giant* (1989) was to wrench Tolstoy away from the clutches of the Cold War divisions and to put him in dialogue with the masters of modernism (e.g., Joyce and Hemingway) and with dissident and émigré Russian literature and thought (e.g., Solzhenitsyn).[8] In a tide-turning forum of leading Western and Russian Tolstoy scholars in 1996, convened on the theme of brotherhood, Richard Gustafson admitted that Tolstoy's values are unavoidably no longer the values of our morally relativist, technologically determined, postcolonial world of mass culture and consumption obsessed with celebrity and wealth elitism. In his rather pessimistic comments, Gustafson found three links between Tolstoy's world and the coming world of the twenty-first century that put Tolstoy in need of reevaluation as an artist *and* moralist *and* religious thinker. These three links are our shared mortality (finality), our facticity (Gustafson borrows Heidegger's term to explain our existence as our membership in being), and the ethics of our mutual responsibility for all creation (Gustafson, "Tolstoy," 142–46).

A further step in the millennial elaboration of the Tolstoy problem was an introduction written for the volume *Tolstoy: Pro et Contra* (2000) by the Russian philosopher Konstantin Isupov. Isupov notes there that the creative life of Tolstoy is built on the principle of eclecticism that even in reading time through a biblical viewfinder sidesteps the commonsensical and aligns itself with the syncretism of the defamiliarized methods of seeing (Isupov finds Tolstoy comparable with Scriabin's synesthesia, Malevich's suprematism, Einstein's theory of relativity, the twelve-tone serialism of Schönberg, and with Georg Cantor's set theory, among other kinships). In short, Isupov sees the profound value of Tolstoy's problems in terms of their always transcending the possibility of final definition, despite the precision with which Tolstoy formulates them.[9] The general tendency of the past fifteen to twenty years has been to allow a prerogative of creative cooperation of Tolstoy the artist, thinker, and man. Most recently, there has been a recurrence of the opinion that Tolstoy the thinker is only occasionally relevant, and that it is only to a limited extent that his art could be judged as useful to the solution of our concrete plights.[10] To John Burt Foster, a charitable recent critic, the benefit of Tolstoy in the twenty-first century is how easily he can be read cooperatively, amenably, and "transnationally."[11]

❋ ❋ ❋

Anyone who reads Tolstoy's letters or his diary of any period of his life can immediately see that Tolstoy is not interested in fashionable or transient causes, that he isolates neither crises and disasters nor positive changes from the primary tasks and plural challenges of life. His creative work has always meant and will continue to mean different things to different readers. Quality and attentiveness of interpretation and a will to understand matter the most according to Ludwig Wittgenstein, who once observed, "Tolstoy: the meaning (meaningfulness) of a subject lies in its being generally understandable. That is true and false . . . Rather it is the contrast between the understanding of the subject and what most people want to see. Because of this the very things that are most obvious can become the most difficult to understand."[12] For Tolstoy, automatism of reception and uncritical adulation are enemies of understanding. These two come from our tendency to become slaves of the moment and easy prey to mass hypnotism.

What makes us slaves of the moment is an inability to commune with the eternal, which had begun with Hegel's relentless critique of Spinoza's notion of *sub specie aeternitatis* (Spinoza, *Ethics*, V, XXIII, Scholium), his umbrella term for the fusion of consciousness with a "rigid unyielding substance" in the shapeless abyss of the pantheist absolute, which obviates the need of a point of view, a perspective of the "understanding in act," and undermines "an eternal and infinite eventuality of thought."[13] The phenomenological turn in the study of the absolute presented in the fulcrum of what Tolstoy called, with contempt, a "historical point of view" (*istoricheskoe vozzrenie*) was perhaps Hegel's most lasting influence and one that Tolstoy had started protesting in his very first pieces of published work on education in the early 1860s. He was especially adamant in refusing to "live taking into consideration the demands of the time"[14] and accepting that works like *The Iliad* may be just the informative parameters for construing their relevance to our historical moment and an expression of the points of view of their historic past: "Based on this, the historical worldview not only does not argue about whether freedom is necessary for a human being, about whether there is or there is no God, or whether *The Iliad* is good or bad, not only does it do nothing for the attainment of the freedom that you desire, nothing for either persuading or dissuading you regarding the beauty of *The Iliad*, but it only points out the place that your inner demand, your love for truth or beauty, is occupying in history" (8:326).

Another enemy of free understanding for Tolstoy was hypnotism. He had studied hypnotism—a form of intellectual dramaturgy for conduction and influence—for decades and considered it overall an unscrupulous manipulation of consciousness used widely in the modern world.[15] In a diary entry of October 9, 1900, Tolstoy wrote of hypnotic inspiration (*vnushenie*) and indoctrination as obstacles to independent thought: "It is becoming clearer and clearer to me that the weaker the power of the sensation of an independent thought the easier it would be for man to imbibe what is being transmitted" (54:47). It would be even easier to influence a child. One way to resist hypnosis and to understand the subject is to practice defamiliarization, a term Victor Shklovsky introduced exactly a century ago without having considered Tolstoy's interest in employing defamiliarization as a tool of resistance and change, a device of creative decentering and disambiguation, the function of "freedom consciousness" (*svobodosoznanie*), one's resource of resistance to hypnosis.[16] Tolstoy offers the following conclusion to his rumination about why we do not question our automated actions, a conclusion that Shklovsky overlooked despite being otherwise inspired by Tolstoy's disdain for automatism: "Without consciousness there is no freedom, and without freedom there can be no consciousness. (If we are being subjected to violence and have altogether no choice as to *how we will endure this violence then we will feel no violence*)" (53:141–42; emphasis added). In what follows, we can witness how Tolstoy employs, in his late work "On the State" (1909), the same device to challenge the unquestioned status of the power of state institutions:

To think up the explanations for the existence of such a *strange institution*, where the will of one or several people may be the cause of all kinds of suffering, death, or, worst of all, the corruption of the many, to think up various reasons for this strikingly human institution, which is contrary to feeling and reason, is indeed very difficult, and the most abstract abstractions [*samye otvlechennye otvlechennosti*] are needed so that the simple, crude truth, the crude violence of man over man, the coercion by one man of the higher qualities of another would not be visible.[17]

✿ ✿ ✿

As our situation is becoming more precarious (environmentally, economically, politically), more dependent on the moment, on technologies, technologists, and administrators of the invisible forces that infiltrate our daily lives, interfere with our aspirations (which are far from confined to matters of electoral choice), we can find empowerment in that Tolstoy's problems compel us to develop fair and effective principles of organizing life that successfully trump the powers that hack our energies. Tolstoy's problems are those of the Aristotelian long-duration category, those from which we can continue to learn something new, and they still permeate our contemporary world, ever more powerfully and in a range of ways that go beyond literature and the literary. Addressing material and spiritual conditions, labor, art, love, the delivery of justice, and the scale of human needs—including the primary need, to be free and happy—they offer a possibility of a fresh evaluation of the ways we live, work, commune with nature and art, practice spirituality, exchange ideas and knowledge, become educated, and speak and think about social change and our historical future.

In this volume, we adopt some of the problems and part of the title from *Tolstoy and His Problems* (1901), Aylmer Maude's collection of essays written in the years 1896 to 1901 that represents one of the first comprehensive discussions of Tolstoy's worldview taken as a complex set of inseparable problems.[18] Maude was first drawn to Tolstoy out of skeptical curiosity; he wanted to talk to him and to understand his intention to reform the fast-changing world, the world of inequality, wars, persecutions, and injustice, on a pacifist, just, and nonviolent pattern. Maude was to become a translator, publisher, and Tolstoy's best biographer in English for life, and he was a dedicated, though not uncritical, friend. A liberal gentleman and an Englishman to the core, as he liked to repeat, Maude witnessed in Tolstoy's problems alternatives to the accepted social regimen, which, since they were "not . . . final revelations of the truth attainable by man, may and should be subjected to criticism, *and to re-examination from other points of view.*"[19] Maude applies these "other points of view"—his own and other critics'—to an examination of Tolstoy's nihilism and mysticism; his political economy, which wages a nonviolent war on the leisure class with a view to ending poverty; his defense of minorities, small nations, and dissenters; his consideration of populist passions; and the education of children. Maude sees in Tolstoy a healthy antidote to general compliance with authority, to stupefaction by fashion and by cultural stimulants, and to the imperceptible hypnotic effects of power, the consumer and entertainment industry, received ideas, and the educational and institutional establishment. It is here that Maude includes Shakespeare and other hypnotic masters of stagecraft and stage arts, the majority of the literary-cultural canon, and the fashionable causes of the age.[20] Maude understands very well the inseparability of Tolstoy's problems and their plurality, and he grants Tolstoy the right to own them and take responsibility for them (note Maude's use of the possessive in his title).

✻ ✻ ✻

The contributors to this volume come from different linguistic and disciplinary backgrounds: they are classicists, specialists in education, historians, Slavists, literary scholars who are not Slavists, and Tolstoy scholars who teach at the intersections of the social sciences and the humanities. However, we have resisted the methodology of expressing our views and perspectives from these disciplinary standpoints. This volume is not a concert of disciplines converging on one problem but a concert of problems converging on their great author, Leo Tolstoy. We take issue with a simplistic branding of Tolstoy. We therefore offer two essays on the two most enduring tags of Tolstoy's reception: nihilism and mysticism. We consider how he practices laughter for increasing the plurality of perspectives, especially those concerning questions of power and authority; how he modulates laughter to exercise restraint when laughter violates ethical boundaries and disrespects human dignity. We examine how he deals with serious social and political problems of his time, those of poverty and the "Jewish question." We investigate how he elaborates modes of disambiguation and defamiliarization for the sake of resistance to harmful external interferences in matters of education, aesthetic experience, and cooperative coexistence. Finally, we look at the benefits of slow reading and the slow elaboration of problems promoted by Tolstoy.

The sets of problems discussed in the volume are focused on two central themes: Tolstoy's resistance to instruments of what he regards as bad hypnosis (manipulation for the sake of monitoring, infiltration, and interference) and his promotion of an idea of good infection, or good influence, that respects distance and empathetic resistance that can be achieved through critical defamiliarization and detachment from the norms of obedience to the dictates of this moment: the state, institutions, cultural icons, and automated habits (which must have influenced the idea of the good infection held by C. S. Lewis). We consider in this regard the use of artistic devices as instruments of social analysis and reform. When we establish resonances between our way of living and Tolstoy's, we do *not* treat his formulations as prophetic predictions or failures in forecast. We treat them as guidelines for thought and interpretation rather than according them an absolute value located in Tolstoy's conflicts or answers.

The volume begins with an essay on Tolstoy's nihilism by Jeff Love, who takes Tolstoy's nihilism to task for its rebellious yet ingenious radicalism. Love strips Tolstoy's nihilism of dead clichés: he is no simple naysayer, no simple anarchist, no simple realist who perfected the power of analysis to the level of the exhaustion of content and form and thus brought it to the point of negation. Nor does Love portray Tolstoy as a respectful apophatic theologian. Love thinks that Tolstoy, the great realist, might be a nominalist—that is, someone who denies the possibility of offering adequate sets of meanings to words, of naming things in only one way, and of offering straightforward continuums. In doing so, Love echoes Isupov's recommendations. He places Tolstoy in the venerable company of other radical reformers of the notion of nihilism (Jacobi, Nietzsche, Heidegger, and Cantor). Love shows how Tolstoy practices the principles of the eternal return in revaluing the errors of creation with which we are doomed to live by suggesting routes of alternation between Homeric rage and divine apathy. Love's special focus is Platon Karataev, the "cunning 'Russian' god" of Tolstoyan nihilism, the emblem of divine indecision and indifference, and his companion, the purplish "cynic" peregrine, his nomadic dog. Love argues that Tolstoy's "nihilism" is an anguished philosophical search for a more adequate definition of what it is to be human.

Michael Denner turns to Tolstoy's long and rarely discussed work *What, Then, Shall We Do?* (1882–86), in which Tolstoy describes his experiences as a volunteer worker for the census in Moscow. This episode required that he set foot, for the first time in his life, in tenement houses in the poor sections of the old capital. By analyzing this complex narrative that recovers from Tolstoy's initial shock by way of offering some radical and wide-ranging recipes for social improvement, Denner explores Tolstoy's narrative strategies for representing the rich and the poor, and he shows that Tolstoy is at his best and most relevant when, like a social scientist, he theorizes about how social practices and institutions should cooperate in sustaining and enhancing the quality of personal life, leisure, work, and the amount of hours that we spend in public each day, choosing active forms of disengagement from the functions of the state built on violence and oppression. Denner examines Tolstoy's strategies of resistance to enslavement, analyzing the examples of extreme poverty and waywardness and arriving at a determination about the similarity of Tolstoy's solutions to poststructuralist economic thought. Love and Denner both ask, is it Tolstoy's language or his ideas that are more radical? Both offer illuminating discrimination with respect to this question, and both defend a necessary connection between rhetoric and action. G. K. Chesterton observed in 1903 that Tolstoy's radicalism tends toward "going mad" because Tolstoy lacks in one significant quality: mysticism. Here is what Chesterton wrote:

> The truth is that Tolstoy, with his immense genius, with his colossal faith, with his vast fearlessness and vast knowledge of life is deficient in one faculty and one faculty alone. He is not a mystic: and therefore he has a tendency to go mad. Men talk of the extravagancies and frenzies that have been produced by mysticism: they are a mere drop in the bucket. In the main, and from the beginning of time, mysticism has kept men sane. The thing that has driven them mad was logic.[21]

In that same year—1903—Tolstoy responded to the atrocities against the Jews in the pogrom in Kishinev and started writing his long critical reflection on Shakespeare. The year 1903 was a meaningful one for several essays in this book. Was Tolstoy a mystic or a logic-driven rationalist, after all?

The next contribution, by Vladimir Paperni, confronts these persistent myths about Tolstoy: that his thought is a form of either anarchism or detached mysticism. Paperni examines Tolstoy's religious thought from the perspective of mystical Gnosis and follows Tolstoy and his heroes on their roads of *unio mystica*. He demonstrates that they arrive at a paradoxical optimism of misunderstanding in progress, the liberating *countermysticism* that prompts the possibility of unfinalizable discovery rather than dead-ended disappointment. The essay argues that instead of presuming any knowledge of the inner life of a particular deity, Tolstoy concentrates on elucidating the process of human awareness as a developing openness toward interpreting God's will. This will is expressed in the discovery and practice of moral law for which no known mystical teaching shows any interest. Paperni demonstrates fruitful points of application of the myth of Tolstoy's mysticism and its counterarguments for the concerns of this century. To illustrate Tolstoy's conclusions and broaden their reach beyond the reading of *War and Peace*, toward the end of his essay, Paperni provides examples from a few of Tolstoy's well-known works of fiction, as well as examples from his underappreciated religious writings and diaries as indicators of Tolstoy's conflicted mysticism.

Out of the several examples that Paperni mentions, consider the Hindu principle of *Tat tvam asi* ("You are me") (Paperni essay, page 78), which implies the connection of every being and thing with ultimate reality and with their other. Another example Paperni mentions is the seemingly sudden outburst in Tolstoy's diary on December 18, 1899, against "a vulgar, personal Jewish God" [*grubogo, evreiskogo Boga lichnogo*] (53: 232) (Paperni essay, page 84). Is the latter outburst a sign of Tolstoy's latent "rationalist" Christian intolerance against Judaism? And is the former embrace of the Brahmin principle a sign of his spiritualistic paganism, uninformed by ethics?

Fruitful points of application of Tolstoy's complex mysticism are explored in the contributions in the volume that follow. Let's begin with the principle of *Tat twam asi*, references to which are scattered throughout many pages of Pelevin's *T*, which is filled with psychedelic dreams of lost identity. The same principle inspired the real Tolstoy to serve a humanitarian and political cause when he composed in 1903 three new stories describing the works and effects of that principle—stories that he donated to the relief of victims of the Jewish pogrom in Kishinev.[22] Mystic dreams and political action are united for Tolstoy under the aegis of ethics. This is exactly how he understands the Sanskrit phrase, by making a statement that recognizes our own being in every injured, murdered, and persecuted Jew.

"You are me" is not the original translation of *Tat twam asi*. Literally, the phrase means "This art thou." Tolstoy must have been led to this principle by one of his favorite thinkers on matters of compassionate ethics, Arthur Schopenhauer, with whose chief writings he had become well familiar since the late 1860s when he was finishing *War and Peace*. We can see that Tolstoy develops the formula of a concrete ethical imperative for action out of Schopenhauer's more general discussion of *Tat twam asi*. Schopenhauer explains the principle as one individual's "again recognizing in another his own self, his own inner nature," a reminder to each of us who is fearful of death that "we are all one and the same entity" (210–11).[23] Schopenhauer bases his reading of *Tat twam asi* on the assumption of our shared fear about our mortality, and thus our compassion is a response to the threat of suffering and finality. Why, then, does Tolstoy, who radically rewrites *Tat twam asi* as a call for action contained in the reworked translation of the phrase, "you are me," reject as vulgar and crude the idea of a personal God in Judaism? The answer is both existential and political. In the same diary reflection in which he rejects the personal Jewish God, Tolstoy shows that he is really looking for how "to conquer death by what is not death" [*pobedit' smert' ne smert'iu*] (53: 232). By rethinking the source of authority in Judaism, he is rethinking pathways for achieving imperishable brotherhood.

In the essay "Tolstoy's Jewish Questions," I consider Tolstoy's role in the elaboration of the Jewish question, arguing that Tolstoy opposed the process of politicizing national, ethnic, and religious problematics. He was unwilling to enclose Jews in an exclusive pale of interpretation and therefore replaced the notion of the "Jewish question" current in his time with plural sets of questions he learned from Judaism and the Jews whom he came to know. The Jew of Tolstoy's imagining is neither marginal nor mainstream, is exempted from messianic tasks yet is ethically commanding. The ethical dimension of Judaism is especially significant for Tolstoy, as are its tropes of obligation in the face of such historical challenges as ghettoization, dispersal and migration, and assimilation. And thus, with the ethical vector in mind, Tolstoy speaks of the plurality of human questions prompted by Judaism rather than of *the* Jewish question. Adamant in his condemnation of pogroms, antisemitism, and anti-Jewish measures, Tolstoy is not driven to guilt-provoked exultation of Judaism, nor is he motivated by a sense of stone-faced propriety covering up contempt. In lieu of a tasteless "ethnic joke," his complex attitude toward Jews relies on moral wisdom, traditions of religious laughter, and historical anecdote and represents an instructive case of overcoming prejudice responsibly. Atrocities against the Jews and their persecution elevated Tolstoy's awareness of the need of humanity without borders and of brotherly, global citizenship.[24] When Tolstoy speaks against the authority of the personified Jewish God, he speaks in favor of the unassuming Jesus, whom Tolstoy calls the "Hebraic Yid" (Medzhibovskaya essay, pages 109, 118). In Tolstoy's treatment of the dialogue between Jesus and Pilate on truth, Jesus's rejection of the authority of the Roman Caesar invites a critical and nonviolent defamiliarization of power, it disempowers power.

Approaching Tolstoy's problems from the point of view of a critical defamiliarization that creates a space for irony, humor, and laughter, Jeffrey Brooks wonders why Tolstoy is so often considered a humorless writer—a dull, overbearing, and "fun-challenged" dogmatic. Brooks's essay is a cross-cultural exploration of the processes through which high culture becomes part of popular culture using the vehicles of humor, satire, the comic, and caricature. Tolstoy emerges from Brooks's description as an author who would enjoy a much wider readership if he were writing today, specifically because of his unusual employment of cartoon, mass print media, and "social humor." When Tolstoy has a policeman tied to a bear and floated down the river in *War and Peace*, he straps the symbol of the enforcement of earthly power to the mercy of the elemental whim of the force of nature; it is easy to predict what will happen if the floating structure capsizes. Such an approach allows us to see how Tolstoy subjects the perception of the power of authority as inviolable to withering humor, in the process imagining a well-functioning, self-correcting, and self-governing humanity without need of a monitoring, censoring, or coercing institutional body. In addition to Tolstoy's ability to undermine persistent myths, Brooks sees in Tolstoy precisely the sense of humor that he is customarily denied: a levity that nonetheless does not upend the seriousness of Tolstoy's realism. This humor is pluralistic and it gives hope.

The problem of authority certainly looms large in matters of education and pedagogy. Both were evidently among Tolstoy's lifelong interests, but his thoroughly innovative views on them, yet again, have been examined incompletely and in frequently distorted ways. A common mistake has been to assume that Tolstoy's pedagogical articles on his Yasnaya Polyana school experiment published in the 1860s were the end of his work in the field of education. Drawing upon all of Tolstoy's educational writings, including those of the 1870s to 1910, Daniel Moulin-Stożek synthesizes five key principles of Tolstoy's educational thought (Truth, Freedom, Spirituality, Experimentation, and Relationship). Based on his experience conducting the international project "Religion and Civil Society" and on theoretical and practical work on education from a twenty-first-century perspective, Moulin-Stożek shows that Tolstoy's principles of mutual influence between teacher and learner are extremely useful for thinking about ways to resolve the challenges faced by educators and students today. The five principles engage teacher and learner in the creation of a space for freedom founded on love. This is Tolstoy's contribution to what we are only beginning to explore as a form of what we now call sanctuary space.

Stephen Halliwell investigates the potentials of a notion of aesthetic freedom built on Tolstoy's discrimination between infection and hypnosis. Tolstoy's aesthetics is best known, albeit in the main only from the ideas expressed in *What Is Art?* (1897–98), as a conduit of infectious love (echoing here the gist of his views on pedagogy). But isn't Tolstoy's theory of infection itself a form of aesthetic manipulation? Rather than treating Tolstoy's ideas about artistic infection as little more than a kind of simplistic transcript of Tolstoy's own views of the art form, or as the topic of a debate on the privileging of artistic and performance genres over one another, Halliwell's essay identifies new access points to Tolstoy's theory of infection (which the author believes Tolstoy ensured would be ultimately unanswerable). These tensions take us to the roots of the paradoxical nature of all aesthetic seduction that transcends states of bodily arousal, psychological loss, trancelike receptivity, and exuberant "agapeism." Aesthetic estrangement is a form of escape from the erotic bestiary, with its key instincts of expropriation for the sake of capture, conquest, or destruction. It is also a way toward the attainment of a self-enriching otherness, which is a process rather than a single state. Halliwell maintains that infection and defamiliarization (estrangement) are both creative forces of freedom, nonreducible to a single argument from the side of moral autonomy or relativism.

Why did Tolstoy hate Shakespeare? Caryl Emerson's essay argues against a deep-rooted fallacy that Tolstoy's "On Shakespeare and on Drama" (1903–4) is his sole—albeit strategically elaborate and verbose—outburst against Shakespeare from a Lear-like old man. The standard view is that this essay is not worth attention on account of its being the mean and laborious prank of an old and unhappy Lear-Tolstoy (the famous essay by George Orwell is thus also a memorable mistake). Emerson instead builds a case for Tolstoy's rational and principled animosity toward Shakespeare, who represents to Tolstoy the epitome of false art: infatuation with his own verbal virtuosity, vacuous attachment to derivative and formless plots acted out through endless and similar-sounding speeches. The characters who deliver them all look and sound the same because they are as divorced from real-time concerns and as utterly morally illiterate as their creator.

Emerson finds that Tolstoy is in excellent company when it comes to Shakespeare's "immoral jokes" and partners Tolstoy with George Bernard Shaw. In particular, she depicts the role Shaw played in offering a new fuse to Tolstoy's never-dormant anti-Shakespeare combustible by sending him a copy of his *Man and Superman* at the end of 1906 (two years after the completion of "On Shakespeare and on Drama") followed by *The Shewing-Up of Blanco Posnet: A Sermon in Crude Melodrama* (1909), the play set in Protestant and hypocritically intolerant America, forwarded to Tolstoy by Shaw in March 1910.[25] Shaw thus enacted an epistolary debate with the older master he admired. But, as Emerson shows, Shaw mistook the adages of the Falstaff-like soldier Mitrich from *The Power of Darkness* and Tolstoy's tragicomic appearances in his autobiographically inspired dramatic cameos of later years for talented fun making.[26] How the seriousness proper to the highest demands of art could coexist with jokes and humor is what Emerson scrutinizes, giving special attention to the discussion of "Bardolatry," a term Shaw coined in refusing to laud Shakespeare as a holy and untouchable cultural icon canonizing the mix of the high and the low. Tolstoy's responses to Shaw's impiety against Shakespeare, with which he agrees, reveal an important difference from the Irish playwright: while not accepting Shakespeare's jokes, Tolstoy declines Shaw's type of humor as well; it is only witty and superficial, not serious.[27] Emerson sees the riddle of Tolstoy's hatred of Shakespeare in his privileging the silent or stuttering jokes of life over the voluble pathos and jesting elegance of Shakespeare's stage. The devil's advocate here is Shaw, who believes in jokes and the comic as one must believe in the force of life: Tolstoy has some of the comic—and then he doesn't, and that's tragicomic. Emerson sees the importance of Tolstoy for this century in his call on drama to exercise the emptying of nonsense and to "serve the clarification of religious consciousness," "the only principle that permanently unites human beings" (Emerson essay, pages 208–9).

In the last essay in this collection, Ellen Chances explores Tolstoy's supreme force as a great simplifier to overcome art with artlessness, by, for example, pointing at pigeons and gingerbread—figures that helped to break open the strictures of Tolstoy's didactic severity. These little characters come from responses to Tolstoy written by late twentieth- and early twenty-first-century authors. Chances assumes a very unusual task: she answers the question about Tolstoy's problems for the twenty-first century by analyzing the lessons carried out of her own attempted reading of all ninety volumes of *The Jubilee* edition. This reading cannot be done on a fast schedule or in a linear fashion, volume after volume in sequence. Chances finds herself constantly drawn to external conversations in which she sees resonances with Tolstoy—with, for example, Pablo Neruda, Woody Allen, and a number of authors who attempted to rewrite Tolstoy in other genres or to complete sequels to his famous works. From this paradoxical sum of influences, Russian and foreign, the essay turns to thoughts about what an individual reader in the present day might learn from reading Tolstoy's fiction and nonfiction, bearing in mind today's American nonfiction books of the mass-market category that are as far from the academic standards of *The Jubilee* edition as can be. The issue at hand is the haste and loss of ability to slow down plaguing this century. This is the same issue that Maude was referring to when he began to approach Tolstoy's problems: Tolstoy writes a lot, and he is not easy to understand at once.

In addition to her advocacy of slow reading, Chances adds another important discussion to the themes of the volume, on the possession of this century by ageism. Chances speaks about the wisdom of older age, free of the dictates of appearance, and focuses on how this theme is portrayed by Tolstoy alongside his descriptions of the accepting and trusting openness to the world shared by old people and children. The art of good aging is one of the key problems that Tolstoy tackles with luminous openness, according to Chances. She further addresses the obsession of our century with enhanced performance and speed. As the performance-drug industry flourishes and the dependence on the substances it produces are at an all-time high, Tolstoy's caution against stupefaction (and hypnosis) comes up yet again at the conclusion of the volume.

❊ ❊ ❊

A few words are due in closing regarding the relationship of eternity to the twenty-first century and problem-solving. For fear of becoming outdated in his treatments, Aylmer Maude—a carpet trader in his first vocation—tried conscientiously to revise his definition of Tolstoy's problems. He sought to rewrite Tolstoy's project to the nearest demands of the market and in reflection of the changing political reality. He started by releasing the second edition of his *Problems* book three years after the first was published, and he considered publishing updated volumes of the book every few years. Yet the changing reality, he came to appreciate soon enough, should seek in the legacy of great artists practical solutions hidden in eternity. Maude realized the futility of this craving to update and retrofit Tolstoy's problems, letting them take their due course on their own terms in their afterlife. Maude issued no further volumes of *Tolstoy and His Problems*. His methodology in respecting the integrity of Tolstoy's persisting questions is helpful. And it was fully shared by Anton Chekhov. Chekhov explained his relationship toward artistic problematics during his exchange in 1888 with Alexei Suvorin, the editor of *Novoe Vremia* and a mentor of Chekhov's in his early career: "By demanding a conscientious attitude toward his work from an artist you are in the right. But you are confusing two notions: the solution of the question and a correct posing of the question. The second is obligatory for an artist. In *Anna Karenina* and *Onegin* not a single question has been resolved, but they quite satisfy you only because all questions have been posed correctly. The court is obligated to pose the questions correctly and let the jury judge, each to his taste."[28]

Almost two decades into the twenty-first century, the jury is still out. The essays collected here are not a compendium of all the problems of the twenty-first century, big and small, immediate or long-standing. Nor do they constitute a sourcebook on where to locate these problems in the vastness of Tolstoy's legacy. We focus here instead on Tolstoy's earnest practices of peaceable war against violence and indoctrination, against mass hypnosis, against enjoying anything worse than the truly best in art, education, economy, and forms of faith.

We also focus on a number of methods followed by him to liberate the good instincts that spark the energy for living with critical attention and yet spiritually, reverently, justly. On the question of the eternal, Aristotle considered the potential answers that one might receive from philosophy, history, and poetry. It is most interesting therefore that he ultimately chooses to address "problems" to poets directly (read: "writers," more broadly). From poets, more is expected: poets should represent things "either as they were or are, or as they are said or thought to be or to have been, or as they ought to be. All things he does in language, with an admixture [. . .] of strange words and metaphor" (*Poetics* 1460b7–12; *Complete Works* 2:2337).

Improving the world by defamiliarizing it, with the help of "strange words and metaphor," is one of Tolstoy's contributions we examine in this book. Following Konstantin Leontiev, we thank Tolstoy for all the good hypnosis, the only form of acceptable coercion, and echo his words: "I kneel before Count Tolstoy even for that coercion he carried out on me by forcing me to know as living and love as close friends such people who seem almost contemporaries to me" (131). But completely reverent we could not be, instead choosing to "laugh with the count" through the epic roars of *War and Peace*, through his Jewish jokes and Shavian barbs, and with the neurotic New York genius of Woody Allen, the mind-altering horse whispers in Pelevin, and the stuttering wisdoms of Akim.

During the several years that it has taken to complete the book, we remembered the words of Baruch Spinoza, Tolstoy's fellow excommunicate, and his recommendation for living and thinking when in doubt or in peril under the aegis of eternity. We tried our best not to overlook any sightings of the eternal, viewing its allure as we ought to from the ineluctable points of view of our time. This volume submits new formulations of Tolstoy's problems and new questions in which all the important illusions were welcome to stay.

NOTES

Epigraph: S. N. Bulgakov, "Filosofiia khoziaistva. Rech' na doktorskom dispute" [The philosophy of economy. A doctoral dissertation defense presentation" in S. N. Bulgakov, *Sochineniia v dvukh tomakh* [Collected works in two volumes], ed. S. S. Khoruzhii (Moscow: Nauka, 1993), 1: 307.

1. Viktor Pelevin, *T* (Moscow: Eksmo, 2009). *T* won the All-Russian Reader's Choice Award and the Big Book Prize soon after its publication. Subsequent citations to this work appear in the main text as parenthetical page numbers.

2. "Rublevka" is a reference to Rublev Highway (Rublevskoe Shosse) outside Moscow, indicating the residential compound of the new Russian aristocracy (of oligarchs, government officials, and other important forces in Russia's power structures).

3. Aristotle, *The Complete Works of Aristotle*, ed. Jonathan Barnes, 2 vols. (Princeton, N.J.: Princeton University Press, 1984), 1:169. Subsequent citations to this work appear in the main text as parenthetical page numbers.

4. In his classic essay "Tolstoy as the Mirror of the Russian Revolution" (1908), written on the occasion of Tolstoy's eightieth birthday, Lenin identifies objective historical causes behind Tolstoy's problems that had shaped his worldview.

5. Tolstoy's contradictions are a frequent topic of interest of such brilliant literary scholars of classical Marxist and Hegelian leanings as Georg Lukács and Boris Eikhenbaum.

6. Konstantin Leontiev, *Analiz, stil' i veianie: O romanakh gr. L. N. Tolstogo* [Analysis, style, and tendency: On the novels of Count L. N. Tolstoy], intro. Donald Fanger (Providence, R.I.: Brown University Press, 1968), 50–51, 132, 134–35. Subsequent citations to this work appear in the main text as parenthetical page numbers.

7. S. M. Breitburg, "Predislovie k tridtsat' deviatomu-sorok vtoromu tomam" [Preface to volumes thirty-nine through forty-two]. The preface was placed at the beginning of volume 39 of *The Jubilee*, which was published in 1956 and overseen by V. S. Mishin, 39: v–xxxviii.

8. See especially the introduction to Hugh McLean, *In the Shade of the Giant: Essays on Tolstoy*, ed. Hugh McLean (Berkeley: University of California Press, 1989).

9. K. G. Isupov, "Chary troianskogo naslediia: Lev Tolstoy v prostrastve pri-

iatiia i nepriiatiia" [Charms of the Trojan heritage: Lev Tolstoy in the space of acceptance and non-acceptance], in *Lev Tolstoy: Pro et contra*, ed. K. G. Isupov (Saint Petersburg: Izdanie Russkogo Khristianskogo Gumanitarnogo Instituta, 2000), 28; see also 7–32.

10. "Even Tolstoy's thought remains relevant, especially but not exclusively as expressed in his fiction," writes Donna Orwin, questioning whether it transcends the confines of nineteenth-century realism (Donna Tussing Orwin, ed., *Anniversary Essays on Tolstoy* (Cambridge: Cambridge University Press, 2010), 6. In her newest book, however, which is an introduction for general readers to Tolstoy's life and major works, Orwin makes a case for an integral version of Tolstoy. See Donna Tussing Orwin, *Simply Tolstoy* (New York: Simply Charly, 2017).

11. John Burt Foster Jr., *Transnational Tolstoy: Between the West and the World* (New York: Bloomsbury Academic, 2013).

12. Ludwig Wittgenstein, *Philosophical Occasions, 1912–1951*, ed. James Klagge and Alfred Nordmann (Indianapolis, Ind.: Hackett, 1993), 161.

13. G. W. F. Hegel, *Lectures on the History of Philosophy*, trans. E. S. Haldane and Frances H. Simson, intro. Tom Rockmore (Atlantic Highlands, N.J.: Humanities Press, 1991), 498, 650.

14. "Progress i opredelenie obrazovaniia" [Progress and the definition of education, 1862], 8:330.

15. In his letter to V. Anokhin of April 1910, he writes, "Hypnotism is sham and stupidity" (81:293). A copy of a study of the phenomenon of hypnotism, its significance and its future, is preserved in Tolstoy's personal library: A. Tel'nikhin, *Gipnotizm i ego znachenie v nastoiashchee vremia i v budushchem* [Hypnotism and its importance at the present time and in the future] (Saratov: N. P. Shtertser, 1888).

16. Victor Shklovsky, "Iskusstvo kak priem" [Art as device], in *O teorii prozy* [On the theory of prose], 7–23 (Moscow: Federatsiia, 1929), 12–13.

17. "O gosudarstve," 38:294; emphasis added.

18. Tolstoy's excommunication from the Russian Orthodox Church in 1901 inspired Maude to put together a volume of essays on Tolstoy: Aylmer Maude, *Tolstoy and His Problems: Essays* (London: Richards, 1901); Aylmer Maude, *Tolstoy and His Problems: Essays*, 2nd rev. ed. (New York: Funk and Wagnalls, 1904).

19. From Maude's unpaginated preface to *Tolstoy and His Problems*; emphasis added.

20. It seems that beginning around 1873–74, Tolstoy had started to become guarded against the capacity for hypnosis in Shakespeare. On May 10, 1874, philosopher and critic Nikolai Strakhov wrote to Tolstoy with complaints about the inability of modern fiction to touch and infect, pointing to the example of Shakespeare, whom he said would easily "drown the stage with tears." Contrary to the

habitual practice of their correspondence of many years, when every point raised in their letters to each other was discussed in detail, Tolstoy did not respond to Strakhov's remark on *Hamlet*. His deferral is telling and may suggest that Tolstoy was not yet ready in the seventies to produce a strong statement on Shakespeare and the hypnotic infection of his work. For Strakhov's letter in question, see A. A. Donskov, L. D. Gromova, and T. G. Nikiforova, eds., *Leo Tolstoy and Nikolaj Strakhov: Complete Correspondence*, 2 vols. (Ottawa: Slavic Research Group, 2003), 1:160–61.

21. G. K. Chesterton, "Tolstoy," in G. K. Chesterton, G. H. Perris, and Edward Garnett, *Leo Tolstoy* (New York: James Pott and Company, 1903), 6; see also 1–5.

22. Tolstoy explains his use of this principle—the mystical formula of Buddhism he employs for social change and social relief—in his letters to the great Jewish author Salomon (Solomon) Naumovich Rabinovich (Sholem Aleichem), on August 22 and 25, 1903 (74:166–67). Tolstoy's source for *Tat twam asi* was the German translation of the principle (*Das bist du*) in a Buddhist parable he found in the journal *Theosophischer Wegweiser zur Erlangung der göttlichen Selbsterkenntniss* 5 (1903): 163–6.

23. See especially paragraph 22 of Schopenhauer's *Über die Grundlage der Moral* (1839): Arthur Schopenhauer, *On the Basis of Morality*, trans. E. F. J. Payne, intro. David E. Cartwright (Providence, R.I.: Berghahn Books, 1995), 209; 210–1. The same idea about the "great word" of the Sanskrit formula *Tat twam asi*—this kernel of the "highest human knowledge and wisdom"—is developed in both the early and late parts of *The World as Will and Representation* (see Arthur Schopenhauer, *The World as Will and Representation*, 2 vols., trans. E. F. J. Payne [New York: Dover Publications, 1969], 1: 220, 355, 374; 2: 600).

24. When a teacher, A. Vinokur from Zvenigorod, asked Tolstoy in a letter of May 16, 1903, what he was supposed to tell Jewish children—his students— about the pogrom in Kishinev, Tolstoy responded that as an educator Vinokur was to focus on dispelling the fear that was being impressed upon Jews and the Russian people alike and with which they had been hypnotized into enmity, and on encouraging them to carry out the one eternal law of God, of unification and love, where hatred and suspicion are no more (74:134). Tolstoy had previously shared similar advice about the dire need of impressing universal humanistic ideals on children out of respect for the same law with a future prominent ophthalmologist, Naum Botvinnik, on December 30, 1898 (71:519–20).

25. Tolstoy's impatience with British and Irish wit can be explained by his general aversion to what Gary Saul Morson has called the refined sides of wit that had a place in the aristocratic or cultured salon (Gary Saul Morson, *The Long and Short of It: From Aphorism to Novel* [Stanford, Calif.: Stanford University Press, 2012], 87–89). About Shaw in particular, Tolstoy repeated more than once, each time in English, "He's got more brains than is good for him."

This is not to say that Tolstoy could not muster a classy joke: the many examples in his works of high-society witticisms spoken by dozens of superb aristocrats make the case.

26. Shaw applied his now-famous terms "tragicomedy" and "tragicomedian" to Tolstoy, the author of the unfinished play *And Light Shineth in Darkness* (*I svet vo t'me svetit*, 1896–1902), immediately recognized as Tolstoy's send-up of his own spiritual biography. In light of what has been said about Tolstoy's attitude toward the Jewish question and other national questions, it is interesting to note that Shaw thought of national questions as a strange matter, a form of high-pitched farce. As he famously wrote, he was "not only disinterested, but disengaged" in relation to the Irish question (Bernard Shaw, *How to Settle the Irish Question* [Dublin: The Talbot Press, 1917], 5).

27. Herman Bernstein recorded the following about Shaw on Tolstoy: "'Tolstoy was a prodigious genius,' he went on as he reclined on his couch, with a smile. '*But he was devoid of any humor or fun. That's why he could not understand me*'" (Herman Bernstein, *With Master Minds: Interviews by Herman Bernstein* [New York: Universal, 1913], 74–75; emphasis added).

28. A. P. Chekhov, *Polnoe sobranie sochinenii* [Complete works], ed. S. D. Balukhatyi, 20 vols. (Moscow: Goslitizdat, 1944–51), 14:207–8.

Jeff Love

Prologue
Tolstoy's Nihilism

> Such is literature: one builds a complete logical
> structure upon an erroneous first premise.
> —António Lobo Antunes

NIHILISM HAS A bad reputation. The notion of a vertiginous loss of horizons so commonly associated with nihilism in the twentieth century is a formidable contributor to the predominantly negative associations that the term has gathered since it was first used in 1799 in F. H. von Jacobi's objection to Fichte's making a science out of the principle of negativity.[1] Nietzsche of course lent the term additional grandeur and ominousness when he was in fact describing precisely the opposite of both, the collapse of the deadened bourgeois into the permanent slumber of tedious routine best described in the figure of the last man who seems capable of little more than bland blinking.[2] But in the popular imagination it is the notion of nihilism as a loss of horizons, as a kind of mourning for the assurances of another, ostensibly more secure time, that has predominated, resolving itself into a commonplace.[3]

My intent is to upend this commonplace interpretation by attempting a different evaluation of nihilism in the context of Tolstoy's attitude toward narrative, an attitude complicated by the fact that so much of its content must be inferred from Tolstoy's extraordinarily diverse narrative practices. My primary claim is that Tolstoy's narrative practices reveal a brand of nihilism that differs dramatically from the commonplace interpretation, referring back to different strands in the Western tradition while also seeming to pursue a reevaluation of the basic notion of loss associated with nihilism that has affinities with both Buddhism and the modern Heideggerian project. Briefly put, in Tolstoy there is a fascinating valorization of indeterminacy, which takes one to the center of Tolstoy's contentious relation to narrative.

Since it is nothing new to speak of Tolstoy and nihilism, I begin my discussion with a brief, thumbnail sketch of a certain tradition—indeed, legend—in the critical practice that considers Tolstoy a nihilist. I then provide a different interpretation of what the tradition has offered up as nihilism by maintaining that Tolstoy's nihilism has much more in common with nominalism. Finally, I examine one aspect of this nominalism as it appears in Tolstoyan narrative, in particular in *War and Peace*. In this context, I emphasize Tolstoy's "decisionism," which throws the very problematic consequences that nominalism has for action or narrative into bright relief. By proceeding in this way, I hope to reveal a different aspect of what emerges, with great irony, as Tolstoy's sustained polemic against narrative.

One may of course object that this is simply a counterintuitive exercise or playful provocation. Is it not Tolstoy, after all, who writes one of the longest modern novels? What kind of polemic can this be? In this regard, I think it is extremely important to keep in mind the characteristically paradoxical manner of Tolstoy's creative output: it is not axiomatic in any loose sense but certainly quite valid to say of Tolstoy's literary production that it evinces both a tremendous attachment to and distrust of language and "mere" linguistic constructions.[4] Moreover, one may be hard-pressed to recall another writer of similar stature who builds such imposing narrative edifices while all the time expressing the most excoriating doubt about their authority, capacity for truth or beauty, or, more humbly, any of the simple tasks allotted to narrative. Tolstoy's narrative art—if one wishes to refer to it so—rests on what we have come to call tensions that remain unresolved and, perhaps, unresolvable, hence their continued vitality or power to puzzle. For if Natasha, that darling of a certain Tolstoyan audience, can be said to form little more than a cliché of a bygone era riven with cliché,[5] the narrative that surrounds and overcomes her, with resolute irresoluteness, simply cannot coalesce into cliché other than by critical misprision or fiat.

Now, to the matter itself.

*   *   *

Maksim Gorky played an important role in the iconography of Tolstoy's nihilism. His justly celebrated *Reminiscences of Tolstoy* surely count among the most interesting portrayals we have of a major writer, easily rivaling the numerous memoirs of Goethe and no doubt surpassing them in acuteness of observation and stylistic brio. Gorky not only created an image of Tolstoy that underlined the distance between the public figure and the private individual but also established the latter's apparent lack of belief as a foundational aspect of that distance. Moreover, Gorky did so by emphasizing Tolstoy's silence, his reticence to broach certain themes, even his wooden treatment of what he appeared to cherish most as the Christian militant he had become by the time Gorky first met him.[6]

Gorky compares Tolstoy to a god, not an Olympian god but a cunning Russian god. The accent on cunning (*khitrost'*) sets the tone for what amounts to a revelatory portrait of the majestic nihilist hidden under the mantle of the prophet: Tolstoy speaks of Christ without enthusiasm, as if the latter would be laughed at by village girls if he appeared among them; Tolstoy holds great silences—he is afraid of what he knows; he sings many songs, being variable and contradictory; indeed, Gorky has Tolstoy suggest that we become aware of ourselves as such only through contradiction. About what we become aware, Tolstoy is, of course, silent.

Gorky creates a mythic wisdom figure, one who, having seen and done it all, has realized the ultimate futility and emptiness of life, the fragility of norms and the perennial hopes of salvation they reflect. As Donald Fanger records in an appendix to his translation:

> Walking in the woods Tolstoy once said to me: "It was in this very spot that Fet recited his verses. Fet was a ridiculous man."
>
> "Ridiculous?"
>
> "Yes, of course ridiculous—all people are ridiculous. You're ridiculous too. So am I—we all are." (79)

Tolstoy looks upon life as urgent, ridiculous, repetitive spectacle and plays the noble game of silence—*omnia vanitas*. Of course, this claim itself expresses a terrible cliché about Tolstoy, the writer who gave up writing, the desperate, mythic seeker who died in a small room at a stationmaster's house after one last attempt to liberate himself from his own achievements, to become, as it were, reborn. Instead, he cut a strikingly sad and ridiculous figure, as he himself seemed to know—from a more mythic perspective, his end was both tragic *and* comic.

Isaiah Berlin is obviously seized by the same mythic imagination as Gorky, the same desire to raise Tolstoy to the position of a god. But Berlin also makes Tolstoy do some good practical work for the basically nominalist view of history he explores in his famous essay "The Hedgehog and the Fox."[7] Berlin delights in descriptions of Tolstoy's magnificent giftedness, his capacity to see things in their—pardon the oxymoron, which belongs to Berlin anyway—unique particularity as no one had seen them before.[8] He also delights in the skeptical view of generalities to which this giftedness leads Tolstoy and mentions how his contemporaries were compelled to view this giftedness negatively, referring to Tolstoy as a *netovshchik*, a "naysayer." Berlin emphasizes the distinction between Tolstoy's capacious heterogeneous talent and his far less capacious and heterogeneous intellect, and in this— yet another persistent cliché about Tolstoy—he follows Gorky, the latter once remarking that the "real drama of Tolstoy lay in the constant struggle of his enormous talent with his mind, which was, comparatively speaking, not a large one" (70).

Gary Saul Morson radicalizes and recasts Berlin's view, referring memorably to Tolstoy at one point as an "epistemic nihilist."[9] But Morson gives far more credit to Tolstoy's intellect than do either Gorky or Berlin and, in so doing, tends to avoid the simplistic and clichéd distinction of "great artist and poor thinker" that seems to have gained such a foothold in the critical reception. Morson makes the best case for a far more aggressive Tolstoy, one whose astutely skeptical manipulation of narrative conventions does not seek to conceal itself behind pregnant silences or insincere professions of faith. While Morson's aggressive Tolstoy is confined largely to *War and Peace*, one could easily extend Morson's argument, suggesting that Tolstoy merely varies or refines his approach to narrative form after *War and Peace*: one could even claim that such changes in approach to form are the real substance of the so-called conversion.

Is there a gist to these claims, then? A red thread that draws them together despite their differences as to Tolstoy's forthrightness? I think there is, and it comes to light most distinctively by referring to Tolstoy's nihilism as a brand of nominalism.[10] But what do I mean by that?

o o o

I would respond poorly to the subject matter by attempting to do what nominalism claims one cannot do: provide a neat, discretely comprehensive definition.[11] Instead I suggest that one define nominalism as the claim that any definition is equally possible and impossible, equally true and untrue, equally valid and invalid. The assumption that underlies this rather callow playfulness is twofold: (1) no definition can be complete and (2) any definition, to be a definition, must be complete: such a definition must be universal.[12]

Complete? Universal? Are they the same? Is absolute better? As one can see, we now have an unfortunate proliferation of terms on our hands. Why is that so? What is the underlying problem?

This is a predictably vexed matter, but I shall make my bets on history, and on a specific model of knowing that puts us in a grave predicament. Martin Heidegger gives an admirably clear account of this model in his 1928 summer course on Leibniz.[13] There Heidegger makes the seemingly simple claim that the highest kind of knowing is intuitive, an immediate apprehending of all that is. He also shows that this kind of knowing has been traditionally attributed to God, as divine intuition, the *visio Dei* or, for those Kantians among us, the *intuitus originarius*.[14] Use of the word "intuition" here is hardly fortuitous, for intuition finds its root in the Latin verb *intueor*, "to look, see." The nearest analogue for this kind of knowing would thus be immediate visual apprehension.

What kind of knowing can this be? Heidegger's point is that immediate knowing cannot really be a kind of knowing. One might be able to define it negatively, analogically—indeed, we must—but an immediate knowing is no closer to knowing as we might use the term than an immortal being is to a mortal one, all negations, analogies, and anthropomorphism aside.[15]

But, crucially, the standard is thereby raised to the level of impossibility: that to know is to know everything, completely and absolutely. This means that we not only have a quantitative disparity, the criterion of completeness: we can never survey enough to know all because we cannot come to a stop, ever—there is always more time, at least for the living, who cannot know their own deaths. But we also have a qualitative disparity, the criterion of absoluteness or universality: we cannot know immediately, for we must think, and thinking means division, and division means distinction, and distinction means difference. Why is difference a problem? Difference means negation, limitation—that something is x because it is not y, what Kant refers to as an infinite judgment.

How does one come to know the infinite? In Tolstoy's day this was not a vexed question: one could not come to know the infinite, other than through some sort of revelation or intuition or memory that must evade description, the territory of monkish mystics, madmen, and monsters, like the infinitely memorious Ireneo Funes of Borges's famous tale—and that was that. Now, in our twenty-first-century landscape, matters are not so clear.

I suggest that the kind of infinity that nominalism presupposes is of still a different order, what Georg Cantor, in his revolutionary theory of aleph-null, might have associated with the absolute infinite, a special continuum beginning at the beginning, and negating limits. This infinity "diverges" rather than ends or closes and completes the set.[16] Put in more traditional terms, this infinity is akin to "pure" multiplicity itself, admitting of no cuts, no rules, no encroachments by finite practices: both quantitative and qualitative ascriptions must fall asunder. The definition of this infinite is necessarily negative, for it must evade definition to be what it is; its definition is thus a sort of nondefinition, a failure of definition in the face of *potentia absoluta* (absolute power).[17]

Failure preoccupied Tolstoy as much as it did Pascal and the great medieval nominalists before him, from Ockham to Biel.[18] And Tolstoy was just as unable to free himself of its implications, something his remarkable inaugural work of the so-called late or postconversion period, *A Confession*, amply proves. If the late Tolstoy indulged in long silences, he did so based on what he thought he knew of what neither he, nor any other mortal, could possibly know, for "in the infinite there is nothing either simple or complex, nothing before or after, nothing better or worse."[19] One might say that there the nothing, the *nihil*, is or, as Heidegger put it memorably, *das Nichts . . . nichtet*, "nothingness nothings," perhaps an even more intriguing play on words in English than in German.[20]

This might seem a fanciful connection, but it is nonetheless a useful one. For Heidegger also claims that the fear of nothingness is in fact a fear of indeterminacy, of the failure of all definition or, at the very least, of definition's precarious inadequacy (Heidegger, "What Is Metaphysics?," 101). In this sense, infinity is an ironically definite description of ineradicable indefiniteness, which haunts our claims to know and, as we shall see, the claims of narrative to give form to what is, to create what we call experience by explaining what can never fully belong to any experience. What is overpowers us always: it is the "great all or nothing"—the nothing that is all—as Prince Andrei says regarding the infinite sky that swallows him in his reverie of a wounded man at Austerlitz.

❆ ❆ ❆

Hence, it seems to me that the line of thought culminating in Morson's claim of epistemic nihilism needs to be taken very seriously indeed. But a further, perhaps banal, problem emerges that I have already hinted at earlier in this essay: the charge of nihilism, whether it be epistemic or otherwise, does not seem to square well with Tolstoy's prodigious output, which becomes, if anything, more vast and experimental the more intoxicated with infinite impossibility Tolstoy's vision becomes. The common response—one tirelessly repeated in regard to claims made about another author of monstrous epics, James Joyce, that, say, *Finnegans Wake* is a mere joke—has plenty of force: why write so terribly much to reveal the ostensible futility of doing so? Adepts of philosophy's two most notorious contemporary *graphomanes*, Jacques Derrida and Heidegger himself, will also recognize this old saw, which needs to be put on the dissecting table: no one wants to be accused, after all, of "fetishizing failure."

In this respect, Morson's argument, that Tolstoy engages in a violent act of destruction, that his immense narrative endeavor is an act of positive, ideologically charged negation or "negative narration," as Morson calls it, seems fitting, but somehow incomplete. Indeed, I have argued elsewhere that Morson's view gives us access to an intriguing inconsistency in Tolstoy: to argue demonstratively that a narrative is wrong means to argue at some level that one's countervailing narrative is right, even if in the negative, as refutation.[21] But how can one do so if the supposed basis of that argument is that no narrative can be right and still be a narrative? In other words, what authority can a negative narration claim if it cannot even claim the authority of refutation? For to claim the authority of refutation is to remain within the parameters for authority set by what one refutes; refutation being merely opposition that must retain the model of authority whose current guise it undermines as a condition of being able to do so. Hence, a refutation without claim to authority, a negation that is not also in some sense a position, cannot make any claim to authority at all: if it is ever possible, it must be merely arbitrary and, thus, fail.

What, then, are we to make of Tolstoy's nominalism, as I have described it, as a kind of nihilism? Why create narratives if none of them can have any greater purchase on authority than any other, the infinite swallowing all, including itself, equally in its infinite indifference?

But one might question why there needs to be a connection between nominalist nihilism and infinite indifference. Why does one connect, that is, the sheer impossibility of the latter with the valuation that seems to be offered by the former? Can we not speak of infinite indifference positively as a sort of cultivation of nothingness? Why must we speak of it negatively?

This is a crucial issue in Tolstoy's fiction where the cultivation of nothingness emerges ambiguously, both as a high form of life and as one that seems impossibly high because it sets no standards for authority but rather blithely ignores them all—to live without authority, this is the basic meaning of the nihilism of Tolstoy. And, as such, is it really nihilism? After all, to live without authority is to live in a radically egalitarian manner by setting aside the principal mechanism of injustice: the exercise of authority itself. To live without authority is to live without permanence, in a sort of perpetual fusion of distinctions. To live without authority is a kind of freedom so radical it may be incapable of representation—and this is indeed Tolstoy's gambit, a source of irony and adventure that amounts to the attempt to represent in narrative form what withdraws from form.

❖ ❖ ❖

To return at last to the beginning: a fruitful way of gaining access to this perspective on Tolstoy is decision. And I argue that *War and Peace* in particular creates a hierarchy at whose summit rests a life of infinite indifference, an equanimity that marks freedom from decision as well as the temptation to narrative that depends on it, infinite indifference being a cultivation of nothingness as unaware of itself as it is of the need for authority that is the wellspring of narrative.

By this I mean to suggest that infinite indifference, a perfectly egalitarian rejection of the priorities imposed by the imperative of choice, an imperative we can hardly escape as beings limited by a series of basic necessities, is as close as we can come to the freedom our tradition associates with divinity: indifference is divine, radically infinite and free. But it is also impossible to attain, even to imagine, and, hence, the imperative of choice, to decide, prevails: we seem to be creatures condemned to authority, needing narratives, paths of decision, that we can neither completely tolerate nor abandon.

Decision is thus a child of necessity: only gods have no need to decide anything, to tell stories other than to relieve themselves of a boredom they also cannot experience since they are timeless, experiencing nothing (at least other than as a virtual parody of what mortals experience).

Platon Karataev is the cunning "Russian" god of Tolstoyan nihilism, of divine indecision and indifference in *War and Peace*. One of the most penetrating exoteric figures associated with him is that of the wonderful dog described during Pierre's captivity.[22] I call this figure exoteric because it alludes to the dilemma of the nihilist sage, that his way of being cannot be explained directly in propositional form, as positive assertion, but only via a mediation, a figure, that can do little more than point:

> On the sixth of October, early in the morning, Pierre stepped out of the shed and, on his way back, stopped by the door, playing with a long, purplish dog on short, bowed legs that was fidgeting around them. This dog lived in their shed, spending the nights with Karataev, but occasionally went to town somewhere and came back again. It had probably never belonged to anyone, and now, too, it was no one's and had no name at all. The French called it Azor, the storytelling soldier called it Femgalka, Karataev and the others sometimes called it Gray, sometimes Floppy. Its not belonging to anyone, and the absence of a name and even of a breed, even of a definite color, seemed not to bother the purplish dog in the least. Its fluffy tail stood up firm and rounded like a panache, its bowed legs served it so well that often, as if scorning to use all four legs, it raised one gracefully and ran very deftly and quickly on three. Everything was an object of pleasure for it. Now it lolled on its back, squealing with joy, now it warmed itself in the sun with a pensive and meaningful look, now it frolicked, playing with a wood chip or a straw. (*W&P*, 1009)

This passage—one of the most beautiful in the novel—ends perfectly by ending abruptly. The sentence that follows the last sentence of the quote simply takes up a different topic. Indeed, this little figuration comes and goes in the text almost as a digression: it both fits and does not fit. Or, indeed, it could fit almost anywhere. And that is, of course, precisely the point. For the dog fits and does not fit; the dog has no particular home in any one context but can fit into multiple contexts. In this sense, the dog has a generic identity, a universality that points generously to the ever-elusive identity of the nihilist sage, the Karataev who is at home everywhere and nowhere.[23]

Digressiveness here does not affirm a particular narrative: essentially promiscuous, it can at once affirm and not affirm any one narrative. Here is an image of pure, transient narrativity itself, narrativity whose capacity to form multiple links in multiple narrative forms resists the kind of coalescence required to create a single, unifying narrative, a definite singular way of coordinating things. Perhaps we should not even call this inchoateness narrativity since it has no definite narrative identity, and narratives as we conceive them, at least since Aristotle, cannot be narratives in any other way: they must have a definite identity or refuse identity. Thus, to allow multiple possibilities, to entertain a series of possible "ghost" narratives,[24] is to undermine the narrative cohesion—the necessity of actuality—that was of such significance to Aristotle as well. There is, in other words, no narrative without authority expressed as a unifying center directing all the narrative parts to engage in the maximal self-expression of that center, which, in Aristotelian terms, is akin to the *causa finalis* or telos of the entire narrative structure. To imagine a narrative without such authority is to engage contradiction.

Here we see in miniature another example of the hostility to the interpretation of narrative as a purely causal construct that courses through many other parts of the novel and comes to expression perhaps most polemically in the famous reflections on history. In those reflections a central thesis emerges according to which any narrative that purports to be complete based on its taking count of all the causes must lie because the causes are always in excess of what any one account can count. Put more simply, the narrator insists on the reductiveness inherent in any single narrative account, and the remarkable resistance of the narrative to singular emplotment, perhaps epitomized by the narratively promiscuous dog, is of course one of the most noteworthy aspects of the novel as a whole, almost endlessly commented on in the reception, and negatively so, this negative commentary reflecting the perplexity of the critics before a work that may not authorize any one reading of its own plot.[25]

* * *

From the acme of Karataev, we encounter myriad forms of decline, of narratives striving to articulate and thereby establish their authority—as if that were the only object to pursue. In Tolstoy's novel, narrative has this sort of archaeological quality: it is the primary way that the characters attempt to explain and justify their decisions to themselves, why they act the way they do. This feature of the novel has been examined extensively, most pointedly in regard to the way war narratives take shape in accordance with a very specific notion of authority—that of the select or great man. But it is also the case that some of the ostensibly domestic narratives reflect a need for authority residing not in a great individual but in fate (as in Natasha's own interpretation of her love for Prince Andrei Bolkonsky) or a divine sign of some kind, like the comet Pierre Bezukhov finds so fascinating. Indeed, it would not be idle to examine the dense texture of narratives in the novel to ascertain the various forms of authority they reflect.

Narrative, from the point of view of the nihilist sage, is decadence, the inability to live without authority, to live without the lie that must accompany any construction of authority. Tolstoy's novel shows just how difficult it is to live without the lie. This difficulty is arguably most apparent when one is confronted with one's own death, with that about which it is most difficult not to be decided, the only authority from which there is indeed no escape. Hence the temptation to ask why and, thus, to seek justification is almost—and perhaps this "almost" is mere pleonasm—ineluctable. We would rather live in flattering falsehood than unflattering truth: there is a right way, a proper way, a sure way. Yet what are all these ways in the face of death? Mere diversions? A sort of febrile pragmatism?

This is where Morson's notion of negative narration is most persuasive. The novel becomes a kind of failed theodicy, an attempt to justify the world in the face of death, that ends up unstable, edging closer to ironic—thus comic—than heroic pathos.[26] But this failure fails to explain the vehemence of that attempt given the equally vehement skepticism about all such attempts. With the exception of Karataev and his epigones, the sense of death hangs over the novel, as the passion of the infinite, and the hope of a final authority other than death.

Here we have the immense conflict of the novel, its peculiar and enduring *aristeia*, a battle to overcome an infinitely productive skepticism, one that ever returns, refreshed and renewed by death. This is what we might also call the novel's tragic edge that emerges with particular vividness in the novel's most exploratory characters: no matter how they try to find reasons for why they decide and act as they do, they cannot; and this inability seems to compel them to try further, to "fail better," in the words of one of Tolstoy's most interesting successors in the twentieth century.[27] The tragic way is that we are compelled to decide and, thus, to find ways to act—and new explanations for those actions, a compulsion whose most powerful representative in the novel is Napoléon himself, the great conqueror who must believe in his own authority, that he quite literally authors himself, in order to live freed of the necessity that haunts him. But the same could be said for Prince Andrei and Dolokhov, two significant characters who enact the Napoleonic grand narrative to make sense of themselves as beings delivered from necessity—and death.

The other way is of course the comic way: that of skepticism, of the synoptic view that recognizes the vanity of synoptic views. From this point of view (which seeks to free itself of all points of view), Napoléon is a most comic creature, as the narrator's descriptions of him attest, especially during the Russian campaign. But, if Napoléon is ignobly comic, other characters seem to be less ignobly so. Karataev is the most extreme representative of this view, but we find it expressed in other characters like Kutuzov, Pierre, and even Princess Marya. And there is some irony in this, for the others I mention here all live in the space of narrative—they are unable to live in the manner of Karataev because they cannot free themselves from necessity (even Karataev's liberation is suspect)—they remain risible if not as squalidly risible as Napoléon.

This inability is of interest since it also applies to those characters whom I have associated with the tragic. Both cases end in a kind of failure, whether it be the radical refusal of Prince Andrei that precipitates his death or the enthusiasm of Pierre at the end of the novel, an enthusiasm that has very little to do with the lessons he learned from Karataev. And how can one accept failure, one's own poverty?

❊ ❊ ❊

I have discussed these connections extensively elsewhere.[28] Hence, I should like to examine them and the problematic they reveal in the context of another crucial character in the novel about whom all too little is said: the narrator. For, one could argue, the narrator of *War and Peace* is at once the most and least remarkable character in the novel.

This narrator is a strange creature. Assuming mask after mask, notionally sexuated and sexless, within (in-sistent) and above (ek-sistent) the text,[29] dogmatic and supremely ironic, the narrator seems to weave in and out of characters, to write perfectly conventional novelistic passages and long essays that have tested the patience of generations of readers. The narrator's ever-shifting presence in the most innocuously and conventionally narrative portions of the novel is belied by the aggressively omniscient ostentation of the essays. The narrator both reveals and hides "itself" in giving reasons for the way the narrative is being constructed, reasons the narrative will both support and put in question. The narrator thus shows how we are constantly forced and tempted to create lies that we are able neither to discard nor retain, this being the source of irresolvable instability and fecundity in the novel. In so doing, the narrator gives us the tragic and comic views with great intimacy.

Let me offer three examples, one rather obvious, one more curious, and one most unusual: these are the shifting perspectives in battle scenes, Lavrushka's meeting with Napoléon, and Prince Andrei's death. I present these examples in severely truncated form, both for reasons of economy and because I can extract what is relevant in them fairly directly.

Tolstoy is justly famous for his battle scenes, which created a novel syntax for the representation of battle. These scenes show battle as a kind of chaos. Thus, they involve themselves in a very Tolstoyan paradox, since they are formal descriptions of the violence of war; on a more abstract level, one might say that they are caustically formal descriptions of the dissolution of form, a subtle sort of grotesque. The narrative creates a sense of chaos by breaking the battle scenes into small narrative chunks that do not seem to fit into one overall syntactic pattern. At the same time the narrative binds them together by using different perspectives that can be linked into a comprehensive view. Thus, at any of Schöngraben, Austerlitz, or Borodino, a plurality of views, from various ranks and locations on the battlefield, are wound together retrospectively as a unity in the narrative voice. But this unity does not have the "fit" necessary to dispel doubt.

The Lavrushka episode is notorious. Tolstoy takes one of his roguish characters, the unscrupulous Lavrushka, and has him meet Napoléon. This might seem innocent fun, except that Tolstoy casts this Lavrushka in the role of a Cossack soldier whose meeting with Napoléon Thiers records in his history of the campaign in Russia. Tolstoy then claims that Thiers misunderstood the meeting, thus showing Thiers's—and by extension French historians'—ruinously partial judgment in regard to the campaign. In simpler terms, Tolstoy attacks their authority. But what authority does he offer in its stead? That of a seemingly arbitrary, whimsical narrative, a mere thought experiment, an exercise in the power of narrative imagination. The narrator plays at polemics by taking the unassailable role of a god in them, hardly fair and, indeed, assailable because the authority of the fictional narrative belongs only to the narrator.

Prince Andrei's death scenes are among the greatest in world literature. This is a standard and worthy judgment. They have that authority based, however, on the narrator's great skill in taking on Prince Andrei's view as well as a view that explodes Prince Andrei's and can hardly belong to an individual. The narrator imagines death and describes the strange consciousness, if it can be called that, that Prince Andrei enters once he has died. Significantly, this consciousness is "of"—if the preposition could possibly be appropriate here—a sort of love, divine love, that is inseparable from the love of all and none also identified with Karataev. If Karataev acts in that manner, and under the limitation inevitable in trying so to act, Prince Andrei picks up the other, more sharply ironic aspect: that he can achieve pure equanimity, the blessed indifference of the nihilist sage, only in death.

In all these examples, the narrator shifts from part to whole, from the most partisan comradeship to a position that is like that of a god.

But his most godlike turn, perhaps, is in the essays themselves, where he suggests that we look at the universe in a new way. What is most godlike about these essays is that the complicated edifice he constructs in them has no grounding outside the bare assertion of the narrative itself, this construct being the abstract analogue and perhaps fulfillment of the voice that occurs throughout the narrative. The irony here is that the narrator is silent about this grounding; not a word, other than a quickly dismissive one, is said about it. And with good reason, since the narrator's introduction of the infinite ensures that no such grounding can possibly be found: the greatest claim to authority in its infinite reach undermines all authority.

This is decisionism at work. The novel viewed, retrospectively, as the demonstration of a thesis based not on grounds, which cannot convince, but on a largely hidden, never explained choice: a decision, a beginning, that, as such, cannot but withdraw from what it begins, as such both taunting and tempting.

❋ ❋ ❋

What, then, is Tolstoy's nihilism? I might say that nihilism for Tolstoy describes that perfect indifference to life or death, infinitely perfect, which seems to come into view most clearly with Karataev. [30] Of course, I have to be ironic here because to speak of perfect indifference, of its coming into view, shows how I cannot speak of it without corrupting its perfection. And this is the same problem that disturbs Tolstoy's great novel. If one must fail, and if narratives are that failure, then what does one do? One might argue then that one can judge failure; after all, one might "fail better." But is that really so?

Tragic and comic modes of presentation are nourished on this hope, that one might indeed fail better. Critical approaches to the novel are infected by the same hope. Some emphasize the heroic aspect of the novel, the terrible beauty of failure, a beauty whose warlike ethos belongs as much to Homer as it does to Hitler. Some emphasize the comic in the good old Christian sense of loving the everyday, the ordinary, the merely interesting. To them grand abstractions are violent, leftovers of our dangerous aristocratic past. Others may emphasize a different, more Greek, notion of the comic as the essentially impassive gaze of the god on the ridiculous spectacle of human striving.

But is one better than the other? Is Christian love to be chosen over Homeric rage or divine *apatheia*? This question, at least to me, remains undecidable in the novel, which, doffing the mask of the Epilogue, might start all over again just to respond to it.

NOTES

1. Martin Heidegger, "European Nihilism," in *Nietzsche*, vol. 4, *Nihilism*, trans. Joan Stambaugh, David Farrell Krell, Frank A. Capuzzi (New York: HarperOne, 1991), 3.

2. For a helpful account of nihilism and Nietzsche's role in shaping current views of the concept, see Michael Allen Gillespie, *Nihilism before Nietzsche* (Chicago: University of Chicago Press, 1995).

3. We can in fact identify three basic notions of nihilism: (1) a complete loss of foundations or justifications regarding *any* norms directing human action, the so-called everything is permitted variant that finds nothing to orient (or limit) human action; (2) the triumph of unfettered subjectivity whereby all things become products of human will and nothing beyond what is created by human will

exists; and (3) the combination of the two preceding accounts whereby human beings create the world and themselves without any external limitation. It is indeed relatively easy to see that the central issue is limitation, since nihilism is in all cases connected to the absence of limitation, viewed either as terrifying or liberating. Tolstoy's case is extremely complex since people like Gorky consider Tolstoy to be a nihilist who fits into the first category. Yet this supposed nihilism may well be considered the beginning of emancipation for Tolstoy, as I suggest in the remainder of this chapter. As to a few sources: Gillespie pays due regard to both the first and second categories, whereas Stanley Rosen sees the first as decisive, as does Conor Cunningham. Gianni Vattimo takes the position that nihilism is simply liberating. Heidegger is closer to Tolstoy, decrying the second category as the essence of modern nihilism. See Conor Cunningham, *The Genealogy of Nihilism* (London: Routledge, 2002); Stanley Rosen, *Nihilism* (New Haven, Conn.: Yale University Press, 1969); Gianni Vattimo and Santiago Zabala, *Ethics, Politics, and Law* (New York: Columbia University Press, 2004).

4. Liza Knapp, *Anna Karenina and Others: Tolstoy's Labyrinths of Plots* (Madison: University of Wisconsin Press, 2016), 173.

5. By this I mean the cliché of "Russianness" that Tolstoy creates and Orlando Figes interrogates. See Orlando Figes, *Natasha's Dance: A Cultural History of Russia* (New York: Picador, 2003).

6. Maksim Gorky, *Gorky's Tolstoy and Other Reminiscences*, trans. Donald Fanger (New Haven, Conn.: Yale University Press, 2008), 15–82. Subsequent citations to this work appear in the main text as parenthetical page numbers.

7. Isaiah Berlin, "The Hedgehog and the Fox," in *Russian Thinkers*, ed. Henry Hardy and Aileen Kelly (Harmondsworth, U.K.: Penguin, 1978), 22–81. Subsequent citations to this work appear in the main text as parenthetical page numbers.

8. For a delightful parody of this notion, see Jorge Luis Borges, "Funes the Memorious," in *Labyrinths*, ed. Donald A. Yates and James E. Irby (New York: New Directions, 1962), 59–66.

9. Gary Saul Morson, *Hidden in Plain View: Narrative and Creative Potentials in "War and Peace"* (Stanford, Calif.: Stanford University Press, 1988), 109.

10. There is of course nothing new in this view. Fredric Jameson emphasizes Tolstoy's nominalism in his recent article on representation in war, "War and Representation," *PMLA* 124, no. 5 (2009): 1532–47.

11. Nominalism can be defined as grounding or expressing the impossibility of final definition itself. And, without a final or complete definition it is questionable whether any definition is anything other than a regulatory and salutary fiction.

12. The best source for a discussion of nominalism is still Hans Blumenberg, *The Legitimacy of the Modern Age*, trans. Robert M. Wallace (Cambridge, Mass.: MIT Press, 1985), 145–79.

13. Martin Heidegger, *The Metaphysical Foundations of Logic*, trans. Michael Heim (Bloomington: Indiana University Press, 1984), 43–47.

14. Heidegger writes, "*Intuitus* means a direct insight, a knowledge that comprehends the whole of time in a single stroke without succession. *Visio* as *praesens intuitus* is a look which must be taken to range over the whole, as present before God who has everything existing presently before him. God's present intuition reaches into the totality of time and into all things that are in any time whatsoever, as into objects present to him" (Heidegger, *Metaphysical Foundations*, 45).

15. Intuitive knowing cannot be knowing at all because knowing for us is necessarily temporal, sequenced, and discrete. Intuitive knowing is silent, a void; it is the visual equivalent to silence.

16. Joseph Warren Dauben, *Georg Cantor: His Mathematics and Philosophy of the Infinite* (Princeton, N.J.: Princeton University Press, 1990), 47–76.

17. I allude here to the nominalist distinction between the *potentia absoluta* in God and His *potentia ordinata* expressed in the structure of creation. The tension between the two is obvious, since any structure is a restriction of God's power, which, as absolute, is necessarily a self-restriction. Thus God can intervene any time He wants to change the structure, and we can assume that the only reason He does not is to show his benevolence. The deeper tension between power and benevolence here is equally troubling especially given the benevolent character of the nature that kills us and makes us suffer.

18. Heiko A. Obermann, *The Harvest of Medieval Theology: Gabriel Biel and Late Medieval Nominalism* (Grand Rapids, Mich.: Baker, 2001).

19. L. N. Tolstoy, *A Confession*, trans. David Patterson (New York: Norton, 1983), 36.

20. Martin Heidegger, "What Is Metaphysics?," in *Basic Writings*, ed. David Farrell Krell (New York: Harper Perennial, 2008), 103. The awkward English translation of the phrase given in this edition is "The nothing itself nihilates." It is not clear why the translator chose to render the verb (to be sure, unusual in German) by the Latinate "nihilates." For Tolstoy's struggle with "all or nothing" and his dealing with Schopenhauer's negativity of privation, see Inessa Medzhibovskaya, *Tolstoy and the Religious Culture of His Time: A Biography of a Long Conversion, 1845–1887* (Lanham, Md.: Lexington Books, 2008), 242–44.

21. Jeff Love, *The Overcoming of History in "War and Peace"* (New York: Rodopi, 2004), 13.

22. The nomadic dog may be a reference to the Cynics, whose name derives from the ancient Greek *kúnes*, nominative and vocative plural of *kúōn*, "dog." There are many aspects of Cynic thought that emerge in Tolstoy, and one wonders to what extent Tolstoy may have picked up traces of Cynic thought through Rousseau. See the useful collection R. Bracht Branham and Marie-Odile Goulet-Cazé, eds., *The Cynics: The Cynic Movement in Antiquity and Its Legacy* (Berkeley: University of California Press, 1996).

23. That the dog may not be so free, that, indeed, such freedom may not be possible, is suggested by the howl it makes upon the death of Karataev. The homelessness of the dog and, by extension, of the nihilist sage may be exaggerated.

24. By "ghost" narratives I mean a series of possible narratives that may coexist along with any one choice of a principal narrative (if, indeed, such a choice is possible). In other words, in a highly indeterminate text that may allow various constructions of the principal narrative, none of which can be conclusive, the others remain as possible principal narratives as well. Put in formalist terms, ghost narratives presuppose a *siuzhet* that does not permit conclusive determination of an underlying *fabula*. Indeed, in Tolstoy's case, the polemic relating to causality in *War and Peace* has the effect of undermining a primary means of constructing a *fabula* as a causal construct.

25. A. V. Knowles, ed., *Tolstoy: The Critical Heritage* (London: Routledge, 2010), 89–211.

26. We might note in this regard that Blumenberg does not hesitate to connect theodicy with nominalism. Blumenberg in fact suggests that theodicy as devised by Leibniz is a response to the more disturbing aspects of medieval nominalism, in particular the tension that nominalism identifies between will or power and benevolence. From a nominalist perspective, the order of the world derives from God's benevolence, not a restriction on God's power—the upshot is that God retains the power to transform or modify his order at any time. Leibniz, by asserting the principle that God can only will the best, in effect asserts the very restriction that nominalism puts in jeopardy. See Blumenberg, *Legitimacy of the Modern Age*, 161–62.

27. Samuel Beckett, *Worstward Ho!*, in *Nohow On* (New York: Grove Press, 1980), 89.

28. Love, *Overcoming of History*, 157–81.

29. Martin Heidegger, "On the Essence of Truth," in *Basic Writings*, 132. The terms "in-sistent" and "ek-sistent" describe the differing senses in which we are actively in the world and also capable of taking distance from our immediate absorption in the world. Likewise, Tolstoy's narrator shifts from what seems to be a perspective exterior to the novel (as essayist, as capable of giving an overview not available to the characters) while also frequently seeming to be fully in the narrative, a feature most distinctively realized in the novel's tendency to emphasize a temporality of the constant present rather than of retrospective narrative.

30. The Franco-Russian philosopher Alexandre Kojève makes this point very effectively in his book on Kant. There Kojève insists that the perfect sage cannot truly be free (and thus perfect) while remaining alive because no one who is alive can be perfectly indifferent (the need to preserve one's life itself being a sign of servitude, to life itself, and thus of imperfect freedom). Hence, Karataev, despite his ostensive indifference, is hardly perfect and cannot be so. Within the terms of this chapter, he is only an imperfect or "defective" nihilist.

See Alexandre Kojève, *Kant* (Paris: Gallimard, 1973), 47. Tolstoy confronts this problem in his later work (e.g., "Father Sergius") as a problem of egoism, since it is impossible to free oneself of egoism—to truly free oneself of sin—while remaining alive, the prerogative of self-preservation carrying with it a pervasive and indefatigable egoism.

Michael A. Denner

Tolstoy as Social Theorist

WHAT FOLLOWS IS an analysis of the social model developed by Leo Tolstoy in *What, Then, Shall We Do?* That work, written on and off between 1882 and 1886, reveals the emergence of a completely new stage in Tolstoy's thought, his first attempt at social and political philosophy through an interrogation of social practices and state institutions. The sparse scholarly attention to the text has been devoted mostly to the first chapters of the book, where Tolstoy engagingly and artistically recounts his experiences with urban poverty and the Moscow census of 1882.

Although I examine the first part of the work from a narratological perspective, my real focus bears on the second half, beginning with chapter 12, in which Tolstoy examines state authority. He consciously engages in an ancient debate about regime authority that begins with Plato, a debate that pivots on principles of justice and the origins and proper role of government. This emphasis on the state, particularly on its use of coercion and violence, sets *What, Then, Shall We Do?* off from other works written during this decade—*A Confession, The Four Gospels Harmonized and Translated, What I Believe*—that are explicitly theological in nature. *What, Then, Shall We Do?* offers Tolstoy's first statement on the formal use of state coercion[1] and his exploration of points d'appui from which it might be successfully thwarted. His exploration of poverty and coercion in the faubourgs of Moscow is a historical and contemporary account of the interaction between imposed order and reactive disorder.[2]

From *What, Then, Shall We Do?* onward, Tolstoy's oeuvre shifts from arenas of dominant culture described in his previous works of literature—the estate, the parlor, the patrimony and history of Great Russia—to the borderline and dissentient. Themes of exile, sickness, and dispossession pervade nearly all of Tolstoy's works during this period. They feature antiheroes: prostitutes, beggars, drunkards, murderers, thieves, hermits, anarcho-Christians, Bashkirs, Chechens, Jews, heretics, revolutionaries, and monk-apostates. As a (former) member of the dominant system, Tolstoy explored these arenas of subalternity seeking a qualitatively different reality and ultimately a means of escape from his own condition.[3]

Michael A. Denner

TOLSTOY AND THE MOSCOW CENSUS

The prompt for writing of *What, Then, Shall We Do?* dates to 1881, when the Tolstoy family began wintering in Moscow in the posh Prechistenka-Arbat area; the next year they moved to the Khamovniki district, at the time on the edge of a rapidly sprawling Moscow.[4] Struck by his chance encounters with the urban Muscovite underclass, Tolstoy volunteered to oversee the census count in several poor areas close to his new home. To aid the cause, in advance of the census he read publicly and published "On the Census in Moscow" in January of 1882 (25:173–82). In this short address, he recommends taking advantage of the momentary "communion" between those who stand on the "highest rung of the ladder"—the enumerators and directors of the census—with the "thousands who stand on the lowest." He recommends that the census organizers "join to the business of the census a task of assistance" and, using the information gathered by the census, work to ameliorate "all the wounds of society, the wounds of poverty, of vice, of ignorance" that they will find. He recommends giving the truly desperate a bit of money (25:178–79) and

> then let assistance be rendered to all those unfortunates . . . Let those laborers who have come to Moscow and have sold their clothing to buy food, and who cannot return to the country, be dispatched to their homes. Let the abandoned orphans receive supervision. Let the weak old men and indigent old women, living off the charity of their comrades, be liberated from their half-famished and dying condition . . . All the evil may not be exterminated, but there will be some understanding of it, and the battle against it will not be by police methods but by internal ones—by the brotherly intercourse of the men who see the evil, with the men who do not see it, because they dwell within it. (25:180)

Biographers have observed that this public address and article mark the beginning of Tolstoy's "crusade to bring Christian principles into the lives of educated Russians."[5] This observation is, however, incorrect. The hortatory "On the Census in Moscow" reminds one of, say, a well-meaning Rotary address or a lecture at the local Unitarian church. Urban poverty, according to "On the Census in Moscow," is a problem that can be solved by the application of social science and compassion, with a little transfer of wealth from the upper to the lower classes. It is, I would argue, the *last* public statement Tolstoy made before or after his conversion in which he professed belief that contemporary social institutions could reform themselves, what Inessa Medzhibovskaya has rightly called his profound intellectual and artistic involvement in the problem of radical politics.[6]

THE NARRATIVE STRUCTURE OF *WHAT, THEN, SHALL WE DO?*

It is vital to understand the structure, context, and manuscript history of *What, Then, Shall We Do?* Tolstoy started it immediately after participating in the Moscow census in January 1882, about a month after publishing and reading "On the Census in Moscow." Initially, he was writing a report to the donors and the public on the work of the census; the first dozen chapters of *What, Then, Shall We Do?* therefore describe his encounters with the urban poor while working as a census supervisor.

However, his views on the cause and cure for poverty undergo a profound change in the course of the book: what started as a naive program for social amelioration—the "brotherly intercourse" of the rich trying to fix the problems of the poor—becomes, interestingly, an argument *in favor* of poverty and against the educated and wealthy. This transformation is depicted in the sprawling work, which organizes and depicts the unfolding of Tolstoy's sharply changing views from January 1882 to January 1886, a tumultuous period that he described as an internal reconstruction in *A Confession* finished exactly in 1882. (Indicative of the complexity of the work and Tolstoy's exertions over it, the manuscript description and history of the writing of *What, Then, Shall We Do?* in *The Jubilee* edition cover more than a hundred pages.)

The first dozen chapters betray a peculiar generic and stylistic structure. While the book is not exactly a literary work, these chapters vividly recount adventures in lower-class Moscow street life. We trek across unfamiliar ground with a familiar Tolstoy, the same indefatigable tour guide who accompanied us in the Sevastopol stories and the battle scenes of *War and Peace*. Because his views on the social institutions and poverty change so radically during its composition, *What, Then, Shall We Do?* is a palimpsestic work: Tolstoy rarely excised his initial impressions and beliefs in the book; instead, subsequent observations and anecdotes complicate, contradict, or clarify previous ones.

The resulting structuring of various narrative voices separated by time and experience bears a great deal of similarity to the polyphonic "pseudo-autobiographical" structure that Andrew Wachtel identifies in *Childhood*:[7] The first voice, the protagonist-guide, presents unproblematically and in vivid detail what he sees in a tenement or street scene. The second voice, the philanthropist Tolstoy, comments and interprets the scene, particularly his feelings of confusion and guilt at the sight of poverty. This second voice is the author of "On the Census in Moscow"—naive, guilt-ridden, but optimistic that he might find a way to help the downtrodden. The third voice, the one with the final word, is Tolstoy the radical, who emerges in the second part of *What, Then, Shall We Do?* and returns to earlier parts of the text to prime the reader for the analytic work that uncovers the true source of poverty and proposes solutions. He corrects the philanthropist's analysis and extrapolates about the "true" relationship between the philanthropist and the problem of urban poverty, inculpating the former in the latter. The first voice inhabits the immediate present and does not analyze. The second voice is subsequent, but contiguous, to the first; it has access only to partial truths. The third voice is absolutely separated from the first two and passes verdict on them. This narrative technique, where various voices with differing levels of self-consciousness and authority comment upon one another, is common in Tolstoy's oeuvre; one finds it, for instance, in his early war stories.[8]

Since Tolstoy bases his analysis of poverty in the second part of the book on his experiences that he recounts in the first part, it will be useful to give some examples of his adventures among the urban poor. The examples also demonstrate the interplay among the three voices.

* * *

Curious about the plight of the urban poor, he took what we call nowadays a ghetto bus tour on the advice of his Moscow friends. After several false starts—"several times I set out to Khitrov market, but each time I felt uncomfortable and ashamed" (25:187)—he finally made the trip in December 1881. Unsuccessfully posing as a vagrant, he attempts to infiltrate the infamous Lyapinsky flophouse; the crowd immediately recognizes him as out of place. The men's stares make him uncomfortable, and he finally engages them in conversation, buying them glasses of *sbiten'* and recording their stories of woe. Moved by their needs, he gives them alms, and, in a scene repeated several times in the book, he is quickly swarmed by mendicants— "I was besieged by the crowd"—who take all his money. The doors open and he enters the flophouse with the crowd, barely making it inside before fleeing at the sight of the men to whom he had earlier given alms. The second voice, the guilt-ridden philanthropist, comments on this reaction remarking that he was ashamed "as if I had committed a crime." Tolstoy returns home to "a five-course dinner, served by two lackeys in dress clothes with white ties and white gloves" (25:189–90).

At this point, the third, dissenting voice interrupts, explaining the ultimate source of shame. Tolstoy recounts how, thirty years earlier, he had attended a public execution by guillotine in Paris, and its effects on him. Although he had heard all the "arguments in defense of capital punishment," as soon the head was separated from the body, he realized that he had, by his "presence and nonintervention . . . approved and shared in" murder.

> In the same way now, at the sight of the hunger, cold, and humiliation of thousands of people, I not with my mind nor with my heart but with my whole being understood that the existence of tens of thousands of such people in

Moscow—while I and thousands of others overeat ourselves with beefsteaks and sturgeon and cover our horses and floors with cloth or carpets—whatever all the learned men in the world might say about its being necessary, is a crime, not committed once but constantly. (25:190)

This third voice castigates the philanthropist, remarking that the *sbiten'* and handful of rubles that he had given the men was not enough, and that he ought to have given away all he owned, otherwise he would share "in a constantly repeated crime." In recounting this memory of the guillotine in Paris, this dissonance of voices introduces and links the various topics of the second half of the work; state authority, violence, poverty, property, and unconscious inculpation will come to define Tolstoy's model of society.

What, Then, Shall We Do? then shifts to a recounting of Tolstoy's participation in the census. Tolstoy's census site was the notorious Rzhanovsky tenements. Although he expected "a den of most terrible poverty and vice," he finds the residents rather different: men and women working "cheerfully" and "skillfully": "Everywhere we were greeted cheerily and kindly" (25:203). His first aborted foray into the Lyapinsky flophouse turns out to have given him a false impression of urban misery. The industrious poor, it turns out, need no help. Scattered among them, however, were some few "tattered, fallen, idle ones" in "crying need." Tolstoy groups these real "unfortunates" into three categories: former aristocracy, "wayward" (*rasputnyye*) women, and children. The former aristocracy, he reports, are "the most degraded and unhappy" denizens of the Rzhanovsky tenement house: "The present appeared to them unnatural, abhorrent, and unworthy of attention. None of them had a present [*net nastoiashchego*]. They had only recollections of the past and expectations of a future." Though he tries and fails to help some of them, in retrospect Tolstoy realizes that these people are no different from his upper-class acquaintances. Like those fallen Rzhanovsky nobility, his Moscow friends are "dissatisfied with their position, regret the past and want something better . . . namely, positions in which they can do less work and make others do more for them" (25:207). The downtown noblemen and the uptown noblemen, observes Tolstoy the radical, are equally irredeemable—an absent present is their common lot.

Tolstoy next examines the loose women. The scene at the first bordello is vivid and by far the most commonly excerpted passage from the book. He asks a woman wearing a "pink blouse loose in front and tight behind" what she does for a living. She replies that she "sits in a tavern." The landlord imperiously corrects her, using and relishing the foreign word *prostitutka*. Tolstoy, offended by his contempt, cries out, "It is not for us to reproach them but to pity them." The interplay among the three voices is particularly clear in this passage and so bears quoting in extenso:

[Protagonist-guide's voice:] I had only said this when, from the hole [*kamorka*] from which we'd heard the laughter, the boards of the beds squeaked, and over the partition that did not reach the ceiling arose a disheveled woman's head with small, swollen eyes and shiny red face, and behind her another and a third. Apparently, they had stood up on their beds, and all three of them stretched their necks and, holding their breath, with concentrated attention, silently looked at us.

The student, smiling at all this, became serious; the landlord was embarrassed and lowered his gaze. The women, not drawing a breath, looked at me and waited.

[Tolstoy the philanthropist:] I was more abashed than any of them. I had not at all expected that a word casually dropped would produce such an effect. It was just like the field of death, strewn with bones, would shudder from the touch of the spirit, and the dead bones would stir. I had spoken an accidental word of love and pity, and it had acted on all as though they had only been waiting for that word to stop being corpses and to come alive. They all looked at me and waited for what would come next. They waited for me to speak those words and do those deeds that would cause the bones to come together and grow flesh and come to life again. But I felt I had no words or deeds to continue what I had begun; I felt in the depth of my soul that I had lied: that I had nothing more to say or do, and I began to write on the card the names and occupations of all the people in the apartment. [Tolstoy the radical:] This event led me to believe that we could help these unfortunates also. It seemed to me then, in my self-deception, that this would be very easy. I said to myself, Let us note down these women also, and *afterwards we* (who these *we* were, I did not stop to consider), when we have noted everybody down, we will take care of this. I imagined that we, the very people who have for several generations led, and are still leading, these women into that condition, would one fine day take it into our heads suddenly to fix it all. (25:209–10)

Tolstoy and his university students next find a woman rocking a baby in her arms. She tells him that she is a wench (*devka*). Sensing an opportunity to rescue her, Tolstoy presses her for details. The child, it turns out, belongs to another prostitute, dying in the next room. The first prostitute, at her own expense, is caring for both mother and child. Wanting to save this decent woman, Tolstoy asks whether she would not rather become a cook. She replies, "'A cook! But I can't bake bread!' and she laughed . . . I saw by the expression of her face that she did not wish to be a cook and considered that position and calling to be a low one." The third voice, Tolstoy the radical, offers commentary:

This woman, who like the widow in the Gospels had in the simplest manner sacrificed her all for a sick neighbor . . . had been brought up to live without working and in the way that was considered natural by those around her . . . These prostitutes have lived from childhood among other such women, who they know very well have always existed and do exist and are necessary for society: so necessary that government officials are appointed to see that they exist properly. They know moreover that they have power over men and can often influence them more than other women can. (25:211–12)

Tolstoy soon hears of another woman selling her thirteen-year-old daughter and rushes to save the child, planning to "speak to some ladies who take an interest in the wretched position of such women" and send them to rescue the girl. They meet with only confusion, since neither mother nor daughter sees anything wrong with the transaction: "I should have understood that in [the mother's] action there was absolutely nothing bad or immoral: she had done and was doing all she could for her daughter—that is to say, just what she herself considered best." Tolstoy the radical wonders whether his society friends would be able to save the girl:

Had I thought of that I should have understood that the majority of the ladies I wished to send here to save that girl themselves live without bearing children and without work, serving merely to satisfy sensuality and deliberately educate their daughters for such a life. One mother leads her daughter to the taverns, another takes hers to court or to balls, but both share the same view of life: namely, that a woman should satisfy a man's lusts and that for that service she should be fed, clothed, and cared for. (25:212–13)

Tolstoy himself rescues a member of the final class of "unfortunates," children, by bringing one back home. The twelve-year-old orphan, Seriozha, is left in the Tolstoy family kitchen for the cook to care for: "Was it possible to put a lousy boy taken from a den of depravity among our own children?" (This is clearly the voice of Tolstoy the naive philanthropist.) He dutifully finds a peasant—the sectarian Siutaev, whom Tolstoy had recently befriended—willing to adopt the boy. The boy demurs and, after a week at the Tolstoy home, runs off to join the circus. The third, radical voice reflects on this experience:

If I took him from a *den* [iz *vertepa*] and brought him to a good place, he was right to assimilate the views of life existing in that good place; and from those views he understood that in a good place one must live merrily, eating and drinking sweet things without working . . . And he understood this and did not go with the peasant to herd cattle and live on potatoes with kvass but went to the zoo to dress as a savage and lead an elephant about for thirty kopecks. (25:214)

In the tenth chapter, Tolstoy relates one final, nighttime visit to the Rzhanovsky house for the census, accompanied by curious society friends who "had dressed specially in shooting jackets and high traveling boots, a costume in which they went on hunting expeditions . . . They were in that special state of excitement people are . . . for a hunt, a duel, or to start for the war." To obtain an accurate count of nightlodgers, the gate of the house is locked, causing a near riot among the poor. Tolstoy is grief-stricken and tries to reassure the masses, to no avail. The third voice reemerges: "It was as hard for them to believe this as it would be for hares to believe that dogs had come not to catch them but to count them" (25:218–19).

SCREWED UP: TOLSTOY'S SOCIAL CONTRACT

Tolstoy ends chapter 11 with the story of how he had failed to find satisfaction even in distributing thirty-seven rubles. He had received twenty-five rubles from the government for his work as a census taker and another dozen donated by the students who had worked with him during the census. (From his many "genteel acquaintances," his Moscow neighbors, he claims to have received not a single ruble of the many thousands that had been promised [25:218].)

In chapter 12, he observes that he has not touched the manuscript for three years (1882–85) and returned to it only when his mind had "sufficiently sharpened" (25:225). He worked furiously on it throughout 1885 because, he explained in a letter to Chertkov dated October 15–16, "I've got to cough up what is stuck in my throat" (85:267). In this second part of *What, Then, Shall We Do?* the ongoing dialogue between Tolstoy the philanthropist and Tolstoy the radical ends, and much of the rest of the book explains why Tolstoy's philanthropic efforts could never have worked:

> I wanted to write an article about everything that I had experienced and to tell why my undertaking had failed . . . No matter how hard I worked on it, no matter the abundance of material, no matter the frustration I experienced in writing it, I could not manage to write the article until this year [January 1886] because I hadn't experienced what I needed to experience to correctly relate to this matter, and, most important, because I clearly and simply had not realized the cause of it all, a reason that is very simple, one that had its roots in me. (25:225)

46

One's views on the causes of poverty control the methods for solving (or not solving) the problem. Simplifying things for the present purpose, poverty theories are usually rooted in either individuals or aggregates. Conservatives largely indict the individual, while progressives blame the system. (Most thinkers fall somewhere in between these extremes.) Conservatives claim that the poor do not participate in the practices that make up the everyday life of the dominant class because poor people are lazy, inferior, and immoral. Progressives argue that the poor are excluded from such practices because the social system distributes wealth unequally and unjustly.[9] Tolstoy is neither progressive nor conservative. Based on his observations of urban poverty, he claims that the wenches, ruined noblemen, and intransigent orphans participate in precisely the *same* practices, expectations, and assignments of energy that make up the everyday life of the dominant class. What unites the whores and society ladies, Tolstoy's own children and Seriozhka (the lousy orphan), is the temptation of and tendency for parasitism, a desire to enjoy the fruit of others' labor without expenditure of one's own. The working urban poor and Tolstoy's beloved peasants *are not the problem*; they have "a present" and lead lives of dignity and security precisely because they do not "enslave" others, they do not expropriate labor. Poverty does not need to be solved—wealth and leisure do.

In the second half of the book, Tolstoy investigates *how* the few are able to coerce the many into unjust and immoral relationships, asking questions that we recognize as very contemporary ones: How, practically, does dominant culture—the one symbolized, complicatedly, by whores and society ladies—assert itself? Why do subalterns (the workers and peasants) so predictably and uniformly subordinate themselves, providing their labor for the indolent? How do the fraudulent institutions and false beliefs, those that lure the toiling masses to a life of pointless sloth, arise and persist? In short, why, if the toilsome life that Tolstoy claims is both natural and superior, is it so difficult to change social organization? On a related note, why does society countenance the rebellious behavior that it does countenance? Culture is not monolithic, and some alternative and even oppositional modes and practices are allowed, and Tolstoy seeks to oppose the system from those loci. In the fringe of the city, in the faubourg of Khamovniki, he finds a source for new order and a refuge from the center.

Tolstoy begins his analysis, in chapter 17, with the question of money (25:247), what had seemed to him the very solution to the problem of urban poverty in his census speech. Clearly, he remarks, it is the *vehicle* of parasitism. We can enslave others because money purchases, directly or indirectly through goods, others' labor: "To simple people it seems indubitable that the proximate cause for the enslavement of some people by others is money" (25:254).[10] Tolstoy wonders, though, what invests money with this power to enslave others: "I can, with a whistle, gather in any civilized town a hundred people who, for those three rubles, are ready to do my will and perform the most laborious, repulsive, and degrading tasks. This is not because of the nature of money but because of the very complex conditions of our economic life" (25:242).

These chapters, with their ambitious intellectual, geographical, and historical scope, and their open scorn for experts, are strongly reminiscent of Tolstoy's attacks on professional historians, nearly twenty years earlier, in *War and Peace*. They are additionally genetically linked to his attacks on art critics and professional artists in *What Is Art?*, which he began a decade later, in 1896. In *What, Then, Shall We Do?* Tolstoy asks reasonable if simplistic questions about why things happen as they do and not otherwise: "What is money?" (25:242). "What is property?" (25:249). "Where does money come from?" (25:255). To answer these questions, he surveys the classic and contemporary literature on political economy—Malthus, Darwin, Comte, Kant, and Spencer—and finds their answers to be little more than addled tautologies when measured against the reality he recounts in the first part of *What, Then, Shall We Do?* Reading these attacks on economists and political theorists, one recalls Berlin's grudging compliment in *The Hedgehog and the Fox* for the dismantling of historiography in *War and Peace*: "The irritated awareness at the back of his mind that no final solution was ever, in principle, to be found, caused Tolstoy to attack the bogus solutions all the more savagely . . . Tolstoy's purely intellectual genius for this kind of lethal activity was very great and exceptional."[11]

Finding no satisfaction in the explanations of experts, Tolstoy develops an original social-contract theory, an intellectual construct that explains the natural state of man, the origin of society, and what constitutes legitimate and illegitimate authority. These deductions are defended using largely his personal experience, based on his contact with the urban poor and the peasantry. He weaves more of their stories, and references to the stories from the first part of *What, Then, Shall We Do?*, into his model.

Like other social-contract theorists, Tolstoy imagines and recounts the history of the world from "precivilizational" natural man to the economic and political order of his own "civilized" day. Each successive stage, he claims, is defined by a certain method of violence. With each stage, the reach of authority broadens, and more and different people become enmeshed in the system. Each successive method more effectively wields violence, and the total systemic use of violence increases. The extent to which the population is conscious of the violence, however, decreases.[12]

Tolstoy finds the start to his social contract in Genesis, in the story of Joseph's rule over Egypt (Gen. 39–47). Enslavement begins with the "first method," the earliest, the one in place before Joseph's elevation to vizier of

Egypt: "Warriors [*voiny*] who constantly ride among the inhabitants, and, under threat of death, they make sure that orders are obeyed." The strong-man (*silnyi*) and his warriors control the oppressed masses through violence. This "primitive method" of demographic management (25:271) gives way to a new one when Joseph directs his men to gather up and store the "fruit of the field" during seven years of plenty. When famine arrives, this stored food allows Joseph and the Pharaohs to extract a system of permanent tribute and land ownership, without resorting to direct violence. In addition to warriors, oppressors now need assistants, "great and little Josephs," "managers and distributors" to preserve the stores of grain and police the land. They all "become sharers in the advantage of the violence used." This second method, the political use of hunger and land, is a great "advance" over the first for the strongman: although the spoils have to be shared (great and little Josephs), the oppressor (*nasil'nik*) no longer needs to exercise his authority through "exertions" (*usiliia*) (25:275), and he can exercise his violence against a larger population. The oppressed (*nasiluyemyye*) prefer the second method since they are no longer subject to "brute force" (*grubaia sila*) and can now hope "to pass over from the ranks of the oppressed to the ranks of the oppressors," albeit "they can never more escape from some measure of coercion" (25:276). This new, second method, however, eventually fails to keep pace with the increasing complexity of life's conditions, so a third method of enslavement is devised—monetary taxation (*dan'*): "The oppressor demands from the slaves a certain amount of money tokens, which he himself possesses. To obtain them, the slaves are obliged to sell not only [food] but also articles of prime necessity: meat, skins, wool, clothes, fuel, even buildings, and thus the oppressor always holds the slaves in subjection not only by hunger but also by thirst, want, cold, and all other kinds of privation" (25:276).

Money, which Tolstoy had at first thought was the solution to poverty, instead provides the means by which labor is appropriated by the few. This form of slavery is founded on the implicit *threat* of physical violence. The strongmen says, I can "shoot each of you, or . . . kill you by taking the land that feeds you . . . but that is inconvenient and unpleasant for me, and therefore I allow all of you to arrange your own work and your own production as you please, so long as you give me so many money tokens" (25:276). Under this third method, an even more complex administration is required, so the oppressor has to share with more people. However, no one can now evade being subjected to the system's violence, directly or indirectly wielded—anyone with money, even in other countries, participates.

Unlike grosser forms of physical coercion, monetary taxation also maximizes the labor that can be taken: "Money tax is like a screw—it can easily and conveniently be turned a bit at a time to the utmost limit that does not kill the golden hen." The oppressed, incorrectly, perceive the third method as an improvement: he has more *personal* freedom, "he can live where he pleases, do what he pleases, and sow or not sow grain; he is not obliged to account for his work, and if he has money he can consider himself quite free" (25:278). However, since there are relatively more oppressors—more "great and little Josephs"—living without laboring, the burden of supporting them falls on a smaller number. The total violence required to maintain the system always increases.

All three methods coexist in modern society—the military maintains the first, landowners and capitalists the second, and the state the third. These "screws" can be alternately relaxed or tightened. People are "thrust into the worst slavery, more terrible than ever before" (25:284). Yet having been slaves so long, they are "not conscious of their condition and consider slavery to be a natural condition and regard the changes in forms of slavery as an alleviation" (25:282). The oppressors eventually come to consider themselves, and be considered, as emancipators and benefactors when they loosen one screw while tightening another. This pattern, Tolstoy maintains, has been repeated, over time, throughout Europe and the "ancient world"; in his day, it was exported from Europe, with the recent history of colonialism in Fiji offering a perfect example of the pattern that originated with Joseph in Egypt (25:256–66).

Tolstoy's "story" of how we have passed from a state of nature to the present "complex conditions of our economic life," his social-contract theory, dismisses outright the existence of a "primitive uncorrupted perfect human society" as something philosophers "dream up" (25:266); warriors have always ridden among us, violence and any systematic organization are coeval. Tolstoy's social contract thus begins with a Hobbesian state of war, one in which a few, the strong, predate the weak, peaceable, self-sufficient, agrarian, and communitarian communities; it ends with a worse, more diffuse but more totalizing and inescapable *bellum omnium contra omnes*, where everyone is either a slave or a slaveholder. (More exactly, nearly everyone, save those very few who make no use of another's labor, is *both* a slave and a slaveholder.) Such a state has been made possible by the invention of money and the subsequent growth, in scope and power, of the state.

One aspect of Tolstoy's methodology for developing his social theory merits mention: this network of unconscious violence succeeds because it is abetted by institutions that share an interest in maintaining these illusions of freedom, choice, and progress. This insight animates Tolstoy's later attacks on natural science, art, organized religion, and nationalism—all of which he condemns for their complicity and collaboration with the system. In *What, Then, Shall We Do?* his specific target is the "science of economics," which constructs elaborate explanations to valorize a system in which the few exploit the many: "One can make a man a slave, make him do what he considers bad for himself, but it is impossible to make him think that while suffering violence he is free, and that this obvious evil that he is enduring is for his own good. That seems impossible. That is just what has been done in our time through science" (25:285).

VIOLENCE AND FREEDOM

With its search for totalizing explanations for human behavior and the interplay of lexically related terms like "coercion" (*nasilie*), "strongman" (*sil'nyi*), "exertions" (*usilie*), "oppressors" (*nasil'niki*), and "oppressed" (*nasiluemye*), Tolstoy's analysis of the formation of state organization furthermore clearly recalls the discussion of force and freedom in the second epilogue of *War and Peace*. There, Tolstoy wonders, "What force [*sila*] moves people?" and ransacks the historian's concept of power or authority (*vlast'*) attributed to authority figures like Napoléon and Alexander. To the two central questions of history, "(1) What is authority (or 'power' [*vlast'*])?" and "(2) What force [*sila*] produces the movement of people?" (i.e., what makes history happen as it does), Tolstoy answers,

(1) Authority is that relation of a certain person to other persons in which the person who takes the lesser part in the action is the one who expresses opinions, propositions, and justifications for the jointly accomplished action.

(2) The movement of peoples is produced not by authority, not by intellectual activity, not even by a combination of the two, as historians have thought, but by the activity of *all* the people taking part in the event and joining always together so that those who take the most direct part in the event take the least responsibility upon themselves, and vice versa. (12:322)

The historian's concept of "authority" masks his ignorance of the causal chains that determine our every act: "Napoléon ordered the army to go to war," and therefore a war began (12:316). In fact, an inverse relationship obtains between claims to direct or to be responsible for a given action— the Napoléons and Alexanders—and that person's actual importance and responsibility. The greater our sense of agency and responsibility for the "course of events," the less our actual importance and influence on it. This relation between sense of freedom and actual agency leads Tolstoy to his well-known conclusion regarding determinism: the true force of history is an individual's "relation" and "connection" to everything and everyone around him, the catchall concept of infinitesimally small and pervasive "influences." A person may, perhaps must, believe he is free, but that sense of freedom is false, for "to the extent that we see these influences, to that extent our notion of his freedom decreases and our notion of the necessity he is subject to increases." We may have power over some of our choices on certain, highly circumscribed levels, but we are unfree when we act collectively; perhaps we are always and utterly unfree, for even the "light that falls on things" exerts an influence and therefore deprives us of some of our freewill (12:329–30).

Tolstoy never finally resolves the question of freedom in *War and Peace*. Whatever the case, since we cannot live without a sense of agency, and since we can never know *all* the forces that condition our acts, we preserve some, perhaps illusory, sense of freedom.

It is critical to understand that the social theory in *What, Then, Shall We Do?* echoes and refines these interconnected notions of force and the freedom that circulate in the epistemological project of *War and Peace*. The operating terms and concepts are unchanged: authority and force, freedom and enslavement, great men and the "swarm life" of ordinary people, conscious and unconscious action, and, generally and perhaps most important, our awareness of those forces that subvert our freedom. The model in *What, Then, Shall We Do?* fully answers the question from *War and Peace*: what is this force (*sila*), that moves people, "joins them together," and produces their actions, the same force that ultimately renders them (unconsciously) unfree? The force (*sila*) is coercion (*nasilie*) (the two words are directly related in Russian), be it direct physical violence or the sublimated violence of the state facilitated by economic transactions.

The same topsy-turvy world of "exceptional" individual and the swarm life found in *War and Peace* persists in *What, Then, Shall We Do?*: the great do nothing yet receive the credit, while the rest do everything useful, yet their stories are rarely if ever told. The higher in the system a person's position, the less he directly participates in the coercion, the fewer "exertions" (*usiliia*) he is required to make, because he relies on the pyramid of "little Josephs." Yet the less he participates, the more this person in authority profits from the system that arrogates the fruits of the labor of the many. These "little Josephs" are the aristocrats, the addressees of Tolstoy's census article, the parasites who subsist on others' labor. At the other end of the spectrum exists the swarm, the industrious residents of the Rzhanovsky Tenement and Tolstoy's peasants. The humbler a person's position in *What, Then, Shall We Do?* the more alike she is to the true heroes of the resistance during the Napoleonic campaigns in Russia, those people who were "guided only by the personal interests of the day" and were therefore "the most useful" (12:14). Whereas the laboring masses are most immediately and relentlessly exposed to coercion, no one who participates in the system can escape its coercion.

At the end of chapter 21, Tolstoy offers a Tolstoyan analogy, comparing the problem of the system with a leaky wooden bucket. The bucket clearly has a hole, and no amount of trying to patch it from the outside will solve the problem. Stopping the leak requires finding the hole and patching it from the inside:

> The same holds true for the proposed means for stopping the unjust division of wealth, for the stopping up of the holes through which the wealth of the people leaks. They say—just organize workers' associations, make capital public property, make the land public property! All this is only external plugging of the places from which the water seems to leak. To stop the leakage of the workers' wealth into the hands of the leisured classes it is necessary to find, from the inside, the hole through which this leakage takes place. This hole is the coercion that armed men exert on the unarmed; the violence of troops by means of which the people themselves are taken from their work, and the land is taken from the people, and the produce of people's toil. As long as there exists a single armed man who believes it is his right to kill any other man whatever, so long will there be the irregular distribution of wealth—that is, slavery. (25:290)

What, then, shall we do? Tolstoy answers that question directly in the final chapter of the book.

A WOMAN'S PLACE

The discussion of female procreativity at the end of *What, Then, Shall We Do?* likely takes the reader by surprise. While the first thirty-nine chapters of the book deal directly and unambiguously with poverty, the final chapter abruptly changes tack, addressing directly women "of our class"—Tolstoy's class, and the likely class of his readers, then and now—with a detailed analysis of, and prescriptions for, dominant-class female sexual practices. If we reasonably assume the answer to the title's question lies in the book's conclusion, then, here is what "we" shall do about poverty: on the last pages of the book, Tolstoy tells "our" woman to give birth to as many babies *herself* as she can, "nurse them *herself*" personally (without the use of a wet nurse), "prepare food," "sew" and "wash," and "teach her own children" (the prescription rhymes in Russian: *i shit', i myt', i uchit'*), "sleep and talk with them." If you lack the inclination or requisite organs for all this, you are part of the problem: Tolstoy dismisses women who practice birth control as "whores" (*bliadi*) and all men "of our circle" without exception as "scoundrels and cowards." "The salvation of the world" lies in the hands of bourgeois mothers "more than in those of anyone else" (25:411).

Tolstoy begins his address to women-mothers in chapter 40 by remarking that men "of our class" have long ignored the biblical injunction to live by the sweat of our brows. They are irredeemable. Our women, though, might still be salvaged, since they have always lived their destined lot, bearing children. They have maintained their "reasonable understanding of life." Their salvation is threatened, however, by science, which has made available "among the wealthy classes dozens of methods of preventing pregnancy . . . and appliances for preventing childbirth" that have "become common accessories of the toilet." These "barren women" seem to be mastering men with their "shoulders and curls," but they are really being "perverted by men, descending to his level," "letting slip" their true power "[instead] to compete with streetwomen" (25:406–7).

Throughout the book, Tolstoy's obvious fascination with the "prostitutes" (*prostitutki*) at the flophouses and the "lady-whores" (*damy-bliadi*) in his own social set is animated by how their sexual practices illustrate the central themes of the book: an aversion for honest work and a pursuit instead of pleasure and leisure; our dual roles as slaves and enslavers (prostitutes are both); our willing submission to systemic violence, a violence that money structures in such a way that we are unaware of our victimhood; and the role of governmental authority and science in maintaining these relations. The "woman-mother"(*zhenshchina-mat'*), however, rejects the interconnected causes Tolstoy identifies of poverty—money, coercion, and leisure—and therefore remains outside the interconnected systems of coercion that Tolstoy has explored:

> [A woman-mother's] business is to serve life, and therefore she will not seek distant paths for that service but will only not neglect those near at hand . . . Such a mother will not ask others what she shall do; she will know it all and will fear nothing and will always be at peace, for she will know that she has done what she had to do . . . If there are doubts for men and for childless women on the path to fulfilling the will of God, for the woman-mother this path is firmly and clearly defined; if she humbly and in the simplicity of her soul fulfills it, she stands on the highest point of perfection a human being can reach; she becomes a guiding light [*putevodnoy zvezdoy*] for all people. (25:411)

If reform and revolution are useless and participation means corruption, then the only reasonable relationship to a system is a passive one: nonaction, noninterference, nonparticipation. In the mid-1880s Tolstoy spends his days reading Laozi, Confucius, and the Buddha stories—he writes "Chinese Wisdom," and he retells the Buddha tales while taking a break from writing *What, Then, Shall We Do?* His paean of childbearing and rearing clearly resonates with the quiescent virtues he finds in the Tao, the Path.

In the description above, note the emphasis on how the woman-mother has found "the path"; throughout the book, Tolstoy has clearly been fascinated by the women in the tenements who have "lost the path" (the etymological meaning of the word *rasputnyi*, "wayward").[13] Women-mothers live in the absolute present, the present that the nobility—in the Lyapinsky house or in Tolstoy's parlor—lack. Their pleasure *is* labor, and their labor, pleasure. A mother's work is immediate, intuitive, beyond culture, beyond science, beyond authority, and beyond control and, therefore, outside the system of violence that is our social system.[14]

SOME CONCLUSIONS ABOUT TOLSTOY'S SOCIAL CONTRACT THEORY

1. In *What, Then, Shall We Do?* Tolstoy proposes that in state formation, consent is far more effective than violence but that consent is always and ultimately obtained through the implicit threat of physical violence that the state alone can legally wield. The armed military and police guarantee the state's right and ability to use physical violence. It is important to note that as the overt exercise of violence decreases, the total amount of coercion available to the state, and wielded by it, increases. Tolstoy develops this theme in a later treatise on state violence, *The Kingdom of God Is within You.* Because money represents one person's arrogation of another's labor, it is itself a form of coercion. Tolstoy calls it "monetary-taxational coercion" (*denezhno-podatnoe nasilie*) and claims that it is "strongest" and "most important" because it is "impersonal" (25:289).

2. Modern authority is unavoidable, terrible, and productive precisely because we are mostly unconscious of its underlying potential for physical violence. (Recall Tolstoy's experience at the execution in Paris.) Systemic power operates most effectively when it does not outright or violently repress dissentient forces but instead organizes and channels them through systems of exchange that offer the illusion of freedom and improvement. The prostitutes Tolstoy tries to "save" are quite happy to be prostitutes, and the state oversees their welfare because they are part of one system.

3. Anyone who participates in any economic system—wherever one person is "not working, not because others work for him lovingly but because instead of working himself he transfers, using coercion, that work onto others"—is enslaved (25:288). Since we are each exploiting the other through economic relationships, we are all victims and perpetrators of what Tolstoy calls an unconscious conspiracy. We deceive and abuse one another but do so, as it were, while sleeping. How can we stop, if we do not awaken to our true state, if we remain ignorant of the violence constantly enacted upon us? It would be difficult to overstate the importance

of this concept for Tolstoy's later spiritual and political thought. It is precisely in this sense that his social theorizing is itself anarchical: it represents an attempt to undermine dominant value systems by revealing the complex ways in which specifically Western institutions—particularly liberal, pluralistic democracy and "civilization"—control and compromise people.

4. Modern dominant culture is not an externally imposed ideology, nor the overt exploitation of the many by the few, nor some blatant and violent oppression of the masses. People believe, mistakenly, that they are free and see their masters as liberators. Modern sciences, the arts, and religion all collaborate and confirm this false reality as the real one. These dominant values and practices organize the life of most people and constitute their only sense of reality. How does one rebel against reality? Ivan Ilyich perhaps sensed the irreality of his reality in the final moments before his death.

5. If it were as simple as the few oppressing the many, revolution might work and change might be easy. Since any new form of society will simply repeat and extend the relationships of violence, reform and revolution are equally useless. All reformers inevitably become "little Josephs." The uselessness of political reform gets most fully developed in Tolstoy's late political thought, particularly in "The End of an Age" (1905) and "On the Meaning of the Russian Revolution" (1906).[15]

6. Therefore, nonparticipation, nonviolence, and nonaction offer the only true forms of dissent.

7. Tolstoy's insights into state coercion and co-optation take part in a nineteenth-century tradition of systemic investigation of authority and state that leads directly to what we would now call, broadly and incompletely, poststructuralist social theory.

NOTES

1. This concern with authority, the state, and coercion arises in some earlier works, notably in "Progress and the Definition of Education" (Progress i opredelenie obrazovaniia, 1862), where the state's ability to intentionally improve the lot of the populace is examined. Tolstoy returns to the subject in part 2 of the epilogue to *War and Peace*, where the discussion has less to do with state and institutional authority than with individual authority and its influence on history. The question of the state and coercion is central, in part 8 of *Anna Karenina*, when Prince Shcherbatsky and Levin discuss the Russian Volunteer Movement and the Balkan Question with Katavasov and Sergei Ivanovich (18:387–92).

2. The margins of cities as nexuses of imposed order facing popular resistance is something of a commonplace in demographic history. My recounting

here relies heavily on John M. Merriman, *The Margins of City Life: Explorations on the French Urban Frontier, 1815–1851* (Oxford: Oxford University Press, 1991), 3–30, and James C. Scott, *Seeing Like a State: How Certain Schemes to Improve the Human Condition Have Failed* (New Haven, Conn.: Yale University Press, 1999), 53–84.

3. For more on Tolstoy's master plots of antiheroes, dissent, and revolution, see Inessa Medzhibovskaya, "Terror Un-Sublimated: Militant Monks, Revolution, and Tolstoy's Final Master Plots," *TSJ* 22 (2010): 17–38.

4. S. A. Tolstaya, *My Life*, ed. Andrew Donskov, trans. John Woodsworth and Arkadi Klioutchanski (Ottawa: University of Ottawa Press, 2010), 312.

5. Rosamund Bartlett, *Tolstoy: A Russian Life* (Boston: Houghton Mifflin Harcourt, 2011), 294.

6. Inessa Medzhibovskaya, *Tolstoy and the Religious Culture of His Time: A Biography of a Long Conversion, 1845–1887* (Lanham, Md.: Lexington Books, 2008), 141, 265–66.

7. Andrew Wachtel, *The Battle for Childhood: Creation of a Russian Myth* (Stanford, Calif.: Stanford University Press, 1990), 26–35.

8. John Givens, "The Fiction of Fact and the Fact of Fiction: Hayden White and *War and Peace*," *TSJ* 21 (2009): 22–24. Biographers (e.g., Ernest Joseph Simmons, *Tolstoy* [London: Routledge and K. Paul, 1973], 356–58) often quote passages from the book as direct, factual descriptions of Tolstoy's activities in Moscow in the early 1880s, failing to properly qualify for the fact that the passages are drawn from a book with complicated generic motivations. (Similar problems arise when biographers accept *Childhood*, e.g., as Tolstoy's unproblematic autobiography.)

9. This schematic and necessarily simplistic rendering of the opposing views on the sources of poverty is based on chapters 1 and 3 of John Kenneth Galbraith, *The Affluent Society* (Boston: Houghton Mifflin, 1998).

10. This section of *What, Then, Shall We Do?* was excerpted and published in several editions and languages at the end of the 1880s and beginning of the 1890s by the Swiss publisher Elpidine. Along with *A Confession*, its publication abroad brought Tolstoy's philosophical and social program a worldwide audience.

11. Isaiah Berlin, *The Hedgehog and the Fox: An Essay on Tolstoy's View of History*, ed. Henry Hardy, 2nd ed. (Princeton, N.J.: Princeton University Press, 2013), 41.

12. Tolstoy's historical analysis of inequality aligns significantly with current anthropology and social theorists. For a very similar history of how growing societies and intense competition for resources lead to despotism and inequality, see Kent V. Flannery and Joyce Marcus, *The Creation of Inequality: How Our Prehistoric Ancestors Set the Stage for Monarchy, Slavery, and Empire* (Cambridge, Mass.: Harvard University Press, 2012).

13. He describes the prostitute caring for her dying colleague's baby as "a woman living a wayward life [*zhenzhchina, zhivshaia rasputstvom*]" (25:205); one of the three classes of truly needy in the Rzhanovsky tenement was the "wayward women [*rasputnye zhenshchiny*]" (25:205); he mentions a former servant who had an affair with a lackey and ended up dying at twenty in a "house of wayward women [*v rasputnom dome*]" (25:232). There are numerous other examples of this phrase.

14. The best overview of Tolstoy's interest in China in particular and Eastern metaphysical traditions generally is Derk Bodde, *Tolstoy and China* (Princeton, N.J.: Princeton University Press, 1950). On the topic, see also Michael A. Denner, "Tolstoyan Nonaction: The Advantage of Doing Nothing," *TSJ* 13 (2001): 8–22, which touches directly on Tolstoy's idea of inaction and complete quiescence as a panacea for all social problems.

15. Tolstoy's essays "Konets veka" (1905) and "O znachenii russkoi revoliutsii" (1906) were both published in 1936 in *The Jubilee*, volume 36, overseen by N. K. Gudzii, pages 237–77 and 315–62, respectively.

Vladimir M. Paperni

The Transformation of the Mystical Tradition in Tolstoy's Art and Religious Thought

BOTH DURING HIS LIFE and after, Lev Tolstoy was often labeled a mystic. Tolstoy himself rejected this label and said so openly on several occasions. In his treatise *The Kingdom of God Is within You* (1890–93), Tolstoy recalls with disdain and sarcasm how certain "foreign critics" had called him a "Russian mystic" (28:37). He gave the treatise the subtitle *Christianity Not as a Mystical Doctrine but as a New Conception of Life.*

In the religious and philosophical rhetoric Tolstoy deployed in his writings on Christianity in the years just before and after the turn of the twentieth century, the word "mysticism" and its derivatives appear often and always carry the same negative valence. For Tolstoy, the term denotes vagueness, arbitrariness, incomprehensibility, hostility to the demands of reason, inanity, and falsity—all common to traditional religious doctrines. Thus, in his *Harmonization and Translation of the Gospels* the word is used thirteen times and always with the range of meanings suggested above. The Trinity, God incarnate, sin offering, the resurrection and ascension of Christ—Tolstoy labels all of these, as well as their theological interpretations, "mystical."

Already in Tolstoy's time, in positivistic cultural circles devoid of religious interests, the concept of mysticism was interpreted broadly and associated with such disparate phenomena as theological religion, occultism, spiritualism, theosophy, and so forth. All of this was "mysticism": incomprehensible, outdated, confusing, and unnecessary. And the late Tolstoy used the word in precisely this way, in the spirit of positivism. In so doing, he stripped his discourse of any ability to distinguish mysticism as a unique form of religiosity from church religion. But this in no way meant that Tolstoy did not recognize the uniqueness of mysticism as a religious movement.

In a letter to Alexander Herzen dated March 14, 1861, Tolstoy describes the main character of a new novel, a Decembrist returning from exile, as "an enthusiast, a mystic, and a Christian" (60:374). As we know, this idea was ultimately realized as *War and Peace*, while the Decembrist was transformed into the Freemason and mystic Pierre Bezukhov. And it was precisely around Pierre that Tolstoy organized a vast amount of thematic material describing the phenomenon of Russian mysticism at the beginning of the nineteenth century, a phenomenon called directly by name in the text. The word "mysticism," in its standard meaning in the period Tolstoy depicts, appears three times in the text, and the adjective "mystical" shows up another three times.[1]

In the mid-1850s, when Tolstoy began to display some interest in Russia's political and cultural history from the end of the eighteenth to the beginning of the nineteenth century, he became acquainted with several representative works of Masonic literature. While working on the early drafts of *War and Peace*, Tolstoy used these sources time and again. And at the end of 1866, when the overall structure of the text was essentially complete, he began to study the esoteric Masonic manuscripts housed in the Rumiantsev Museum archive in Moscow. He ordered copies of several of these manuscripts. Lengthy fragments of Masonic manuscripts—the protocols of the Masonic student lodge and the notes of P. Titov and of S. Lanskoy—were worked into the text of *War and Peace*, thus providing material for Bezukhov's diary, for descriptions of his mystical dreams, for the episode of his initiation into Freemasonry, and for some other episodes.[2]

Tolstoy in no way identified the Russian Freemasons he depicts in *War and Peace* with mysticism. He presents the Freemasons not as a community of mystics but as an organization whose members strive to achieve the most diverse moral, social, political, and material ends; only some of them are in fact involved in seeking out mystical secrets. On the whole, Tolstoy represents both the mystical doctrine the Freemasons profess and the mystical rituals they perform as being divorced from real Masonic practice and bereft of meaning. Tolstoy saw Freemasonry as an integral part of "high society," a part that functioned according to the false laws of convention that were just as applicable to the salon as they were to the Masonic lodge.

In *War and Peace*, direct, authorial descriptions of Masonic ritual and social practice are accompanied by scathing irony. Tolstoy's private remarks about the Freemasons were even more negative. In a letter of November 15, 1866, he writes to his wife, "Went to the Rumiantsev Museum and sat there until three. Read Masonic manuscripts—very interesting. And I cannot explain to you why reading them has made me feel an ennui I haven't been able to rid myself of all day. It is sad that all these Freemasons were fools" (83:129). One should note, however, that this strictly negative view did not extend to the philanthropic tendencies of Masonic ideology or to their mystical religiosity. These aspects of Freemasonry invoked in Tolstoy a deep, if limited, sympathy.

Tolstoy's reflections on Masonic mystical religiosity were concentrated around its fundamental characteristics. The distinguishing features of different movements within Russian Freemasonry, its history, and other similar questions of a historical nature were of little interest to Tolstoy. His studies of Masonic sources led him to a specific intellectual and social microcosm of Russian Freemasonry and, at the same time, opened the doors to the macrocosm of the centuries-old tradition of mystical Gnosis from which Masonic mysticism had grown. It was this tradition Tolstoy sought to understand and explain, in the context both of Russian history at the beginning of the nineteenth century and of the universal history of religion.

The twentieth century proved fruitful for historians of religion in the study of mystical traditions, to which Freemasonry was closely related. When Tolstoy was writing *War and Peace*, he had almost nothing to rely on aside from Masonic semilegendary narratives about Freemasonry's connection to mystical traditions of the past. At the same time, Tolstoy did not consider it necessary to include any historical narration on the Masonic movement in his novel. As he suggests more than once in *War and Peace*, the true tasks of historical investigation lie in studying the "laws" according to which historical events take place, not in creating narratives about the causal connection between these events that then made up the activity of professional historians. Against the positivistic historicism of his epoch, Tolstoy proposed a method of reconstructing the historical past in all its vivid glory with the aid of artistic narration, thereby showing that "historical" events and events concerning the private lives of people happen according to the same laws. Using this method, Tolstoy embedded in his narrative about the individual lives of his Freemasons entire images of Russian Freemasonry and mystical religiosity. Like other images Tolstoy created in *War and Peace*, these images reflect a strikingly high level of historical accuracy.

❄ ❄ ❄

According to Harold Bloom,

> The dominant element in Western religious traditions . . . tends to be institutional, historical, and dogmatic in its orientations. This is true for normative Judaism, for Islam in its Sunni and Shi'ite branches, and for Christianity, whether Roman Catholic, Eastern Orthodox, or mainline Protestant. In all of these, God essentially is regarded as external to the self. There are mystics and spiritual visionaries within these traditions who have been able to reconcile themselves with institutional authority, but there always has been an alternative convention, the way of Gnosis, an acquaintance with, or knowledge of, the God within, that has been condemned as heretical by the institutional faiths. In one form or another, Gnosis has maintained itself for at least the two millennia of what we have learned to call the Common Era.[3]

61

For all the diversity of the mystical doctrines and practices that have been developed by different Gnostic movements over the course of centuries, common to them all is the use of general concepts. The key concept of Gnosis is *mystery*. The Gnostic is a mystic striving toward mysterious knowledge inaccessible to laymen and the uninitiated. The very word "mysticism" goes back to the ancient Greek mystery cults and their initiatory rites. (The Greek word *mystikos* originates from *mystes*, which means "the one who has been initiated.")

For all mystical movements, initiation is a crucial stage that the layman must pass through in order to become a mystic. Initiation gives access to the process of knowing the mysteries of Divine Reality, the mysteries of Godhead, gods, and spirits. For the mystic, these mysteries are unrevealed and cannot be revealed in the doctrines of religious teaching. Even when the mystic accepts such doctrines, they remain for him only a part of knowing God, only one element of mystical Gnosis. Concerning religious knowledge, the mystic's criterion for truth is not correspondence to a doctrine but rather the fact that this knowledge has been received from special, mystical sources. Such sources for him are canonical mystical literature (of the tradition to which he belongs) and the personal religious experience of mystical revelation, which also has literary sources, for in their visions mystics generally see what they have read about in books.

The knowledge a mystic acquires is mysterious, secret, esoteric, and occultic (all these adjectives are practically synonymous). The mystic is called upon to conceal his religious experience and to respect it himself as a mystery. The books he reads and the knowledge he receives by word of mouth are secret. The language he uses should be mysteriously complicated and incomprehensible to the uninitiated. The community of mystics and their gatherings should be mysterious, and their rituals should be like their language: incomprehensible to those on the outside.

Mystical Gnosis has an archaic, mythological nature. It is not knowledge as a certain epistemological practice in which the one who strives to know and the object of knowledge are separated. Rather, it is a kind of magical practice called in some traditions *via mystica*. The mystic proceeds along the *via mystica*, performing as he does so specific magical and symbolical acts that are meant to change his human nature, to liken him to the Divine object of his knowledge. In the course of this movement, the mystic develops a magical *force* with the aid of which he finds the possibility of reaching the end of the *via mystica*: contemplation of the Godhead, merging with Him (*unio mystica*), and in some mystical traditions also influencing Him.

The idea of *unio mystica* is based on an ancient mythological concept that Mircea Eliade defined as "man's overcoming of his human status." Eliade also noted the most important traditional symbols through which this concept is realized. Primary among them are mythological images of *crossing over*: ascent of a mountain or ladder connecting sky and earth, entrance into a holy place or temple, ascent to the heavens, temporary death and rebirth, and resurrection. The mythological symbolism of enlightenment by divine light has an analogical meaning: the Godhead (or a divine entity representing the Godhead) emits light, standing before the mystic. Taking the divine light into himself, the mystic is enlightened and thus becomes a part of the Godhead himself.[4]

❅ ❅ ❅

In *War and Peace*, the ideas described above are absent on the explicit, conceptual level of authorial reflection, but they are very much present on its implicit, narrative level, one that transforms the fictional narrative into a means of understanding historical reality.

The key moment depicting Masonic religiosity in the text is the story of Pierre Bezukhov, which is consistently rendered as the story of a mystic. But Tolstoy's Pierre is a mystic of a different order: he is a failed mystic, one who in fact fails more than once. Three times Pierre sets out on the *via mystica*: first in the context of his Masonic career and then twice when he acts on his own fear, at his own risk. And in each case, his *via mystica* is interrupted and ends in failure.

Discussing the *via mystica* of early Christian and Islamic mystical movements, Margaret Smith noted the concept, shared among all the mystical doctrines she examines, of the three stages constituting the *via mystica*: (1) purification, (2) enlightenment (*illuminatio*), and (3) unification (*unio mystica*) with the Godhead.[5] We find something similar in Tolstoy's version of the *via mystica*, which, incidentally, Tolstoy uses in *War and Peace* as well as in later texts. But everything begins, of course, with the description of Pierre's first *via mystica*, which takes place in the Masonic lodge.

Tolstoy presents Pierre's first *via mystica* as resulting from a coincidence. In a state of despair after his duel with Dolokhov and break with his wife, Pierre happens to meet the Freemason Bazdeev, who, sensing Pierre's dejection, proposes to him the path of salvation: the path of the Freemason.

Tolstoy bases Bazdeev's speech to Pierre on Masonic documents. Tolstoy chose his sources carefully, with the result that Bazdeev distinctly describes mysticism as a certain *type* of religiosity.

Practically from the start of their conversation, Bazdeev speaks about God and the Freemasons' construction of a "temple that is meant to be a dwelling worthy of Almighty God" (10:68). Pierre admits that he does not believe in God. This response does not perturb Bazdeev but rather emboldens him, and he explains to Pierre that when speaking of God, it is not faith that is important but knowledge (i.e., mystical Gnosis). It is precisely because Pierre "does not know" God that he is so unhappy with his life (10:69). As Bazdeev explains, knowledge of God is a mystery inaccessible to the uninitiated, and to penetrate this mystery is the goal of many generations of Freemasons that have been building the temple. Contact with the mysterious knowledge of Freemasonry, he adds, is impossible without *purification*: "The highest wisdom and truth are like the purest liquid . . . Can I receive this pure liquid in an impure vessel and judge of its purity?" (10:70).

The story of Pierre's Masonic conversion is told in a double perspective—from Pierre's point of view, full of naïveté and incomprehension, and from the narrator's point of view. The narrator constantly underscores Pierre's extreme confusion and gullibility. From the very beginning, this psychological backdrop defamiliarizes the depiction of Masonic behavior, rituals, and doctrine. In the first episode of the story, the point of view of the narrator is absolutely neutral. Bazdeev is presented in an impartial manner, as a historically typical image of a Masonic teacher (as is well known, the prototype of Bazdeev was a prominent Russian Mason Osip Alekseevich Pozdeev). In the following episodes, the point of view of the narrator becomes more and more ironical. The Freemasons are drawn to Pierre's wealth, which is why they quickly lead him through the stage of purification and do not place great demands on him. In the course of a single week, Pierre stays at home and does nothing but read one book: Thomas à Kempis's *The Imitation of Christ*.[6] It is said to have been sent to Pierre "by an unknown person" (10:73)—that is, its arrival is ironically described as a (pseudo)mystical event. As he reads, Pierre is filled with "a pleasure he had not known before: to believe in the possibility of attaining perfection and in the possibility of practical brotherly love between men, as revealed to him by Bazdeev" (10:73). This essentially moral "pleasure" is disconnected from Bazdeev's mystical pathos on which Pierre places his own hopes. Pierre is led into the world of Masonic mysticism by unfounded hopes and his characteristic weakness. Pierre says yes in answer to the two questions that Willarsky poses to him: yes, he is ready to enter the order, and yes, he believes in God. As the author notes, Willarsky comes to Pierre "with the same official, solemn air as Dolokhov's second" (10:73). The importance of this detail cannot be emphasized enough. Entering the Masonic lodge, Pierre is essentially just as much a slave to circumstance as he was before the duel with Dolokhov and, even earlier, before his marriage to Hélène Kuragin. All these and the subsequent life-changing events are accompanied by a paralysis of will.

In the next major episode dealing with Pierre's initiation into Freemasonry, the narrator's perspective combines defamiliarizing irony and sharp scrutiny of the nuances of the Masonic ceremony, their special mystical and mythological semantics. As is well known, the archaic mythological concept of initiation—the altering of the initiate's human state as a result of passing through temporal death and rebirth or resurrection—lies at the foundation of Masonic initiation rituals. (Since the Masonic movement grew from medieval Scottish builders' communities, Masonic initiation rituals stemmed directly from the archaic magic rituals of these communities). Superimposed on this semantics of initiation are the mystical symbolism of enlightenment, illumination by divine light (*illuminatio*), and the Gnostic symbolism of the receiving and transmitting of mysterious divine knowledge. Tolstoy lacked the analytical vocabulary necessary for describing such phenomena. He dealt with this task by writing a highly sophisticated narrative instead.

Pierre's initiation begins with his being blindfolded and left alone for five minutes, symbolizing immersion into the darkness of death before enlightenment and new life. Acting according to instruction, Pierre removes the blindfold when he hears a knock at the door and sees a lamp illuminating a human skull, the Gospel, and a coffin full of bones: all symbols of death, the unity of life and death, and divine immortality. Then Pierre's door is opened,[7] and the tyler enters. The tyler, who says Pierre is "one who does not believe in the truth of the light and who cannot see the light," promises Pierre "wisdom, virtue, and enlightenment." He apprises Pierre of the aims of the order, the "first and principal" of which is the "preservation and handing down to posterity of a certain solemn mystery . . . that has come down to us from the most ancient times, and even from the first man." He explains the meaning of the seven Masonic virtues and says that the order discloses its doctrine using not only words but also hieroglyphs. After this, the initiation proper begins. At first, Pierre is asked to undress and confess his primary temptation,[8] after which he is subjected to additional symbolic machinations. Once again, his eyes are covered and uncovered, and he is shown first the "lesser light" and then the "full light." The Freemasons instruct him to lie before the altar, "to lie prostrate before the gates of the temple." Then he is given the Masonic accoutrements: a white leather apron, a trowel, and three pairs of gloves and is asked to listen to the charter of the order (10:74–83).

In this passage, which the author treats with increasing irony, the initiation ceremony seems to consist of dead symbols. Tolstoy understands the meaning of these symbols well, but he simultaneously suggests that for the participants the rituals are nothing more than a formality, a dead letter, a hieroglyph. The aim of any religious ritual is the spiritual transformation of the participants, their crossing over from the profane to the sacred. This is what Pierre expects, but as the author indicates, no such transformation happens to any of the participants.

The absence of any crossing over into sacred space is underscored not only by the ritual described above but also by Pierre's feelings at the time. For Pierre, the whole ritual is strange and summons up feelings of shame and doubt: "Where am I? What am I doing? Are they laughing at me? Won't

I be ashamed to remember this?" (10:81). Suppressing his feelings, Pierre continues to participate in his initiation. But as Tolstoy indicates, Pierre does this not because the initiation has any sort of spiritual benefit for him but because his will is paralyzed.

The key moment in Pierre's reception of Masonic doctrine is his re-action to the tyler's teaching of the seven virtues. Inwardly, Pierre accepts the first six: humility, obedience, morality, love for mankind, wisdom, and generosity. But though he accepts these essentially secular virtues, he rejects the seventh, which is religious and mystical and therefore primary: the love of death. Pierre initially accepts the virtue as incomprehensible but later forgets entirely what it is all about (10:78). He forgets because he does not want to know anything about death, and so the fundamental meaning of the Masonic initiation as a symbolic passage through death and rebirth remains incomprehensible and has no value for him.

Tolstoy is merciless in his evaluation of the effects of Pierre's turn to Freemasonry. Striving to embody the philanthropic ideal of Freemasonry, Pierre attempts to free his serfs. His efforts fail, and he is unable even to improve their lives. Failure awaits his attempts at self-improvement as well. In Kiev, he indulges in his "primary weakness": women. Over time, Pierre returns to his former way of life, bereft of genuine spirituality. Attempting to make his life conform to Masonic morality, Pierre starts a journal, but this means of self-perfection does not have the anticipated results.

Summing up Pierre's sober and rational reflections on his disappoint-ment in Freemasonry after a two-year stint, Tolstoy notes that "his heart was not in the mystical side of Freemasonry" (10:172). However, the practical conclusion Pierre draws from his reflections turns out to be neither sober nor rational but completely in conformity with Tolstoy's maxim in the Epi-logue: "If we grant that human life is governed by reason, then the possi-bility of life is destroyed" (14:239). In the face of his entire experience with Freemasonry, Pierre concludes that the reason for all the problems lies in the fact that Russian Freemasonry "had taken a wrong turn and deviated from its source," and so he goes abroad in search of true Freemasonry. As Tolstoy venomously notes, Pierre "gained the confidence of many people in high places, discovered many mysteries, and was raised to a higher level" (10:173). Upon his return, however, Pierre presents his "brothers" not with new mystical mysteries but with a fantastic and dangerous project for politi-cizing Russian Freemasonry. He calls on them to strive toward "creating a form of supreme government" (10:176). The Freemasons' rejection of the plan effectively marks the end of Pierre's Masonic activities.

Tolstoy traces Pierre's various failures to the impracticality, fantastic nature, and even falsity of the Masonic program. Tolstoy views the Free-masons' politics, philanthropy, and morality as ideological fictions, just as conventional and divorced from reality as their rituals.

As we shall see once again, the idea of man's spiritual rebirth after his encounter with death is important to Tolstoy in *War and Peace*. However, from the author's perspective, this encounter must be real, not symbolic, as it is in Freemasonry. Tolstoy does not believe that the real needs of the spiritual life can be satisfied symbolically. In order to be reborn, Pierre must really face death.

❊ ❊ ❊

Pierre's second attempt to walk the *via mystica* takes place like the first: suddenly, accidentally, and in spite of his will. Trying to satisfy his curiosity, Pierre finds himself in the Russian army at Borodino, and chance leads him to the most terrifying place on the battlefield: Raevsky's Redoubt. He witnesses the meaningless and awful mass slaughter, which paradoxically lends meaning to his life. The carnage becomes for Pierre a mystical *purification* and prepares him to receive mystical *enlightenment*, which takes place in Pierre's consciousness early in the morning, the day after the Battle of Borodino, when he wakes up in Mozhaisk. Slowly falling asleep, Pierre thinks about his primary impression from the day: the "simple," "steadfast," and "calm" soldiers. "These strange people he had not known before" fascinate him because, unlike Pierre, they do not know the "horrible and shameful" fear of death, and Pierre begins to dream about being a simple soldier and joining the "common life" of outer men that soldiers live. And these dreams lead him to think about the Freemasons. Pierre thinks about the necessity "of casting off everything superfluous, everything sent by the devil, the whole burden of the *outer man*."[9] He recalls the main events of his past: the dinner at the English Club, where he challenged Dolokhov to a duel; his encounter in Torzhok with his "benefactor" Bazdeev; and his visits to the Masonic lodge. All these recollections and thoughts merge into his vision. Pierre finds himself at a grand dinner at the English Club, situated between two radically different spiritual powers. The first, "evil" power, representing the "superfluous" and "everything sent by the devil," consists of the screaming and singing Dolokhov, Anatole, and company. The second power, that of the "common life of all creatures," is represented by "*them*": the simple soldiers who "do not see or know" Pierre. The meaning of all this is explained to Pierre by Bazdeev, supposedly dead but now seen alive (i.e., *resurrected*). From Bazdeev Pierre learns of his own thoughts. As the author notes, Pierre "*did not understand* what his benefactor was saying, but he *knew* . . . that he was speaking about good, about the possibility of being what *they* were." Pierre learns the same thing from the *mysterious voice* that reveals to him the "mystical truth" about the sameness of submitting to God and the acceptance of death: "War is the most difficult subjection of man's will to the laws of God . . . Simplicity is submitting to God's will . . . And *they* are simple . . . Man can master nothing so long as he fears death. And the man who does not fear death possesses everything" (11:290–91). Like Bazdeev, this mysterious voice is nothing less than Pierre's double, his unconscious, revived Ego.

Pierre's vision has a mystical dimension (the allegorical events and mysterious voice) and is concentrated around a theme of the Masonic initiation—the disciple accepts the secret knowledge regarding the necessity of experiencing death from his Masonic teacher. Only in one respect does the vision depart from Masonic mystical ideas: it has real-life content; it is Pierre's encounter with death, one that comes before him not as the mystic's symbolic death but as the cruel and awful mass death of people at war.

What does Pierre do with the knowledge he receives from death itself? As the author explains, he simply loses it in order to return to his meaningless life. Roused from his dream, "Pierre was horrified to realize that the entire meaning of what he had seen and thought in his dream was destroyed" (11:292). Pierre's transition to a wakeful state is also a transition to a false, "temporal" life and a spiritual dormition accompanied by a forgetting of his experience with death, itself an imprescriptible part of true, eternal life. On the road from Mozhaisk, Pierre receives news of the deaths of his brother-in-law Anatole Kuragin and Prince Andrei. In Moscow, he learns of the imminent surrender of Moscow to the French and of his wife's intention to marry. All this befuddles Pierre, and his confused thoughts rise to the surface of consciousness before he falls asleep: "*They*—the soldiers in the battery, Prince Andrei killed . . . the old man . . . Simplicity is submitting to God's will. Need to suffer . . . the meaning of everything . . . need to unify . . . wife is getting married . . . Need to understand and *forget* . . ." (11:298).

At this point, Pierre's *via mystica* is broken off, and once again he gives in to the false life of the "outer man." The culmination of this new stage of Pierre's path is his intention to remain in occupied Moscow in order to kill Napoléon. Pierre's decision to perform this "great feat and great happiness" of liberating the world from Napoléon is based on his pseudo-Cabalistic calculations. Pierre adjusts these calculations to mean what he wants them to. Having completed the intended adjustment, Pierre discovers that the numerical meaning of the words "l'empereur Napoléon" is equal to that of the Beast of the Apocalypse (666) and to his own, albeit grammatically incorrect, title "L'Russe Besuhof" (11:77–79). Pierre's second *via mystica* concludes with this absurdity.

But the law, to which Pierre's fate is subjugated, acts with inexorable consistency: although he runs from his encounter with death, the author redirects him again and again. His new encounter with death takes place soon enough. After fires begin to flare up in occupied Moscow, Pierre is accused of arson and arrested. Miraculously escaping death, he becomes a witness to an execution of "arsonists." As the first two pairs of arsonists are killed, Pierre turns aside and closes his eyes, not wanting to watch. But as the last of the arsonists (who happens to be standing in the pair with Pierre)[10] is executed, Pierre *"could no longer turn away and close his eyes"* (12:41–42; emphasis added).

This entire series of events turns into a spiritual catastrophe for Pierre. He feels "as if the mainspring of his soul on which everything was balanced and seemed alive had been torn out, and everything had collapsed into a pile of meaningless rubbish. Although he did not realize it, his faith in the order of the universe, in men's souls and his own, and his faith in God had been destroyed . . . the world had collapsed before his eyes, and only meaningless ruins now remained" (12:44).

What happens to Pierre here is nothing other than immersion in death: physically, he is alive, but spiritually he experiences death as something he has gone through before.

For Pierre, this experience means purification, from which his third *via mystica* begins; and the moment of enlightenment comes soon. Pierre finds another "benefactor" among his fellow Russian prisoners: Platon Karataev. In contradistinction to Bazdeev, Karataev does not teach Pierre Truth but rather himself becomes for Pierre the embodiment of Truth. The enlightening Divine Revelation appears to Pierre in the form of a dirty soldier reeking of sweat, a former peasant whose identity has been effaced and who immediately forgets the very wisdom he articulates. Pierre interprets his encounter with Karataev, for which his experience with the "folk" at Borodino has prepared him, as an epiphany that leads him to spiritual resurrection, to *unio mystica*. Listening to Platon sleeping, Pierre feels "that the ruined world was stirring in his soul, with new beauty and on new, unshakable foundations" (12:51).

For Pierre, Platon Karataev is the mystery of the world revealed, the *"incomprehensible,* round, eternal personification of the spirit of simplicity and truth" (12:50; emphasis added). He embodies that fear-releasing dissolution of identity in the "common life" characteristic of the folk—something that had occurred to Pierre in Mozhaisk. Karataev "loved his comrades, loved the French, and he loved Pierre, his neighbor. But Pierre felt that Karataev . . . would not be sad even for a moment if they were to part ways. And Pierre began to feel the same way toward Karataev" (12:50). Pierre attempts to learn from Karataev this universal, impersonal, and futile love akin to death.

But in the end, Pierre turns out to be just as bad a student of Platon Karataev's as he was of Bazdeev's. This is strikingly apparent in his reaction to Karataev's death. Pierre witnesses a French soldier killing Karataev, but he refuses to acknowledge what he sees. He refuses precisely because he has failed to conquer his fear of death ("Pierre feared for his life" [12:157]) and his individual, not impersonal love for Karataev.

Pierre's fear of death disappears, however, in his dream in which the mystical and peaceful meaning of death is revealed to him. The "long forgotten, gentle old geography teacher" appears to Pierre. This new double of Pierre's, a mystical teacher and "benefactor," presents to Pierre the world as a "living, shimmering ball," whose surface consists of drops of water moving about, flowing together and separating. "God is in the middle, and each drop tries to expand in order to reflect Him on the largest possible scale . . . Here he is, Karataev. He has been absorbed and has disappeared" (12:158).

This image of the world has as its foundation one of the key concepts for the entire tradition of mystical Gnosis: the concept of the unity of Cosmos, God, and Man. This concept is given form in Pierre's consciousness and in several other images connected with this tradition. Thus, in an earlier episode, when he is leaving Moscow with his fellow prisoners, we learn of Pierre's reaction to the French soldier who blocks him from going to the other side of the road. Pierre "sat on the cold ground . . . and spent a long time sitting motionless and thinking . . . Suddenly, he burst out laughing . . . 'Ha, ha, ha!' laughed Pierre . . . 'The soldier wouldn't let me through. They've captured me and locked me up. They're holding me prisoner. Me? Me? My immortal soul! Ha, ha, ha!'" (12:105–6).

In this passage, Pierre's feeling of absolute inner freedom comes to him when circumstances unambiguously point to his external unfreedom. With this sense of freedom, Pierre looks at the sky and undergoes a kind of mystical ascension that allows him to merge with the fullness of the divine world: "The full moon stood high in the luminous sky . . . the bright, *shimmering*, beckoning, infinite distance was visible. Pierre glanced up *at the sky*, at the play of stars receding into the depths. 'And all this is mine, and all this is in me, and I am all of this!' thought Pierre. 'And they've captured all this and put it up in a shed and boarded it up'" (12:105–6; emphasis added).

Pierre's feelings and thoughts here are presented like the experience of the *unio mystica* and, at the same time, of unity between the man as the *microcosm* and the Universe as the *macrocosm*. Ancient mythological ideas regarding the macrocosm and microcosm held significance for most of the mystical traditions. One of the Freemasons' primary teachers, Jakob Böhme, expressed this idea in the following way: "Men were made out of nature, the stars, and elements; but God the creator reigneth in all: even as the sap doth in the whole tree."[11] Depicting Pierre's *unio mystica*, Tolstoy underscores the submergence of his hero's consciousness in the mystical tradition.

The concept of the unity of Godhead, Cosmos, and Man is expressed by another means characteristic of the mystical tradition: the image of *the ladder of nature*. Pierre uses this image in his enthusiastic speech to Prince Andrei during their trip from Bogucharovo to Bald Hills. Trying to convince Prince Andrei of the truth of Masonic teachings, Pierre says, "Don't I feel in my soul that I am part of this large, harmonious whole? Don't I feel that in this large quantity of beings in which the *Deity* is manifest—a higher power, if you wish—that I am one link, one step connecting lower and higher beings? If I can see, I clearly see this *ladder* running from plant to man, then why do I suppose that this ladder ends with me rather than leads further and further? . . . I feel that spirits exist above me." In response, Prince Andrei says, "That is Herder's doctrine" (10:116–17; emphasis added). The remark is meant to be malicious: Prince Andrei suggests that Pierre is merely paraphrasing the German philosopher.

And indeed, G. V. Krasnov has shown that Tolstoy has Pierre retell a few passages from an article that summarized and translated parts of Herder's *Ideas for the Philosophy of History of Humanity*. Published in 1804 in *Vestnik Evropy*, the article in a sense finds readers in Pierre and Prince Andrei.[12] Tolstoy makes Pierre a follower of Herder's *Naturphilosophie* because he, with characteristic insight, recognized in this Herder's teaching on substantial features of the Gnostic understanding of Nature, which arrived in Russia along with Freemasonry and German *Naturphilosophie*.[13]

As Moshe Idel has shown, the concept of the *ladder of nature*, itself an allegorical interpretation of Jacob's Ladder (Gen. 28:12–16), was first formulated by the Arabic mystic and Neoplatonist Al-Bataliawsi. Jewish mystics (Cabalists) borrowed it from him, and then through their mediation the concept found its way to Renaissance mystical *philosophia naturalis* (Pico della Mirandola, Giordano Bruno, and others).[14] I cite, as one of the possible sources of Pierre's retellings of Herder, an excerpt from Bruno's *De magia*:

> Magicians take it as axiomatic that, in all the panorama before our eyes, God acts on the gods; the gods act on the celestial or astral bodies, which are divine bodies; these act on the spirits . . . the spirits act on the elements, the elements on the compounds, the compounds on the senses; the senses on the soul, and the soul on the whole animal. This is the *descending scale*. By contrast, the *ascending* scale is from the animal through the soul to the senses, through the senses to the compounds, through compounds to the elements, through these to spirits, through the spirits in the elements to those in the stars, through these to the incorporeal gods.[15]

Mystical *philosophia naturalis* with its idea of a cosmic ladder had many followers, as recent as Vladimir Vernadsky and Pierre Teilhard de Chardin in the twentieth century. Tolstoy in no way sympathized with this type of philosophical thought. He merely links Pierre's mystical ideas to the cultural context to which his hero belongs. Pierre's experiences are not Tolstoy's.

At the end of volume 4 of *War and Peace*, Tolstoy includes a story about Pierre's final break with the world of mysticism. At once surprising and typical of Tolstoy, the passage is structured like a *via mystica*. Right after his return from captivity, Pierre falls ill, and his sickness brings him to the brink of dying. Similarly, his recovery recalls the passage through death, rebirth, resurrection, and acquisition of divine truth.

Tolstoy depicts the "resurrected" Pierre's spiritual state thus:

> The very thing that had tormented him previously that he had sought, the purpose of life—this did not exist for him now . . . He could have no purpose because now he had faith—not faith in any sort of principles or words or ideas but faith in a living, always perceptible God. Previously, he had sought Him in the purposes he had assigned himself. This search for purpose had really been a search for God, and suddenly he had realized during his captivity . . . something that his old nurse had once told him: that God is here, everywhere. In captivity, he had realized that Karataev's God was greater, more infinite, and unfathomable than the Architect of the universe revered by the Freemasons. (12:205)

Tolstoy continues, "The question that had previously destroyed his carefully structured thinking—Why?—no longer meant anything to him. Now, in his soul, he always had a simple answer to the question why: because God is, and without His will not a hair shall fall from man's head" (12:206).

As can be gathered from the citations above, the truths Pierre discovers not only do not correspond to the mystical idea of truth as knowledge but also directly contradict this idea. To Pierre are revealed not the truths of mystical Gnosis but the truths of faith. And having found faith, Pierre understands that if there is a living God Who concerns Himself with man, then man has nothing to seek out, no questions to ask, no paths along the *via mystica* to walk.

But Pierre's fate does not belong to Faith or eternal life. Pierre deviates from the path of faith just as he did from the *via mystica* in order to plunge into the stream of daily routine—chaotic, irrational, temporal but also attractive and full of "secular" family, societal, and political interests. As we learn in Epilogue I, Pierre's political interests—Decembrist in orientation and hostile to authority—make him critical of Tsar Alexander's infatuation with mysticism. This is because it is now the authority that promotes mysticism. In Epilogue I, Pierre announces, "This is the situation in Petersburg: the Tsar no longer does anything. He is completely absorbed in mysticism." This pronouncement is followed by a short and acidic narrator's commentary: "Pierre no longer forgave anyone for mysticism" (12:283). Tolstoy was very well informed about interpenetrations of the Decembrists' "secret societies" and Masonic lodges. But he preferred to present his Decembrist, Pierre, as an enemy of mysticism.

* * *

Just as he does with Pierre, Tolstoy puts his second "spiritual" hero, Prince Andrei, face-to-face with death several times. Prince Andrei, too, experiences these encounters as rehearsals of the *via mystica*.

Prince Andrei's entry onto the *via mystica* takes place on the field of Austerlitz. Seized by the impulse to be a hero, he runs at the enemy with a banner, attempting to inspire the soldiers to go with him. However, his attempt is suddenly interrupted and he falls supine after being injured.

The hero's physical *fall*, notably, takes place on Pratzen *Heights*. Recall that, in the broader mythological and mystical traditions, mountains symbolize the passage from earth to sky; the ascent of a mountain represents a mystical ascension, while the sky is the highest spiritual and sacred existence, which abolishes the lower, material, earthly, profane human existence. This entire mythological symbolism is present in Tolstoy's text. Prince Andrei sees the sky precisely as the embodiment of a higher spiritual world that cancels out all the values of the material world. He sees the sky and nothing else and suddenly understands that "everything is empty, everything is illusory, except for this infinite sky. *There is nothing, nothing*—that's all there is. But even that doesn't exist. *There's nothing* except for stillness, peace" (9:341; emphasis added). Thinking about the sky cures Prince Andrei of his need for "grandeur," his need to be like Napoléon. Seeing Napoléon and looking him in the eyes, Prince Andrei thinks of the "insignificance of grandeur and life, the meaning of which no one could understand, and also of the greater insignificance of death, the meaning of which no one among the living could understand" (9:356). At this stage on his path, Prince Andrei in no way interprets his revelation as a demand for the complete renunciation of earthly life. He still hopes to live, and he identifies this hope with the "quiet life and peaceful family happiness at Bald Hills" (9:357). It is his fate to descend from the sky back to earth, where much more awaits him, before he will prefer death and the complete liquidation of his identity to the most modest, humble, but still material, life.

His injury at Borodino once again finds Prince Andrei in a state of elevated heroism. The grenade that lands "two steps" from him injures him because he considers it shameful to fall to the ground in order to save himself. His heroic behavior is informed by his sense that even at the risk of dying "he remembered that he was being watched" (11:251). The last remark is of critical importance. For Tolstoy, individualistic behavior of any sort, especially heroic, is by nature false insofar as one performs it for others and not out of true feeling. In *War and Peace* and other of Tolstoy's texts, the rejection of individualistic behavior and self-consciousness in the face of death signals a return of a human being to his authentic, presocial, primordial self, to himself as a naive child. Thus, on the brink of dying Prince Andrei assumes an "innocent, boyish look" (11:380).

As the narrator emphasizes, Prince Andrei dies as a result of his own free will. He thinks before his death, "Love is God, and what dying means for me, one small part of love, is to return to the common and eternal source" (12:63). And death underscores by its presence these mystical reflections linking love, God, death, and the universal unity of the world. Death appears to Prince Andrei in a dream as a mysterious entity. However, given the context there is nothing extrapsychological about this entity—it is described as Andrei's unconscious self that only reassures him of the truth of his thoughts. Tolstoy's approach in depicting Prince Andrei's "mystical vision" is the same one he used for Pierre's dream at Mozhaisk. The content of these visions is also much the same.

Prince Andrei's vision begins with his seeing himself speaking and arguing "about something unnecessary with many different people" (recall the noisy "outer people" in Pierre's dream). Then these people—*others*—disappear, leaving him face-to-face with death. And for Prince Andrei now "all that is left is the question of closing the door": death is breaking in through the door, and he, battling for his life, tries to keep it closed. But death wins out: it enters, and Prince Andrei dies. But at the moment he dies in his dream, he is awakened in reality, and this awakening brings him to the realization that even death is an "awakening" (12:63–64).

For Prince Andrei, his acceptance of death becomes a mystical *purification* from "worldly" life, and it brings him to that "remoteness from all things *worldly* that seems so horrible to a living person" (12:57; emphasis added). The personal love he feels for his fiancée, son, and sister is gone. In its place is the "eternal" and impersonal love for all people preached by the Gospel and described by Tolstoy as being completely similar to Platon Karataev's version of love.

In the depiction of Prince Andrei's dying and death, which Tolstoy explicitly calls a "mystery" (12:65), one finds direct parallels with Pierre's initiation into Freemasonry. The door through which death tries to enter in Prince Andrei's dream recalls that moment in the initiation when Pierre hears the loud knocks at his door. Remember that it is through this door, which symbolizes the gates of the temple and truth, that the tyler, the bearer of truth, enters. During the ceremony, the initiate is shown the symbols of truth regarding the merging of God, life, and of the Gospel teaching: the burning lamp, *the Gospels*, the skull, and coffin full of *bones*. A candle burns next to the dying Prince Andrei, and he himself reads the Gospel (11:381, 12:59), and his body is said to be torn up, rotting, and dying: during his operation "*bones*" and "pieces of meat" (11:255) are extracted, and afterward his wound emits the "stench of rotting meat" (11:381). But the parallels between the two scenes also put into relief the differences between them. It is as if Tolstoy were urging the reader to contrast the false mystical initiation of Masonic ritual with life's authentic initiation.

The Masonic mystical motifs that recur throughout volumes 3 and 4 were edited and in some cases completely incorporated at that stage of his work that followed his study of Masonic manuscripts. As Zaidenshnur notes in her essay on the creation of *War and Peace*, Tolstoy wrote the scene of Pierre's initiation and put the finishing touches on the "mystical episodes" in volumes 3 and 4 almost simultaneously.[16] Naturally, a textual coincidence does not explain Tolstoy's reasons for using Masonic mystical motifs in depicting the spiritual lives of Pierre and Prince Andrei. His reasons lie in the fact that he presents both characters as Freemasons. In the final redactions of the text, Tolstoy removed an earlier mention of Prince Andrei's admission to a Masonic lodge. He preserved, however, the reference to Prince Andrei's membership among the Freemasons. Prior to Prince Andrei's courtship of Natasha Rostova, he asks Pierre to give Natasha his Masonic gloves, which are to be entrusted to one's beloved (10:218).

War and Peace ends with these words: *"It is essential to renounce the false sense of freedom and accept the dependence we cannot feel"* (12:341; emphasis added). This maxim, which Tolstoy develops throughout, is the guiding principle not only of his philosophy of history but also of his poetics. In the novel, the religious life of people at the beginning of the nineteenth century is depicted not as the result of their free choice but rather, in its complex conditionality, determined by psychology, age, gender, social position, history, and culture.

As Pierre observes the general reverence for the Holy Mother of Smolensk icon on the eve of Borodino, he is struck by the "solemn expression on the faces" of the soldiers and militiamen, "all gazing greedily at the icon" (11:194). Pierre tries to learn such simple faith from the folk and from Platon Karataev and even acquires it for a time, but he cannot retain it because it is incompatible with the "conditions" that have determined his life. But this simple, unselfconscious faith, so inaccessible to Pierre and "enlightened" society, turns out to be accessible to the "enlightened" Kutuzov. Like the simple soldiers, Kutuzov bows down with complete faith before the Holy Mother of Smolensk icon (11:195). Receiving news of Napoléon's desertion of Moscow, he turns to the "far corner of the hut, which had been blackened by the candles around the icons," in order to thank God ("Lord, my Creator! You have heard our prayer. Russia is saved"), and weeps. Kutuzov has simple faith because he is an old man whose personal aspirations have all been extinguished (and for many other "countless" reasons, as Tolstoy often writes). Thus, his faith is not his choice but his fate.

When Prince Andrei dies, he thinks of Princess Marya's simple faith, founded on the Gospel. The faith he finds before dying, however, is not at all identical to his sister's. Princess Marya's religiosity is determined by the whole web of "conditions" in which she is caught. Princess Marya is a noble girl who is also lonely and unattractive (with no hopes of getting married). She has aged early and is oppressed by her despotic father. She naturally seeks comfort in religion by immersing herself in the Gospel, prayer, and the typically Russian world of Orthodoxy as represented by "God's people": the pilgrims who visit holy places and tell of miracles performed by holy icons and saints' relics. One episode is indicative: recall when Julie Karagina sends Princess Marya a copy of *Gefühle und Tempel der Natur* [*Key to the Mysteries of Nature*] by the eighteenth-century German mystic Karl von Eckartshausen, a book that was extraordinarily popular among the Freemasons. Princess Marya refuses to read the book because "mystical books awaken doubts in people's minds . . . Let us read the Apostles and the Gospel" (9:109–14).[17] It is impossible to determine whether Princess Marya does the right thing in censoring her reading for fear of losing faith, or whether her atheist father knows best in allowing her to read the mystical book because he doesn't meddle in religion.[18]

All this allows me to summarize briefly Tolstoy's stance toward mysticism in *War and Peace*. His is a three-sided perspective. As a writer studying history, Tolstoy interprets the mystical tradition as a part of the historical past that does not need to be praised or censured but explained. As a thinker concerned with the meaning of life, Tolstoy values mysticism's pathos in its idea of man's belonging to the world's spiritual unity, but he is simultaneously skeptical of mysticism's ways of conceptualizing the world. Finally, as an artist and storyteller, Tolstoy finds in mystical texts an abundance of literary material he can use. In depicting the religious experience of his mystical characters, Tolstoy naturally transfers some elements of mystical rhetoric to his own plane of literary discourse. But insofar as he does not preach any particular religious worldview in *War and Peace*, he refrains from preaching any sort of mystical worldview.

❖ ❖ ❖

As is well known, one of the consequences of Tolstoy's spiritual crisis in the late 1870s was his transformation into a religious teacher. I have already noted that the late Tolstoy rejected out of hand attempts to qualify his teaching as a kind of mysticism. Objectively speaking, however, his religious and philosophical system was strongly connected, albeit in a complicated and contradictory way, to the tradition of mystical Gnosis.

Responding in March 1901 to his informal excommunication from the Orthodox Church, Tolstoy wrote, "If we understand the afterlife as a second coming, hell with eternal torments, devils, and heaven as eternal bliss, then it is absolutely fair to say that I do not acknowledge the afterlife. But I acknowledge life eternal and retribution here and everywhere, now and always, to the point that, standing in my late years with one foot in the grave,

76

I must often make the effort not to wish for *death in the flesh—that is, to be born to new life"* (34:248–49; emphasis added).

The obviously Gnostic concept that death is man's passage from temporal "fleshly" life to its eternal spiritual form was exceptionally important in the late Tolstoy's religious views. In his religious and philosophical works and diary entries, Tolstoy expresses this idea as a rational concept and persistently tries to prove its truth. In "The Posthumous Notes of the Elder Fedor Kuzmich" (1905), the hero of the tale, strongly associated with Tolstoy, summarizes the idea thus: "In this alone, the approach of death, is man's rational desire. The desire is not for death, for death itself, but for life's movement that leads to death. This movement is freedom from the passions and temptations of that spiritual principle that lives in every man. I feel it now, now that I am free of the greater part of that which hid the essence of my soul from me—its unity with God—and hid God from me" (36:72). At the same time, in his narrative prose, Tolstoy presents the concept not in terms of philosophical reflections but in terms of mystical narratives about his characters' "revelations of death," to borrow Lev Shestov's accurate formulation. And these narratives are based on the model of the *via mystica* Tolstoy had used in *War and Peace*.

In his two stories "The Death of Ivan Ilyich" (1886) and "Master and Man" (1895), Tolstoy deploys "revelations of death" as he describes his dying characters. Ivan Ilyich is inoffensive, just, and amoral just like everyone else, a judge doomed to die after being afflicted by illness. Ivan Ilyich interprets his illness, physical suffering, and inevitable death as a terrible injustice, so outrageous that although he has never thought about God before, he suddenly begins to do so. He not only remembers God but also rebels against Him Who has condemned him to death. It even seems to Ivan Ilyich that in destroying him, God is destroying the entire world. "I won't exist, but what will? Nothing" (26:91). Recalling the famous syllogism—"Men are mortal, Caius is a man, therefore Caius is mortal"—Ivan Ilyich refuses to acknowledge that he is like Caius because "he was not Caius and not man in general; rather, he was always quite, quite separate from other beings" (26:92–93).

Tolstoy, however, impels Ivan Ilyich to realize that it is in his separateness that the source of his pain, and indeed all those evils and misfortunes that had constituted his life since childhood, had been hidden. Ivan Ilyich recalls being not "separate" only in childhood, when he felt a part of the common world. Among the people who surround him, only his servant, a former peasant, Gerasim, and his young son are endowed with such understanding. It is they who aid in Ivan Ilyich's purification: his exit from his "separate" world into the common world of people united in love. Right after his son, who loves and pities him, kisses his hand, "Ivan Ilyich fell through, saw the light, and it was revealed to him that his life had not been what it should have been." Ivan Ilyich sees the light of enlightenment that brings knowledge—

knowledge not only that it is necessary and good to reject the "fleshly life" but also that the law of death brings not evil but good: liberation from evil, pain, and suffering. We learn of Ivan Ilyich's last word: "He also wanted to say 'forgive me' but said 'let me go,' and no longer strong enough to correct himself, he waved his hand, knowing that the one who needed to understand him would." Ivan Ilyich's plea for forgiveness from his wife, whom he had so hated, becomes simultaneously a plea to God (Who had revealed to him that death does not exist) to be admitted into the world of eternal life. "There was no death. Instead of death there was light" (26:112–13).

Like Ivan Ilyich, the hero of "Master and Man" is the rich, impudent, successful merchant Brekhunov, a man like everyone else, who knows nothing and does not want to know anything other than his "separate" world. And as was the case in "The Death of Ivan Ilyich," death comes to Brekhunov unexpectedly and in the most accidental, absurd, and terrible way: in a snow-covered field where Brekhunov and his servant Nikita get stuck during a blizzard. The similarities between the two stories continue: Brekhunov at first does not accept death and tries to find a way out by saving *himself*. And Brekhunov, too, enters onto the *via mystica*, accepting "fleshly death" in order to plunge into the world of eternal life.

Brekhunov's *via mystica* begins with *purification*. His fear of death "completely subsides," and he "suddenly" lies on top of his freezing servant Nikita, whom he had planned on letting die not long before and whom he now tries, at all costs, to warm and thereby save. "*Nikita is alive, which means I am alive, too*" (emphasis added). The meaning of these words (which go back to the mystical Hindu phrase *Tat twam asi*, "You are me") lies in the idea that man's true life is beyond his egoism. Only when man is purified through love, through unity with *others*, does he begin to live his true life.

Brekhunov then comes to the stage of *enlightenment*. Or rather, it comes to him in a vision before he dies. It begins with the disappearance of time ("he didn't see how time had passed") and the merging of all his impressions from his former life "into one white *light*" (emphasis added). And then God emerges from this light. He appears to Brekhunov as a *joy* and *fulfillment of his innermost hope*, as "the very person he had been waiting for" (emphasis added). And Brekhunov hears the *voice* of God calling him, "the Very One Who had called his name and instructed him to lie on Nikita." Brekhunov's encounter with God becomes an awakening: he "wakes up and is no longer the person he was when he had fallen asleep." In the wake of this encounter, Brekhunov acquires true *knowledge* (he refers to his former self as being ignorant, but says about his new self: "*now I know*" and *liberation* ("he is free" [29:43–44, emphasis added]). Like Prince Andrei, Brekhunov has a mystical vision in which he passes through death, leaves death behind, resurrects, and unites with God just before his physical end.

78

Commenting on Tolstoy's "revelations of death," Lev Shestov writes, "It was he who revealed to us things about the *nox mystica* which even the great saints had not seen, St. Bernard of Clairvaux, St. Theresa, or St. John of the Cross."[19] One cannot argue with this, but one can and should argue with Shestov's interpretation of Tolstoy's *nox mystica*. According to Shestov, "Both Ivan Ilyich and Brekhunov are outside reason: they die in absolute solitude. Tolstoy cunningly cuts them off from all society, all action."[20] And yet, as I have already shown, the most important event in Tolstoy's characters' *nox mystica* turns out to be the overcoming of absolute solitude: discovering *others* through love. And for Tolstoy himself, his *nox mystica* was the result neither of a solitary monk's irrational yearning nor of a skeptical philosopher's inability to join the lives of ordinary people. Rather, it was Tolstoy's vision of life, based upon his belief in Reason and in his grandiose social mission of religious enlightenment of humankind, the goal of which was freeing the world from the plague of violence.

In some instances, the narrative component based on the concept of *via mystica* comes not at the end of the text, as in my previous examples, but in the middle. In such cases, the characters experience a symbolic death.

Such is the case in "Father Sergius" (1898). Revered for his miraculous ability to heal the sick, Father Sergius commits a disgusting sin: he copulates with the deformed and mentally ill daughter of a merchant who has been brought to Father Sergius to be healed. For the hero, this act signifies the end of the life he has devoted to God. He interprets it as a spiritual death, which requires his immediate physical death: suicide. But from the author's perspective, the sin has another meaning: it is Father Sergius's purification. Father Sergius's egoism, his "separate," solitary, and proud world without people is broken and destroyed by his sin. And coming to see himself not as a righteous holy man but as the last, worthless sinner, he in effect proves ready to move on to the next stage of the *via mystica*: enlightenment.

In the text, this transition is presented as a series of mystical perceptions and visions that take place on the borderline of dream and reality. Father Sergius suddenly remembers his meetings with his old acquaintance, Pashenka, and then he sees an angel who "came to him and said: 'Go to Pashenka and learn from her what you are supposed to do, what your sin is and what your salvation is.'" Upon awakening, Father Sergius "decided that this was a vision from God" (31:37–38). His visit to Pashenka, whose identity is completely defined by her service to people, enlightens Father Sergius and directs him to take the path of an anonymous and homeless wanderer who devotes himself to serving others. For the late Tolstoy, this is the only means by which a person who has not yet crossed the threshold of "fleshly death" can attain unity with God.

In his late prose, Tolstoy uses many of the mystical motifs first found in

War and Peace, although they serve a different function. They are no longer part of the cultural and social backdrop he describes in his texts. In contradistinction to Pierre Bezukhov, Brekhunov, Ivan Ilyich, and Father Sergius are not Freemasons, nor do they know anything about Gnosis. Mystical motifs are not the driving force of their spiritual experience. Rather, their stories are about the "real" mystical experience Tolstoy writes for them. Mysticism, it turns out, is part of the author's religious position.

Brekhunov, Ivan Ilyich, and Father Sergius represent Tolstoy's position only obliquely. By contrast, several other "mystical characters" from the late prose are largely autobiographical.

In 1884, Tolstoy began the story "Notes of a Madman." He returned to it several years later but never completed it. Tolstoy conceived of this story as a fictional account of his own spiritual rebirth. It is well known that the main character experiences Tolstoy's own "Arzamas horror," which took place on the night of September 4, 1869. However, there are other events that reflect real-life episodes from Tolstoy's spiritual biography, which he discusses at length in *Confession*. The hero's "Moscow night," which proved worse than the "Arzamas horror," corresponds to Tolstoy's 1875 crisis that led him to the brink of suicide. Like Tolstoy, the hero of "Notes of a Madman" seeks but does not find religious comfort in performing Orthodox rituals, in reading Holy Scripture, and in the *vitae* of saints. Again like Tolstoy, he finds truth only by rejecting the Church. One should note, however, that Tolstoy does not simply describe events from his biography in his text—he reworks them to conform to the *via mystica*.

The most important moment in Tolstoy's reworking of the *via mystica* in "Notes of a Madman" is the description of the hero's "mystical purification" as a long, but interrupted, process. The hero's "madness," which constantly returns during this process, reveals to him again and again that his life, like everyone's, is haunted by death and therefore insufferably horrible. At first, this recurring revelation comes to the hero during that same Arzamas night when death appears: "There is nothing in life but death, and there should not be death . . . It is awful, terrifying, it seems one is afraid of death, but you think about it and remember that one is afraid of dying life. Somehow, life and death have merged into one. Something was trying to tear my soul into pieces and couldn't do it" (26:470). This purification ends with the crossing over into what the hero calls "complete madness." The hero writes that during mass "it suddenly became clear to me that this shouldn't exist, that it doesn't exist, and if it doesn't, then death and fear don't exist, and I don't feel the tearing anymore, and I'm no longer afraid of anything. Here the *light illuminated* me, and I became what I am. If this nothingness does not exist, then that everything in me does not exist. At the parvis, I gave away everything I had (thirty-six rubles) and went home, talking to the people"

(26:474; emphasis added).[21] The hero's enlightenment quickly leads him to *unio mystica* in its characteristically Tolstoyan form: transformation into a wanderer who rejects material possessions.

Strange as it may seem, there is one more autobiographical character worth mentioning: the hero of "The Posthumous Notes of the Elder Fedor Kuzmich," the former Russian emperor Alexander I, who wanders across Siberia. Tolstoy knew very well that the real Alexander I was a practicing, enthusiastic mystic. However, he writes nothing on this topic and designed his hero's spiritual personality as similar to his own. In his story, Tolstoy elaborated the famous legend claiming that Alexander I did not die in 1825 but secretly escaped to Siberia and lived his new life there as a wanderer for many more years. And this elaboration is built around the concept of *via mystica*: Alexander imitates his death and disappears; his body in a coffin is replaced by the body of a soldier who had been executed by military authorities. Having died symbolically, Alexander passes through his mystic death. By inaugurating his own new life, he symbolically grants resurrection not only to himself but to his victim as well. The meaning of all these events is purification of the hero. His long years in Siberia are described as *illuminative* life, slowly moving to its true goal—to death as the unity with God.

The symbolic and allegorical discourse that Tolstoy borrowed from mystical tradition makes its way organically into his prose. However, this discourse did not become part of his religious and philosophical treatises, which he structured to be completely rational and cleansed of everything that might deviate from logical argumentation.

Following his emergence from his crisis, Tolstoy, over the course of seven or eight years, wrote a series of religious and philosophical works. Three of them were especially significant. In his *Harmonization and Translation of the Gospels*, Tolstoy formulated his understanding of Christian doctrine, providing a new translation from the Greek and redacting the canonical texts from a rationalist perspective. He excised all the miracles, all the "mystical" (read irrational) moments, and presented the content as a unified and rational moral system. Indicative of his procedure is his translation of *logos*, from the first verse of the book of John, as "intelligence" (*razumenie*). This opening verse was rendered thus: "The beginning of everything was the intelligence of life, and the intelligence of life took the place of God" (24:25–26). In announcing God the universal spiritual beginning identical to "intelligence"—that is, reason in action—Tolstoy, in his *Critique of Dogmatic Theology*, attacked the teachings of the Orthodox Church and other Christian faiths. He condemned them primarily for their lack of reason and for their irrational mysticism. Finally, summarizing the metaphysical principles of his teaching in *On Life*, Tolstoy declared reason to be fundamentally self-evident: "Reason is what defines everything else . . . not only do we know this, but reason is the only thing we know" (26:347–48). Reason for Tolstoy is also a moral law: "Reason is that law recognized by man and by which his life is led" (26:347). All human life should conform to reason. Following Kant's teaching of "religion within the confines of reason alone," Tolstoy definitively subordinates even religious faith to reason: religion cannot be founded on faith because "man always understands everything through reason, not through faith" (26:439).

Tolstoy's collection *Wise Thoughts for Every Day* contains the following noteworthy aphorism that Tolstoy himself composed: "If you have not reached the stage when you see two truths contradicting each other, you have not yet begun to think" (40:120). This aphorism essentially negates one of the cornerstones of rationalist thought: the principle of noncontradiction. And indeed, in the years separating *On Life* (1887) and the aphorism (1903), the boundaries of Tolstoy's rationalism became increasingly narrow, and his thought increasingly turned to concepts of an irrational and, in particular, mystical nature.

In the first decade of the twentieth century, Tolstoy conceived of a "philosophical summary of true life" (54:154), which was supposed to replace the religious metaphysics of *On Life* that no longer satisfied him. Tolstoy made notes of different ideas concerning his new metaphysics in his diary and notebooks, where he felt free of the obligation to be logically consistent—something he tried to observe strictly in his treatises and journalism. One of these notes is relevant to our discussion.

On June 13, 1904, Tolstoy wrote in his diary as follows:

> God is He Whom I do not so much perceive or understand as He Whose existence for me is inevitable, although I cannot know anything about Him, aside from the fact that He is, this God for me is eternally "Deus absconditus," unknowable. I perceive something timeless, nonspatial, causeless, but I have no right to call this God . . . It is only that higher essence to which *I am privy to*. But the Principle, *principium*, of this essence can be and should be something totally different and completely inaccessible to me . . . There is no God of Whom I can make requests or Who is concerned with me, but I am not a creature that has randomly appeared by someone's whim—*I am an organ of God*. He is unknown to me, but my purpose in Him is not only known to me, *my belonging to Him* constitutes the unshakable foundation of my life. (55:51; emphasis added)

In this reflection, "two truths contradict each other." The first is the truth about God's being unknown. Although Tolstoy uses Pascal's well-known formula "Deus absconditus,"[22] his unknowable God is not Pascal's personal, biblical "God of Abraham, Isaac, and Jacob, not of philosophers and scholars" and to Whom he appeals. Tolstoy defines his unknowable God precisely as the "God of philosophers and scholars," the God of *the rationalistic Gnosis*, to Whom it is pointless to appeal. Tolstoy understands the unknowability of God in the spirit of Kant, who interpreted God as a thing-in-itself, something man lacks the appropriate sense organ to know.

Tolstoy never rejected the God of Kant and other "philosophers and scholars." His diary entry for January 4, 1903, which is connected to his conception of a "philosophical summary of true life," is indicative: "In order for my understanding of life to be comprehensible, one must adopt Descartes's perspective that man undoubtedly knows only that he is a thinking, spiritual creature, and one clearly understands that the most rigorous and scientific definition of the world is that the world is my representation (Kant, Schopenhauer, Schpir[23])" (54:153).

But in the diary entry for June 4, 1904, one finds a "contradictory truth" alongside the truth of the rationalistic Gnosis about the unknowability of God. Referring to personal experience (to sense perception!), Tolstoy writes that he is personally "privy" to God, that he is His "organ" and lives only by Him. It goes without saying that such assertions cannot pass any sort of Kantian or Cartesian inspection. Here we have arguments typical of *the mystical Gnosis*.

On August 12, 1891, Tolstoy recorded the following in his diary: "Somehow while praying it became clear to me that God is precisely a *real being*, love . . . and not a feeling, not a sense, but a real being; and I perceived it" (52:56). Tolstoy has many similar diary entries. In his attempts to conceptualize his immediate, living, existential religious experience, Tolstoy wrote in the first years of the twentieth century a series of "definitions of life" in which he increasingly gravitated toward the idea that God and only God is reality, while everything else is nothing more than an illusion. Tolstoy dictated the last of his definitions of life to his daughter on October 31, 1910, at the very place where he would die a week later: at Astapovo. Here he says the following: "God is that limitless *the All* of which man perceives himself to be a limited part. Verily, only God exists. Man is a manifestation of Him in matter, time, and space. The more the manifestation of God in the man (life) is united in the manifestations (lives) of other creatures, the more the man exists. The unity of this life with the lives of other creatures is accomplished by love. God is not love, but the more love there is, the more the man manifests God and the more he truly exists" (58:143; emphasis added).

In this passage, Tolstoy makes use of one of the ancient Hindu religious metaphysical doctrines. According to this doctrine, *ātman* (the human self, Tolstoy's "man") and *brahman* (the impersonal absolute Being, Tolstoy's "God as the All") are identical. From a typological perspective, this Hindu conception is Gnostic: the metaphysical idea behind it does not know God beyond the Cosmos and looks at God, Cosmos, and man's Self as components of a single, "mysterious" spiritual reality that exists beyond the sensual, material world. Tolstoy's religious and metaphysical thought arrived at similar conclusions, and that is partly why he set such great store by the aphorisms of Hindu sages, even as he ignored or condemned Hindu mythology.

As is well known, Tolstoy thought much of Taoism and the teachings of Laozi. In Taoism, Tolstoy found the mirror image of his own idea that the foundational function of "God as the All" consists in establishing an absolute moral law (the Tao, or "Way").

In the Hindu and Chinese religious traditions, as in the tradition of Western mystical Gnosis, Tolstoy found a teaching about God and man concordant with his own thought. Tolstoy rejected the primary postulates of the Judeo-Christian religious tradition: God is a personal Being and He is the Creator of the Cosmos that exists beyond as well as within Himself. Tolstoy considered such faith not only a metaphysical mistake but also a moral evil. He wrote about this more than once. Here is one such reflection, his diary entry for December 18, 1899: "One of the main reasons for the evil in our lives is the faith, cultivated in our Christian world, in a vulgar, personal Jewish God. Meanwhile, God's primary characteristic (if one may express oneself thus) is that He is not limited by anything, therefore He is *im*personal" (53:232).

※ ※ ※

All the above allows us to conclude that in the religious philosophy of the late Tolstoy there was an exceptionally important component that was typologically and historically related to mystical religious metaphysics. But it would be a mistake to go further and conclude that the late Tolstoy was a mystic. Tolstoy's position regarding mystical tradition might be better characterized as *countermysticism*. Adopting some of the general metaphysical postulates of mysticism, Tolstoy rejected the content of all the mystical stories of the inner life of the Godhead. The result of his reflections on the mystical traditions was not mysticism but an alternative to traditional mysticism. This countermysticism carried some of the features of mysticism but was essentially different (incidentally, one could say the same about "Tolstoy's religion": it is not so much what people generally call religion as it is a *counter-religion*, an alternative to religion that is somewhat similar).

Tolstoy never adopted any specific mystical teaching in its wholeness. In the 1860s, he took a skeptical view of the Masonic mysticism he had studied. The late Tolstoy was just as well versed in the primary mystical movement of his time: theosophy. Among the holdings in his library at Yasnaya Polyana are numerous books and journals on theosophy. Tolstoy used some ancient Hindu texts published by theosophists for his literary needs. But the theosophists' attempts to convert Tolstoy to their faith, however, inevitably led nowhere, and Tolstoy never accepted their "secret doctrine."

For Viacheslav Ivanov, Andrei Bely, and many of Tolstoy's younger contemporaries, theosophy was a kind of revelation. Books and journals on theosophy presented readers with an encyclopedia of mystical knowledge gathered from the most diverse mystical traditions, from Hindu mysticism to the Jewish Cabala, from the Corpus Hermeticum to Rosicrucianism, from alchemy to astrology, from the ancient Gnostics down to Jakob Böhme, and so forth. In this encyclopedia, one could learn about the mysteries of the creation of the world, Lucifer, Ahriman, *ātman*, Osiris and Horus, Ouroboros, and many other gods, demons, spirits, and cosmic powers. And all these occult mysteries were available to anyone with a small sum of money to buy a book. Mysticism was essentially dragged out onto the street and put on display.

Of course, this vulgar mysticism, which was attractive to people from a bourgeois and decadent background, had little chance of winning over Tolstoy with his refined aristocratic tastes. But this was not the defining factor. Tolstoy was a radical rationalist who did not believe in God as the Personality, and still less in personal gods, demons, and spirits inhabiting the mystics' universe. Mysticism is full of myths and magical concepts. In the era of decadence and symbolism, myth and magic were reborn and became culturally fashionable (but let's not forget that they also became the object of scientific inquiry and the content of great art). Tolstoy did not accept this fashion. To his last days, Tolstoy was in many ways a man of the Enlightenment, an enemy of religious deceit, prejudices, and superstitions. And he could see the mystics' tales of the mysteries of the Godhead and spirits only as manifestations of religious deceit and false faith. Theoretically and practically, Tolstoy was convinced that the mysteries of God were precisely that— mysteries that man cannot and should not know. Tolstoy was thinking about just this subject when, a week before his death, he dictated to his daughter his last "definition of life." I cited the first part of it above, so here I cite the concluding part where Tolstoy essentially speaks about the superfluity and harm in mysticism's attempts to penetrate the mysteries of God: "God, if we wish to use this term to clarify the phenomena of life—in such an understanding of God and life there can be nothing grounded and solid. These are just pointless reflections that lead nowhere. We know God only through the consciousness of His manifestation in us. All the conclusions from this consciousness and the guide to life on which it is founded always completely satisfy the man in knowing God Himself and in guiding his life founded on this consciousness" (58:143–44).

NOTES

This essay was translated into English by David Houston.

1. Z. N. Velikodvorskaia, ed., *Chastotnyi slovar' romana L. N. Tolstoy "Voina i mir"* [A dictionary of frequent word usage in L. N. Tolstoy's novel *War*

and Peace] (Tula: Tul'skii gosudarstvennyi pedagogicheskii institut im. L. N. Tolstogo, 1978), 93.

2. For a general description of Tolstoy's work on Masonic and mystical sources while writing *War and Peace*, see E. E. Zaidenshnur, "Istoriia pisaniia i pechataniia 'Voiny i mira'" [The history of the writing and publication of *War and Peace*] (16:61, 99–100, 141–42). For analysis of usage of some specific Masonic sources (books and manuscripts) in the novel, see N. D. Bludilina, "Zapiski I. V. Lopukhina kak odin iz istochnikov 'Voiny i mira'" [Notes of I. V. Lopukhin as one of the sources of *War and Peace*], *Russkaia slovesnost'* 5 (1994): 10–15; V. Shcherbakov, "An Unknown Source of *War and Peace* (*My Notes* by Freemason P. Ia. Titov)," *TSJ* 9 (1997): 66–84; and R. Faggionatto, "Iescho o masonskikh istochnikakh 'Voiny i mira' (zapisnyje knizhki Sergeia Lanskogo)" [Another account about the Masonic sources of *War and Peace* (the notebooks of Sergei Lanskoy)], *Russkaia literatura* 1 (2012): 112–24. For historical and literary analysis of the Masonic theme in the novel, see V. V. Pugachev, "K istoricheskomu fonu 'Voiny i mira' (Masony v Rossii pervoi chetverti XIX veka)" [Regarding the historical background of *War and Peace* (Masons in Russia in the first quarter of the nineteenth century)], in *L. N. Tolstoi. Uchenye zapiski; Stat'i i materialy* [*L. N. Tolstoy: scientific proceedings; articles and materials*], vol . 6 of Uchenye zapiski series (Gorky: Gor'kovskii gosudarstvennyii universitet imeni N. I. Lobachevskogo, 1966), 149–74; L. Katsis, "Sny masona P. Ia.Titova i sny Piera Bezukhova v 'Voine i mire' L'va Tolstogo" [Dreams of the Mason P. Ia. Titov and dreams of Pierre Bezukhov in *War and Peace* by L. N. Tolstoy], *Isvestiia RAN: Seriia I literatury i iazyka* 64, no. 5 (2005): 46–55; P. A. Buryshkin, "Masonstvo v romane L. N. Tolstogo 'Voina i mir'" [Masonry in the novel *War and Peace* by L. N. Tolstoy], in *Masonstvo i russkaia kultura* [Masonry and Russian Culture], ed. V. N. Novikov (Moscow: Iskusstvo, 1998), 344–50; A. A. Shuneiko, *Masonskaia simvolika v iazyke russkoi khudozhestvennoi literatury XVIII–nachala XIX vekov* [Masonic symbolism in the language of Russian literature of the eighteenth and the beginning of the nineteenth centuries] (Khabarovsk: Izd-vo DVGGU, 2006), 290–305; S. Shargorodskii, "'Vsiak iz nas dolzhen byt' Bemom . . .' (Masonskii tekst 'Voiny i mira')" [Each of us should be a Böhme (The Masonic text of *War and Peace*], in *Lev Tolstoi v Ierusalime. Materialy mezhdunarodnoi nauchnoi konferentsii* [Lev Tolstoy in Jerusalem. Academic Conference Proceedings], ed. Elena D. Tolstaya, intro., Vladimir M. Paperni. (Moscow: Novoe literaturnoe obozrenie, 2013), 177–90. For more general analysis of the Masonic theme in the novel, see G. Ya. Galagan, *L. N. Tolstoy: Khudozhestvenno-eticheskije iskaniia* [L.N. Tolstoy: Artisitc and Ethical Searchings] (Leningrad: Nauka, 1981), 109–22; Kathryn B. Feuer, *Tolstoy and the Genesis of "War and Peace,"* ed. Robin Feuer Miller and Donna Tussing Orwin (Ithaca, N.Y.: Cornell University Press, 1996), 98–99, 244–45; and Vladimir Paperni, "Lev Tolstoy i mistitsizm" [Lev Tolstoy and Mysticism], in *Lev Tolstoi v Ierusalime*, 157–76.

3. Harold Bloom, *Omens of Millennium: The Gnosis of Angels, Dreams, and Resurrection* (New York: Riverhead Books, 1996), 1–2.

4. Mircea Eliade, *Patterns in Comparative Religion* (Cleveland, Ohio: Meridian Books, 1965), 99–108; Mircea Eliade, *The Two and the One* (New York: Harper and Row, 1965), 19–77.

5. Margaret Smith, *The Way of the Mystics: The Early Christian Mystics and the Rise of Sūfīs* (Oxford: Oxford University Press, 1978), 6–9.

6. As V. V. Ivanov has noted, at the end of the eighteenth century Russian Masonic teachers designated this book not for "students" such as Pierre but for "masters." See V. V. Ivanov, "Rossiia i gnosis" ["Russia and Gnosis"], in *Izbrannye trudy po semiotike i istorii kul'tury* [*Selected studies in the semiotics and history of culture*] (Moscow: Iazyki russkoi kul'tury, 2003), 4:297.

7. The door motif symbolizes the opening of the gates of heaven and of the temple, as well as the revelation of divine truth.

8. Both moments signify the Old Adam's shedding of his fleshly clothes in preparation to be reborn into the spiritual New Adam.

9. As Shuneiko has pointed out, the contrast between the "inner" and "outer" man is an important part of the freemasons' worldview, as reflected in the text. See A. A. Shuneiko, *Masonskaia simvolika* 292, 304; emphasis added.

10. Tolstoy underscores this moment: Pierre is about to be killed.

11. Jacob Boehme, *Aurora: That Is, the Day-Spring or Dawning of the Day in the Orient or Morning Redness in the Rising of the Sun*, trans. John Sparrow (London: Watkins, 1914), 27.

12. G. V. Krasnov, "Filosofiia Gerdera v tvorchestve Tolstogo" [The philosophy of Herder in Tolstoy's creative work], in *L. N. Tolstoi, Uchenye zapiski; Stat'i i materialy*, vol. 4 (Gorky: Gor'kovskii gosudarstvennyi universitet imeni N. I. Lobachevskogo, 1961), 162–65. It seems to me that Krasnov's argument (and that of others who have written on this topic) is unfounded. The facts suggest only that Tolstoy used a number of Herder's ideas as "material," to borrow Shklovsky's term, for his novel.

13. Tolstoy apparently knew nothing of the exact sources of Herder's ideas in the mystical tradition. It remains unclear whether Tolstoy knew that Herder was a Freemason.

14. Moshe Idel, *Ascensions on High in Jewish Mysticism: Pillars, Lines, Ladders* (Budapest: Central European University Press, 2005), 167–204.

15. Giordano Bruno, *Cause, Principle, and Unity: And Essays on Magic*, trans. Robert de Lucca and Richard J. Blackwell (Cambridge: Cambridge University Press, 1998), 108; emphasis added. Bruno calls all bearers of "secret knowledge" magicians: "The trismegistes [*sic*!] among the Egyptians, the druids among the Gauls, the gymnosophists among the Indians, the cabalists among the Hebrews, the magi among the Persians (who were followers of Zoroaster), the sophists among the Greeks and the wise men among the Latins" (105). Jacob's ladder, on which angels ascend and descend, is interpreted in this context both

as a structure of the Cosmos and as a *via mystica*. Like other mystics, Bruno hypothesized that the mystic's soul ascends to the heavens and descends from them repeatedly.

16. Zaidenshnur, "Istoriia pisaniia."

17. The title *Gefühle und Tempel der Natur* is usually translated into English as *Key to the Mysteries of Nature*.

18. The Old Prince declares: "As for me, I don't interfere in anybody's matters of faith" [A ia ni v ch'iu veru ne vmeshivaius'] (9: 108). On matters of faith in *War and Peace* at large, see chapters 4 and 5 in Inessa Medzhibovskaya, *Tolstoy and the Religious Culture of His Time: A Biography of a Long Conversion, 1845–1887* (Lanham, Md.: Lexington Books, 2008), 83–130. On the Eckartshausen episode, see 85–88.

19. Lev Shestov, *In Job's Balances: On the Sources of the Eternal Truths*, trans. Camilla Coventry and Carlile Aylmer Macartney (London: Dent, 1932), 110.

20. Shestov, *In Job's Balances*, 117.

21. The fact that the hero's enlightenment is linked to his overcoming of Orthodox religiosity is singularly important. For Tolstoy, Orthodoxy and the Church are perhaps the primary manifestations of spiritual death's evil power, which prevents people from breaking through to "true life."

22. "Hidden God"; Tolstoy uses quotation marks in his own text to indicate when he is citing.

23. African Schpir (Spir) (1837–90) was a German neo-Kantian of Russian descent. He served at the same time as Tolstoy in the defense of Sevastopol but later emigrated to Germany. Tolstoy became acquainted with his works (written in German) in 1896 and was greatly impressed by them.

Inessa Medzhibovskaya

Tolstoy's Jewish Questions

IN 1912, EIGHT RUSSIAN intellectuals belonging to the philosophical group Put' joined forces to publish a collection titled *On the Religion of Lev Tolstoy*. The authors explained in their three-page introduction that ten years following Tolstoy's excommunication from the Russian Orthodox Church by decree of the Holy Synod in 1901 and a year after his death in November 1910, it was time to reexamine his life-in-God, complicated as it was by its "sick dislocations" (*boleznennye vyvikhi*).[1] On account of these dislocations, at least two of the contributors to the volume spoke of Tolstoy's Jewishness and his Judaism. The symbolist poet Andrei Bely focused on Tolstoy's ostracism from the settled nests—the pale, as he called it—of contemporary culture. The Christian existentialist Nikolai Berdiaev found in Tolstoy a distinctive progeny of the Old Testament prophets. (Neither Bely nor Berdiaev were supportive of Tolstoy's rejection of the state and the chief tenets of Russian Orthodox Christianity.)

Bely set up his argument about Tolstoy's supposed Jewishness by extending a convoluted network of associations and analogies—those of expulsion, territorial restriction, and exile—told via an anecdote in which professors of sociology, aesthetics, and philosophy meet to discuss where Tolstoy belongs. Each tries to foist him off on another and each, in turn, refuses to give him shelter, casting him off onto religion: "We know how men of religion dealt with Tolstoy: they literally deported him, forced him out of the pale of religion. And Tolstoy stands before them like the Eternal Jew, a restless refugee from the Pale of Settlement of contemporary culture and the state."[2] Tolstoy's departure from home in November 1910 was the last leg in his lifelong wanderings to the Promised Land where reason and faith would again reign as one (166). Bely uses characteristic vocabulary: the "Pale of Settlement" (Cherta Osedlosti), a "restless refugee" (*neuspokoennyi izgnannik*), and even, further on in the text, the "dust of Babylon" (*prakh Vavilona*) (171). Shielding their protectorates from the hordes of barbarians pressing at their gates, the bureaucratic agencies run by "fiefdom lords of Aryan culture" find no place for Tolstoy within the demarcated constituencies they oversee. If his eternal Jewishness can have any residency at all after the exit from Babylonian captivity it is in the catacombs of early Christianity, not in the modern world where passports are stamped and permission of domicile is required.

A different but no less symbolic Tolstoy emerges from the pages of Berdiaev's essay: "The life of Tolstoy, his searches, his riotous criticism are a great phenomenon of worldwide scale. It requires being examined *sub specie* of eternal values rather than temporary utility."[3] The utility at which Berdiaev points flags the difference of the Put' group from ultraconservative critics who denounced Tolstoy and banned him and the Jews together as ally servants of the anti-Christ (172). Berdiaev thinks that evaluations of Tolstoy's religion should pay no heed to the scores Tolstoy and the ruling spheres had had to settle and should ignore the strife between the Russian intelligentsia and the Church that drove Tolstoy outside the pale of Orthodoxy. Nonetheless, Tolstoy—this mystic who contemplated sub specie aeternitatis and who "muffled down his rationalism" to prepare for his flight, the "final *up*heaval," is, Berdiaev declares, a providential genius of Russia: "Without L. Tolstoy Russia is unthinkable . . . Russia cannot deracinate him" (195; emphasis added).

I leave aside for now Bely's future sympathies with Aryan mythology and Berdiaev's extraordinary rebuttal to antisemitism and Nazi ideology in his essay "Christianity and Antisemitism" (Khristianstvo i antisemitizm, 1938). Bely's and Berdiaev's intense sense of history leads to their realization that Tolstoy's ostensible "Jewishness" is not accidental. How shall a Russian breakthrough into messianic history making become materialized? By following the path traveled by the Jews over forty centuries? Together or apart from the Jews? Through wanderings or cultural settlement? Through peace or upheaval? This is the range of questions that the leaders of the Russian intelligentsia united to ask in their eagerness to define their attitude toward Tolstoy by means of his proximity to the Jewish question and Judaism.

It is time to revisit a discussion of Tolstoy and the Jewish question taken as a complex set of tasks.[4] Myths, legends, and tags of unqualified polarity about Tolstoy's attitudes toward the Jews and the Jewish question existed in his lifetime. He was suspected of either hidden antisemitism or excessive Judeophilia. For the monarchist press and the Black Hundreds in the years between the two proletarian revolutions (1905–17), Tolstoy was the satanic drummer in league with the Jews, with forces plotting against Russia. The ultranationalists of today continue to hold Tolstoy responsible for his alleged contribution to deposing the country from its former position of greatness. From the other side, paraphrasing Lenin's famous metaphor about Tolstoy, "the mirror of the Russian Revolution," one zealous critic calls Tolstoy "the mirror of the antisemitism of the Russian intelligentsia."[5] Such commentar-

The artists from the Black Hundreds' periodical *Veche* (no. 105, 1908) created a poster titled "The Satanic Drummer" [Osatanelyi barabanshchik]. The drummer is Tolstoy, shown barefoot, drum and drumstick in hand, marching in front of a motley crowd, which he is rousing against the Holy Russia of the tsars. The drummer's gang and its leader are drawn up to appear repulsive. Their features are hyperbolically "Jewish": enormous hooked noses, thick lecherous lips, short insectlike legs, and disfigured trunks. The cowhide on Tolstoy's drum has three patched sections bearing the following titles, clockwise from the top: "False Teaching"; "Puffed-Up Popularity"; "Hot-Air Twaddle." Reproduced from N. N. Apostolov, *Zhivoi Tolstoy: Zhizn' L'va Nikolaevicha Tolstogo v vospominaniiakh i perepiske* [The living Tolstoy: The Life of Lev Nikolaevich Tolstoy in reminiscences and correspondence] (Moscow: Izdanie Tolstovskogo Muzeiia, 1928), 473. The caricature is signed "M. Taganrogsky."

ies tend to present a long list of accusations and indictments against Tolstoy. Yes, he may have signed petitions of protest against the pogroms, but he did not put everything aside to focus exclusively on the Jewish question; according to rumor, he was overheard to say that Jews were not pleasant. He found time to write so much in general, and yet he wrote so little on the Jewish question, and so on.[6] Western studies of Tolstoy and Judaism and the Jewish question barely exist. A short piece by Harold Shefski, "Tolstoy and the Jews" (1981), accuses Tolstoy of indifference toward the Jewish plight and holds him responsible for failing to create a memorable Jewish type in his fiction (not even a caricature with a possible dose of "rabid antisemitism").[7]

Direct testimonies of Tolstoy's attitude toward the Jewish question are scattered across his voluminous written legacy and in memoirs and notes about him. Once assembled and scrutinized for accuracy, they present an image of a liberal humanist and a cosmopolitan with the convictions of a Christian Universalist. In a conversation among close family and friends at his home, which Alexander Borisovich Goldenveizer recorded, Tolstoy defined the categories of Jews and the fates of their self-determination in the contemporary world based on their degree of commitment to the Law:

> L. N. said this about the Jews.— There are three categories of Jews. The first are the religious believers. They honor their religion and strictly observe its customs. The second are the cosmopolitans, who stand on the higher step of consciousness. Finally, the third, the middle category, and arguably the most numerous part, at least among the Jewish intelligentsia, are the people who conceal their Jewishness, are even ashamed of it, and are at the same time hostile to other nationalities, but as if hiding their hostility up their sleeve. As much as I sympathize with those in the former two categories, I have little sympathy with those in the third.[8]

This conversation in which Tolstoy gives preference to observing Jews and to cosmopolitans obedient to the Law over the assimilated and the atheists—those disconnected from the religious bonds of ethical obligation—took place on September 3, 1903. This was five months after the history-changing pogrom on April 3, 1903, over Easter in the Bessarabian capital, Kishinev (Chişinău), Goldenveizer's hometown. Tolstoy's support of Judaic piety and cosmopolitan tolerance after the pogrom, especially after his swift responses to the Kishinev massacre in April and May 1903 that made instant headlines worldwide, were circulated in print and by word of mouth. Tolstoy's response to the pogrom in Kishinev in April 1903 is known in detail from his letter to his Jewish acquaintance David Shor, a professor at the Moscow Conservatory—which he also sent to the dentist Emmanuil Linetsky of Elisavetgrad and to the writer Sholem Aleichem—and from the protest note Tolstoy sent to the mayor of Kishinev, Karl-Ferdinand Schmidt, which was signed by Tolstoy and ten others.[9] (After Tolstoy's substantial editing, the final version of the forwarded text was essentially Tolstoy's.) On the spur of the news of the pogrom, Tolstoy wrote to Linetsky on April 27, 1903: "The criminal outrage in Kishinev is only a direct consequence of the propagation of lies and violence conducted by the Russian government with so much strain and tenacity. And the reaction of the government to the same event is but another proof of its crude egoism, which would not stop at any cruelty when it comes to cracking down on a movement deemed danger-ous to it . . . and of its complete indifference . . . as long as its interests are not concerned" (74:106–8). Nonetheless, Tolstoy disagreed with Linetsky's suggestion that Jews should organize a military response: Jews should "fight the government nonviolently (let's leave violence to the government alone)" (74:108). Tolstoy furthermore warned against putting too much volatile pro-test language into print: clichés tire attention. Used frequently, such lan-guage makes habitual the feeling that impending atrocity always lies in wait for targeted groups, Jews in this case (74:107). On April 27, Tolstoy explained to Professor Storozhenko, the initiator of the protest, that "burning Christian shame" is precisely a cliché that did not belong to the language of strong condemnation (74:110). And, as he put it in the letter to Sholem Aleichem on May 6, 1903, there are only one or two words for calling a crime a crime; one could of course keep adding the word "hideous" to it, but "what I have to say and to wit, the government is the sole culprit not only in the horrors of Kishinev but also in the whole discord that resides in a small part of the Rus-sian population—and not in the common folk. Unfortunately, this is some-thing I cannot say in a legal Russian edition" (74:118–19).[10]

With unprecedented speed, the seventy-five-year-old Tolstoy ac-complished in 1903 results typically afforded only by the social media net-works of today: he rapidly transmitted copies of his protests and responses to private individuals and, bypassing legal channels in Russia, condemned the outrage, shamed spineless officials and burghers who tried to condone the pogrom, and spoke words of courage to the Jews.[11] The text of the pro test note sent to Kishinev City Hall in Tolstoy's final edit read as follows: "Deeply shaken by the heinous crime committed in Kishinev, we would like to express our feeling of empathetic pain toward the innocent victims of the crowd, our horror before this beastly act committed by the Russian people, as well as our inexpressible revulsion and disgust toward the instigators and abettors of the crowd and an immeasurable indignation against the conniv-ers of this terrible act" (74:110). Michael Davitt, the well-known labor leader and a collaborator with Charles Parnell, put together a book detailing the di-sastrous situation of the Jews in Russia that came out at the end of 1903. Da-vitt's volume included Tolstoy's letter to Linetsky and Shor, in which, despite

Tolstoy's disclaimers to Linetsky and Shor about his lack of competence to participate in expert coverage of the Jewish question, Tolstoy's words about leaving violence to the government and its criminal lieutenants at the head of the mob resonate particularly strongly, especially given that they were placed next to recantations by John of Kronstadt, who initially condemned the Easter killings but soon accused Jewish victims of a sly conspiracy: by getting themselves killed they gave themselves the right to spill more Christian blood.[12]

The *New York Times* made a point of printing regular (sometimes not very accurate) statements on Tolstoy's responses to the pogrom with his words of consolation and advice to the Jews.[13] Despite infelicities in details, such blemishes could not mislead a clearly and honestly thinking person into error about Tolstoy's unequivocal and passionate condemnation of the crimes committed by the immediate perpetrators, the instigators, local authorities, the government of the Russian Empire, perfidious hierarchs like John of Kronstadt, and the tsar. The world knew that Tolstoy donated his stories for the relief of the victims in Kishinev to the illustrated collection in Yiddish titled *Gilf* [Help], insisting that they should first appear in Yiddish and in no other language. Following the publication of the stories in *Gilf*, Tolstoy allowed all those capable and willing to translate the stories from Yiddish into any language and publish them and use the proceeds at their discretion for additional measures of relief.[14]

Five years after the pogrom, on the eve of Tolstoy's eightieth birthday, the rising star of American journalism Herman Bernstein had Tolstoy in mind to be the first person he should interview for a series of responses on the Jewish question. At the time, Bernstein was an international correspondent covering the condition of Jews in Russia, eastern Europe, and Palestine. In his capacity as the editor of the *Jewish Tribune* and as an international correspondent for the *New York Times* and the *New York Sun* in Europe, Bernstein was authorized to arrange interviews with the most outstanding contemporary thinkers and writers, and he promptly received permission to visit Tolstoy. The Tolstoy interview later appeared as the opening to the volume in which the newspaper versions of the published dispatches were collected.[15]

Since this rare statement on the Jewish question by Tolstoy has not been given attention, it is worthwhile quoting it at length:

> I asked Tolstoy to express his views on the Jewish question in Russia. He said:
>
> "Most of the things ascribed to me as my expressions on this question are exaggerated. To me all questions are solved by my religious view of life. All people are alike. Therefore, there should be no such thing as a Jewish ques-

tion. It is as if you asked me about the Russian question, the German question, or the Japanese question. There should be no Jewish question, no Polish question, no Russian question—all people are brethren.[16] It is very sad and painful if we must make an effort to realize this. If there are any bad traits in the Russian Jews, they were called forth by the horrible persecutions to which we have subjected them. How do I account for the anti-Jewish feeling in Russia? We often dislike more those whom we harm than those who harm us. This is exactly true of the attitude of the Russians towards the Jews."

At dinner Tolstoy brought up the Jewish question once more. He said: "Herzen used to tell a story of a dispute he had heard between a Greek Catholic, a Roman Catholic, and a Protestant. The Greek Catholic declared that all the witches came from Kiev. The Roman Catholic said that the witches came not from Kiev, but from Tchernigov. And the Protestant swore he was sure that the witches came neither from Kiev nor from Tchernigov, but from Vologda. He was asked to settle the dispute. His answer was: 'I cannot answer your question, for I do not believe in the existence of witches.' That is how I look upon the Jewish question. Just as I do not believe in witches, so I do not believe in these various national and political questions." (20–22)

Bernstein had heard many responses to this question before, but Tolstoy's struck him with its contrarian honesty. How seriously can this denial of the question be weighed against more politically correct and cautious responses or merely rhetorical compliments meted to Jews by other interviewees with whom Bernstein met to talk? Tolstoy surely knew what he was saying in commenting on the Kishinev event.

In Europe, the solution to the Jewish question in the nineteenth century was usually seen as a choice between assimilation, with the presumption of equal rights and duties and full integration into the host culture, and the separation of the Jews inside an artificially maintained state-within-a-state in a variety of segregation packages (the so-called *status in statu* introduced by Fichte in 1793).[17] But the state of the question in Russia was more complicated. Tolstoy grew up during a recession phase in Russian politics and public discourse and the formalization of the Pale of Settlement in 1835.[18] He was an officer in the artillery during the Sebastopol debacle serving under Admiral Nakhimov until Nakhimov's heroic death in action defending against the allied siege. (It had never been a secret that Nakhimov was Jewish by birth.) The flowering of Tolstoy's literary career and fame coincided with the temporary liberalization of Jewish life during the Great Reforms and the remission of the early counterreform era. The disastrous war against Turkey unsettled the Jews in the Balkans, parts of Romania, and Bulgaria (Jews had been vassals of the sultans for five centuries). At this time, Tolstoy was completing part 8 of *Anna Karenina* with its indictment of the "Slavic question" in the name of which the war had been fought. The assassination of Alexander II on March 1, 1881, brought in its wake a wave of pogroms in the southwest of the empire in 1881–82. As Tolstoy was completing *A Confession* and working on his commentary on and translation of the Gospels as well as *The Critique of Dogmatic Theology*, the institution of the so-called May Laws (1881–82) decreed by the minister of the interior, Count Nikolai Pavlovich Ignatiev, was ending for good the ability of the government to liberalize Jewish life in imperial Russia, despite the considerable effort of many public servants. As Count Ivan Tolstoy, vice-president of the Russian Academy of Sciences, put it in his introduction to his and Gessen's *Evreiskii vorpos v Rossii* (1907), "The injustice of our legislation toward the Jews, its absolute impracticability in the cause of achieving its final goals, and the fact that through it only the most deleterious results were being reached—and not only for the Jews per se but also for the whole country, for Russia—all of this was becoming clearer and clearer to me every day."[19]

By the 1880s, the Jewish question had become one of Russia's "cursed questions" and was discussed as such very actively in the Russian press. The most famous exponent of the state-within-a-state proposal among Russian writers was Dostoevsky, whose "A Propos of the Jewish Question" (1877)— his double bill written in vicious jest for *The Diary of a Writer*—would continue to cast a dark shadow over his legacy.[20] To paraphrase the words of Saltykov-Shchedrin, published in the democratic *Otechestvennye zapiski* (Notes of the fatherland) in issue 8 of 1882, the Jewish question was the most depressing and shameful of its cursed questions, now a responsibility of all Russian society rather than only a matter of government policy; it constituted one of its worst headaches.[21] However Tolstoy preferred to frame his attitude to the Jewish question to Bernstein, it should *not* be called into question that from his youth he had been very familiar with the three categories of Jews he described to Goldenveizer and his family in 1903. Before Sebastopol and the Crimea, Tolstoy served in the Danube Army (Dunaiskaia Armiia) and was billeted for several months in the Danube basin on the territory of Romania and Bessarabia, including several monthlong stays in Iaşi and Kishinev and in the agrarian provinces of southeastern Europe, coming into close contact with the town life of eastern European Jewry. There, he was witness to the reality of the shtetl, and he experienced what sutlers' liquor-selling carts and roadway inns with pubs run on franchise by Jews really amounted to. He mentions these encounters briefly, without dwelling on them except for pointing out, with a few vivid details, that both the military and local population treat Jews with dastardly contempt and heartless cunning. Jews are called kikes or Yids in these earlier appearances in Tolstoy's works and his diary: the appellations normally come from characters whose hearts and minds are not to be trusted, while pity for Jews is expressed by characters whose minds and hearts are in the right place.[22]

96

TOLSTOY'S JEWISH ENCOUNTERS: PEOPLE AND HOLY SCRIPTURE

After resigning from the army on November 26, 1856, and during his two trips abroad and extensive travels through Italy, Switzerland, France, Belgium, Germany, and England in 1857 and 1860–61, Tolstoy gained more insight into the results of cultural assimilation than he could in eastern Europe. This is where life in the historical ghettos and the poorest quarters of European cities was already combined with the growing participation of western-European Jews in the cultural, economic, political, and ideological life of nation-states.[23]

But Tolstoy could see "Russian Jews" with sufficient frequency and communicated with them only after his family moved to spend the autumn and winter months in Moscow in 1881, which followed the assassination of Tsar Alexander II and a wave of pogroms in the southwestern provinces of the Russian Empire during the preparation and implementation of Ignatiev's May Laws. Some statistics are necessary here. In the entire Tula gubernatorial region where the Krapivensky District with Tolstoy's estate, Yasnaya Polyana, was located in 1858, there lived only 700 Jews. Their number grew somewhat to reach 1,023 in 1880–81. Only at the turn of the twentieth century did the Jewish population of the Tula Gubernia finally exceed 2,000. The township of Aleksin, known as the Jewish *mestechko* (shtetl) outside the Pale, was famous for its Jewish artisans and repairmen, and yet of its 3,465 inhabitants, only 56 were Jews.[24] It follows from the testimony of Dushan Makovitsky, the resident doctor in the Tolstoy household from 1904 onward, that the writer was in close contact with various economic strata of the Jews of Tula, who were also divided by their religious and political convictions. Tolstoy would speak warmly of the banking clerk whose last name was London and who would later move to America.[25] Tolstoy's remarks on the categories of the Jewry in Makovitsky's recording of April 11, 1906, follow quite closely the earlier evidence by Goldenveizer discussed above. Note Tolstoy's emphatic protest of the lack of rights and the persecution of Russian Jews, which explain not only the enterprising spirit through which Jews are frequently perceived but also the radicalization of Jewish youth:

> L. N.: They have *fervor* because they do not have the same rights as others. This also wins the Russians to their side. I am against quotas in schools, against the Pale of Settlement. All ethnic groups living on the earth have the right to live where they wish. Why should we be allowed to live at Yasnaya Polyana while others have to live in Mamadysh?[26] I stand for the abolition of all laws of exception [*iskliuchitelnykh zakonov*] relating to the Jews. These laws are a disgrace! [Emphasis added.]
> A. A. Bers:[27] They [the Jews] are useful.

97

L. N.: I wouldn't know whether they are useful or not, but one must not restrict the rights of men. The best of the Jews whom I have known was London. There are three categories of Jews: the first one, like London, consists of those who do not abandon their religion, the believers, who adopt the moral teaching from the Talmud. The second category are the atheists, the Jews who have strayed away from Judaism but have not drifted toward Christianity, *sans foi ni loi*—Warszawer[28]—the most unpleasant type, but he is always for the Jews. The third category are the cosmopolitans, for whom all people are equal, like Berkenheim.[29]

Andrei Lvovich: But they do not exist.

L. N. thought and could not recall others. Then he named Nazhivin's wife.[30]

L. N.: Those Jews straying away from the Talmud and not joining Christianity should strive at least toward this cosmopolitanism. Baskin-Seredinsky could be one of those.[31]

In an exchange of letters in which he introduced himself to Tolstoy, Ivan Nazhivin had mentioned that he was going to marry a Jewish woman. Tolstoy's blessing for Nazhivin to marry Anna Zussman is very instructive. It is possible that to practice medicine or to have her marriage to Nazhivin formally registered, Anna Zussman had to convert to Russian Orthodoxy. Tolstoy writes on December 3, 1902, "I wish from the bottom of my heart that you find a kindred believer [*edinoverka*] in your bride and wife—and then she will be a helping friend" (73:340). The first, bureaucratic meaning of the word *edinoverka* is "coreligionist." This is *not* how Tolstoy means the word, however. He means precisely a "kindred believer," a spiritual ally and friend. There are many religions under God, but one faith. Tolstoy's ideal is unity in faith, mutual understanding, cooperation, brotherhood.

This conviction explains Tolstoy's open approach in his communications with the Jews of Moscow. The Tolstoys' Khamovniki town manor was located not far from a section of Moscow that was home to many Jews who had been able to move to the old capital during the reforms of the 1860s and in the decade of counter-reforms that followed in the 1870s.[32] The most numerous part of the Jewish community of Moscow had settled in the Zariadie district, which was not too distant from the city center, on account of the construction of the first choral synagogue in the city at the corner of Bolshoi Spasoglinnishevsky Lane and Soliansky Drive. It is into that latter section of Moscow that Tolstoy would walk from his home to study ancient Hebrew during the period of his intense biblical studies conducted through 1884 with the remarkable Moscow rabbi Solomon Minor. Tolstoy immortalized Minor in his banned work *What Do I Believe?* (1884), quickly known worldwide from its French title (*Ma réligion*). Tolstoy remembered being taken aback and not yet ready to formulate the principles of his emerging teaching of nonviolence when Minor had asked him whether it is true that all those who call themselves Christians turn the other cheek (23:313–16).[33] And Tolstoy agrees that it is Jews who turn the other cheek more frequently when Christians come to beat them (23:15–16).

The theological dispute between Tolstoy and Minor must have centered on the points that had caused Tolstoy's passionate objections to certain positions in the Five Books of Moses and that had arisen during his commentary on the Gospels and their harmonization a few years earlier, in 1880–81:

> In the Gospels: not only no to killing anyone, but it is forbidden to harbor resentment against anyone. In the Five Books: kill, kill, and kill—wives, children, and cattle.
>
> In the Gospels: wealth is evil; in the Five Books—it is the greatest boon and reward.
>
> In the Gospels: purity of the body—have one wife; in the Five Books—take as many wives as you wish.
>
> In the Gospels: all people are brethren; in the Five Books: all are foes, only Jews are brethren.
>
> In the Gospels: no ritual worship of God; the greater half of the books defines the details of how to ritually serve God.
>
> And yet they assure us that the Gospel teaching is the complement and sequel to the Five Books (24:101).[34]

Tolstoy's objections to the relatedness of the Old Testament and the Gospels in 1880–81 recall the objections made by Kant to Moses Mendelssohn, who had translated the Torah into the German vernacular.[35] It is known that Kant's attitude toward Judaism was critical, but his criticism rested on a single cliché that he adopted according to which Judaism is the religion of law whose major principle is retaliation. In Kant's treatment, the Psalms bring the idea of vengeance to frightening extremes.[36] According to Kant, the idea of messianic teleology is not interpreted by the Jews in moral terms but in political terms—specifically, with a utilitarian bias. Further, according to Kant, through the idea of the messianic end goal, the Jews place themselves in relation to God as they would in relation to their ruler.

In view of the fact that many years of dedicated study are necessary for mastery of the Tanakh and especially the Talmud, Tolstoy's initial immersion in Judaism in the early 1880s must be deemed superficial. Despite his suspicious rejection of Judaism at this stage and whether or not this was a result of the superficiality of his acquaintance, it is most instructive to notice how through Tolstoy's reading of the Christian Gospels themselves Jesus arises as a rebellious prophet of heroic nonviolent resistance. This Christ, in Tolstoy's reading, causes a conversion of those minds that split human history into halves, the latter according to which the Sabbath is for man rather than vice versa (Mark 2:27). Traces of this anarchic Christianity that Tolstoy reads from the internal strife in Judaism are visible in his equally anarchic reading of the excerpts from the Talmud and the Bible in annotations he wrote in 1878–80, such as "blessed are the persecuted."[37] In the commentary to *The Four Gospels Harmonized and Translated* (1880–81), Tolstoy associates the attainment of the Holy Land with the spiritual unification of human purpose with Christ's awareness (*razumenie*). In addition to humanity's sharing a universal condition of sonhood to God the Father, every human being holds a unique relationship toward the world and yet is interconnected with all other human beings. Life renews and resurrects from ruin as a continuous process independent of one's physical or historical placement in the world. Those left outside the Holy Land so understood are those who had not changed internally and remain as they used to be (*ostaiutsia kakimi oni byli*)—unable or unwilling to live by way of love (24:372). Finally, Tolstoy blames the poor or deliberately malicious interpretive skills of John Chrysostom for the perpetuation of the hateful libel concerning Jewish guilt for the death of Christ, the deviation from truth "repeated for one thousand years" (24:373).

Tolstoy made it publicly known in Moscow in the early to mid-1880s that Jesus was a Jew killed by Roman soldiers at the order of the Roman governor for refusing to respond to evil with evil. This is exactly what Tolstoy told a nineteen-year-old Nikolai Nikitich Ivanov (1867–1913) in 1886, who was at that stage assisting Tolstoy with the compilation of biblical parables and stories for inexpensive readers: "Jesus is that Jew whom about two thousand years ago people flogged and stretched in this way on a pole (Lev Nikolaevich spread his arms wide apart), nailed him to the pole, and condemned him to the most terrible capital punishment of all only because he never had done any evil to anyone and preached a teaching about how people can become kind and happy."[38]

It is precisely the questions of how to practically construct a nonviolent kingdom of God on earth and how to reach the symbolic Promised Land by finding one's place of service in this world that occupied Tolstoy almost entirely from around 1879 and that brought him to the attention of younger Jews in Russia. These young Jews were either disillusioned or did not sympathize with socialist and revolutionary ideas. For them, the Tolstoyan teaching rang familiar tones of ethical obligation but was not as restrictive and binding as the religion of their Orthodox fathers and rabbis. Tolstoy revived the ideal of agriculture that was presented in the stories of the Bible. What he understood to be the biblical kind of agriculture is when labor is induced by an inner need rather than forced by the conditions of the Pale or the strictures that the kahal imposed. Such an ideal also satisfied the young Jews' thirst for a freedom of conscience not overseen by rabbinical authority.

The imposition of new restrictions against Jews in 1881–82 brought extraditions from the cities, expulsions from the universities and other institutions of learning, the revocation of licenses and professional bans, and restraints on travel and mobility and on choice of domicile. This wave coincided with the campaign led by progressive rabbis promoting nonviolent forms of auto-emancipation. It also coincided with the circulation of Tolstoy's first postconversion works. The authorities banned these works. Tolstoy and his followers suffered the same measures of restriction and threats of retaliation as the revolutionary Jewish youth and reformers. As such, the Jewish reformers and Tolstoy understood each other.[39] From this point on, Jews regularly sought personal correspondence or meetings with Tolstoy. They included Jews emigrating to America, assimilated professionals, those unsure whether to convert, and, very slowly—since there were still too few of them—Russian-Jewish intellectuals and artists.

In 1885, a young Jew named Isaak Feinerman moved to Yasnaya Polyana with his wife, intending to become a teacher at its school. The story of Isaak (as he was known there) is as exemplary as it is sad.[40] Tolstoy was very fond of him and, with his domestics, took an immense interest in Feinerman's fate. He supported Feinerman's ardor for farming and cooperative labor; he especially welcomed Feinerman's developing passion for retelling Bible episodes for peasant children. And yet he could support neither Feinerman's beggarly tendencies nor his disregard of his duties toward his wife and child. Feinerman constituted an experiment open to peasant ridicule and judgment on the estate and in the Tolstoy circle. While most critics condemned Feinerman's abandonment of his wife, in whose fate Tolstoy's family became invested, Tolstoy was especially troubled by Feinerman's literal-mindedness in his understanding of "Christian behavior," which led to the cooling of their relations toward the late 1880s and the complete dissolution of them after 1900.[41]

Concerning Feinerman's intended Christian baptism (in 1885) so that he could be allowed to teach, Tolstoy took a different stand than in the case of Nazhivin's wife, Anna. In August 1885, he wrote to Vladimir Chertkov, "I do not judge Feinerman's conversion to Christianity. It seems to me I could not have done that because I cannot imagine a situation in which it would be better not to speak the truth and not to act in truth. But I know that there used to be times when I could" (85:250). In other words, as he relates directly to Feinerman in November 1886, Tolstoy thinks that Feinerman should rather adhere to Judaism and follow the ethical commandments of his forefathers dictated by a sense of inner emancipation: "Act only then when you cannot act in any other known way . . . Man cannot help but act in a given way only when he feels that unless he does he would kill his self, his divine reasonable being" (63:412).[42]

Following the financial collapse of the agricultural commune in Kherson Gubernia where he had gone to work after the ongoing scandals with his abandoned wife, Feinerman was issued an official order from the authorities to move to Poltava. Tolstoy would treat with ever-increasing criticism Feinerman's decision to convene congresses of Tolstoy followers at which, as Feinerman hoped, Tolstoy himself would deliver keynotes.[43] An even more serious split began to form between the teacher and his disciple when Feinerman attempted to stylize Tolstoy into a sort of rabbinical sage in his literary excursions and various memoirist sketches that he started publishing, in Tolstoy's lifetime, using the pen name Teneromo. Tolstoy's disillusionment with Isaak reached a zenith in a cold denial that he even knew Feinerman (under his pseudonym of Teneromo): "I am not familiar with his writing and I do not communicate with him."[44] Tolstoy caught as well the early signs of Feinerman's lack of talent for precise expression. In his writing, Teneromo attempted to create a synthetic narrative combining the very distinct styles of the Old and New Testaments. The result was cacophony. Teneromo's prose and dramatic fictions attribute to Tolstoy the role of an exuberant prophet who speaks on the borderline of Christian and Judaic anarchism. It is through a particular exercise of his modest literary merit that Teneromo attempts to tell the story of the Jews' fate in Russia and in the contemporary world, combined with a self-confident but inadequate mettle for social exposure—a ridiculous "twinity" (*dvoitsa*), as Tolstoy wittily put it (68:261–62).[45] Tolstoy appreciated just as little Feinerman's caricatures of emancipated life outside the Pale.[46]

The rejection of Teneromo's mythology can be read as a self-condemning guilt felt by Tolstoy for his Pygmalion-like failure to mold a plausibly cosmopolitan Jew. It hurt Tolstoy to see that under the guise of a literary hack profiting from the legends of patriarchs his much-beloved Isaak was achieving relative success as a journalistic parvenu writing for pay.

EMANCIPATING THE COVENANT

In 1889, a young Jew, Simon Dubnov, who was enormously impressed with Tolstoy's *A Confession* (*Ispoved'*), resolved to investigate rumors about Tolstoy's refusal to come to the rescue of the Jews of Russia.[47] Dubnov addressed Tolstoy directly and, with the writer's permission, made his responses public.[48] In his response to Dubnov, Tolstoy explained that he considered the solution of a state-within-a-state to be "the worst of all evils," an unacceptable attempt to "separate people from one another" with borders

(140–41). Dubnov had found that Tolstoy's awe of the Old Testament prophets was complete and that the system of ethical monism read by Tolstoy from Judaism was lucid, logical, and simple (140–41). In his brief note, Dubnov expressed a wish that Tolstoy would confess this love for the Jewish people in print so as to bury for good and shame the malicious lies about his hatred of Jews (141).

This was the whole point. It was not in Tolstoy's character to write any *forced* assurances of an ethical nature on commission or under pressure. In his diary of November 23, 1888, he comments on the falsity of what may be described as ethical commission for a good cause (50:3–4). A few months after Dubnov's interview, Tolstoy had to abort a draft titled "An Appeal" (Vozzvanie) that he hoped would open the eyes of men on the cause of the "misery of the people of our time" (27:738).[49] The contribution of the Jewish "teachers of humanity" on the topic of escaping woe—alongside "Indian, Chinese, and Greek" teachers (27:530), and most clearly Christ—foreground the entire discussion, but the draft was abandoned by Tolstoy because of a lack of mental energy (50:85–86). But he did not lose interest in the topic of Jewish thought or Jewish history. We know that only a few days after the abandoned draft on June 1, 1889, Tolstoy read *Histoire du peuple d'Israël* by Ernest Renan and was thinking about the effects of Israel on the origin of Christianity.[50] The topic of Jewish thought and history clearly preoccupied Tolstoy, although he showed himself to be reluctant to write on the topic under pressure.

Several months later, in February 1890, the philosopher Vladimir Soloviev and the Irish-English journalist Emile Dillon, who was investigating the state of the Jewish question in Russia, solicited an address from Tolstoy to the government "written individually, in your own name," to avert new strictures against the Jews that were rumored to be forthcoming.[51] By this stage, Soloviev was an old hand with the Jewish question, having published in 1884 an essay titled "The Jews and the Christian Question" (Evreistvo i khristianskii vopros).[52] Tolstoy doubted that this was a job for one person, however. Agreeing, in a letter to Soloviev on March 15, 1890, to add his signature, he thought that Soloviev and Dillon, the initiators of the project, should write the following explanation: "The basis for our repugnance at the measures of persecution against the Jewish people is one and the same, the consciousness of a brotherly connection among all nations and especially so with the Jews, among whom Christ was born and who have suffered so much and are suffering from the heathen ignorance of so-called Christians" (65:45).

It is at this point around 1890 that pressure on Tolstoy to write on the Jewish question intensified. Although his signature tops the list of the other forty-nine signatories to the Soloviev-Dillon address, Tolstoy felt that the Jewish question was beginning to be a theme assigned to him by others (*zadannaia tema*) (65:45).[53] Soloviev turned to Faivel-Meer Goetz (1853–1931), a historian from Wilno who had been Soloviev's adviser since 1881 on all theological and linguistic matters concerning biblical Hebrew. The idea of the address might have originated with Goetz, who was an aggressive proselyte much inspired by Soloviev's dream of a theocratic kingdom with a strong bedrock in Judaism and a special role for the chosen people in its construction.[54] Goetz persisted in his attempts to get Tolstoy involved in this theocratic enterprise, which would lead to a polemically charged and intermittent correspondence between the two lasting almost two decades.

Tolstoy's message to Goetz on May 25–26, 1890, was that the moral teaching of the persecuted Jews and their life practices "stand beyond any comparison above the moral teaching and practice of our quasi-Christian society" (65:98). He added that the Jewish question was part of a network of problems concerning *all* persecutions in Russia and worldwide (in the same letter, Tolstoy cites the expulsion of the Chinese from America and restrictions on their immigration and employment status; 65:98–99). And thus, while "the persecutions to which the Jews are being subjected" are not only "unjust and cruel but also insane," the topic cannot "hold an exclusive or preferential place" over his other thoughts or feelings (65:98) until the root of all injustice is defeated. Tolstoy clarified that the "very same [institutions] in the name of which the current persecutions are happening" are inspired, first, by the Judeo-Christian preference of "the poor of your town before the poor in another land,"[55] and second, by the adherence protected by the state to the *lex talionis* principle derived from Mosaic Law (65:99).

Tolstoy does not think that Jews or Judaism are to blame for the enduring presence of these archaic principles of exclusivity and vengeance, but he holds both Jews and Christians responsible for leaving the state of affairs concerning retaliation unchanged. Left unrevised, the principles of vengeful justice, exclusive entitlement, and order built on violence would continue to exert harmful effects on societies, among other things giving rise to contemporary nationalism along with the artificial creation of national questions themselves. In a letter to Goetz of June 30, 1890, Tolstoy pressed Goetz on the necessity to give up on the messianic obstinacy that, as he wrote, "the Jews are attributing to themselves" and that, on top of the restrictions imposed on Jews from above, is "setting the Jewish people" even further "apart" (65:117–18). Here, Tolstoy relies on his favorite idea that Christ intuited his individual mission rather than fulfilled the prophecy: "The nation need not know its mission, just as man need not know his predestination" (65:117–18).

Goetz returned with a confrontational program of his own publishing in 1891, "The Accused Speaks!" (Slovo podsudimomu!). At the beginning of this collection, Goetz reprinted Tolstoy's correspondence with Soloviev and Dillon of 1890, adding to it statements from legal historian and statesman B. N. Chicherin and democratic writer and public intellectual V. G. Korolenko concerning proposed measures of legal protection for Russian Jews, as well as the letters Goetz had received from Tolstoy and Soloviev.[56] Tolstoy's letters were printed in excised form, and his motivations for refusing to write on commission were dropped from the printed text. But Goetz published Soloviev's letter of March 5, 1891, in its entirety. Soloviev optimistically asked the question, "After this amazing forty centuries' long life of Israel [why] should it fear some antisemites?"—a question that appealed to Goetz far more than to Tolstoy with his antiprovidential stance.[57] The alarm sounded by Soloviev did not concern the Jews but rather Russia, which was rising up against the forty-century-old Israel relocated by the force of Providence on the territory of the Russian Empire: "It is not in vain that Providence installed in our fatherland the most numerous and the strongest part of Jewry."[58] Goetz was pleased by this approach since he was attempting to substantiate the desired integration of the Jews of Russia into Russian life by reference to the fact that Jews born on all territories of the Russian Empire could not be considered aliens, minorities, or migrant arrivals.

Failing to find in Goetz a productive interlocutor on the question of ethics, Tolstoy felt overjoyed upon receiving a letter from the twenty-four-year-old Vulf Kanter, a recent graduate of the Technical Academy in Moscow, who wrote to Tolstoy in March 1890, seven months before his emigration to America.[59] Kanter informed Tolstoy that he was ready to reject the principle of retaliatory justice, but he asked Tolstoy to expand on the ways of active practice of nonviolence in an unstable world that was far from just. In his letter of April 9, 1890, Tolstoy addresses Kanter as a kindred believer untouched by religious formality and revolutionary liberalism alike, exactly the kind of Jew who is ready to abandon his belief in *lex talionis*. Kanter had a question: Should this abandonment of *lex talionis* be absolute? Or can there be compromises? The response that Tolstoy provides is one of his most succinct formulations of nonresistance: Yes, it should be absolute in idea because compromises will inevitably occur in practice: "One should not commit the very evil that one is combating" (65:70) or interpret the phrase "do not resist evil" as an invitation to be complacent toward evil (65:71). Tolstoy summarizes, "The rule about nonresistance is uttered as a rule about how to combat evil most successfully. It is said, You are used to combating evil with violence, with retaliation. These are evil and bad means. The best thing to do is not to retaliate but to respond in kindness" (65:71).

The years 1890–94 were, for Tolstoy, a period of reconsideration and recontextualization of the unsolved paradoxes of nonviolence. In a brief reflection found in his diary of July 19, 1893, Tolstoy busied himself with deciding why the principle of "tit for tat" persists in human society. The exemplary groups on which he settles are Jews and women. He thinks that they are comparable because of a frightening longevity of these two groups' repression. What causes the vitality of aggressor instincts in their oppressors? Tolstoy thinks that it is the fear of retaliation that necessitates that the oppressors maintain their capacity for coercion with artificial and distracting questions, bureaucracy, and specially designed institutions. These are the societies in which an individual is sacrificed "for his own welfare" to the idea of national-historical or state interest—societies that Tolstoy calls pagan that were founded on slavery (from ancient empires and Israel all the way down to modern colonial powers and nation-states).[60] In such societies, alongside other comparably oppressed groups, women and Jews enslave others in recompense for their own enslavement with whatever measures are afforded to the weak (52:95).[61] These measures only increase with emancipation, enabling the newly empowered to act "rapaciously" in recompense for the losses that they had suffered (28:192–93). Yet emancipation cannot and should not be stopped because it puts limits on oppression.

Noah's paternalist justice, Mosaic Law, and the Talmud all identify *what evil is* most correctly (28:202). It is the ways of restitution of good from evil that are incorrect. Inner and auto-emancipation should consist in the nonviolent reinterpretation of the conditions for following the covenant between God and his chosen people. Those choosing emancipation choose the giving up (for-give-ness) of sins and errors. True emancipation is guaranteed when the symbolic power of the seat of Moses (*sedalishche Moiseevo*) as that of retributive judgment (Matt. 23:2) becomes the idea of loving purification from sin at the seat of mercy (Heb. 9:5)[62] in human awareness and social practice. The problem lies in that the Pharisees and Scribes running the functions and operations of modern churches, science, intellectual life, governments, and state affairs "sat on the seat of Moses [*oni seli na sedalishche Moiseevo*]" (39:15).[63] The hoarded ballast of hostility and the tallying of the scores of guilt hinder progress. The Christian historical mission as interpreted in Tolstoy's texts of 1890–94 brings to a decisive conclusion Isaiah's complaints that Tolstoy highlights in the Old Testament. The complaints Tolstoy remarks on are those against the legalistic imprisonment with "rule upon rule" in Yahweh's system of Law (28:40–41) and the acceptance of the oppressor's matrix of permanence in which Cain always kills Abel, the cunning Jacob always escheats the trusting Esau, Caiaphas and Pilate always prevail over Christ. Taking their cue from these emblems, English colonizers subdue Indians and Russian bureaucratic and militaristic autocracy violates the basic rights of "alien peoples" (*chuzhie narodnosti*): Jews, Poles, Latvians, and native Russian muzhiks themselves (28:192–93). Yet retaliate in kind one must not.

Tolstoy had decided by 1896 that the existence of men in uniform whose job was to carry and use arms in the name of the state was the cause of Jewish pogroms. Such is the conclusion reached in the second draft of a sketch of Tolstoy's given the notable title "Carthago delenda est" (1896).[64] The draft attempted to describe the scene of a pogrom in which Russian officers with soldiers under their command had looted the home of a Jewish miller and tortured his family. There were casualties, but the incident was given *no* coverage in the press. How is the punishment of the murderers and the destruction of the irreparable Carthage to be delivered by nonviolent means? The Jews were tortured at the mill after they had stood up to drunken hoodlums by tearing off their epaulettes—that is, their distinction of power. Twelve officers were demoted for this crime. In their defense, they claimed that they were fighting for the national honor symbolized in their uniforms, their safe conducts for crime, Tolstoy argues (39:217–18).[65]

The idea that the magnificence of the Mosaic sense of historical purpose with high ethical obligation is cheapened by the arrival of petty and manipulative national questions handled by the man in uniform dates back to Tolstoy's historical reflections in the Epilogues to *War and Peace* (EII, 1; 7:310) and to the concluding chapters of *Anna Karenina*, in which national interests are reassigned from Moses and Joshua of Nun to "monarchs and journalists" and unfit but bloodthirsty volunteers in whom "the soul of the nation has found a way to express itself" (VII, 1; 19:350–51). Thus, this idea is not completely new for Tolstoy. But the idea that the historical being of humanity should consist of finding a nonviolent route to the Promised Land *every day*, where one is borderless, dispersed, "scattered," and owes one's pledge of allegiance only to the ethical sense through the brotherly link in God, is developed by Tolstoy most fully only in his major texts completed between 1893 and 1898.[66] A remarkable letter to John Kenworthy summarizes Tolstoy's dream of the kingdom built from inner emancipation of the dispersed, of humanity without borders (67:171–72). The primitive Galilean nomads eighteen centuries earlier, Tolstoy writes in *The Kingdom of God Is within You*, were able to overcome the boundaries of the old law and followed Christ (Tolstoy names the tax collector Zacchaeus, the profligate son, the wayward woman, and the robber on the cross). He is pleased to include in the ranks of these first Christian Jews "Russian semiprimitive muzhiks like Siutaev, Bondarev, and the Russian mystic Tolstoy," the "impracticable dreamers" relative to the Galileans, who are without counterparts in the modern world (28:37).[67]

Tolstoy's new version of the Kingdom of Heaven is thus a drastic revision of the positions of the Old Testament regarding prophecy and predestination: "Moses could enter with his people into the Promised Land, but Christ could in no way see the fruit of his teaching" (diary entry for July 17, 1898, 53:203). And thus, while the Rousseau follower in Tolstoy claimed in his pedagogical writings of 1862 that the Old Bible had to be read because "our ideal is behind us, not ahead of us" (8:301–24), the Tolstoy of the 1890s writes, in a letter to Goetz of June 14, 1898, that history "does not move backward" (71:378). This rather curt response was sent to Goetz after he had anonymously published "An Open Letter to Count L. N. Tolstoy" (Ot-krytoe pis'mo k grafu L. N. Tolstomu) in which, hiding behind the signa-ture "N. N.," he took issue with Tolstoy's attempts to revise Mosaic Law. Goetz claimed its superiority over Christian law, a mere derivative already contained in the Jewish Holy Scripture.[68] Tolstoy abruptly halted Goetz's proposals according to which if Tolstoy is a true Christian he is originally a Jew: "Like the majority of the educated, sincere, and believing Jews you are trying to prove that all that we see in Christianity is already contained in Judaism" (71:377). This is not yet the case, says Tolstoy—not until he sees the abolition of the principle of retaliation and the idea of historical exclusiv-ity that are assumed by the Jews in exchange for God's protection in the cov-enant. He is ready to greet this change in Judaism that would bring it closer to Christianity: "Let it be new Judaism, or the Talmud cleansed and clarified, and let the Christian Church be called heathen paganism as I consider it to be. But in order for me to call by the name new Judaism or the Talmud the understanding of life that is dear to me and by which I live it is necessary for me to find this understanding of life to be clearly and harmoniously ex-pressed in the Jewish book" (71:377–78).[69]

THE WISDOM OF THE TALMUD AND THE POUND OF FLESH

Years before Bely's and Berdiaev's comparisons in Put', Jewish intellectu-als had noticed similarities between Tolstoy and radical Jewish reformers like Spinoza, and Christ himself, in his readiness to cleanse the Talmud in a similar way that Tolstoy had done to the Gospels.[70] In 1890, the young journalist Khaim Flekser, known by his pen name Akim Volynsky, published a review of Tolstoy's philosophical work *On Life* (1887).[71] Tolstoy's work pri-oritized a sense of life characterized by a direct line of spiritually conducted service, where true life, ontologically speaking, really does, for Tolstoy, come before personal, social, and world-historical obligations. In these solutions, Volynsky notes two strands that spell out Tolstoy's connection with "the line of Judaic prophesy" as well as the direct connection with certain episodes in the history of Judaic thought: an affinity with Spinoza's pantheism and ethical didacticism and an affinity with the morality of and the eagerness to follow into "the kingdom *not* of this world" (36–37). Volynsky thought that Tolstoy's progress in that direction was still unclearly defined. In May

1894, Tolstoy indeed wrote to Volynsky on the importance of designing the language of the new sermon that would "shame the persecutors and . . . liberate the persecuted" and that would serve the truth "that is ahead and not the truth that used to be true some time ago" (67:129). "Are you ready for this?" he asked Volynsky (67:129). It appears that Tolstoy soon realized that not even Volynsky, an assimilated Jew with his relatively high literary standing, could accomplish the task of such a reform. During times in which the Dreyfus affair was possible in one of the most civilized of nations, external help from leading cultural figures in the nation was still needed—one good example of which is Zola's *Pour les juifs* (1896).[72] In an anecdote that Tolstoy features in *On Life*, a Russian and a Jew enter into a theological dispute about the meaning of life. When they run out of good arguments, the Russian simply slaps the Jew on his bald pate, feeling unable to respond to the other's religious "subtleties" and feeling that, first, he will get away with this way of argumentation and, second, that only this way of argumentation will be heard (he is satisfied by the sound of the smack on the head and even asks the Jew about what action of his had produced the sound) (26:315).

The best argument for nonviolent resistance according to Tolstoy was made by a Jew named Jesus. In the summer of 1890, Tolstoy found a perfect model of peaceful resistance to violence in the artistic treatment of Christ by his painter friend, Nikolai Gay. Gay's piece, *Christ before Pilate* [*Khristos pered Pilatom*], is a rendition of the famous conversation between Christ and Pilate about truth, which Tolstoy recommended for acquisition to art collector Pavel Tretiakov's newly founded Tretiakov Gallery in Moscow. Tolstoy wrote the following to Tretiakov about the painting: "Christ sees that he is facing a deluded man overflowing with fat, but instead of deciding to cast away this man judging him by his looks alone, Christ begins to relate to this man the gist of his teaching. But the governor has other things to do and he says: 'What was that about truth?' And he leaves. Christ looks with sadness at this impenetrable human being" (65: 125). At the end of the summer of 1890, Gay's painting was awaiting shipment to go on a planned tour of North America and Tolstoy wrote to many of his acquaintances in the United States to advocate for their support and every kind of assistance that they could provide for Gay. The most remarkable letter Tolstoy sent in this regard was to George Frost Kennan, author of the by then already finished two-volume study, *Siberia and the Exile System*, which Tolstoy deeply respected. In this letter, Tolstoy recommends Gay's Christ to Kennan by describing the perception of Christ by Pilate: "It is not interesting for him to go on listening to the nonsense of this Hebraic little Yid [etot evreiskii zhidok] or anything he could possibly say [. . .] It is distressing for him that this tramp, this tattered beggar, this boyish young lad" could talk to him about truth—to him, Pilate, "a friend and interlocutor of Roman poets and philosophers" (65: 140).

The examples above illustrate vividly that Tolstoy regarded Jewish thought as ethical above all, in terms of choosing to do good over doing well,[73] but also as passive and pessimistic in its secular expressions. When Eduard von Hartmann was willing "to get free from the Jewish religious worldview," Tolstoy notes, he did so by falling into the trap of Buddhism (39:12). In a diary entry for June 11, 1904, we find an intriguing reflection by Tolstoy on Spinoza's philosophical mind and his Jewish literary style in comparison with Pascal's maximally epigrammatic and paradoxical Christian brevity: "I have stopped writing down my profession of faith and spent two days translating Pascal. He is very good. I have read Spinoza and made selections. The Jew Spinoza—love of God above all. There is no sincerity and he is young; rather, he is young and therefore artificial and not quite sincere—not, for instance, like Pascal, who writes with the blood from his heart" (55:104).

The selections that Tolstoy mentions have to do with his work on the reader he was compiling, *Thoughts of Wise People for Every Day* (*Mysli mudrykh liudei na kazhdyi den'*). How are we to interpret Tolstoy's reference to Spinoza's being excommunicated from the Jewish community of Amsterdam for his Latin adage *Deus sive Natura*? One does not get excommunicated for half-hearted or artificial language but for heterodox views.

The principles Tolstoy used to compile his *Thoughts of Wise People* and subsequent collections of this nature such as *The Cycle of Reading* and *The Path of Life* were to find consonance and harmony in the heterodox thoughts of other sages with his "understanding of life," as he puts it. He did not hesitate to alter and adapt quotations during selection and translation and thus did not recommend looking for the exact source of quotations in the multilingual originals. Frequently, Tolstoy did not indicate the source at all. It is therefore most illuminating to notice how such principles are put to work in relation to Jewish thought. In the collection *Thoughts of Wise People*, quotations from Pascal (styled by Tolstoy "Vlas," à la Russe, rather than "Blaise"), the Talmud, and "L. T." (Lev Tolstoy) prevail. The sole quotation ascribed to Spinoza and placed in this collection has to do with mastery of language. The tone for understanding this tactic is set by the Talmudic selections known for their spurning of linguistic exuberance, wordy artificiality, and preference for silence in pledging obedience to and carrying out the will of God. This is the phrase Tolstoy ascribed to Spinoza: "Experience teaches us all too frequently that there is nothing that people have less power over than their language" (40:211). This is Tolstoy's wish-fulfillment version of Spinoza, the Spinoza who would rather have submitted to the Logos of the Word instead of submitting the Word to the Logos of his system. In Tolstoy's thought after 1880, Spinoza's God and Nature cannot be one. In the introduction Tolstoy wrote around the same time to the collection of thoughts of

Jean de La Bruyère, he reproaches Aristotle, Spinoza, and Hegel for their prideful wish to coerce into a given unity all phenomena and laws of human life through the rationalistic discourse of their systems (40:217).

In its own right, the language of the Talmud resisted Tolstoy's skill as an adapter for a long time: he experienced great difficulty trying to find the right tone for the conveyance of its registers running through the description of rules and rituals for everyday behavior, but also covering the ethical, folkloric, philosophical, historical, and theological themes within its enormous structure. No artificial unity was imposed here; one had to discover it. Tolstoy's frustration was recorded by Makovitsky on December 17, 1906, when Tolstoy was working on his compilations for *The Cycle of Reading*: "There is nothing of interest in the six volumes, and in the seventh there is a little ethical teaching, 'Pirke abot'; all that is found in *The Cycle of Reading* (from the Talmud) has been taken from there."[74] When one looks closely at it, the "little selection" is worth volumes, given the proportion of space it takes in *Thoughts of Wise People*. Of the one hundred and ten selections Tolstoy made from the Talmud for the Russian publication by the Jewish press in Odessa of a brochure collection, *The Wisdom of the Talmud* (*Mudrost' Talmuda*, 1904)—edited at his publishing firm, Posrednik—quotations about the love of God, love of neighbor, love of labor, generosity, and selfless joy prevail.[75]

These selections with "nothing of interest" in them almost completely match the selections Tolstoy made from the Talmud for *Thoughts of Wise People*. Tolstoy's voice has a clearer and louder resonance in *The Wisdom of the Talmud*, blending with Hebraic and medieval Jewish *chokmah*. Even excepting the many examples of quotations that could easily be identified with the Talmud, which Tolstoy included without attribution, there are almost two hundred citations that reference the Talmud in Tolstoy's own hand in his collections *Thoughts of Wise People*, *The Cycle of Reading*, and *The Path of Life*. None of these have even a hint of retribution, vengeance, or messianic exclusivity. Tolstoy corrected his older convictions of 1880–81 that Judaism praises and encourages murder, vengeance, lust, and ritual sacrifice. Tolstoy's selections from the Talmud of 1904 onward praise and encourage *self*-sacrifice, ethical responsibility for others, empathetic kindness, charity and relief work, grateful treatment of the earth and the land on which we live, work, and from which we eat. The Talmud becomes "his" book. Most curiously, beginning with *The Cycle of Reading*, Tolstoy does not even announce or attribute quotes from the Talmud, signing many Talmudic sayings with his own initials, "L. T."[76] Lev Talmud? The Talmud selections were never terminated nor excluded. But Tolstoy internalized their wisdom to such a degree that his sense of authorship was dissolved. As the single phrase from Maimonides that he included in all three major collections of wisdom intones, "If you are receiving an income that you haven't earned, somebody else is earning it without having received it (Maimonid[es])."[77] Tolstoy both earned and received his Talmud.

What about the "pound of flesh"? Tolstoy's reference to Shylock occurs toward the end of "Carthago delenda est" (1896)—Tolstoy's first attempt to write a longer narrative against pogroms as an example of state-sponsored violence—in a paragraph where Tolstoy appeals to an imagined audience by quoting the words of General Mikhail Dragomirov, a known antisemite and a staunch defender of wars and the prerogative of men in uniforms to exercise ferocity against the enemies of Russia. As Tolstoy quotes Dragomirov, he uses the opportunity to expose the perverse mind frame of someone who supports the idea that justice is guaranteed by armed force: "What gives the obligatory power to gentle sentences like years of hard labor, the dispossessing of a family sent begging, for the satisfaction of a 'lawful' claim of some Shylock? It must be confidence in the fairness of a judge, the inviolability of the written law, isn't that so?" (39:220). Shylock stands here either for all the greedy rich or all the greedy Jews. Then Tolstoy remembers that it is Shylock who is on trial, and that the hair of his own head (2 Sam. 14:26) and the flesh of his own bone (Luke 24:39) are neither his call nor his claim. The abandonment of the draft at this point is not owing to Tolstoy's hatred of Shakespeare but to his realization that his parallel was not ethically equivalent and thus unethical in its own right.

In the following concluding comments, I assemble Tolstoy's "Jewish questions" together and read them against any uncomfortable oversights based on the material already discussed and also bring in several corrective details for final comparisons.

1. In examining Tolstoy's evaluation of Judaism as a worldview, it is important to appreciate the extent of dialectics in his thinking about the progress of religions through history, in which every later religion supersedes its predecessor. Goldenveizer again supplies an indispensable piece of evidence in his records of conversations held on September 2, 1903: "For me personally Christianity stands above all religions, but I am speaking about Christianity here only as a historical phenomenon and not as the highest religious-moral teaching. And there is much in common at the point where extreme opposites meet: Judaism and Muhammadanism strictly adhere to monotheism; there is no drunkenness in one or the other, but in the historic Christianity of the Church there is no monotheism[78] and all kinds of darkness and cruelty."[79]

2. Tolstoy denies that the Jewish question exists separately from the task of achieving universal emancipation and brotherhood in the kingdom of God, where "the equality of all people is an axiom," as he put it in a letter

to Goetz of June 30, 1890 (65:117). National and ethnic questions of any sort are artificial constructs created for promoting emotions, traditions, and policies of exclusivity and hostility.

3. The press and writers themselves are often complicit in the processes described above. Tolstoy's favorite example is the Dreyfus affair, of which he speaks at length in "On Shakespeare and on Drama" (1903–4). The affair acquired its valence thanks only to the hypnotic effect borrowed by the press from the theater (this is how Dreyfus and Shakespeare can become unexpectedly comparable). Although hardly a household was left in Europe where its members would not be "divided for or against Dreyfus," "everyone had a thousand affairs more intimate and interesting than the Dreyfus affair"; these households, for Tolstoy, were, as such, really victims of hypnotic agitation (35: 260–61). It is certainly harder to stand up for an anonymous victim not featured in headlines. The Dreyfus trial was far from a banal affair, but the fashion for Dreyfus was. It is for this reason that Tolstoy likens it to other transient fashions and predicts correctly the fast cooling of interest in Dreyfus right after the media coverage of the affair winded down.

4. Volatile excitement over "questions" and "affairs" with real indifference or hidden animosity at its base is dangerous. It takes only a little manipulation to direct the propaganda blades in reverse and accuse the undeserving recipient of sympathy of their own stubborn marginalization. Tolstoy's position here is the polar opposite of Dostoevsky's. Famously beholden to a set of old anti-Jewish prejudices, in his conversation with Tolstoy on January 12, 1908, Makovitsky attempted to draw on Dostoevsky's irony in an attempt to seed doubt in Tolstoy's mind concerning the possibility of brotherly love for the Jews, in view of "their evil qualities." He means one of the chapter subheadings, "But Let There Be Brotherhood," in the two anti-Jewish chapters of *The Diary of a Writer* (1877). Tolstoy retorts, "It is more of a possibility to treat one person with prejudice than an entire nation."[80]

5. With the exception of the responses to the Kishinev pogrom that he sent out for publication abroad, it is quite extraordinary that despite having a high number of Jewish correspondents, Tolstoy never published even a semblance of "A Letter to the Jew" similar to such letters extracted from his private correspondence with representatives of other nationalities that Tolstoy decided should be made public (consider his "Letter to a Hindu," "Letter to a Man from China," "Letter to a Polish Woman," published by him after a practice of timing such statements to moments of national reawakening and hence to moments of choice between peaceful means or armed struggle). However, the ethnically unmarked "The Letter to a Student on Right" in which Tolstoy argues for his preference for

the Kantian categorical imperative and the biblical notion of conscience over the modern-day science of right was sent to a Jewish youth, Isaak Krutik.

6. Never after the birth of terrorism in 1878 would Tolstoy underscore the frequently Jewish origin of revolutionaries. By not highlighting the "nationality" of the revolutionaries, Tolstoy maintains his point about revolution being a natural human response against oppression. Despite his frequently negative remarks about such odious figures as the socialist revolutionary Gershuni, as well as other unprincipled political radicals, Tolstoy never highlights that they were also Jewish. On the contrary, Tolstoy does highlight that Simonson and Rozovsky in *Resurrection* are Jewish revolutionaries who sacrifice themselves to the curing of life from evil, both nonviolently. The teenager Rozovsky's request for chamomile tea to relieve a sore throat as he is being led out for execution by hanging is one of the most powerful scenes in the novel.

7. In contrast to the revolutionaries, Tolstoy is keen on emphasizing traces of "Jewish philosophizing" in Maimonides, Mendelssohn, Spinoza, and Eduard von Hartmann (despite their differences in style and their degree of philosophical optimism, they are always serious about God and ethics). He disbelieves that an antirationalist Shestov, whose thought operates in the sphere beyond good and evil, could be Jewish.[81]

8. Tolstoy became increasingly intolerant toward everyday antisemitism. Goldenveizer was impressed by the strict standards against antisemitism in Tolstoy's household. When Onisim Denisenko, Tolstoy's grandnephew who was then still a young child, called somebody a Yid at the table, Tolstoy checked him and explained that unlike the word "Jew," which is respectful, the word "Yid" is derogatory.[82] Making an effort to understand why antisemitism is born and stays rooted in people, Tolstoy undertook a correspondence with a rather backward Bessarabian landlady, Eleanore Stamo, pointing out an incompatibility of her professed Christian piety with her hatred toward the Jews. Tolstoy wrote to her that he would prefer to be a laughingstock in the eyes of the world even if he still had to learn to love the Jews at eighty—if such a thing is laughable (Stamo thinks it is).[83] As regards the fabled but superficial antisemitism of Dushan Makovitsky, which can be sensed through the jealous exchanges above, Tolstoy had a theory that God wanted to test his friend by giving him one temptation without which he would be without sin.

9. Tolstoy's stance on historical antisemitism differs from that of most Russian writers. He differs from Dmitry Merezhkovsky, who thought that the Russian people needed to purge their guilt before the Jews by taking on a historic mission from the Jews and making their salvation a key moment of this mission. He is likewise very far from metaphoric resolutions

in which the Jewish question is understood as the fulfillment of *all* history (treated as such by Soloviev and by Vasily Rozanov). Tolstoy is more optimistic than Saltykov-Shchedrin, refusing to agree that as one of the worst "cursed questions," the Jewish question cannot be positively solved. Finally, Tolstoy did not direct his attention to describing the devastating *results* of hatred, which were at once soul-searching and picturesque in various forms of investigative journalism (Vladimir Korolenko, Alexander Kuprin, and Maxim Gorky are good examples of this approach).[84]

10. Unique to Tolstoy's position was his sometimes overstated and even irritating tendency to evade invitations from Jews in which he would fulfill the role of a mouthpiece for the reigning culture on the grounds of his alleged incompetence. He, too, must have been a little dismayed by the carefully coy voice of a downtrodden Jew that Aleichem had assumed when he wrote to Tolstoy on April 27, 1903, with a request to give *Gilf* something, "at least a letter of a consoling quality."[85] Tolstoy sent to Aleichem much more than he had asked for: three of his new artistic works, tales drawn from international folklore. All of Tolstoy's three selections ("The Assyrian Tsar Asarkhadon" [Assiriiskii Tsar' Asarkhadon], "Three Questions" [Tri voprosa], and "Labor, Death, and Illness" [Trud, smert' i bolezn']) feature the response of world folklore to violence in an artistic demonstration that violence is not only a crime of man against other men but also a satanic folly committed against the whole of creation. His gesture to Aleichem's *Gilf* was therefore not that of "the Great Writer of the Russian Land" who graced a pariah colleague writing "in jargon" with a hand-me-down.[86]

11. In his insistence on the primacy of ethical responsibility commanded by Judaism, Tolstoy differs from other deniers of the existence of the Jewish question in the West: obviously from the openly antisemitic and Nazi-favored Eugen Dühring but also from Karl Marx, who thought that emancipation would arrive for Jews qua citizens when they exchange religion for civic rights.[87]

12. In his consistent condemnation of hate crimes and of all persecution and crime targeted at Jews, Tolstoy presages Karl Jaspers's famous words spoken during his radio statement after Nuremberg: the crime against Jews is a crime against all humanity.[88]

In sum, in his evaluation of the Jewish question Tolstoy is neither with "the Greek" nor "the Jew." The Jew, according to Tolstoy, is neither a marginalized type nor a dangerous extremist at the heights of despairing determination; neither a historic hegemon nor a mythic villain; neither the biblical forefather nor the messianic son. Although made exempt from any messianic tasks, the Jew is associated, for Tolstoy, with an absolute ethical intention; he embodies the categorical imperative of service, life transformed by ethics, the thou-shalt of everyday action. Tolstoy considers the creation of such an enduring human type by Judaism to be its most valuable contribution to world history. For Tolstoy, the Jew had never been a feeler tool for finding the extreme limits of human freedom but a model of loving God. He would therefore not be too impressed by Jean-Paul Sartre's brilliant argument exposing the cowardly existential Manichaeanism of modern antisemites who allowed only to the Jew the absolute freedom to choose; for Tolstoy, this would be only satanic freedom to extend and strengthen evil.[89] It is worth noting that considering the high number of Tolstoy's prose and drama adaptations of picaresque legends and *lubok* plots about petty devils, hell, drunkenness, and drunks, not a single Jew or Jew-like character is featured among wine distillers, pub owners, or within the unclean force itself.[90]

It is important to observe the transformation of the figure of the Jew in Tolstoy's art. In his later fiction beyond popular genres and folk tales, Tolstoy lets his leading but controversial male characters experience in liminal situations—at times of despair or on the verge of making fateful decisions—the behavior of their own prejudiced perception, of men "of the Jewish type." Unlike the examples from his earlier fiction discussed above where the word *zhid* is used exclusively, in Tolstoy's later work the word "Jew" (*evrei*) prevails.

Tolstoy creates an atmosphere of displacement and marginalization for these Jews by emphasizing their harried and hurried nervousness, unctuous attentiveness to the reactions from interlocutors lest something wrong is said, garrulous and gossipy chattiness, talking with an accent that Hannah Arendt identified with upstarts and parvenus who were ashamed about their origins and uncomfortable about the sense of their "fit" in assimilated environments.[91] For example, consider Pozdnyshev's overhearing a Jewish blabbermouth in a dirty train car on his way to murdering his wife in *The Kreutzer Sonata* and Nekhliudov checking in with an edgy Jewish-looking court clerk upon his lackadaisical arrival to serve on the jury. Let us be careful not to confuse the literary "type" of the Jew with the "Jewish question," however. Tolstoy does not confuse the question with the ready clichés: instead of world capital, usury, the wine trade, and the like, there is here anxiety, fear, and uncertainty about one's disoriented life.[92]

It would give Tolstoy special pleasure concerning his theory about Jews and women that the middle-aged Stiva Oblonsky, who was an irresponsible husband and father, cadged fifty rubles from his wife, Dolly—whom he systematically mistreats and deceives—in order to go to Saint Petersburg and plead with the "railroad Jews" for a position that would allow him to keep on with his squandering habits.[93] What could be better than this double humiliation? Alas, and thank God, unlike Karenin, who had had to "wait-yid" for him while he was coaxing his mogul Jews, Stiva can never be humiliated and can never fall into a state of vengeance (or undergo transformation). The miraculous transformation into the holy man happens to the murderer Stepan Pelageiushkin in Tolstoy's *The False Coupon* (1904) when he hears a sermon against vengeance from a Judaizing dissenter Chuev and his pointing at the superscript of the crucifix, the symbol of persecution: "This is the tsar of the Jews" (36:38).[94] Conversely, the brash Butler in *Hadji Murad* (1904) keeps drinking, gambling, and blaming Jews, from whom he needs to keep on borrowing to go on drinking, gambling, and womanizing after his participation in the killing of Hadji Murad. The money borrowed from the Jews for these purposes helps him muffle the call of conscience, "defer the unsolved problem," and prolong his hate for Jews whom he must blame for the torture of his uniform, his obligation for murder (35:106–7). The question of radical versus pedestrian antisemitism was, for Tolstoy, much the same as it was for Hannah Arendt: never metaphorical but painfully banal, a result of having become a tool prescribed by professional code, true as much for Tolstoy's loyal soldier Butler and for Arendt's version of Eichmann, an honest servant who fulfills all orders coming from above, resulting in the refusal to bear responsibility for the life of another as it was ordained in the fourth chapter of Genesis.[95]

On April 30, 1908, the peasant G. E. Bychkov asked the "kindest grandfather Lev Nikolaevich" whether Jews were to be considered good or evil: "What do they bring to humanity, without a doubt these future masters of ours—happiness or evil?" (78:341). Tolstoy's response on May 18, 1908, consisted of six words in Russian: "There can be no masters above saints [*Nad sviatymi ne mozhet byt' gospod*]" (78:341). A saint Tolstoy was not. Neither did he want to be anyone's master.

Let us return to the comic intermezzo staged in Tolstoy's tract *On Life* (26:315). Two people are facing each other, but instead of the expected ethical dialogue, the Buberian and Levinasian "face-to-face," the Russian and the Jew resort to facetious and clever tricks to avoid seeing eye to eye. There are several types of ethical encounter with the Other that Tolstoy is interested in: face-to-face (becoming aware of one's responsibility for the Other and carrying this responsibility regardless of one's religion); about-face (turning away from the Other and from one's responsibility by means of conversion [artificial identification], resulting in the reduction of one's responsibility to the extension of its similarity, which amounts to abandoning ethics); and facelessness (assimilation by way of obsessive acculturation, the loss of one's identity and of one's individual sense of responsibility). Tolstoy's vision of the Jewish question was forward-looking, constantly developing and changing, and it was not immune to error. His insistence on nonviolent resistance was of his time; Tolstoy did not live long enough to hear about important courageous acts of defiance that would happen in the future, such as the tragic dignity of the Sobibór Uprising. As Theodor Adorno pointed out, intellectual honesty is not achieved by a simple wish to be able to speak the truth after Auschwitz. The way to truth proceeds through "a network of prejudices, opinions, innervations, self-corrections, presuppositions and exaggerations, in short through the dense, firmly-founded but by no means uniformly transparent medium of experience."[96] The assumption of the role of the carrier of intellectual honesty is itself dishonest. A propos Judaism and Christianity, Tolstoy stands in the role of their dynamic attractive-repulsive "hyphen," as Jean-François Lyotard conceived of it. He will never be completely one or another but always at some point in between; in the "phrases in dispute" in which God is taken for an addressee, truth is sought in place of the "designated reality," and prophesy is distrusted. Only a Hitler-like mindset would conceive of a "destiny" in which "jews" (*sic*)—the displaced and wandering lowercase aliens of this world, in the words of Lyotard's description, and whom Tolstoy noted were dismissed as what he called transnational "Hebraic Yids"—(*sic*) would always threaten his *Weltraum* (life space) and disrupt his *Ordnung* (order).[97]

NOTES

1. Andrei Bely, Nikolai Berdiaev, et al., "Ot izdatel'stva Put'" [From the publishing house Put'], in *O religii Lva Tolstogo* [On the religion of Lev Tolstoy] (Moscow: Put', 1912), i–iii.

2. Andrei Bely, "Lev Tolstoi i kul'tura" [Lev Tolstoy and culture], in *O religii L'va Tolstogo*, 161–65. Subsequent citations to this work appear in the main text as parenthetical page numbers.

3. Nikolai Berdiaev, "Vetkhii i Novyi Zavet v religioznom soznanii L. Tolstogo" [The Old and New Testaments in the religious consciousness of Lev Tolstoy], in *O religii L'va Tolstogo*, 172. Subsequent citations to this work appear in the main text as parenthetical page numbers.

4. This chapter is an expanded and reworked version of talks delivered by me in Russian at the Hebrew University of Jerusalem, October 24–25, 2011, and at Gakuen University, Kumamoto, Japan, November 6, 2010. The text of these earlier presentations appeared in Russian as Inessa Medzhibovskaya, "'Evreiskii vopros' Tolstogo" [The "Jewish question" according to Tolstoy], in *Lev Tolstoi v Ierusalime. Materialy mezhdunarodnoi nauchnoi konferentsii* [Lev Tolstoy in Jerusalem. Academic Conference Proceedings], ed. Elena D. Tolstaya, intro., Vladimir M. Paperni (Moscow: Novoe literaturnoe obozrenie, 2013), 73–108.

5. Nehama Shvarts [Berkenblit], "Lev Tolstoy kak zerkalo antisemitizma russkoi intelligentsii" [Lev Tolstoy as the mirror of the antisemitism of the Russian intelligentsia] (2009), http://world.lib.ru/s/shwarc_n/tolstoy.shtml.

6. Savely Dudakov usually cites Tolstoy as a typical case of someone with a squeamish reluctance to get involved with Jewish troubles. See S. Iu. Dudakov, *Etiudy liubvi i nenavisti* [Études of love and hate] (Moscow: RGGU, 2003), 7–79, and S. Iu. Dudakov, *Paradoksy i prichudy filosemitizma i antisemitizma v Rossii: Ocherki* [The paradoxes and fancies of philosemitism and antisemitism in Russia: Essays] (Moscow: RGGU, 2000), 91–218. An example of a positive evaluation is Vladimir Porudominsky, "Ravenstvo vsekh liudei-aksioma" [The equality of all people is the axiom], in *O Tolstom* [On Tolstoy] (Saint Petersburg: Aleteia, 2005), 247–58.

7. Harold K. Shefski, "Tolstoi and the Jews," *Russian Review* 41, no. 1 (January 1982): 1–10. Many Russian-Jewish writers would disagree with Shefski concerning the popularity of the connection between Jews and Tolstoy. Take the example of Tolstoy's judgments on whether or not individual Jews should convert rendered in S. Ansky's humorous sketch, "Go Talk to a Goy!" [A Goisher Kop(f)], which appeared in the same year as the collection *O religii L'va Tolstogo*—1912. In the story, the Russian revolutionary Anastasia Stephanova, a fanatical Social Democrat living in Berne in political exile, makes a clandestine return to Russia. On party orders, she settles in St. Petersburg under the assumed name of Hannah Henia Floigelman, which is stamped in her new "Jewish passport." The thinking of her party comrades was for her to pose as a Jewish Madame running a registered business from her rented apartment where frequent visits of male "clients" (aka revolutionaries), who would come in droves for conspiratorial meetings, would not cause suspicion. Alas, Stephanova was blonde and good-looking. The police inspectors decided they wanted to visit, too, under the pretext of needing to check the legality of her Jewish passport and her right of residence. To put an end to these visits, the party decided that she should "convert" to Russian Orthodoxy. Suddenly, Stephanova decided to resist the pressure from her comrades who were accusing her of talking like a Tolstoy follower (many of these revolutionaries were Jews living in the capital as Russians with fake passports and fake Slavic names): "'You sound like a follower of Tolstoy [. . .] If you think that pretense is immoral, why do you constantly deceive the government?' 'A policeman is not someone's God,' she replied." The story initially appeared in the February issue of *Die yidische welt* (1912). I have used the translation of the story in S. Ansky, *The Dybbuk and Other Writings*, ed. and intro. David G. Roskies, trans. Golda Werman (New Haven: Yale University Press, 2013): 145–50; quoted passage, 150. S. Ansky, the pen-name of Shloyme-Zanvl Rappoport, had an uncle in Tula whom he frequently visited. For an excellent recent biography of Ansky and his absorption of Tolstoy's ideas, see Gabriella Safran, *Wandering Soul: The Dybbuk's Creator, S. An-sky* (Cambridge: Harvard University Press, 2010).

8. Alexander Goldenveizer, *Vblizi Tolstogo.Vospominaniia* [Near Lev Tolstoy. Reminiscences] (Moscow: Zakharov, 2002), 103.

9. Throughout his career in general, Schmidt enjoyed a good rapport with the Jews in Kishinev, and he praised the Jewish contribution to the city's prosperity. See Brighita Kovarski, "Schmidt, Carol/Şmidt, Karl-Ferdinand," in *Chişinău Enciclopedie* [Encyclopedia of the city of Chişinău], ed. Iurie Colesnic (Chişinău: Museum, 1997), 410. However, upon receiving news of the pogrom, he behaved in the most cowardly fashion, locked himself in his house, and did nothing. On Schmidt, see Edward H. Judge, *Easter in Kishinev: Anatomy of a Pogrom* (New York: New York University Press, 1995), 26, 39, 62, and the most recently published book by Steven J. Zipperstein, *Pogrom: Kishinev and the Tilt of History* (New York: Liveright, 2018), passim.

10. Tolstoy means to say that a truthful coverage of the pogroms and the Jewish question is impossible in a legal Russian edition. "A legal Russian edition" is the kind of publication that Russian censors allowed to be published.

11. On May 10 (23), 1903, Tolstoy sent a cable to the *North American Newspaper* in Philadelphia, in which he writes, "Guilty is government firstly excluding Jews as a separate cast [*sic*] from common rights, secondly inculcating by force to russian [*sic*] people an idolatrous faith instead of Christianity. Tolstoy" (74:125). He followed up with a letter expressing the same idea: "Dear Sir, I have sent today by telegraph my answer to your question; but being afraid that my answer will not reach you, I repeat it by letter. It is as follows . . . Yours truly, Leo Tolstoy, May 23, 1903" (74:125–26). See as well Tolstoy's letter to Anatoly Butkevich of May 22, 1903 (74:129). Tolstoy's condemnation in his letters of the "propaganda of lies and violence" of the Russian government was "widely reprinted in the Western world" (Judge, *Easter in Kishinev*, 89).

12. John of Kronstadt initially reproached the Christians of Kishinev for the bloody reprisal in the May issue of the *Missionary Observer* (*Missionerskoe obozrenie*), which Tolstoy congratulated in a letter to Butkekvich on May 22, 1903 (74:129). Kronstadt would accuse the Jews in the very next issue of the *Missionary Observer* in June, apologizing to the Christians for his lapse in judgment. See Michael Davitt, *Within the Pale: The True Story of Anti-Semitic Persecution in Russia* (Philadelphia: Jewish Publication Society of America, 1903), 268–77. Chertkov published on the occasion, in his monthly political periodical *Svobodnoe slovo*, also published in French as *Parole libre* [*The Free Word*], scurrilous and tasteless doggerel in blank verse written by A. M. Khiriakov to pillory Kronstadt's recantation of his earlier sympathy for the victims of Kishinev—namely, that "Jews are themselves the reason for the violence against them." The *Free Press* informed readers that the Church of Russia "had made its final choice to serve only Mammon—that is, the government. Such improbable levity in the thoughts of a seventy-three-year-old hierarch caused the appearance of the jocular poem following below that we are printing in its entirety" (*Svobodnoe slovo* 6 [July–August 1903]: 31). Tolstoy sent Chertkov a rebuke in a letter written on September 6–7, 1903: "This is quite beneath you and poor" (88:306–7). Michael

Davitt (1846–1906) visited Tolstoy twice, according to sources that could be verified, but not during Davitt's investigation of the events in Kishinev. Their primary interest in each other's views was based on their shared enthusiasm for the ideas of Henry George about the "single tax" system. Davitt's first visit occurred on June 9 (22), 1904 (as noted by Tolstoy in his diary on June 9, 1904: "Michael Davitt today" [*Michael Davitt nynche*] (55: 47), and then on January 19, 1905 (Russian calendar), when Davitt interviewed Tolstoy on current political affairs in Russia in the aftermath of the events of "Bloody Sunday" [*Krovavoe Voskresenie*] on January 9 (22), 1905, when troops shot at the unarmed procession of petitioners in St. Petersburg, killing at least two hundred and wounding at least eight hundred people. One of Davitt's books is preserved in Tolstoy's library at Yasnaya Polyana, with the inscription "to Count Tolstoi, Yasnia, Russia, with respectful regards and all good wishes, and in recollection of the visit in Yasnia on the 22nd of June, 1904. From Michael Davitt. Dalkey, Dublin, Ireland" (*Biblioteka L'va Nikolaevicha Tolstogo v Iasnoi Poliane: Bibliograficheskoe opisanie* [The library of Lev Nikolaevich Tolstoy at Yasnaya Polyana: A bibliographic catalogue], ed. V. F. Bulgakov et al., 3 vols. [Moscow: Kniga, 1972–99], vol. 3, book 1: 273). The book in question is Michael Davitt, *The Fall of Feudalism in Ireland: The Story of the Land League Revolution* (New York: Harper and Brothers, 1904). On February 3, 1905, London's *The Standard* published Davitt's account of his conversation with Tolstoy of January 19, 1905. The interview—an untitled and unsigned report—appeared on page 4 of the newspaper. In Davitt's summary, Tolstoy gives the same advice to the laboring masses as he did to the victims of the Kishinev pogrom: "Force [. . .] is a remedy up to a certain point for the evils which Despotism brings upon itself," but that it cannot suppress freedom that chooses to abstain from the use of force and from violence (*The Standard*, February 3, 1905, p. 4).

13. Tolstoy's comments that appeared in the *New York Times* on May 25, 1903, are crippled by omissions, inaccuracies, and misstatements. On May 29, 1903, a correction of the earlier report was published concerning Tolstoy's role in fund-raising: "The Novosti today publishes a letter from Count Tolstoi's son in which he denies the published report that his father gave 15,000 rubles for the relief of Jews of Kishineff. He says Count Tolstoi desires a contradiction of the report, not because of lack of sympathy with the Jews, but because he dislikes to be credited with an action he has not performed" ("Denial by Tolstoi's Son," *New York Times*, May 29, 1903).

14. Tolstoy offered clear instructions on this score to Aylmer Maude and Vladimir Chertkov and an interdiction to publish any version of the stories in "Russian, English or in whichever language [*ni po-kakovski*]" (88:305), which could threaten the success of the publication of *Gilf* and thus with it undermine the fund-raising effort (Tolstoy to Chertkov, August 24, 1903 [88:305]; October 6–7, 1903 [88:306]). See also Tolstoy's letters to Maude of October 10, 22, and 24

of 1903 aiming to have Chertkov, Maude, and Sholem Aleichem avoid any misunderstandings and financial arguments as to the rights held to the stories and
their translation and publication (74:204, 209, 213). I highly recommend a
lengthy exchange of letters on *Gilf* scrupulously documented by Roberta de
Giorgi; see "Materiali" [Archival material] section in the just published annual
issue of *Russica Romana* 24 (2017): 121–67.

15. "Leo Tolstoy," in Herman Bernstein, *With Master Minds: Interviews
by Herman Bernstein* (New York: Universal, 1913), 7–25. Subsequent citations
to this work appear in the main text as parenthetical page numbers. Bernstein
would alter only a few words in later reprints of this interview. Most significantly,
he would add the text of a letter he received from Chertkov of July 20, 1908, regarding the state of celebrations allowed by the authorities for Tolstoy's upcom-
ing eightieth birthday and a note of thanks from Tolstoy written in May 1909,
concerning the receipt of Bernstein's translation of Leonid Andreev's *The Seven
Who Were Hanged* and the non-receipt of Bernstein's translation from wise sayings for *The Cycle of Reading* (see "Leo Tolstoy," in Herman Bernstein, *Celebrities of Our Time* [London: Hutchinson, 1925], 7–19, especially the referenced
additions, ibid., 17–19). The only other substantive change regarding Tolstoy's
responses is the substitution by Bernstein of "All people are alike" in the 1913
edition with "All people are equal" in the 1925 edition. See Bernstein, *With
Master Minds*, 20, and *Celebrities of Our Time*, 14, respectively.

16. Tolstoy very consistently repeats this thought in response to other in-
quiries. See, for example, his letter of September 10, 1895, to Marian Edmund
Zdzechovskii (Zdiechowski), professor of Slavic literatures in Kraków, in which
Tolstoy calls the creation of national questions "one of the most common soph-
isms" used to promote nationalism and hostility among people (68:165–70).

17. The literature on this topic is vast. I attend to several meaningful moments within this literature that relate to this discussion at the conclusion of
the essay. The most authoritative and comprehensive general source engaging
with major Western and Jewish voices from antiquity through the creation of the
State of Israel is Alex Bein, *The Jewish Question: Biography of a World Problem*, trans. Harry Zohn (Rutherford, N.J.: Fairleigh Dickinson University Press,
1990). By 1908, when the interview with Bernstein took place, the most fundamental study of the Jewish question in Russia at the time, *Evreiskii vopros v
Rossii*—coauthored by Tolstoy's younger relative, Count Ivan Ivanovich Tolstoy,
and an even younger Jewish scholar, Yulii Gessen—had come out (1907). See
Graf Iv. Iv. Tolstoy and Yulii Gessen, *Fakty i mysli. Evreiskii vopros v Rossii*
[Facts and reflections: The Jewish question in Russia] (Saint Petersburg: Tipografiia t-va Obshchestvennaia pol'za, 1907).

18. See the following by John Doyle Klier: *Russians, Jews, and the Pogroms
of 1881–1882* (Cambridge: Cambridge University Press, 2014); *Russia Gathers*

Her Jews: The Origins of the "Jewish Question" in Russia, 1772–1825 (DeKalb: Northern Illinois University Press, 1986); and *Imperial Russia's Jewish Question, 1855–1881* (Cambridge: Cambridge University Press, 2005).

19. Tolstoy and Gessen, *Fakty i mysli*, vi–vii.

20. See F. M. Dostoevsky, "Dnevnik pisatelia za 1877" [Diary of a writer for 1877], in *Polnoe sobranie sochinenii v tridtsati tomakh* [Complete works in thirty volumes], 30 vols., ed. V. G. Bazanov, G. M. Fridlender, et al. (Leningrad: Nauka, 1972–90), 25:74–92; quoted passage, 25:74.

21. Mikhail Evgrafovich Saltykov-Shchedrin, "Iul'skoe veianie" [The July trend], in *Evrei i zhidy v russkoi klassike* [Jews and Yids in Russian classics], ed. Mikhail Edelshtein (Moscow: Mosty kultury / Jerusalem: Gesharim, 2005), 249–64.

22. Thus, the horrible travails through the snares and greed of "kike" sutlers and "Yid" innkeepers in Austria and eastern Europe are reported through the perspective of Boris and Julie Drubetskoy (book I, part II, chap. 7 and book III, part II, chap. 2; see 4:299 and 6:111 respectively). The kind captain Timokhin, on the contrary, calls Dolokhov a beast for having beaten up a Polish Jew during the Austrian campaign: the demoted and angry Dolokhov "nearly killed a Yid, if you'd be pleased to know" (I, II, 2; 4:151). Prince Vasily Kuragin, an old hand at court intrigue, undertakes to convince his son-in-law, Pierre Bezukhov, of the innocence of his daughter, Hélène, Pierre's wife and Dolokhov's lover. His argument is a carefully chosen double entendre: "I can assure you that Elen is innocent before you like Christ before the Yids" (book II, part II, chap. 5; 5:89). And the final example deals with Tolstoy's service in the Crimea: During one of the horse-changing layovers, the officer Tolstoy was struck by a scene in which a Cossack innkeeper gave a portion of sunflower seeds worth five kopecks to a "little Yid" (*zhidenok*) named Tabun. Although the Jew's real age is not given and it is unclear whether he is a child or an adult of diminutive height, or a Jew and thus a "lesser man," the Cossack woman thinks that no money is appropriate in the exchange since Tabun's family and her uncle's family are "brothers" according to the Cossacks' ethical principle, which she tries to explain to Tabun. Tolstoy is so fascinated by this episode that he writes it down in obvious haste in his diary on October 31, 1853, despite "a difficult day on the road" (46:186–87).

23. Note that the Englishman Aylmer Maude, who translated many of Tolstoy's works into English, has no idea, when translating, in 1903, chapter 5 of Tolstoy's *What Is Religion, and Wherein Lies Its Essence?* (*Chto takoe religiia i v chem sushchnost ee?*, 1902), what the word "goyim" (35:167) might mean. Tolstoy had to explain the meaning in a letter to Maude on September 11, 1903: "The goyim are the non-Jews" (74:186).

24. L. Katznelson et al., eds., *Evreiskaia Entsiklopediia: Svod znanii o evreistve i ego kul'ture v proshlom i nastoiashchem* [The Jewish Encyclopedia:

A compendium of knowledge about Jewry and its culture in the past and at present], 16 vols. (Saint Petersburg: Izdaniie Obshchestva dliia nauchnykh evreĭskikh izdanii Izdatel'stva Brokgaus-Efron, 1906–13), 1:839, 15:44–45, 380, 541–47.

25. A clerk at the Bank of Tula, Solomon London, visited Tolstoy with his granddaughter in August 1902 (54:311) to consult with the writer about London's forthcoming emigration to America. London fell seriously ill en route and wrote to Tolstoy on December 21, 1903, from abroad: "During my illness and the very great physical suffering in Berlin, I never forgot your teaching so dear to me and to all thinking people. And your words recalled during my illness helped me to endure it" (54:621). For unknown reasons, London's letter remained unanswered.

26. Mamadysh, the name of an administrative center in northern present-day Tatarstan, is Tolstoy's favorite epithet to refer to a remote hamlet in a forlorn province, reminiscent of shtetl life, as far as Mamadysh might be from the real Pale.

27. Aleksandr Andreevich Bers (1845–1918) was the younger brother of Sophia Andreevna and thus Tolstoy's brother-in-law.

28. Despite his sympathy for cosmopolitan views, Tolstoy did not find it easy to become friends with Solomon (Romanovich) Warszawer, manager of the Tula branch of the Moscow International Bank, the very "man without faith or law" (*sans foi ni loi*). In a diary entry of May 9, 1907, Tolstoy calls him "difficult" (56:194).

29. Grigory Moiseevich Berkenheim (1872–1919) was one of the doctors invited to Astapovo during Tolstoy's final days and a signatory to his death certificate. "Sweet Grigory Moiseevich," as Tolstoy called him (76:88), was a family doctor and a highly trusted friend to several generations of the Tolstoy family beginning in 1902.

30. Ivan Fedorovich Nazhivin (1874–1940), a young author whom Tolstoy befriended in the early years of the twentieth century, was one of the most loyal of Tolstoy's followers. He married Anna Efimovna (née Zussman), a doctor by training. Tolstoy was very fond of both.

31. D. P. Makovitsky, *U Tolstogo, 1904–1910: "Iasnopolianskie zapiski" D. P. Makovitskogo* [At Tolstoy's, 1904–1910: "The Yasnaya Polyana notebooks" of D. P. Makovitsky], 4 vols. in the series *Literaturnoe nasledstvo* [Literary heritage], issue no. 90, ed. S. A. Makashin, M. B. Khrapchenko, and V. R. Shcherbina (Moscow: Nauka, 1979), 2:104. Samuil Baskin-Seredinsky, a Talmudic scholar and less-than-mediocre poet, visited Tolstoy on November 7, 1906, and then attempted another visit two years later. Tolstoy found him to be a "typical Jew" who wrote bad poetry in Russian. Nonetheless, Tolstoy recommended Seredinsky to the publisher Mikhail Stasiulevich for work in the criticism and reviews section (76:271). In 1908, upon Seredinsky's attempted second visit, Tolstoy was blunter: "The verses of that selection from the poem 'The Prophet Cometh' [Griadushchii

prorok] that you sent me are very weak. I would not recommend that you continue writing poetry. I am very sorry that I have to tell you this. I am now very busy and weak, and today I am feeling completely unwell and therefore am unable to receive you. Please forgive me. Lev Tolstoy, February 29, 1908" (78:76).

32. These were university-degree holders, professionals, successful entrepreneurs, and merchants who were formally allowed or able to procure a domicile permit in the capital.

33. See E. N. Ulitsky, *Istoriia moskovskoi evreiskoi obshchiny: Dokumenty i materialy (XVIII–XX vv)* [The history of the Jewish community of Moscow: Documents and materials (the eighteenth and nineteenth centuries)] (Moscow: KRPA Olimp, 2006) for a history of the Moscow Jewish community and the role of Solomon Minor and the Minor dynasty in their exceptional service as the rabbis of Moscow.

34. In citing Tolstoy's explanation of the reigning interpretations of the Gospels, I have retained Tolstoy's consistent use of the "Five Books" (Piatiknizhie) rather than using the "Torah" or the "Old Testament."

35. These objections were made in Kant's numerous writings on religion. See especially Immanuel Kant, *Religion within the Limits of Reason Alone*, trans. Theodore M. Greene and Hoyt H. Hudson (New York: Harper and Row, 1960). In his seminal work *Jerusalem* (1783), Mendelssohn defended his conviction that Judaism and the Enlightenment are naturally compatible yet maintain the right of difference. See Moses Mendelssohn, *Jerusalem: Or on Religious Power and Judaism*, trans. Allan Arkush, ed. Alexander Altmann (Hanover, N.H.: University Press of New England / Brandeis University Press, 1983).

36. Kant, *Religion within the Limits*, 101, 132, 154–55.

37. Tolstoy writes in notebook 11 (1878–80): "The humble inherit the land in the Bible? Blessed are the meek (the Talmud) Pure of heart (the psalm). Blessed are the persecuted, Ecclesiastes 3:15; The salt of the earth, the sand of Israel; . . . [the] Talmud is liable to the court of Sanhedrin; Be perfect like the Father—the Bible, Deuteronomy 18:13" (48:331).

38. N. N. Ivanov, "U Tolstogo v Moskve v 1886 godu" [At Tolstoy's in Moscow in the year 1886], in *L. N. Tolstoy v vospominaniiakh sovremennikov* [L. N. Tolstoy in the reminiscences of his contemporaries], ed. G. V. Krasnova (Moscow: Khudozhestvennaia literatura, 1978), 1:388.

39. On the aspirations among young Jews in response to the persecutions of Jews in the 1880s, see Yulii Gessen, *Istoriia evreiskogo naroda v Rossii* [The history of the Jewish people in Russia], ed. V. Iu. Gessen (Moscow: Izdatelstvo evreiskogo universiteta v Moskve, 1993).

40. The full story of Isaak Borisovich Feinerman (Teneromo) (1862–1925), one of the most colorful and adventurous Jewish followers of Tolstoy, still deserves to be told. So far, only small parts of it have been given. See Galina Eliasberg, "'Pod nebom Yasnoi Polyany': Epizod 1885 goda i ego otrazhenie v drama-

turgii I. Teneromo" ["'Under the sky of Yasnaya Polyana': An episode in the year 1885 and its reflection in the plays of I. Teneromo], in *Lev Tolstoi v Ierusalime*, 109–46. The pen name Teneromo was used by Feinerman beginning around 1900 and is the Latin translation of his last name in Yiddish. I examine Feinerman's life and writings in a forthcoming volume.

41. Tolstoy's correspondence with Feinerman (mostly on the Feinerman side) has not been published, but a perusal of it in the manuscript section of the Tolstoy Museum in Moscow suggests that Tolstoy continues to use his customary signature "Lev Tolstoy, who loves you" or "fondly, Lev Tolstoy" until about 1900. Feinerman's letters beg for Tolstoy's compliments and exhibit a permanent longing for familial intimacy. Tolstoy accepts familiarity but keeps addressing Feinerman as "Isaak Borisovich," and, in the formal second-person-plural style, regularly chastising him for not taking money for his work, for his careless life habits, for his inconstancy, and for intellectual literal-mindedness.

42. Four years into his postconversion life, Tolstoy considered Feinerman an advocate against conversion and, in a letter to Feinerman of February 18, 1889, recommended that a Jew, "Kh. A.," from Tver whom he was dissuading from converting, should speak with Feinerman (64:227).

43. See, in particular, Tolstoy's letters to Feinerman and M. V. Alekhin, another *tolstovets*, of August 1892 (66:239–42), and Tolstoy's diary entries of the same period (52:69).

44. Feinerman's short books on Tolstoy and *Tolstoy and the Jews* in Tolstoy's personal library at Yasnaya Polyana bear typical inscriptions, usually by Sophia Andreevna: "All invention" (*Vse vydumka*). See *Biblioteka Tolstogo*, vol. 1, book 2:208–9. Many Jews wanted to know if Teneromo's brochures about Tolstoy and the Jewish question were true. Tolstoy's answer was always the same: they were not. On March 10, 1909, for example, Tolstoy wrote on the envelope in which Teneromo's brochure had been enclosed, returning it to the sender, G. Meitin of Ekaterinoslav: "I did not read and do not know this brochure [*Tolstoy on the Jews*] and have no communications with Mr. Teneromo" (79:266). A partial exception to these inventions and embellishments is a possible recording made by Feinerman of Tolstoy's less-reserved comments about the pogroms. See Medzhibovskaya, "'Evreiskii vopros' Tolstogo," 106–8, and Inessa Medzhibovskaya, "Tolstoy on Pogroms? Publication, Translation, and Commentary of the Newly Discovered Archival Document from the Memoirs by Isaak Teneromo," *TSJ* 25 (2013): 78–82.

45. Around November 18, 1895, Tolstoy wrote to Feinerman with a long analysis of his short story "The Court" (Sud), which was bad enough for Tolstoy to say that it was an example of writing that is done "in huge amounts and poorly [*koe kak i mnogo*]" (68:262). Feinerman took offense and spread the word, which came around to Tolstoy, that he had a "non-Christian mind-set." Sometime this same month Tolstoy set to explaining to Feinerman his concept of an impersonal

God and comparing Feinerman's version to a "twinity"—the Orthodox Trinity minus the Holy Ghost (68:272).

46. A copy of Feinerman's "The Seamy Side of the Emancipation" (Iznanka emansipatsii, 1901) in Tolstoy's personal library at Yasnaya Polyana shows no trace of attentive reading or interest. Nevertheless, Tolstoy did seek to help Feinerman when the vocational school where Feinerman worked, "with benefit for the people," closed down on official orders in October 1894 (67:234–35).

47. Semyon (Simon) Dubnov (1860–1941), the great scholar and historian, was the author of the magisterial *History of the Jewish People* (*Istoriia evreiskogo naroda*), which first appeared in a ten-volume German translation in Berlin as *Weltgeschichte des jüdischen Volkes* (Berlin: Jüdischer Verlag, 1925–29).

48. The majority of Dubnov's library and his prized archives perished along with their eighty-one-year-old owner in the Jewish ghetto during the Nazi occupation of Riga. Tolstoy's response is thus quoted from what Dubnov published as S. Dubnov, "Graf L.N. Tolstoy i evrei," *Nedel'naia khronika Voskhoda* 6 (February 12, 1889): 140–41. Subsequent citations to this work appear in the main text as parenthetical page numbers.

49. This unfinished fragment on the evils of exploitation, displacement, and forced migration was jotted down on May 25, 1889.

50. Ernest Renan, *Histoire du peuple d'Israël*, 2 vols. (Paris: Calmann-Lévy, 1887–88). See Tolstoy's diary entry for June 1, 1889 (50:89).

51. Soloviev was the one to ask Tolstoy for this address. See "Perepiska Tolstogo s V. S. Solovievym" [The correspondence of Tolstoy with V. S. Soloviev], in *L. N. Tolstoy* (vol. 2 in *Literaturnoe Nasledstvo* [Literary heritage], issue no. 37–38), ed. P. I. Lebedev-Polyanskii et al. (Moscow: Nauka, 1939), 270. Emile Joseph Dillon (E. B. Lanin) (1854–1933), the future author of Tolstoy's biography *Count Leo Tolstoy: A New Portrait* (London: Hutchinson, 1934), was at the time Russian correspondent for the *Daily Telegraph* (London).

52. *Pravoslavnoe obozrenie*, nos. 8 and 9 (1884).

53. Dillon indeed completed and released his report, with Tolstoy's signature at the top, under his pseudonym E. B. Lanin ("The Jews in Russia," [1890]), which was followed in later years by other investigative reports on Russian affairs. For more details on the protest letter and its publication by Dillon on December 10, 1890, in the London *Times*, see Vladimir Solovyov, *The Burning Bush: Writings on Jews and Judaism*, ed., trans., and with commentary by Gregory Yuri Glazov (Notre Dame, Ind.: University of Notre Dame Press, 2016), 456–58.

54. F. Goetz, *Ob otnoshenii Vl. S. Solovieva k evreiskomu voprosu* [On the attitude of Vl. S. Soloviev toward the Jewish question] (Moscow: Tipografiia Kushnereva, 1902), reprinted from the journal version in *Voprosy filosofii i psikhologii* 56, no. 1 (January–February 1901): 159–98. On Goetz and Soloviev, see Glazov, 218–22.

55. Tolstoy must be paraphrasing Deut. 15:7–11.

56. F. Goetz, *Slovo podsudimomu!* [The accused speaks!] (Saint Petersburg: Novosti, 1891). The maximal fixation on anonymity—the name of the editor is missing from the text's cover—is understandable given the state of censorship in Russia at the time.

57. Goetz, "Slovo podsudimomu!," xxvii.

58. Ibid.

59. I discuss the case of Kanter (variant spelling of Kantor) at greater length in the forthcoming *Tolstoy and the Fates of the Twentieth Century*.

60. *The Kingdom of God Is within You; Religion and Morality* (*Religiia i nravstvennost'*); see, respectively, 28:39–67, 39:8–9, 12, 15, 17.

61. Tolstoy never changed his mind on this decision. See the somewhat earlier rehearsals of the same idea in *Anna Karenina* where Aleksey Alesandrovich Karenin, the scrupulous and righteous bureaucrat placed by the author on the State of Minorities Commission, travels to the provinces in the middle of trying to solve his matrimonial tragedy. Both fronts of work that press the necessity of emancipation are unassimilable to Karenin's well-reputed expertise and efficiency. These explorations continue in *The Kreutzer Sonata* (1889) and *Postlude to "The Kreutzer Sonata"* (1890). Tolstoy resumes them in the diary entries for March 21 and April 12, 1898 (53:189–90), inspired by a conversation with Alexandra Nikolaevna Peshkova-Toliverova on March 21 of that year. In addition to the Jewish question, Tolstoy contests the authenticity of the "woman question," as he noted after speaking with Peshkova: "I was talking with Peshkova about the woman question. There is no such question. There is a question of freedom and equality for all human creatures. The woman's question is fervor [*zador*]" (53:189) just as the Jewish question is about "fervor." Note that Tolstoy uses the same word "fervor" in a conversation about the Jewish question on April 11, 1906, recorded by Makovitsky and discussed earlier in this chapter.

62. The seat of mercy (or mercy seat) is rendered as "purification" (*ochistilishche*), as in the "purification from sin," in the Russian Gospels.

63. See Exod. 18:13; Exod. 40:20; Lev. 16:2; Num. 7:89; Matt. 23:2. Tolstoy's idea about the transformation of the seat of power into the seat of mercy (tolerance) through the reinterpretation of the "holy" element in the Scriptures with some help from Isaiah (34:261) in terms of vengeance and intolerance develops in the works he finished on the eve of his excommunication and immediately afterward in a large number of works written from 1900 to 1902. Tolstoy invokes Moses's injunction not to kill as his argument against the claims by the Church and the state that killing is permitted by God, who is the same as "the general" (34:284, 305).

64. The phrase in Tolstoy's title translates as "Carthage should be destroyed" and belongs to Cato the Elder, who thus concluded every speech delivered by him in the Senate from around 157 to 149 B.C. See my forthcoming essay: Inessa Medzhibovskaya, "Three Attempts on Carthage: Tolstoy's Designs of Nonviolent

Destruction," in *Tolstoy and Spirituality*, ed. Predrag Cicovacki and Heidi Grek (Boston: Academic Studies Press, 2018), 180–211.

65. The draft was left unfinished (39:216–22). Tolstoy completes the thought "let's leave violence to the government" in the discussed letter to Linetsky (1903). Tolstoy's ideas about the organized machinery and technology of violence in relation to the solution of the Jewish question anticipates Zygmunt Bauman's *Modernity and the Holocaust* (Ithaca, N.Y.: Cornell University Press, 1989), 83–116.

66. In this section, I cite most frequently *Religion and Morality* (Religiia i nravstvennost'; 39:3–26) and *The Kingdom of God Is within You*, both completed in 1893. Also of note are *Nondoing* (Nedelanie; 1893), 29:173–201; *The Demands of Love* (Trebovaniia liubvi; 1893), 42:260–64; *Christianity and Patriotism* (Khristianstvo i patriotism; 1894), 39:27–80; *Christian Teaching* (Khristianskoe uchenie; 1896), 39:117–91;"Letter against the persecution of the Doukhobors" (1895), 39:209–15; and the finished version of "Carthago delenda est" (1898), 39:197–205).

67. Vasilii Kirillovich Siutaev (1819–92) and Timofei Mikhailovich Bondarev (1820–98), both dissenters, Bondarev a Judaizer, were peasant friends of Tolstoy's from Tver and the Don Cossack region. In an extraordinary exchange with the American rabbi Joseph Krauskopf of Philadelphia during his visit to Yasnaya Polyana in 1894, Tolstoy supported a plan of resettling the Jews of Russia to the southern reaches of Novorossiya, where they could engage in agriculture and be saved from the cramped conditions of the Pale, pogroms, and other forms of persecution. Certainly the creation of New Jerusalems and Zions, frequent names for agricultural communes of dissenters worldwide, fit into Tolstoy's concept of brotherhood and the kingdom of God. However, the American guest's entrepreneurial approach with respect to earned profit and his readiness to meet potential attackers of the makeshift promised lands with "a fist and a knout," as Tolstoy put it in a letter to Feinerman of July 18–19, 1894, showed that Krauskopf was not very open to nonresistance in Tolstoy's sense (67:177–78).

68. On this and other works in Tolstoy's library by the same title, see Medzhibovskaya, "'Evreiskii vopros' Tolstogo," 96–97.

69. After this exchange, with the exception of two thank-you notes (December 1, 1909, and January 1910; 80:224, 81:42) for the promise of the disbursement of books, Tolstoy wrote no further discourses to Goetz. Witness Goetz's loving memoriam for Soloviev, the ideal Russian intellectual who would forever remain on the list of invested allies of the Jews: F. Goetz, "Ob otnoshenii Vl. S. Solovieva k evreiskomu voprosu," 159, 198. Tolstoy is not mentioned on this list of honorees. The arguments between Tolstoy and Goetz should not be misconstrued as a matter of personal difficulty between the two men. See also Tolstoy's letter to Naum Botvinnik of December 30, 1898 (71:519–20), on the topic of a universalist-cosmopolitan Jewish education that is part of the universal education-in-brotherhood of all humanity.

70. Tolstoy considered the literary skill of the Jahwist superior to that of the Synoptic Gospels and he advised mastering the Vedas and the wisdom of the Brahmins' writings, the Zend-Avesta, Laozi, Buddha, and Marcus Aurelius, Epictetus, and Seneca before reading the Jewish Prophets, especially the first ten chapters of Isaiah. On the techniques that Tolstoy proposes for reading the "not-so-well-written Gospels" with red and blue pencils in hand, see Inessa Medzhibovskaya, "L. N. Tolstoy," in *The Oxford Encyclopedia of the Bible and the Arts*, ed. Timothy Beal, 2 vols. (Oxford: Oxford University Press, 2015), 2:421–26.

71. A. Volynsky, "Nravstvennaia filosofiia gr. Lva Tolstogo" [The moral philosophy of count Lev Tolstoy], *Voprosy filosofii i psikhologii* 5, no. 1 (1890): 26–45. Subsequent citations to this work appear in the main text as parenthetical page numbers. Akim Lvovich Volynsky (Khaim Leibovich Flekser, 1861–1926), the editor of a popular Saint Petersburg journal, *Severnyi vestnik*, paid Tolstoy a visit at Yasnaya Polyana in August 1894. In that year, Tolstoy was able to sway the aforementioned Rabbi Krauskopf of Philadelphia, the outstanding American sermon writer, to speak in his sermons on nonviolence. See Rabbi Joseph Krauskopf, *My Visit to Tolstoy: Five Discourses* (Philadelphia, 1911). On Tolstoy and Krauskopf, see Medzhibovskaya, "'Evreiskii vopros' Tolstogo," 90, and Peter Kupersmith, "How a Meeting of an American Rabbi and Count Leo Tolstoy Resulted in the Founding of an American College," *TSJ* 18 (2006): 70–73.

72. Tolstoy, in a letter to his elder brother, Sergey, of February 25, 1898, shares his depression over the unfolding of the Dreyfus affair and laments the dismal shape of new literature and culture and their inability to achieve the task of repairing the world that is out of joint (71:293).

73. Note that Moses Mendelssohn is the only thinker mentioned by Tolstoy in *What Is Art?* or its drafts, where the former is referred to as one who believes that art is "the bringing of the beautiful knowable only through a vague sensation [*smutnym chuvstvom*] to the level of the true and the good. The goal of art is moral perfection" (30:42). In drafts of the work, Tolstoy notes that Mendelssohn recognizes "the manifestation of goodness and truth through beauty" to be the goal of art (30:314).

74. Makovitsky, 2:333.

75. As Tolstoy confessed in a letter of October 21, 1909, to Rabbi Leiba Meerovich Gordin, "there are more than a few sayings from the Talmud" in *The Cycle of Reading*, which he had sent with the letter (80:153–54). Tolstoy used the following German and Russian translations of the Talmud preserved in his library: *Mirovozzrenie talmudistov* [The worldview of the Talmudic scholars], ed. Fin and Soikin, 3 vols.; a seven-volume edition of the Talmud (Mishna and Tosefta) in the Russian rendition of Perferkovich published beginning in 1898 by Soikin; the one-volume *Zhivaia moral', ili sokrovishchnitsa talmudicheskoi etiki* [The living moral, or the treasury of Talmudic ethics], ed. Gurvich; and the German-language selections from the Talmud by the Stuttgart rabbi Jakob

Stern, *Lichtstrahlen aus dem Talmud* [Rays of light from the Talmud] (Leipzig: Reclam, 1882). This last edition bears extensive notations in Tolstoy's hand.

76. Rabbi Gordin's book, a copy of which Tolstoy received in 1909 (L. M. Gordin, *Chto takoe Talmud* [What the Talmud Is], Wilno: Artel Pechatnogo dela, 1909), contains signs of Tolstoy's approval. Tolstoy gives excellent grades (A+, 5+ in the Russian system) in the margins of a book by O. Gurvich, a selection of the treasury of Talmudic ethics, next to explanations of personal responsibility for acting morally and taking care of others, on not taking offense, on the value of labor, on Moses's attention to God's will, and so forth. See O. Ia. Gurvich, *Zhivaia moral' ili sokrovishcnitsa talmudicheskoi etiki* [The living moral, or the treasury of Talmudic ethics] (Wilno: Tipografiia I. I. Pirozhnikova, 1901), 4–5, 26, 33, 44–47; *Biblioteka Tolstogo*, vol. 1, book 1:227–30.

77. See Tolstoy's readings of April 14 on the unequal distribution of wealth in vol. 1 of *The Cycle of Reading* (1904–8) (41:246), repeated in his February 14 reading of part 1 of *Wise Thoughts for Every Day* (43:82) and *The Path of Life* (*Put' zhizni*, 1910); see also part 5 of *The Path of Life* for Tolstoy's arguments against the justifications of wealth and cupidity (45:155).

78. Tolstoy means the Trinity, his doctrinal target in organized Christianity from the mid-1870s onward.

79. Goldenveizer, 104.

80. Makovitsky, 3:14–15.

81. M. Gorky, "Lev Tolstoy," in *L. N. Tolstoy v vospominaniakh sovremennikov* [L. N. Tolstoy in the reminiscences of his contemporaries], 2:488.

82. Goldenveizer, 99.

83. See Tolstoy's letters to Stamo of December 14, 1907, and April 12, 1908 (77:258, 78:15–16). See also Tolstoy's reference to Stamo in Makovitsky's presence on January 12, 1908, of which Makovitsky made a record on the same day in his notebooks, viz. that five million Jews in Russia should be treated with an even greater love (Makovitsky, 3:114). Stamo had sent Tolstoy in 1907 two volumes of the German edition of Houston Stewart Chamberlain's *Foundations of the Nineteenth Century* alongside Teneromo's inventions about Tolstoy and the Jews. She demanded an unequivocal answer from Tolstoy on his opinion. Tolstoy mentioned that he found Chamberlain's book informative about Jesus's possibly non-Jewish origin, but that this point "constitutes only a small part of his exceptionally well-conceived book" (77:258). How could Tolstoy have liked this future Bible of Alfred Rosenberg's? It appears, upon examination of Tolstoy's notations in his copy of the Chamberlain work, that he never read the more ominous "Teutonic" sections in volume 2 and that his underlining in volume 1 was focused on finding proof that there is neither a Samaritan nor a Jew, that Philo was a neo-Platonist who didn't believe in Yahweh, and what the historical causes separating the Semite from other tribes could have been. See Houston Stewart Chamberlain, *Die Grundlagen des neunzehnten Jahrhunderts, Volksausgabe,*

8th ed., 2 vols. (Munich: Bruckmann, 1907). Chamberlain's argument in volume 1 states that although it is provable that Jesus was not descended from the Jewish people, nothing but the most superficial partisanship could deny the fact that this great figure was inseparably bound up with the historical development of that people (1: 258). Regarding Tolstoy's notations, see *Biblioteka Tolstogo*, vol. 3, book 1:218–19.

84. It is fair to add that age would no longer allow Tolstoy to travel to pogrom sites. Excepting his flight from home in November 1910 and family trips to Moscow, Tolstoy stopped undertaking distant travel after his grave illness in 1901. It is also fair to add that Tolstoy was less interested in befriending the still not too numerous intellectuals of Jewish origin among the writing and publishing members of Russian intelligentsia (e.g., Shestov and Mikhail Gershenzon) compared with artists of Jewish origin (in addition to musician Goldenveizer, he had productive friendships with the artist Leonid Pasternak and with the sculptor Ilya Gintzburg). A curious fact emerges from Makovitsky's records for May 26, 1905, by which stage two years had passed after the pogrom in Kishinev. On that day, Tolstoy's wife, Countess Sophia Andreevna, brought in an old bundle of letters from the year 1887 that she was trying to sort and put into order. Left unanswered by Tolstoy and fished out of that old stack was the letter from none other than Pavel Krushevan, the infamous Bessarabian journalist, one of the instigators of the Kishinev pogrom and an ideological leader of the Black Hundreds. Back in 1887, the young Krushevan—possibly still uncorrupted by extreme nationalism and hatred of the Jews—had sent to Tolstoy the manuscript of his novel *V khaose somnenii* [In the chaos of doubts] (1885). Apparently, Tolstoy had remained so unimpressed that he had abstained from returning even a polite "thank you." See Makovitsky, 1: 296, 516.

85. Aleichem wrote: "The author of these lines not only has the honor of belonging to this forever persecuted, despised people deprived of rights, that is yet great in its own right, but also to be a modest messenger of its feelings, thoughts, and ideals." Aleichem also asked Tolstoy not to "feel squeamish" (*ne pobrezgaite*) reading the letter and some enclosures with samples of his work. See Solomon Naumovich Rabinovich [Sholem Aleichem] to Tolstoy, April 27, 1903 (Russian State Archive for Literature and Arts, f. 1196, op. 1, ed. 22, leaf 1/1ob). The letter is written on letterhead that is embossed as follows: "Solomon Naumovich Rabinovich (Shalem-Aleichem). Kiev. B. Vasilkovskaya 5." I have tried to retain Aleichem's deliberate "Yiddishisms" as they sound in the Russian in which the letter is written. The letter was also published in Sholom-Aleichem, *Sobranie sochinenii v shesti tomakh* [Collected works in six volumes], ed. and trans. M.S. Belenky, 6 vols. (Moscow: Gosudarstvennoe izdatelstvo khudozhestvennoi literatury, 1962), 6: 758–9, but with "improved" punctuation and styles that warp its originality.

86. Tolstoy finished the three Kishinev tales specifically for *Gilf*. With the exception of his more famous story, "After the Ball" (Posle bala), which he thought to be rather too grim for the occasion, he did not complete any other works of fiction in 1903. The great *Hadji Murad* was finished a year later, a work that could not appear in its entirety in legal Russian editions.

87. Marx believed that religion should be a private matter. If the state no longer treats religion theologically but politically, the Jewish question disappears, becoming a question of universal freedom (Karl Marx, "On the Jewish Question" [1843], in *Early Political Writings*, ed. Joseph O'Malley [Cambridge: Cambridge University Press, 1994], 28–56). Close to Marx was Bruno Bauer, who argued in favor of complete emancipation, but on the condition that the Jews relinquish religion, something incompatible with liberal-democratic citizenship; see Bruno Bauer, *Die Judenfrage* [The Jewish question] (Braunschweig: Otto, 1843). Quite close to Dostoevsky, Dühring supported the idea of the disfranchisement of the Jews and their cultural and political seclusion; see Eugen Karl Dühring, *Die Judenfrage als Frage des Racencharacters und seiner Schädlichkeiten für Volkerexistenz, Sitte und Cultur* [The Jewish question as a question of the racial character and its harmfulness to the existence of the people, their customs, and their culture] (Leipzig: Reuther, 1881).

88. Quoted in Hannah Arendt, *Eichmann in Jerusalem: A Report on the Banality of Evil* (New York: Penguin, 1994), 269. Jaspers's point that "the crime committed on government orders" is both "more or less than common murder" (270) resonates with many similar comments by Tolstoy discussed earlier.

89. Jean-Paul Sartre, *Anti-Semite and Jew: An Exploration of the Etiology of Hate*, trans. George J. Becker (New York: Schocken Books, 1995), 39–40, 53.

90. "The First Distiller" (Pervyi vinokur, 1886) is the best example in this regard.

91. Hannah Arendt, *The Jewish Writings*, ed. Jerome Kohn and Ron H. Feldman (New York: Schocken Books, 2007), 42–46, 275–97. Tolstoy's mentions of his dislike for assimilated Jews ashamed of their origin fit perfectly with Arendt's argument.

92. Jews in the plural, as groups, appear in Tolstoy's later prose when his slowly perfecting main characters leave their sinful environment and enter into a new phase of life, frequently falling lower in their social status and thus coming into contact with Russian Jews. Consider the early stages of Katiusha Maslova's escape into freedom from the illusion that she could become a "noblewoman" (part 1, chap. 2; 32:11) in Tolstoy's novel *Resurrection* (Voskresenie) (1889–99). See also the scene of Nekhliudov's sharing his train compartment with Jews and other commoners as he leaves Russia to follow Katiusha into Siberia (part 2, chap. 41; 32:352–53). In a well-known opinion given to Gorky, Tolstoy described Dostoevsky to be one such nervous Jewish type: "There was something Jew-

ish in his blood. He was suspicious, loved himself, was difficult, and unhappy" (Maxim Gorky, *Kniga o russkikh liudiakh* [A book about Russian people] [Moscow: Vagrius, 2000], 483).

93. Stiva thinks he saves face by saying the following to Karenin: "I had business to do with the Yid and wait-yid" (*Anna Karenina*, VII, 16, VII, 20; 19:296–97, 306–10). Rosamund Bartlett is the only translator to have captured the humor concerning the "pun about having wait-yid to see a yid" (Leo Tolstoy, *Anna Karenina*, trans. Rosamund Bartlett [Oxford: Oxford University Press, 2014], 725). Note that Stiva continues to use the word *zhid*.

94. In his later polemical works against violence, Tolstoy regularly supports his arguments with quotes from the Tanakh (especially Isa., Jer., Jos.), the Prophets, Leviticus, and Kings, and Gospels (especially Matt., Luke, and John).

95. I say more on this in Inessa Medzhibovskaya, "Punishment and the Human Condition: Hannah Arendt, Leo Tolstoy, and Lessons from Life, Philosophy, and Literature," in *Punishment as a Crime?*, ed. Julie Hansen and Andrei Rogatchevskii (Uppsala: Uppsala University Press, 2014), 137–61.

96. Theodor Adorno, *Minima Moralia: Reflections on a Damaged Life*, trans. E. F. N. Jephcott (New York: Verso, 2010), 80.

97. Jean-François Lyotard, *The Differend: Phrases in Dispute*, trans. Georges Van Den Abbeele (Minneapolis: University of Minnesota Press, 1988), 18–20, 47; Jean-François Lyotard, *Heidegger and "the jews,"* trans. Andreas Michel and Mark Roberts (Minneapolis: University of Minnesota Press, 1997), 84–89, 92.

Jeffrey Brooks

Laughing with the Count: The Humor in *War and Peace* and Beyond

WHEN A PERSON becomes a bear, vistas open that can lead toward tragedy, comedy, or, at minimum, perplexity. The Greek goddess Hera changed a rival into a bear so her hunter son might kill her, but Zeus saved the pair by placing them a safe distance apart in the night sky as Ursa Major and Minor. Transformation of a person into a bear even in mythology signifies a radical separation and sets up a dynamic tension between the character and his or her circumstances. Such a metamorphosis is cruel and grotesque as well as comic, and the tension can under some circumstances form the foundation for humor.

Tolstoy is not primarily recognized as a humorist. Yet he used humor and was drawn into the humor of his day in ways that have not heretofore been widely recognized. His insertion of a bear into *War and Peace* introduces a comic note that contributes to definition of his hero's character. It also put the author into a comic dialogue, perhaps unintended, with his contemporaries, since the humorists of his day seized on the bear to lampoon the novel, its main character, and even its author. Today's readers of *War and Peace* seriously applying themselves to mastery of the great novel may not be aware that many of Tolstoy's contemporaries would have been chuckling as they turned the pages and would have supplemented their reading by glancing at contemporary cartoons that parodied the main scenes of the book.[1]

Tolstoy wrote *War and Peace* at a time when boisterous humor magazines were a new phenomenon in Russian print culture. The comic aspects of his association of his hero, Pierre Bezukhov, with a bear were quite in keeping with contemporary cultural currents but have been virtually invisible in the subsequent critical literature on the novel.[2] Tolstoy's seriousness has never been questioned and his emphasis on life's moral lessons and choices has usually been assumed to preclude humor. When he began *War and Peace* in 1863 he had already described several potentially humorous situations with such solemnity that even a wry smile seemed out of the question.[3]

Yet when one is open to the possibility of humor in Tolstoy's work, one can see that he occasionally used the kinder forms of irony and laughter, as in his successful first novel, *Childhood* (1852), in which he shows his old German tutor in a friendly comic light. He also drew on the deepest strain of Russian literary humor, that of ridicule and satire with an occasional streak of cruelty. Gogol, Ostrovsky, and Saltykov-Shchedrin often mocked their protagonists without the sympathy that Pushkin, with his gentler wit, showed for a variety of characters.[4] Dostoevsky ridiculed his characters in his funny short novel *The Village of Stepanchikovo and Its Inhabitants* (1859) and in some other works as well, though he, too, could evoke a compassionate laugh. Nevertheless, Vladimir Propp had good reason, writing from a Russian perspective, to describe "ridiculing laughter" as "the main type of human laughter."[5] Tolstoy valued this form of humor. He mentioned Ostrovsky many times in his diary entries of 1857, and he praised Saltykov-Shchedrin as a "serious talent" (47:150).

Tolstoy tried his hand at satire soon after he began *War and Peace* but without great success.[6] In 1864 he wrote *The Infected Family*, a biting but not very effective satirical play about emancipated women that owed something to Turgenev's much-discussed novel *Fathers and Children* (1862). He was able much more successfully to interweave another sort of humor in works with the larger canvas and greater depth of field that characterize his great novels. With so much else happening, it is easy to overlook the humor, but it is clearly there. In the opening pages of *War and Peace*, Anna Pavlovna and Prince Kuragin prattle foolishly about Napoléon while promoting their own petty interests. The socially inept Pierre appears, and Tolstoy departs from realism almost in the manner of Gogol or Dostoevsky.[7] Pierre grabs a bear kept at the Kuragins' home, dances with it, and he and Dolokhov join the bear for a ride in a coach. Pierre and Dolokhov commandeer a policeman, tie him to the bear, and toss the pair into the River Moika.[8]

The episode is so bizarre, unreal, expressive of madcap physical comedy, and subversive of authority that it deserves a closer look. Tolstoy brings on the bear in stages. Prince Kuragin describes Pierre as a "bear" before the incident. "Educate this bear for me," he tells Anna Pavlovna (*W&P*, 15; *SS* 4:22). Later, when Pierre arrives at the Kuragin home, he hears "familiar voices and the roaring of a bear" (*W&P*, 31; *SS* 4:42). A friend pulls the bear on a chain to scare the others. It is a "young bear," not a cub but large enough to intimidate. Before exiting with the bear Pierre embraces it fully, both figuratively and literally: "And he seized the bear and, hugging him and lifting him up, began waltzing around the room with him" (*W&P*, 35; *SS* 4:47). Tolstoy narrates this directly. The anonymous female guest who later relates the episode calls Pierre and his friends "complete bandits" (*razboiniki*), associating their caper with rebellion, which it was (*SS* 4:49).[9]

Pierre's and Dolokhov's violation of a policeman in an autocratic state would probably have sent them to Siberia under the previous tsar. The guest retells the story as follows, adding an unidentified third character: "The three found a bear someplace, put it in the carriage with them, and went to the actresses. The police came to subdue them. They caught a policeman, tied him back to back to the bear, threw the bear in the Moika; and the bear swam with the policeman on top of him. 'Wonderful, the figure of the policeman, *ma chère*,' cried the count, dying with laughter" (*W&P*, 37; *SS* 4:49–50).

She adds that "the poor fellow" was barely rescued. Tolstoy returns to the theme several times and identifies Pierre with the bear. In his own narrative voice, he explains, "Pierre had not managed to choose a career for himself in Petersburg, and had indeed been banished to Moscow for riotous behavior [*buistvo*]" (*W&P*, 52; *SS* 4:68). Tolstoy used the incident to advance the plot. Dolokhov is reduced to the ranks, and Pierre is packed off to Moscow, where much of the subsequent action unfolds. More important, however, was the way Tolstoy opened the novel by reaching out to a wide circle of readers through humor.

The incident with the bear had clear elements of cruelty, but Tolstoy softened it by the use of friendly, good-natured narrators and by his characterization of Pierre himself. Although Pierre roped the policeman to the bear, Tolstoy had already tied Pierre more thoroughly by saddling him with a bear's attributes—clumsiness, strength, size, unpredictability, and ferocity when provoked. He described his awkward hero as "massive," elaborately dressed (evoking a full and furry coat), and larger than other men. Anna Pavlova reacts when Pierre first appears as "at the sight of something all too enormous and unsuited to the place" (*W&P*, 9; *SS* 4:15). Tolstoy contains the ursine image by displacing it: "This fear could have referred only to the intelligent and at the same time shy, observant, and natural gaze which distinguished him from everyone else in the drawing room" (*W&P*, 9; *SS* 4:15). By transposing the characteristics of the bear Tolstoy created a character of surprising otherness; a sympathetic human trapped in the facade of a bear. Pierre moves through most of the novel bearlike, out of place, clueless as to how to behave, often laughably off-key, sometimes violent, and occasionally truly savage. His character thus created is both incongruously comic and simultaneously deeper than comedy, supporting the multiple readings of contemporaries and subsequent generations.

Artists, philosophers, and writers have contrasted humans and animals for centuries.[10] Aristotle characterized man as a "political animal." Less familiar is Jean-Jacques Rousseau's self-mocking description of himself as a "werewolf," with which Tolstoy was no doubt acquainted.[11] Jacques Derrida addresses the question of why the boundary between humans and other animals is fundamental to philosophy.[12] Humans define the essence of human behavior as that which is distinct from animal behavior—that is, mastery over self and desire, organization of political and social structures to control "wild" disorder, and behavioral norms expressing civilization's superiority over barbarism.[13] A "humanlike" captive bear exhibits suffering at its constraint, and a bearlike human skirts perilously close to the line that defines the boundary of humanity, in the process evoking the potential for deprecatory humor. It is tempting to suppose that Derrida may have overstated his case at least for Russia. Yet Ivan Panaev (1812–62), prominent writer in the 1840s and 1850s, used the metaphor of an animal in exactly this fashion. Writing in the poet Nikolai Nekrasov's well-known compendium *Petersburg: The Physiology of a City* (1845), he described the moral decline of a successful hack writer as a descent into an animal-like state. "Gradually, the feuilletonist loses all sense of shame and decency—the last human feeling that distinguishes him from an animal. He has become capable of anything."[14] Tolstoy likewise reminded readers that humans can imbibe the ferocity of animals when Dolokhov quotes a bear hunter before his duel with Pierre. "'How can you not be afraid of a bear?' he'd say. 'But once you see him, your fear goes away, except of letting him escape!'" (*W&P*, 314; *SS* 5:28).

These issues came to the fore in a period when Russia's social and economic development tested many traditional boundaries: the Great Reforms, Russia's defeat in the Crimean War (1853–56), and the crushing of rebellions in the Caucasus and Poland. The resulting changes were of particularly pressing concern to Tolstoy's generation of aristocrats. "Moscow's aristocratic society fell victim to the encroachments of the industrial and bourgeois world," as Dominic Lieven has noted.[15] Bourgeois notions of self and ambition collided with aristocratic excess and sloth in the world in which Tolstoy lived and wrote. The attitudes that Max Weber described as "the Protestant ethic" clashed with aristocratic mores in a rapidly growing urban Russia. The professions, including that of writer, served to undermine notions of an aristocratic life as an end in and of itself. Similarly new notions of mobility, agency, and self among women collided with and undercut patriarchal authority.

The humor magazines gave these themes full scope. They registered tensions about gender by first returning uppity women to their traditional places and then, within a decade or two, by ridiculing those who stood in the way of powerful women. In 1866 a cartoonist in the humor magazine *Budil'nik* used a bear to present two views of captivity. In a first frame, a man in ragged clothes with a spear pokes a snarling bear on a chain. In the second a young bride is escorted down the aisle while the groom and a friend whisper behind them.[16] The caption covering both frames reads, "Jump, you devil, as your master bids you." The first frame is quite straightforward and sets up the subtlety of the second.[17] A first reading of the latter is that the hapless new wife will be the bear on a chain, but a deeper interpretation presents the institution of marriage as one that tames uncouth and undisciplined behavior of young people of both sexes. Another reading would suggest a jibe at the institution of arranged marriages.

Tolstoy was attuned to the changing mores of his time and had personally tried on many of the available male roles, including those of seigneurial sexual predator, serf owner, master of an estate, playboy, bon vivant, colonial officer, and finally successful writer and family man. He experienced the social changes in Russian society from a unique vantage point as a proud aristocrat.[18] Personal discipline was one of his preoccupations, and he was an inveterate maker of lists and a self-improver. He worried about his coarse manner and never circulated in the highest aristocratic society. His references in his journal to his struggle to control his desires and lust also suggest an association with Pierre, who suffered from similarly bearish impulses and riotous behavior.[19] Pierre, too, is a self-improver, as is evident from his adventures with the Masons and other instances. Prince Andrei likewise aspires to self-improvement but without Pierre's tendency to lapse.

Tolstoy's joining of Pierre and the bear gave his readers an ironic portrayal of the aristocracy. Pierre was at once a noble and a bear, and Tolstoy thereby employed what philosophers have described as incongruity theory. The formalist critic Viktor Shklovsky invented the term "defamiliarization or estrangement" (*ostranenie*) or "defamiliarize, estrange, make strange" (*ostranit'*) in 1917 to explain how Tolstoy offered his readers a curiously fresh view of the world.[20] Translators into English have rendered the term as "estrangement," "making strange," "estrange," and "defamiliarization."[21]

Shklovsky's insight can be associated with the incongruity theory of humor, since the odd view of the world and of social codes can also be a source of laughter. He noted that Tolstoy's peers reacted with surprise, discomfort, and outrage to his portrayal of people and events.[22] The phrase he uses to describe Tolstoy's technique is "creation of a special perception of the subject" (*sozdanie osobogo vospriiatiia predmeta*).[23] Shklovsky then points to descriptions that seemed curiously off-key, as, for example, the grotesque outfits worn on occasion by Pierre and Ippolit Kuragin.[24]

Shklovsky saw the connection between incongruity and the novel even if he did not get the joke, or the deeper humor for that matter.[25] He illustrated his 1928 study with pictures from a comic version of the novel published in *Iskra* (1859–73), the popular humor magazine. *Iskra*'s humorists parodied the novel and caricatured Tolstoy in a variety of articles, poems, and cartoons. Most notable were two sets of cartoons, one devoted to Tolstoy and the purpose of the novel and the other to the novel's character and plot. *Iskra*'s humorists revealed the incongruity of scenes and descriptions and used them for satire. They also made much of the bear and the policeman

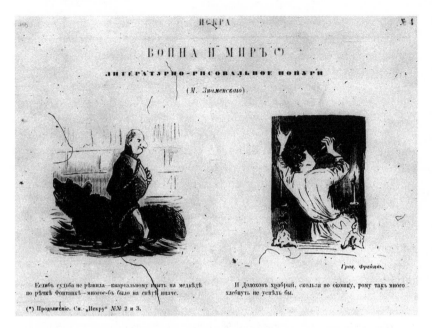

Image from the magazine *Iskra*, 1869. *"War and Peace. A Potpourri of Literary Drawings,"* by M. Znamensky. *Left*: "If fate had not decreed otherwise—that the policeman should float down the River Fontanka sitting akimbo on the bear—much would have turned out differently in the world." *Right*: "And the brave Dolokhov, gliding as he was down the window ledge, would not have managed to take such a good gulp of rum in time."

in the satirical version. Shklovsky used many images from *Iskra* to show how the cartoonists captured the unusualness of Tolstoy's attention to detail and description.[26] In another context Shklovsky considered the power of irony in situations in which the narrator of a story or novel looks askance at the surrounding world.[27] Pierre is Tolstoy's hero, though not his narrator, and he is so oddly placed in one situation after another that he draws irony upon himself while simultaneously opening new ways of seeing the world.

Pierre presents himself as a *bâtard*—"sans nom, sans fortune"—before his friend Prince Andrei (*SS* 4:41). Such self-deprecation represents an ethical form of humor because it is victimless (other than the self), whether authors laugh at themselves or invite readers to laugh at their own faults, as did Gogol on occasion.[28] To the extent that Pierre and the bear create a dynamic of self-deprecating humor they fall into the category that Freud considered as laughter that provides a healthy release of emotion. Freud illustrated the concept in a late essay in which he described a criminal heading to the gallows on a Monday morning who remarks to his jailor, "Well, the week's beginning nicely."[29] This form of self-mockery was familiar to the authors and artists who published in the new humor magazines that appeared both before and after the emancipation. A humorist in *Iskra* evoked a similar form of laughter in a cartoon that paired self-mockery with a challenge to authority.[30] A well-dressed young man asks a policeman if a dark alley is safe, since "there seem to be many rogues there." The policeman answers, "Not at all; I am here alone."[31] The policeman mocks himself, and there is nothing cruel about this form of self-deprecating humor. The cartoonists invite readers to laugh with the policeman and, by extension, at their own foibles. Tolstoy urges readers to laugh along with Pierre, although Pierre might have mocked himself only before equals such as Andrei.

The policeman's self-deprecatory laughter was a modern extension of foolishness, which also had deep roots in Russian culture. Holy fools figured importantly in Orthodox Christianity, and their jokes carried moral force and often deep meanings.[32] The policeman also drew on the tradition of little Ivan the Fool, the hero of folklore, whose innocence conquers evil to the delighted satisfaction of listeners.[33] Pierre has some of the attributes of Ivan the Fool in his naive intentions and inexplicably lucky outcomes. One would not expect readers to identify him with the figure of folklore, but they might sympathize with him as an awkward underdog much as the public for the folktales would sympathize with the character of Little Ivan the Fool. One can follow Pierre's foolishness throughout the novel, from his accidental marriage to the beautiful Helena through his clueless tourism of the battlefield, his involvement with Masons, his later marriage to Natasha, and his association with the future Decembrists. But because Tolstoy was not a folklorist and Pierre was not Ivan the Fool, the character is drawn with an additional layer of self-consciousness. Pierre as a naïf is able to observe and judge himself and others—and depart from the role and express other dimensions of his personality.

Tolstoy applied his comic touches to more than Pierre. His use of humor only upon occasion, to lighten scenes where it would not be expected, was more successful than his earlier and heavier attempt at full-length satire. Tolstoy mocks Napoléon's obsession with his historic role and prefaces Napoléon's appearance in the novel with an ironic characterization of Kutuzov. Kutuzov, whom readers knew had outsmarted Napoléon, appears first as he "walked slowly and indolently past the thousands of eyes that were popping from their sockets" (*W&P*, 117; *SS* 4:139). He then naps off during the council of war and stresses on waking that the most important thing before the battle is a good night's sleep. Only then does Tolstoy show Napoléon pompously addressing his troops and exclaiming, "I myself will direct your battalions" (*W&P*, 269; *SS* 4:339). Tolstoy uses Kutuzov to parody the stereotype of a great general and mocks Napoléon, who tries to live up to the stereotype.

Once we have rediscovered Tolstoy's humor, it is tempting to try to understand it in light of the European high culture of his day, with which Tolstoy was of course familiar, and in which published humor was more prevalent than in Russia. That this would be a mistake can be argued again from the centrality of the bear. Bears featured modestly in European culture at the time, most prominently as benign companions to Goldilocks. They did not, in Europe, carry the force and omnipresence that they held over the Russian imagination and hence did not embody the internal tension that could fuel humor. Tolstoy was part of a cultural tradition that accepted bears as an elemental force. He described them elsewhere not as whimsical figures but as truly savage creatures. He included "The Three Bears" in his children's readers in the early 1870s together with the tale of a tame bear that eludes its master, rides off in a troika, and escapes into the forest.[34] He described the brutishness of bears in his short grotesque tale "The Bear Hunt" (1872), in which a bear nearly devours the hunter-narrator.

Yet bears are powerful and dangerous, lords of the forest and a symbol of Russia.[35] Honoré Daumier, John Tenniel, and others pictured a savage bear menacing Turkey in the era of the Crimean War.[36] Bears also appeared at the time in Russian folklore, circuses, markets, fairs, in the acts of traveling entertainers, and as toys.[37] Tame bears were playthings of tsars and of the gilded youth of Tolstoy's Russia. Bears were objects of an ancient cult and closely associated with humans in folktales.[38] They were given fond nicknames—Misha, Matryona, Aksinia, or Mikhail Potapovich—and in folk wisdom were considered to possess the ability to turn into human beings. As Andrei Sinyavsky explains in his study of Russian folklore, "the folktale bear may marry a woman and have a human son."[39] In addition, people were commonly identified with various animals in Russian folklore, often to highlight their negative qualities.[40] Gogol employed this device in *Dead Souls* when he described Sobakevich ("doglike") as someone who "looked exactly like a medium-sized bear," despite his name.[41] He gives Sobakevich the lethargy, awkwardness, and brown coat of a bear. Pushkin's Tatiana dreams of being helped by a bear and then of being carried by the bear to a gathering of "a horde of monsters in a ring," from which the bear vanishes and Onegin appears.

Tolstoy's bear thus has a clear pedigree traced back to medieval Russia. Russia missed the Renaissance, the Reformation, the Counter-Reformation, and most of the Enlightenment and remained more closely linked to its medieval roots than did the other great powers of Europe. Dancing bears were therefore not unexpected in a novel about early nineteenth-century Russia or even later. Medieval Russian humor survived in Tolstoy's time in holiday celebrations, games, dances, and comic figures such as minstrels (*skomorokhi*), clowns (*balagur*), showmen (*rashniki*), and holy fools.[42] Tolstoy evoked this dimension with the "hussars, wenches, witches, clowns, bears" and mummers at the Christmas gathering in *War and Peace*. The Rostov household maintains a court fool, Dimmler.[43] Princess Marya has her pilgrims at Bald Hills, whom Prince Andrei ridicules before Pierre in chapters 13–14 of book 2, part 2 (*SS* 5:124–30). The same cast of comic characters recurs in the popular songs and folklore of peasant and Cossack rebels, as well as in the *lubok* and *lubochnaia literatura*.[44] Stravinsky evoked Russian folk theater of the eighteenth and nineteenth centuries in *Petrushka*.[45]

The long Russian tradition of the comic was thus alive and readily available to writers and artists working in high culture in Tolstoy's time.[46] Looking back perhaps at traditional Russian culture as well as its legacy in Soviet times, Mikhail Bakhtin celebrated this underworld of laughter and popular amusements and developed its subversive character in his classic study *Rabelais and His World* (1965).[47] Bakhtin identified carnival with a utopian impulse to criticize the established order. As a writer in Stalin's USSR he could not draw direct inference to Russia's and particularly Soviet Russia's experience, but his readers did so. Some critics argue that Bakhtin overstated the opposition between carnival and Christianity in the Western context.[48] But whether opposing or reinforcing, stabilizing or destabilizing, the contrasting manifestations of order and disorder run consistently through Russian culture at all levels, from popular festivals such as Shrovetide (Maslenitsa) to the widely circulated popular prints (*lubki*) that, particularly before they were censored in the mid-nineteenth century, featured bawdy images of naked men and women in the communal bath and drunken gatherings in taverns and bars.[49] The tension between order and disorder recurs as a theme in Russian literature, both high and low, and animated the expression of humor as well.[50] It is no accident that Tolstoy evokes aspects of this tradition in *War and Peace*. The aunt who raised him supported a holy fool, whom Tolstoy wrote about with loving sympathy in his acclaimed debut novel, *Childhood*. Nor is it accidental that Dostoevsky wrote about holy fools and devils, as well as desperate rebels. Both authors explored notions of rebellion linked with early modern Russia as well, Tolstoy in *Anna Karenina* and Dostoevsky in almost all of what he wrote.

How could Tolstoy's readers avoid associating Pierre's life with the pleasures of riotous freedom and the satisfaction of male desire? Tolstoy describes a situation in which the ruling authority was in retreat—namely, war and occupation—and he portrays a bungling outsider of a hero in the person of Pierre who savors the delights of rebellious freedom. As Napoléon's forces advance, Pierre lustfully eyes and then marries the vapid beauty of his circle. Later, in occupied Moscow, in the absence of authority, Pierre fantasizes about assassinating Napoléon but instead saves a French officer from a Russian bullet. Serious critics of the time and some participants in the War of 1812 chided Tolstoy for his version of history, but leading humorists in *Iskra* portrayed Pierre as a comic figure who in one cartoon threatens his wife with a tabletop and also, in an image beside it, as an equally bearish fool shooting Dolokhov in the duel.[51] Only the devils of temptation seem lacking from the series, and they finally appear beside Natasha in the seventeenth and eighteenth issues of the satirical magazine. One grins at her while she awaits her would-be seducer Anatole; another with horns on his head stands by while she drinks poison from a bucket.[52] The satirists had to abort their satire when their editors scrapped illustration in order to publish without prepublication censorship under new postemancipation regulations. Nevertheless, the figure of the devil is revealing.

Freedom meant more than rebellion. With growing social and geographic mobility, freedom implied consumption, the temptations of city life for country people, an escape from the suffocating power of patriarchy and male dominance for women, among younger men from grandfathers and older brothers, and much else. Higher up the social scale, freedom implied the spree or the binge in contrast to "the orderliness in everyday life."[53] Laughter often served as a key to the castle of freedom.[54] On this point, Bakhtin is insightful as well. In his study of Rabelais he stresses "universality" of medieval laughter, "its indissoluble and essential relation to freedom" with respect to fools and other figures of humor, and its "relation to the people's unofficial truth."[55] He emphasizes "the victory of laughter over fear" inspired by religion, nature, and "authoritarian commandments and prohibitions, of death and punishment after death, hell and all that is more terrifying than the earth itself."[56] This was particularly enticing in an era of social mobility, consumption, urbanization, and other changes. Advertisers had no compunction about selling their products as luxuries, offered by a devilish figure representing temptation, in addition to the more conventional alluring male and female figures, children, and clowns. An advertising poster from 1897 features a devilish figure in red, selling perfume.[57]

To see Pierre as a hero of freedom may seem a stretch, but Tolstoy first imagined Pierre as a future Decembrist, a member of that group of young officers who on the death of Alexander I in 1825 rose up against Nicholas I in the hope of establishing one or another alternative form of rule, from a republic to a constitutional monarchy. Tolstoy abandoned this idea, but he nonetheless introduces Pierre as a young man drawn to Napoléon, albeit before Napoléon invades Russia. In this respect, Pierre embodies the meanings of the two words for freedom in the Russian language. The first, *volia*, signified freedom of the will, the will of the individual and the general will—categories stretching back in educated political and philosophical discourse

to Kant and Rousseau. It also meant will and desire more broadly, as in peasants' dreams of land and independence under the tsars. It contrasted with
svoboda, used for civic freedoms of speech and the press, as well as freedom
of trade and the free professions.[58] Parallel to these notions of freedom are
ideas of authority (*nachal'stvo*) and power (*vlast'*). The first is associated with
force, governing, and the person at the top of a hierarchy, from the eldest
in a family and the chief of a village to the ruling authorities. The second is
associated with right, force, power over something, freedom of action, and
order or instruction. As Vladimir Dal (1801–72), the nineteenth-century
folklorist and lexicographer, puts it in his classic dictionary, *vlast'* signifies
right, force, and will (*volia*) over something, as well as freedom (*svoboda*) of
action, also order or instruction.[59]

These concepts were linked with notions of the ruling power and the
tsar in the prerevolutionary era and the idea of law (*zakon*), as in the law of
God. Among peasants and some others as well, order meant the inability to
act as one wished to do. In his great collection of Russian proverbs, Vladimir
Dal grouped authority with obedience and orders to do something, as well
as with proverbs about the tsar, the law, and state service. The first proverb
he lists under authority (*nachal'stvo*) is "two bears cannot live amiably in one
den."[60] Under the heading of "Tsar" he begins with a proverb that suggests
the tsar's unchallengeable power on earth: "God is in the sky, the tsar is on
earth."[61] Dal also collected proverbs warning of the danger of freedom and
pointing up its demonic character, as in "Freedom is its own god"; "Freedom
for the free, heaven for the saved"; and "Freedom corrupts but servitude
instructs."[62] Parallel to these are other proverbs warning of the dangers of
laughter and mirth. Among them are "Where laughter resides sin abides,"
"Sin and pleasure come in equal measure," "He who laughs walks a sinful
path."[63] Thus the association of freedom with humor was inescapable, and
authors used humor as a literary device to bring their readers into the realm
of chaotic imagined freedom.

Tolstoy's literary peers largely missed comic aspects of the novel, or
at least did not find them amusing.[64] Some of their hostile response can be
attributed to literary disputes of the day and professional jealousies, but the
fact that contemporary critics genuinely did not consider misbehavior to be
funny is noteworthy. D. I. Pisarev subtitled his essay about the first three
volumes of the novel in 1868 "Old-Fashioned Lordliness" (Barstvo) but
suggested that Tolstoy had written, perhaps inadvertently, "the best work
on the pathology of Russian society."[65] The social critic and Tolstoy's class-
mate Bervi-Flerovskii described the characters as no better than "coarse
bushmen" (*grubyi bushmen*) and his serf-owning hero, Andrei, as "devoid
of all spiritual nobility [*lishen vsiakogo dushevnago blagorodstva*]."[66] Ivan
Turgenev, Tolstoy's rival, wrote his friend P. B. Annenkov on February 14,

1868, after reading three of seven volumes that dozens of pages "are fully first-class—all mundane descriptions (of hunting, skating at night, and so forth)," but he went on to complain in a note two weeks later that "the historical addition that actually delighted readers" was "a puppet comedy and quackery" in which "there is really no development in a single character."[67] Tolstoy's arguments with Turgenev are well known, but Turgenev was too great an artist to criticize simply from spite.[68] What he appears to have rejected is the humor, such as that with the bear, which he felt did not belong in serious literature.

The critical reception of *War and Peace* and specifically the critics' refusal to recognize comic aspects of impropriety pose anew the question of how humor was integrated into literary life at the time. Literary Russia was a small world. *Iskra* belonged to it and played a double game.[69] As a popular journal it drew on a broad lower middle-class oral culture, but its educated left-leaning staff expressed a critical sensibility. *Iskra*'s allure probably extended down the social scale even to clerks and tradesmen, since it had ten thousand subscribers in 1862–63 and more would have read occasional issues.[70] *Sovremennik*, the leading literary journal of the day, had only six thousand to sixty-five hundred subscribers in 1863–64.[71] *Iskra*'s publishers and staff tapped effectively into a popular sensibility that extended far beyond their actual readers. They captured jokes and sly asides circulating in the oral culture, as well as in flyers and thin magazines that burst on the literary scene during the late 1850s and early 1860s.[72] The wave began with occasional comic sheets that sold well on the street before the emancipation. After irregular street sales were banned, more regular periodicals appeared, some of which were associated with left-leaning critics known as revolutionary democrats. Among the magazines inclined to sharp social criticism in addition to *Iskra* were *Gudok* (1862–63) and *Budil'nik* (1865–1917), as well as some light liberal publications such as *Razvlechenie* (1865–1918) and *Strekoza* (1875–1918).[73] The editors of most of these journals struck at what they considered to be the inconsistencies, injustices, and moral shortcomings of Russian life. Thus the editors of *Gudok*, with a respectable four thousand subscribers, declared in their first issue, "We believe in laughter and satire not in the name of 'art for art' but in the name of life and our future development—in a word, we believe in laughter [*smekh*] as a civic force."[74]

Iskra excelled in its strong team of artists and writers. The Iskraites (Iskrovtsy) arguably found inspiration in the "Nekrasov school" of literature, named after the editor of *Sovremennik* and poet who excelled in civic verse.[75] *Iskra* was founded and edited by caricaturist Nikolai Aleksandrovich Stepanov (1807–77) and the poet Vasilii Stepanovich Kurochkin (1831–75). Stepanov had already published his caricatures in such journals as *Syn otechestva*, *Sovremennik*, and elsewhere.[76] Kurochkin was well known in literary circles after 1858 for his successful translations of the works of Pierre-Jean de Béranger, the French poet and songwriter.[77] Kurochkin was imprisoned for four months in 1866 in the famous Petropavlovsk Fortress for revolutionary activity. Stepanov also leaned to the left and was close to *Sovremennik*.[78]

Radicals at *Sovremennik* wanted art to serve society, and Tolstoy, Turgenev, and some other prominent writers opposed them. In fact, Tolstoy may have consciously taken aim at the *raznochintsy*, or intellectuals of common origins, many of whom did not read French, by beginning *War and Peace* entirely in French. As if to drive home the point he wrote that Prince Kuragin "spoke that refined French that our grandparents not only spoke but thought" (*W&P*, 3; *SS* 4:8).[79] The effect was to evoke the small public of like-minded "reader friends" who shared the same upbringing and culture and on which Russian writers had depended in the first half of the century.[80] From this perspective it is unlikely that Tolstoy embraced the bear in a conscious effort to reach out democratically to a wider audience. Nor was it accepted in that spirit by the staff of *Iskra*. The early Soviet critic Iampol'skii suggested in an essay in 1928 on parodies and caricatures of the novel that *Iskra's* satire was simply an episode in "the struggle of the mixed estates against Tolstoy [*v bor'be raznochintsev s Tolstym*]."[81]

The cartoonists of *Iskra* had already drawn Russian novels and their authors into the irreverent world of contemporary popular culture. They had poked fun at Turgenev and *Fathers and Sons* (1861) and were working on *Smoke* (1867) when they turned to Tolstoy. An anonymous cartoonist in the twelfth issue for 1868 showed Turgenev in a top hat shoving a dirty broom in the face of a child.[82] "The novelist's attitude toward children is truly fatherly," began the caption. Other cartoons were even more pointed and showed Turgenev's famous characters lolling in drunken stupors or embracing in wild abandon.[83] Readers could hardly observe the beastlike caricatures of Bazarov and his bloated lover, Odintsova, without disgust or a mad chuckle.[84] Tolstoy came in for similar treatment. A. M. Volkov, under the pseudonym of Graf. Freind', devoted two spreads of unflattering cartoons to Tolstoy in the sixteenth issue in 1868.[85] In one Pierre stares at a *lubok* print of Kutuzov on horseback, and the caption explains that Tolstoy was inspired by a cheap print titled "War and Peace" that he saw on the wall of a posthouse.

In a second pair of cartoons Tolstoy's characters are shown as toys or figurines that the author plays with above a caption reading, "Literary sources and artistic originals serve the author as material for the creation of his epic."[86] Another shows a scene of gluttony with the explanation, "The modest orgies in the private rooms of Diusso and Boreli provided the author with only the poorest copy of the majestic originals of that heroic time." One man waves two bottles while another lies drunk on the floor and a third has passed out with his head on the table. A further caption reads, "Although the characters are supposedly historical figures from the Napoleonic era, they actually resemble people who can be seen at gatherings and restaurants of Moscow every day." If Tolstoy's readers saw his characters as their contemporaries, then the novel would be a reflection of contemporary society. The bacchanalian celebration could be read as a criticism of the high life of the aristocracy. Tolstoy's readers could see his characters in their historical setting and simultaneously judge their doubles transposed to contemporary life. This was the point Pisarev had made in his critique of the novel.

Iskra pursued Tolstoy and his characters with a doggedness that reflected sustained hostility to the author and recognition that the work held a trove of material useful for satirical comment on contemporary society. The journal ceased to print illustrations in mid-1869 after their eighteenth issue of the year, and the cartoonists ended their sketches with the wounded Andrei in the dressing station at the Battle of Borodino while Anatole Kuragin's leg is amputated.[87] Between the bear and the amputation, *Iskra* presented a visual panoply of twisted scenes from the novel, which the editors described as "*War and Peace*: a literary-graphic potpourri composed of the works of various authors: Count Tolstoy, Homer, Kheraskov, Ovid, Et Al."[88] Pierre's oversized face looms over Hélène and stares down her large bosom; Pierre, like a "cursed bear" chases Hélène with a board; Prince Bolkonsky sports a belly that rivals that of Prince Andrei's pregnant wife. Where Tolstoy brings the reader intimately close to the princess by describing "her pretty little upper lip, on which a delicate dark down was just perceptible," *Iskra* gave her a real moustache, with the caption, "An unusual gift from the author is given to her [*Dar neobychnyi ot avtora dan ei*]."[89] Military terms are matched with funny pictures: "storming" (*shturm*) becomes soldiers rushing a liquor store, "reconnoitering" is a solider grabbing a woman, "casualties" are prostrate drunks, and "state of siege" is shown to be locals of various sorts, including a Pole and a Jew, presumably demanding payment for provisions. The last two cartoons *Iskra* published show a turn to the carnivalesque. In one, Andrei, armed and dangerous, flies through the air chasing Anatole. In the other, he clutches Anatole's boot with the amputated leg still in it.

This was more than satire. A broad and varied comic sensibility had migrated from popular and folk culture to *War and Peace* and then back to popular culture in a reversal of Tolstoy's seriousness. Compare *Iskra's* comic images with M. S. Bashilov's illustrations for the novel in 1866, the first few of which Tolstoy approved.[90] Bashilov (1821–70), a relative of Tolstoy's wife's, never completed the series, but his quaintly realistic and flattering images of the characters have nothing of the grotesque about them. He shows Pierre of ordinary size, though chubby, Dolokhov as charming though unsteady on the window sill, and the women dignified almost to a fault, including Hélène, who stares innocently at the reader in a picture of her beside Pierre. Bashilov ignored the bear and the policeman, though whether he would have included them if his health had not failed and he had completed the series, no one can say.

The critic Iampol'skii stressed in his 1928 essay that the cartoons were "not empty mockery [*ne pustoe zuboskalstvo*]" but a serious critique of the world of the nobility.[91] That Iampol'skii writing in 1928 would politicize the humor was understandable. He was right but captured only a narrow slice of the import of *Iskra's* satire. Henri Bergson in his classic essay on humor stressed "the *social* signification" of laughter—that is, that humor must be linked with life and must suggest "an intellectual contrast" between what is in and what is out of place.[92] This is how the cartoonists interpreted the incident with the bear.[93] Their caption hit the mark: "If fate had not determined that the corner policeman would float down the Fontanka on the bear, much would be different in the world." The cartoonist challenged Tolstoy's fatalism and historical determinism with humor and suggested that infinite possibilities presented alternative directions for the events and characters, an idea that Tolstoy encompassed in the novel.[94] There is also a hint of irony here, since the plausibility of one implausible event implied the plausibility of others.

The cartoonists lampooned the aristocracy with a ferocity and grotesqueness that plumbed below the surface layers of satire and reached a more profound and subversive questioning of life in Russia and the human condition more generally. In this Tolstoy's harsh critics writing and drawing in *Iskra* paradoxically came full circle and met the author on his own ground. They treated Tolstoy, the greatest artistic genius of his day, unapproachable by mere scribblers, much as Tolstoy treated the established order in *War and Peace*. Through their cartoons, they tied Tolstoy to a bear and tossed him into the Moika. They thus fully employed the subversive power of laughter to suggest a counterreality, or a possibility of something other than or in addition to what actually is. The humorists at *Iskra* seized upon this idea of duality in their representation of the policeman and the bear, as well as of Dolokhov drinking his rum.[95]

Is this, or was this, funny? *War and Peace* is profoundly humorous and was so in its day, but it is only rarely funny. Recognition of the comic element unites the work more fully with its contemporaries and provides further insight into how it created waves and echoes in Russia's wider cultural life at the time. In Tolstoy's hand, even levity became greatness. Tolstoy's improbable humor in an age of realistic representation is a reminder of the connections between high and low imaginative forms, as well as of the fact that his generation remained in touch with the traditions of early modern Russia.

NOTES

I thank Edyta Bojanowska, Karen Brooks, Georgiy Chernyavskiy, Barbara Engel, Larry May, and Inessa Medzhibovskaya for their helpful comments. An earlier version in Russian appeared as Jeffrey Brooks, "Neozhidannyi Tolstoi: Lev i medved'; Iumor v *Voine i mire*," *Novoe literaturnoe obozrenie* 109 (Summer 2011): 151–71.

1. For another essay on humor in Tolstoy, see James Rice, "Comic Devices in *The Death of Ivan Ilich*," *Slavic and East European Journal* 47, no. 1 (2003): 77–95.

2. See, for example, Jane Costlow, "'For the Bear to Come to Your Threshold': Human-Bear Encounters in Late Imperial Russian Writing," in *Other Animals: Beyond the Human in Russian Culture and History*, ed. Jane Costlow and Amy Nelson, 77–94 (Pittsburgh: University of Pittsburgh Press, 2010). Pierre's bear does not appear in the rest of the volume either. Vladimir Propp also omitted Pierre and the bear from his chapter "Humans Disguised as Animals," in *On the Comic and Laughter*, ed. and trans. Jean-Patrick Debbèche and Paul Perron, 46–50 (Toronto: University of Toronto Press, 2009). Victor Shklovsky ignores the incident in V. Shklovsky, *Material i stil' v romane L'va Tolstogo Voina i mir* [Material and style in Lev Tolstoy's novel *War and Peace*] (Moscow: Federatsiia, 1928).

3. I discuss this and some other issues in Tolstoy's work in more detail in Brooks, "Neozhidannyi Tolstoi."

4. On the negativity of Gogol and Ostrovsky, see Propp, *On the Comic*, 109.

5. Propp, *On the Comic*, 119.

6. This included the complete play *Zarazhennoe semeistvo* (1864), which was not performed in his time, and the unpublished sketch "Nigilist" (1866) (*SS* 11:593).

7. On the serious character of such departures by Gogol and Dostoevsky, see Dina Khapaeva, *Koshmar: Literatura i zhizn'* [Nightmare: Literature and life] (Moscow: Tekst, 2010).

8. The River Moika is linked with the Fontanka River and encircles part of the central region of the city of Saint Petersburg in the form of a canal.

9. On banditry and rebellion as they relate to Tolstoy in more scholarly detail, see Jeffrey Brooks, "How Tolstoevskii Pleased Readers and Rewrote a Russian Myth," *Slavic Review* 64, no. 3 (Fall 2005): 538–59, and Jeffrey Brooks, "Il romanzo popolare: Dalle storie di briganti al realismo socialista" [The popular novel: From the bandit stories to socialist realism] in *Le forme* [The Forms], vol. 2 of *Il romanzo* [The Novel], ed. Franco Moretti (Torino: Einaudi, 2002), 447–69.

10. There is a long tradition in art of representing humans as part animal. See Martin Kemp, *The Human Animal in Western Art and Science* (Chicago: University of Chicago Press, 2007).

11. Jean-Jacques Rousseau, *Confessions*, ed. Christopher Kelly, Roger D. Masters, and Peter G. Stillman, trans. Christopher Kelly (Hanover, N.H.: University Press of New England, 1995), 526.

12. Jacques Derrida, *The Beast and the Sovereign: Volume 1*, ed. Michel Lisse, Marie-Louise Mallet, and Ginette Michaud, trans. Geoffrey Bennington (Chicago: University of Chicago Press, 2009), 1:14–15.

13. On shared humanity, see Derrida, *The Beast*, 97–114.

14. Nikolai Nekrasov, ed., *Petersburg: The Physiology of a City*, trans. Thomas Gaiton Marullo (Evanston, Ill.: Northwestern University Press, 2009), 301–2. Vissarion Belinsky, Vladimir Dal', and other literary figures of the time also contributed to the volume.

15. Dominic Lieven, *The Aristocracy in Europe, 1815–1914* (New York: Columbia University Press, 1992), 139.

16. *Budil'nik* 6 (1866): 24.

17. The use of a rough Polish or Ukrainian rather than ordinary Russian and of "Pan" may have evoked the 1863 Polish uprising and hence reaffirmed with some readers' notions of order and control within the empire.

18. On Tolstoy's pride as an aristocrat, see Aleksei Zverev and Vladimir Tunimanov, *Lev Tolstoy* (Moscow: Molodaia gvardiia, 2006), 222.

19. Tolstoy writes in his journal on June 15, 1854, "Exactly the interval of three months—three months of idleness [*prazdnosti*] and of a life that cannot satisfy me" (47:3).

20. Shklovsky develops the concept further in *Material i stil'*, 109–10.

21. See the discussion on the translation of the term by Benjamin Sher, "Translator's Introduction: Shklovsky and the Revolution," in *Theory of Prose*, by Viktor Shklovsky, trans. Benjamin Sher (Elmwood Park, Ill.: Dalkey Archive Press, 1990), 18–19.

22. Shklovsky, *Material i stil'*, 71–75.

23. Viktor Shklovsky, *Tetiva: O neskhodstve skhodnogo* [Bowstring: On the dissimilarity of the similar] (Moscow: Sovetskii pisatel', 1970), 230.

24. Shklovsky, *Tetiva*, 91.

25. Shklovsky's *Material i stil'* ignores the incident and does not reproduce *Iskra*'s cartoon of the policeman tied to the bear. Many of the humorous cartoons included by Shklovsky are characterized chiefly by their psychological and descriptive suggestiveness. See especially the illustration and commentary in *Material i stil'* following page 92.

26. Note Shklovsky's explanation beneath the picture: "We see from this caricature how palpable Tolstoy's details are" (*Material i stil'*, 93).

27. Viktor Shklovsky, *Third Factory*, ed. and trans. Richard Sheldon (Ann Arbor, Mich.: Ardis, 1977), 57, points to Leskov's usage in *Steel Flea*: "*Skaz* makes it possible to implement a second, ironic perception of a seemingly patriotic story." Gogol used irony in this manner with respect to the Russian

nation, as pointed out in Edyta M. Bojanowska, *Nikolai Gogol: Between Ukrainian and Russian Nationalism* (Cambridge, Mass.: Harvard University Press, 2007), 221–33. Tolstoy did as well with respect to religion in *War and Peace*, as Inessa Medzhibovskaya points out in *Tolstoy and the Religious Culture of His Time: A Biography of a Long Conversion, 1845–1887* (Lanham, Md.: Lexington Books, 2008), 87.

28. On this aspect of humor, see Jure Gantar, *The Pleasure of Fools: Essays in the Ethics of Laughter* (Montreal: McGill-Queens University Press, 2005), 112–29.

29. Sigmund Freud, *The Future of an Illusion, Civilization and Its Discontents, and Other Works*, trans. James Strachey et al. (London: Hogarth Press, 1961), 161.

30. Mikhail Lemke, *Ocherki po istorii russkoi tsenruzy i zhurnalistiki XIX stoletiia* [Essays on the history of Russian censorship and journalism in the nineteenth century] (Saint Petersburg: Trud, 1904), 77, 79. Many such cartoons appear in 1859, though fewer after the Emancipation of 1861, when censorship tightened.

31. *Iskra* 14 (1863): 200. The cartoon is signed at the top by Ia. Ia. Gromov and under the picture of the wedding party by N. Kurenkov.

32. The literature on holy fools is large. See Sergey A. Ivanov, *Holy Fools in Byzantium and Beyond* (Oxford: Oxford University Press, 2006), chapters 9–12, and A. M. Panchenko, "Smekh kak zrelishche" [Laughter as spectacle], in *Smekhovoi mir drevnei Rusi* [The world of laughter of old Rus'], by D. S. Likhachev and A. M. Panchenko, 91–194 (Moscow: Nauka, 1976). Ewa M. Thompson, *Understanding Russia: The Holy Fool in Russian Culture* (Lanham, Md.: University Press of America, 1987), 126–40, suggests that Pierre has elements of the holy fool. Tolstoy was well attuned to the popular culture of his time, including holy fools, as noted in Medzhibovskaya, *Tolstoy and Religious Culture*, 11–12.

33. Andrei Sinyavsky, *Ivan the Fool: Russian Folk Belief; A Cultural History*, ed. Natasha Perova and Joanne Turnbull, trans. Joanne Turnbull (Moscow: Glas, 2007).

34. See stories and anecdotes about bears in Tolstoy's *Novaia azbuka* [New ABC] and books 1 and 2 of *Russkie knigi dlia chteniia* [First and second Russian readers]. Tolstoy's educational books *Azbuka* (1872), *Novaia azbuka* (1874–75), and four books of *Russkie knigi dlia chteniia* (1874–75) were published in 1957 in *The Jubilee*, volumes 21 and 22, overseen by V. S. Spiridonov and V. S. Mishin. See *Novaia azbuka* and *Russkie knigi dlia chteniia*, 21:2–100 and 102–329, respectively, and especially on bears, 21:114, 357–58, 391, 432. Of special interest is "Medved' na povozke" (A bear on a cart), 21:157.

35. On bears in Russian culture, see Sergei Korolev, "Mif o medvede: Sovremennaia politika vozvrashchaetsya k arkhetipam" [The myth of the bear: Contemporary politics returns to the archetypes], http://sergeikorolev.sitecity.ru/ltext _1602035726.phtml?p_ident=ltext_1602035726.p_0105010644.

36. See "The Crimean War: Turkey and the Russian Bear," part of the on-line exhibit "The Crimean War in the French and British Satirical Press" at the Brandeis University Library website, http://lts.brandeis.edu/research/archives -speccoll/exhibits/crimeanwar/TurkeyBear.html. It is less apparent when Russians adopted the bear as a symbol of the nation.

37. Costlow, "'For the Bear,'" 77–79, describes bears in Russian tradition and the 1866 Imperial Edict on Bear Comedies that banned bear training.

38. See Sinyavsky, *Ivan the Fool*, 102–3, for this and the following observations on bears in Russian folklore.

39. Sinyavsky, *Ivan the Fool*, 103. For one such folktale, "Masha and the Bear," see *Russkie narodnye skazki o zhivotnykh, volshebnye i bytovye: Sbornik skazok dlia chteniia* [Russian folktales about animals—magical and domestic: A collected reader of fairy tales], http://hyaenidae.narod.ru/story1/038.html; for a story about a bear-tsar, see A. N. Afanasiev, *Narodnye russkie skazki A. N. Afanasieva* (Russian folktales [collected by] A. N. Afanasiev), ed. A. G. Barag and N. V. Novikov, 3 vols. (Moscow: Nauka, 1986), 2:74–77.

40. Propp, *On the Comic*, 46.

41. Quoted in Propp, *On the Comic*, 47.

42. On popular theater, see N. Dmitrievskii, *Teatr i zriteli: Otechestvennyi teatr v sisteme otnoshenii stseny i publiki; Ot istokov do nachala XX veka* [Theater and spectators: Homeland theater in the system of relations between the scene and the public; From the origins to the beginning of the twentieth century] (Saint Petersburg: Dmitrii Bulanin, 2007), 60–65; on the broader context, see Likhachev and Panchenko, *Smekhovoi mir drevnei Rusi*.

43. On fools of all sorts, including this one, see Enid Welsford, *The Fool: His Social and Literary History* (London: Faber and Faber, 1935).

44. I describe the evocation of this world of rebellion by Tolstoy and Dostoevsky in Brooks, "How Tolstoevskii Pleased Readers," 538–59, and, in popular fiction, in Jeffrey Brooks, *When Russia Learned to Read: Literacy and Popular Literature, 1861–1917* (Evanston, Ill.: Northwestern University Press, 2003), 166–213.

45. Francis Maes, *A History of Russian Music: From "Kamarinskaia" to "Babi Yar,"* trans. Arnold J. Pomerans and Erica Pomerans (Berkeley: University of California Press, 2006), 221–23.

46. Dostoevsky evoked this tradition in *Notes from the House of the Dead* in describing the prisoners' dramatic performances of *Filatka and Miroshka* and *Kedril the Glutton*. See "The Theatricals," in *"The House of the Dead" and "Poor Folk,"* by Fyodor Dostoevsky, trans. Constance Garnett, 149–67 (New York: Barnes and Noble, 2004). For an overview of Russian cultural tradition and humor, see A. S. Kargin, A. V. Kostina, and N. A. Khrenov, eds., *Chelovek smeiushchiisia: Sbornik nauchnykh statei* [The laughing man (homo ridens): A collection of scholarly articles] (Moscow: Ministerstvo Kul'tury Rossiiskoi Federatsii, 2008).

Jeffrey Brooks

47. Katerina Clark and Michael Holquist, *Mikhail Bakhtin* (Cambridge, Mass.: Harvard University Press, 1984), note Bakhtin's orientation toward Soviet experience. As N. A. Pan'kov, *Voprosy biografii i nauchnogo tvorchestva M. M. Bakhtina* [Questions of biography and the creative scholarship of M. M. Bakhtin] (Moscow: Izdatel'stvo Moskovskogo universiteta, 2010), 362–77, points out, Bakhtin identified Rabelais with "unofficial culture" and folklore more generally, including Gogol in Russia.

48. M. T. Riumina, "O mirosozertsatel'nykh smyslakh karnaval'noi kul'tury" [On the meanings of the worldview of carnival culture], in Kargin, Kostina, and Khrenov, *Chelovek smeiushchiisia*, 78–88; see also Charles Taylor, *A Secular Age* (Cambridge, Mass.: Harvard University Press, 2007), 45–61. Taylor (54–55) emphasizes the place of humor in the creation of an antiworld opposed to the existing order.

49. D. A. Rovinskii, *Russkiia narodnyia kartinki* [Russian popular prints], ed. N. P. Sobko, 2 vols. (Saint Petersburg: P. Golike, 1900), 2:85–114.

50. On these tensions, see Brooks, "How Tolstoevskii Pleased Readers," 538–59.

51. *Iskra* 7 (1869): 86; *Iskra* 9 (1869): 111.

52. *Iskra* 17 (1869): 203.

53. Iurii M. Lotman, "The Decembrist in Daily Life (Everyday Behavior as a Historical-Psychological Category)," in *The Semiotics of Russian Cultural History: Essays*, ed. Alexander D. Nakhimovsky and Alice Stone Nakhimovsky (Ithaca, N.Y.: Cornell University Press, 1985), 124.

54. I. V. Kondakov, "'Dveri smekha': Dialog smekha so strakhom" [Doors of laughter: Dialogue between laughter and fear], in Kargin, Kostina, and Khrenov, *Chelovek smeiushchiisia*, 119–55.

55. Mikhail Bakhtin, *Rabelais and His World*, trans. Hélène Iswolsky (Bloomington: Indiana University Press, 1984), 87–91.

56. Bakhtin, *Rabelais*, 90–91.

57. I. N. Paltusova, ed., *Torgovaia reklama i upakovka v Rossii XIX–XX vv.* [Commercial advertising and packaging in Russia of the nineteenth and twentieth centuries] (Moscow: GIM, 1993), 54. On clowns, children, and women, see 16, 25, 52–53.

58. I discuss this in Brooks, "How Tolstoevskii Pleased Readers," 538–59; see also the entries "volia" and "svoboda" by Vladimir Soloviev in *Entsiklopedicheskii slovar'* [Encyclopedic dictionary], ed. F. A. Brokgauz and I. A. Efron, 86 vols. (Saint Petersburg: Semenovskaia tipografiia I. A. Efrona, 1890–1907), 7: 174–75, 29:163–69, respectively.

59. Vladimir Dal', *Tolkovyi slovar' zhivogo velikorusskogo iazyka* [Thesaurus of the spoken language of Greater Russia], ed. I. A. Boduen de Kurtene et al., 4 vols. (Moscow: Progress/Univers, 1994); see "vlast'" (1:522), "volia" (1:584–87), and "pravo" (3:990–91). In Soviet-era dictionaries published in the USSR,

154

vlast' is normally associated first with the state but also with a certain freedom of action, as in colloquial expressions like "the choice is yours" or "it's up to you" (*vasha vlast'*).

60. Vladimir Dal', *Poslovitsy russkogo naroda* [Proverbs of the Russian people], 2 vols. (Moscow: Khudozhestvennaia literatura 1984), 1:192.

61. Dal', *Poslovitsy russkogo naroda*, 1:189.

62. Dal', *Poslovitsy russkogo naroda*, 2:277–79. The Russian word used in each proverb is *volia*.

63. A. M. Panchenko, "Laughter as Spectacle," trans. Priscilla Hunt, Svitlana Kobets, and Bethany Braley, in *Holy Foolishness in Russia: New Perspectives*, ed. Priscilla Hunt and Svitlana Kobets (Bloomington: Indiana University Press, 2011), 108.

64. The range of sardonic and critical comments with humorous implications is extensive. A recent and stimulating survey is Lev Sobelev, "*War and Peace* as Read by Contemporaries," *Russian Studies in Literature* 45, no. 4 (Fall 2000): 7–61, translated from *Voprosy literatury* 6 (2007): 179–224.

65. D. I. Pisarev, "Staroe barstvo ('Voina i mir,' sochinenie grafa L. N. Tolstogo)" [The old nobility (*War and Peace*, the work by count L. N. Tolstoy], in *Roman L. N. Tolstogo "Voina i Mir" v russkoi kritike* [The novel *War and Peace* by L. N. Tolstoy in Russian criticism], 59–85 (Leningrad: Izdatel'stvo Leningradskogo Universiteta, 1989). The translation is from Leo Tolstoy, *War and Peace: The Maude Translation, Backgrounds and Sources, Criticism*, ed. and trans. George Gibian, 2nd ed. (New York: Norton, 1996), 1099.

66. S. Navalikhin [V. V. Bervi-Flerovskii], "Sovremennoe obozrenie: Iziashchnyi romanist i ego iziashchnye kritiki; 'Voyna i mir,' roman grafa Tolstogo" [A contemporary review: highbrow novelist and his highbrow critics: *War and Peace*, the novel by count Tolstoy], *Delo: Zhurnal literaturno-politicheskiy* 6 (1868): 4. See also Sobelev, "*War and Peace*," 21.

67. N. Gusev, *Letopis' zhnizni i tvorchestva L'va Tolstogo* [The chronology of the life and creative work of Lev Tolstoy] (Moscow: Gosizdat, 1958), 346.

68. I think Zverev and Tunimanov, *Tolstoy*, 226–27, have this right.

69. I. Iampol'skii, "Voina i mir L. Tolstogo v parodiiakh i karikaturakh" [*War and Peace* of L. Tolstoy in parodies and caricatures], *Zvezda* 9 (1928): 93–113. Page 98 provides an incomplete listing of satirical articles and cartoons in *Iskra*.

70. A. G. Dement'ev, A. V. Zapadov, and M. S. Cherepakhov, eds., *Russkaia periodicheskaia pechat' (1702–1894): Spravochnik* [Russian periodic press (1702–1894): A reference guide] (Moscow: Gospolitizdat, 1959), 376.

71. Dement'ev, Zapadov, and Cherepakhov, *Russkaia periodicheskaia pechat'*, 252.

72. If *Punch* is any guide, such comic magazines were a direct conduit from oral to print culture. See Patrick Leary, *The Punch Brotherhood: Table Talk and Print Culture in Mid-Victorian London* (London: British Library, 2010).

73. M. P. Mokhnacheva, ed., *Russkii illiustrirovannyi zhurnal 1703–1941* [The Russian illustrated journal 1703–1941] (Moscow: Agey Tomesh, 2006), 25–27.

74. Dement'eva, Zapadov, and Cherepakhov, *Russkaia periodicheskaia pechat'*, 424–25.

75. On *Iskra*, see also A. V. Zapadov, ed., *Istoriia russkoi zhurnalistiki XVIII–XIX vekov* [The history of Russian journalism in the eighteenth and nineteenth centuries] (Moscow: Vysshaia shkola, 1973), http://www.library.cjes.ru/online/?a=con&b_id=379&c_id=3870.

76. See the entry "Iskra" in *Literaturnaia Entsiklopediia*, ed. P. I. Lebedev-Polyansky et al., 11 vols. (Moscow: Izd-vo Kommunisticheskoi Akademii, 1929–39), http://feb-web.ru/feb/litenc/encyclop/le4/le4-5831.htm.

77. See the entry "Kurochkin" in *Literaturnaia Entsiklopediia*, http://feb-web.ru/feb/litenc/encyclop/le5/le5-7541.htm.

78. See the entry "Iskra" in *Literaturnaia Entsiklopediia*, http://feb-web.ru/feb/litenc/encyclop/le4/le4-5831.htm.

79. Shklovsky, *Material i stil'*, 206–19, discusses the use of French but does not address the issue of whether readers found it off-putting, even though in 1873 Tolstoy provided translations into Russian of most of the French text in the novel.

80. I discuss the "reader friend" in Jeffrey Brooks, "Readers and Reading at the End of the Tsarist Era," in *Literature and Society in Imperial Russia*, ed. William Mills Todd, 97–150 (Stanford, Calif.: Stanford University Press, 1978).

81. Iampol'skii, "Voina i mir L. Tolstogo," 113.

82. *Iskra* 12 (1868): 144.

83. *Iskra* 14 (1868): 171; *Iskra* 15 (1868): 184.

84. *Iskra* 1 (1868): 184.

85. Shklovsky, *Material i stil'*, unnumbered illustration between pages 30 and 31 identifies the cartoon as A. M. Volkov's, who was one of *Iskra*'s regular cartoonists.

86. *Iskra* 16 (1868): 195.

87. This was presumably to avoid prepublication censorship, mandated for periodicals with illustrations.

88. *Iskra* 2 (1869): 23. The cartoon shows Tolstoy under a tree back to back with Kheraskov, author of the late eighteenth-century epic poem *Rossiada*, celebrating the capture of Kazan and other Russian imperial victories. It suggests the glory of empire.

89. *Iskra* 2 (1869): 23.

90. Bashilov's health failed, and the novel appeared without his illustrations. See T. Popovkina and O. Ershova, eds., *Pervyye illiustratory proizvedenii L. N. Tolstogo* [The early illustrators of the works of L. N. Tolstoy] (Moscow: Izobrazitel'noe iskusstvo, 1978), 11–13, figures 1–29.

91. Iampol'skii, "Voina i mir L. Tolstogo," 111.

92. Wylie Sypher, ed., *Comedy: "An Essay on Comedy" by George Meredith, "Laughter" by Henri Bergson* (Baltimore: Johns Hopkins University Press, 1980), 73; Sigmund Freud, *Jokes and Their Relation to the Unconscious*, trans. and ed. James Strachey (New York: Norton, 1960), 107–46.

93. *Iskra* 4 (1869): 2.

94. On this notion of possibilities, see Gary Saul Morson, *Hidden in Plain View: Narrative and Creative Potentials in "War and Peace"* (Stanford, Calif.: Stanford University Press, 1987), 164–69. I thank Inessa Mezhibovskaya for thoughts about these captions.

95. *Iskra* 4 (1869): 2. See note 8 in this chapter. Although Tolstoy has the policeman sent floating down the River Moika in the finished text of the novel, in drafts of the book he had entertained the idea that it could have been the River Fontanka. It is unclear whether Znamensky's mention of the Fontanka was inspired by his possible acquaintance with Tolstoy's work-in-the-making. Known otherwise as the "Venice of the North," St. Petersburg uses its rivers—the Neva, the Big Nevka, the Little Nevka, and the Fontanka—for naval, passenger, and commercial thoroughfare purposes. All of these rivers are connected by channels and an intricate network of canals. It is therefore not surprising that a guest at the Rostovs' relating the anecdote about the policeman and the bear and the Znamensky sketch would have remembered different rivers.

Daniel Moulin-Stożek

Five Principles of Tolstoy's Educational Thought

TOLSTOY LOVED LEARNING, but in many ways he despised scholarship. It therefore risks self-contradiction to suggest that Tolstoy made an unacknowledged but relevant contribution to educational theory. One defining feature of Tolstoy's educational thought—evident throughout his entire oeuvre—is his antipathy toward pedagogues, educational theories, and, not least, universities and their staff. A particularly vehement attack on higher education is given in his 1862 essay "Training and Education" (Vospitanie i obrazovanie).[1] At the university you seldom see "anyone with a healthy, fresh face," Tolstoy writes, the students are "emaciated . . . cigarette smoking, wine drinking, self-confident, and self-complacent" (304); whereas any lecturer fits within just four categories: the stupid but hardworking, the capable but out of date, the corrupt and self-interested, and the fourth and last kind, "the laughing stock of the entire human race, who has been reading out his barbarously written notes for thirty years without stopping" (312).

Tolstoy's disillusionment with university education was founded in his own failed, negative experiences of university, and a comparable negative portrayal of university life is given in *Youth* (*Iunost'*) (1855–157). But by criticizing university scholars, Tolstoy was not referring to the kind of education offered by the innovative institutions he predicted would emerge a hundred years later that would provide "freedom for the generation that is studying" (325). Nevertheless, Tolstoy did mean to attack traditional and elite universities such as Oxford—which he names in "Training and Education" as a good example of an institution whose educative value is yet to be proven. Such universities were for Tolstoy unacceptable bastions of privilege and nepotism that did not cater to the true needs of society but only served the interests of the upper class.

Few would doubt that educational institutions have improved worldwide since Tolstoy's death in 1910. Certainly, the corporal punishment, learning by rote, and enforced catechesis of pupils that Tolstoy abhorred when he toured European schools in 1861 have been rescinded in most countries. Yet many of the problems of education that Tolstoy set out to answer beginning in the 1860s persist despite the ongoing attempts of educators: inequality in education between the social classes; disaffection of children with regard to learning; "coercion" of one form or another; focusing on exams rather than learning; the mal-influence of ideologies, bureaucrats, and governments. It is therefore germane to reconsider what insights into education the great writer can offer us for the twenty-first century. In this essay, rather than presenting a historical or literary analysis, I take on this ambitious task by outlining five key principles of Tolstoy's educational thought likely to be of enduring relevance to the field of education. But before I set these out, I first comment on the reception of Tolstoy's educational writings in the English-speaking world and emphasize some important parts of Tolstoy's overall worldview that are also foundational to his educational thought.

REEXAMINING TOLSTOY THE EDUCATOR

Education was evidently one of Tolstoy's lifelong interests, inextricably linked to his evolution as an artist and thinker, but in the past hundred years this has all too often gone unnoticed, and his views have often been distorted. Richard Gustafson suggested in 1996 that to understand Tolstoy in the twenty-first century, we would need to reappraise the reception of his works because "much of what we think about Tolstoy is based on interpretations by people who were less than objective and often unsympathetic, if not down-right hostile."[2]

And although Gustafson was not referring to it specifically, the reception of Tolstoy's educational views by English-speaking educationists has been especially poor. This is because most accounts and translations of Tolstoy's educational writings are partial and biased and, moreover, are often largely unreceptive to Tolstoy's religious perspective on education.

A common mistake among those Anglophone educationists who read Tolstoy in the twentieth century, with few exceptions,[3] is the assumption that Tolstoy's pedagogical articles of the 1860s were the beginning and end of Tolstoy's work in the field of education[4]—whereas in fact just as Tolstoy was preoccupied with religious and moral questions his whole life, he was also often pursuing educational ones. Tolstoy's periods of teaching were indeed short and resulted in burnout, but it is clear that the premature end of the Yasnaya Polyana school in 1863 was precipitated by the police raid in the summer recess of 1862, not only by his uninterest in education in favor of literature. The raid enraged Tolstoy because, as he wrote in protest to the tsar, his "chosen occupation" was "the founding of schools for the people" (TL, 1:164). And plainly, after marrying and writing War and Peace, Tolstoy again took up this vocation in earnest, first drafting the Azbuka in 1868.

It follows that the texts relevant to Tolstoy's educational thought are much more considerable than those traditionally referred to in much of the Anglophone literature, and some are yet to be translated. The *ABC* (*Azbuka*), *New ABC* (*Novaia azbuka*), and *Russian Books for Reading* (*Russkie knigi dlia chteniia*);[5] the 1875 restatement of his views in the second essay titled "On Popular Education";[6] and his late essay "On Upbringing"[7] are of course the obvious omissions from those commonly presented, in English at least, in many of the most popular editions, from Crosby in 1904[8] to Archambault in the 1960s[9] and Blaisdell[10] in 2000. But in addition to these texts that are needed to understand Tolstoy as an educator, much of Tolstoy's correspondence, many of his diary and notebook entries, his religious essays, and one of his last major works, usually translated into English as *A Cycle of Reading* (*Krug chteniya*), are all essential to understanding his views on education.[11]

Besides these writings, while always controversial among scholars, much of Tolstoy's fiction is obviously relevant to his views on education. Eikhenbaum tells us that both *War and Peace* and *Anna Karenina* grew out of his educational endeavors. Indeed, elements of Tolstoy's entire corpus show a great deal of evidence about his lengthy ponderings over the whys and hows of education. Much of *Childhood, Boyhood, and Youth* is given over to the young protagonist's experiences of education. *The Cossacks*, *War and Peace*, *Anna Karenina*, and *Resurrection* include references and lengthier discussions concerning formal education. Moreover, all of Tolstoy's great novels are centered upon the way characters learn, respond to, and are formed by their experiences as they negotiate themselves through major life events, and the inner realizations that result from them—a kind of analysis of education by life that one commentator has suggested shows a remarkable resonance with the philosophy of John Dewey.[12]

To understand Tolstoy's educational thought, it is important that we draw upon a comprehensive engagement with his writings. A more thorough understanding of Tolstoy's worldview and his attitude to intellectual inquiry enables an understanding of his educational thought. Before setting out five key aspects of Tolstoy's educational thought, therefore, I emphasize some important aspects of Tolstoy's worldview that relate to education, learning, and children—what I call, and indeed what Tolstoy referred to as, the wisdom of children—a discussion of which takes us back to his criticism of scholarship and formal education.

THE WISDOM OF CHILDREN

In all his lifelong interest in education—as it was for religion and philosophy—Tolstoy was interested in truth not pedantry. For example, in his diary in his later years he records his despair at pointless academic discourse, writing, "Man doesn't know what is good and what is bad, but he writes a research paper on a fallen aerolite or the origin of the word 'cowl'" (*TD*, 2:573). However, I must stress that Tolstoy's criticism of scholarship was not a dismissal of all intellectual activity, nor of strenuous thought or debate. Neither was he, in the field of education, opposed to what we would now call educational research. Rather, Tolstoy's attack on the academy was directed against those who obscured and concealed truth rather than searched for it.

Tolstoy's conception of truth was spiritual and moral, and the foundational truths he came to endorse were those of Christianity: love of God and of neighbor; of compassion and goodwill—truths he believed were natural, simple, and easily recognizable but often perverted.[13] Tolstoy was keenly aware of institutions'—particularly the Church and government and their agencies, including schools and universities—capabilities of corrupting the original, simple message of Christianity while purporting to hold and promote eternal religious truths. Such views are expressed in their most heated form perhaps in Tolstoy's late fable "The Destruction and Restoration of Hell" (Razrushenie ada i vosstanovlenie ego, 1902–3). Tolstoy tells us how the truth of Christ's message has been corrupted—the devils of education and science have all played their part in this—and consequently pedantry has overtaken truth as the pursuit of study: theology has become an enterprise with which to absorb men so they would not "think about how to live," and philosophy has become just the study of "everything written by a man called Aristotle."[14]

Tolstoy's view of intellectual inquiry and scholarship is reflected in his fiction. The famous revelations of Levin in *Anna Karenina* serve as a good example of this. Levin, in his existential crisis, rereads the great philosophers Plato, Spinoza, Kant, Schelling, Hegel, and Schopenhauer only to find his questions better answered in the following days by a casual conversation with a serf, Feodor. Levin is excited by the peasant's effortless articulation of life's meaning, given as though it were a truth that everyone already knows— the meaning of life being "plain enough . . . living rightly, in God's way."[15]

But how is knowledge of "living rightly" to be determined? This was Tolstoy's lifelong quest and was at the heart of his educational and religious inquiry. Interestingly, for Tolstoy the answer to this question was to be found in consultation with children. The wisdom of children—not just the title of one of Tolstoy's very last works ("Detskaya mudrost'," a series of dialogues written in 1909 [37:309–47]) but the view it enshrines—resonates on a number of levels with Tolstoy's thought. Tolstoy believed that the child's voice should play a large part in determining pedagogical practice, but he also believed that a child's intuition was useful in determining spiritual truths for the use of adults. This is clearly demonstrated in his method of writing "The Teaching of Christ Abridged for Children" (Uchenie Khrista, izlozhennoe dlia detei, 1907–8),[16] which was written in consultation with a group of village children. Going back forty-five years from that late work, it is clear that Tolstoy learned many things from his profound experiences in the Yasnaya Polyana classroom: not just how to write, as he explains in the famous article "Should We Teach the Peasant Children to Write, or Should They Teach Us" (1862),[17] but also about the power of the Bible on children's imagination and the sacred act of teaching itself. At the time, he wrote to Countess Alexandra that the school had been his "monastery" and "church" (*TL*, 1:160).

The most lyrical account of his belief in the intuition of children is given in Tolstoy's parable "Little Girls Wiser Than Old Men"[18]—the theme of which is taken from Matthew 18:3: "Truly I tell you, unless you change and become like children you will never enter the kingdom of heaven." This verse, and the parable Tolstoy wrote around it, resonates with the belief at the heart of Tolstoy's entire religious and educational thought, and probably his literature too—the natural moral law. Truth and goodness are obvious and easy to understand but often ignored. And neatly, it is on such a premise that his late short stories operate—for how else can a parable work heuristically? It must "tap in" to a moral consciousness that already exists. Tolstoy assumes that a short story can reveal a great truth only if this truth is already known, at least partially, by the reader.

For Tolstoy, then, to establish what is right, as it is to transform spiritually as an adult, is to peel back the lies and deceit promulgated around us, to find those residual truths that we have always known deep down: to, in a sense, return to a childlike state. (And we see many episodes and accounts of this in his literature.) Furthermore, it would also seem that Tolstoy employed a method based on such assumptions in determining how to teach. The needs, volitions, and voices of children become his educator, as so artfully described in the essays of the *Yasnaya Polyana* journal.

FIVE KEY PRINCIPLES OF TOLSTOY'S EDUCATIONAL THOUGHT

In order to present an overall summary of Tolstoy's educational thought, I give five key principles that underlie his writings over a forty-year period. These bring together those things that Tolstoy learned as a teacher.[19] With the possible exception of the *Azbuka*, Tolstoy's writings on education are largely axiological in content, not technical. In matters of method Tolstoy is tentative; but he is always insistent upon the values that should saturate the educational transaction. Indeed, perhaps the most abiding lesson Tolstoy learned about teaching was that education is a *moral* enterprise, and indeed it is from this moral standpoint that his criticism of, and "battle" with, the pedagogues of his day was launched.

I summarize Tolstoy's approach by reference to five main categories: the pursuit of truth, the freedom of the learner, spirituality, experiment, and relationship. Implicit in my statement of these is the view that they are as relevant for educators today as they were in Tolstoy's day. But we should proceed with caution: for the study of any of these concepts in Tolstoy's writings could be the subject of a lengthy thesis, and, furthermore, to argue for the importance of any of them in the world of educational research today would require empirical research of what works and what is effective—something that Tolstoy himself realized in his time, too, for it was only through trial and error that the right educational methods could be obtained. As Tolstoy observed, "It is so easy to talk a great deal in this field [education] without convincing anybody!"[20]

The Pursuit of Truth

Tolstoy believed that the curriculum must be based on the pursuit of the truth. But he also believed that this pursuit should be in the form of a free exploration by pupils—not an imposition of someone else's idea of truth. In the days of the Yasnaya Polyana school, he wrote that schools should answer the existential questions that "life poses to [humankind]"[21] while admitting that educators themselves were not in a position of "knowing what it is that a [person] ought to know."[22] The epistemic uncertainty of the human condition was something Tolstoy wished to bring to the classroom and use as a pedagogical prompt. Education should be an investigation of what it means to be human and to live in the world. But these "truths" of life are not to be communicated as exposition but by the spirit of investigation. For Tolstoy a good lesson was like a good story. It should be lovingly told, immediately appeal to the learner's curiosity, then draw the learner in and, by its end, have helped the learner look at the world in a different way. This is evident from the twists in the short stories written for the *Azbuka* and Tolstoy's in-depth descriptions of his lessons. It was Tolstoy's approach to teaching the Bible, and his attempts in teaching composition followed a similar pattern.

The Freedom of the Learner

Throughout Tolstoy's long involvement in education, he argued that freedom was paramount. Tolstoy became involved in education in the early 1860s to ensure the freedom of "the people," and it is no coincidence that the opening of the Yasnaya Polyana school coincided with the emancipation of the serfs. But Tolstoy was aware that—to be truly liberating—education could not just follow the agenda of the Church or government: it must have at its heart the needs, and liberation, of learners. It has been suggested that Tolstoy's view of educational freedom was complete nonintervention[23]— some kind of anarchic freedom from morality and tradition. But this is not true; what Tolstoy desired to achieve was the equality of all social classes' opportunities to think, learn, and grow—to liberate a people from the fetters of history. And to do this, Tolstoy felt freedom should also become part of the pedagogical process. It was the freedom granted to the child that would allow the teacher to understand how to improve their teaching and how a dialogic, consultative process was to be set in place. In addition, it granted the learner conceptual freedom to develop, test, and reevaluate their own growing understanding of the world.

Spirituality

Tolstoy was a spiritual educator in the sense that he championed a progressive religious education that drew its content from all the main religious traditions of the world.[24] For Tolstoy, the passing on of spiritual truths was an essential function of education, and it is exactly on this premise that one of his last major works, *A Cycle of Reading*, is based. Nevertheless, Tolstoy was strongly opposed to any form of religious education that involved the imparting of doctrine to nonconsenting young people. He writes in his diary that when thinking of the source of evil in the world he "became convinced that the root of it all is religious education. And therefore, in order to eliminate evil . . . [it is necessary] to educate children in the true religion" (May 11, 1901; *TD*, 2:495).

It should be remembered that religious education is a multifarious term ranging in scope from enforced catechesis to "comparative religion," to "religious studies," to something else entirely, like Tolstoy's approach, which seeks to introduce children to the core values of all the world's great religious traditions, recognizing them as exceedingly valuable, but without intending to impede upon children's own emerging worldviews. In England and Wales, because of an ecumenical cultural tradition—one that impressed Tolstoy in the nineteenth century—there is compulsory religious education in all state schools that is specifically designed to be of a nonindoctrinatory ilk but to nonetheless engage children with spiritual concerns, a curriculum subject that Tolstoy's views have much to offer.[25] But beyond England, I think Tolstoy's view of religious education has worldwide significance in the twenty-first century: for while Tolstoy embraced the spirit of all the world's great religious traditions, he also wished to transcend the boundaries between them. For Tolstoy, everyone had a religion as he defined it—"as a relationship to the world or its source"[26]—and when he says children should be brought up in the "true religion," Tolstoy does not mean any *particular* religion but rather the correct orientation of the individual to the world and to those who inhabit it, and this orientation is primarily one of fraternity, love, and respect for others—whatever their religion, nationality, or ethnicity. Any education that fails to enhance or promote a positive relationship between the learner and their world is a bad education. And Tolstoy, through all his life's work, wished to promote such a positive relationship among his students—and readers, for that matter. It follows, then, that although Tolstoy's conception of education is, in this sense, spiritual, it presents a radical, broad-minded alternative to either traditional forms of religious education or purely secular approaches—a position that arguably has much to offer our troubled times.

Experiment

At the heart of Tolstoy's approach was his considered and deeply held opinion that there could never be a conclusive method that could capture all a successful educator would need to know and do. This is key to Tolstoy's conception of education, and it overcomes a number of education's ills he identified: the problem of error in educational method; the problem of epistemological uncertainty over the "truths" that we may believe now but may be proven to be false in time; and the innate, unique differences between learners and their motivations. If education could be made "an experiment with the younger generation which constantly yields new conclusions,"[27] then schools would sensitively move in kilter with the needs and knowledge of the time and also be malleable to the needs of each pupil. A positive result of this dynamic approach, Tolstoy reflected, is that teachers would also be continually learning and improving. And in this respect, Tolstoy's process of pedagogical innovation and continual experiment shows itself as a useful educational research paradigm, a model not too dissimilar to the "action research" or "practitioner research" used by many educators today.

Relationship

Along with the importance of continuing experimentation in education, Tolstoy was also astutely aware of the importance of the human relationship between teachers and their students. He writes that the study of education is best conceived as "the study of the conditions in which the . . . tendencies [of the student and teacher] come together into one aim."[28] Indeed, his complaint about university education was that lectures allowed for no dialogue between student and teacher and therefore no "trust and love"[29] to be formed between them.

For a good relationship to be formed between teacher and student, the teacher must always, Tolstoy believed, be principled and live out what they teach in how they relate to their pupils: it was the educator's very character that had the most pedagogic potency. Learners learn by example, and Tolstoy supposed that if the teacher spent time on their own self-perfection, then everything else would fall into place. To explain his view of the correct relationship between learner and educator, Tolstoy used the relationship between mother and child—a metaphor particularly sacred to him. Such an image reinforces the natural impulses that Tolstoy thought should underlie the pedagogic process. He writes, "A mother teaches her child to speak only so that they can understand one another, instinctively the mother tries to come down to . . . [her child's] view of things, to . . . [her child's] language, but the law of forward movement in education does not permit her to come down to . . . [her child], but obliges . . . [her child] to rise to her."[30] This understanding of learning demonstrates Tolstoy's view that genuine education takes place when the natural inquisitiveness of the child is met by the natural inclination of the teacher to raise the child up to their own level, but also that this process best takes place as part of a nurturing and kind, straightforward and loving relationship. This view is reaffirmed throughout many episodes of Tolstoy's literature—for example, in his description of Levin helping Dolly with her children: "Whatever failings Levin had, there was not an atom of pretense in him, and so the children showed him the same friendliness that they read in their mother's face."[31]

○ ○ ○

In suggesting that Tolstoy offers lessons for twenty-first-century educators, I do not mean to advocate a staunch "Tolstoyan" approach in any hagiographic or dogmatic sense. Indeed, given Tolstoy's recognition that times change and pedagogical fads age—and his view that what is really needed is dialogue and consultation with learners—I do not think Tolstoy's views allow for a strong form of application to educational institutions and pedagogical approaches. Rather, what I would like to suggest is that Tolstoy's writings bring to light some timeless pedagogical values that are relevant for educators today.

Tolstoy writes in *A Cycle of Reading* that "if you know the truth, or think you know the truth, pass it on to others as simply as you can, along with the feeling of love toward them."[32] In this sentence, Tolstoy is giving some final advice on teaching that sums up much of the content of this essay, but it is important to note that he is also stating his conclusion to a lifelong career in literature. These two enterprises often intersected in his life, fed on each other, and as he grew older, he came to believe that the purpose of both must have the same spiritual basis. And it is by referring to Tolstoy's literature that I conclude. Let us recall that famous conversation already mentioned between Levin and the peasant Feodor (although there are many other examples that I could draw upon in Tolstoy's literature from *Childhood* to *Resurrection*). Feodor's comments about "living rightly, in God's way" precipitate an epiphany for Levin: "The peasant's words had the effect of an electric spark, suddenly transforming and welding into one a whole series of disjointed, impotent, separate ideas that had never ceased to occupy his mind. They had been in his mind, though he had been unaware of it."[33]

This passage illustrates Tolstoy's view of learning as spiritual transformation—the ultimate goal of education. But it also illustrates how Tolstoy conceived the psychology of learning. Education involves relating the teachings and words of others to our own individual experience. And it is in this spirit that we should approach Tolstoy's educational views in our present century. That is, by a greater interlocution with Tolstoy's work in education, we should recognize and value the principles in them, but only insofar as they relate to our own reconsidered experience and, more important, only because they contribute to, and resound with, the positive experience of children in schools and of learners and educators everywhere.

NOTES

1. Leo Tolstoy, "Training and Education" (1862), in *Tolstoy on Education: Tolstoy's Educational Writings 1861–1862*, ed. A. Pinch and M. Armstrong, trans. A. Pinch (London: Athlone Press, 1982). Subsequent citations to this work appear in the main text as parenthetical page numbers and in endnote citations as "Training and Education." The title of the collection of Tolstoy's essays on education is abbreviated as *Tolstoy's Educational Writings 1861–1862* in further references.

2. Richard F. Gustafson, "Tolstoy and the Twenty-First Century," in *Tolstoy and the Concept of Brotherhood*, ed. A. Donskov and J. Woodsworth, 142–46 (Ottawa: Legas, 1996), 143.

3. D. Murphy, *Tolstoy and Education* (Dublin: Irish Academic Press, 1992), recognizes the importance of religion to Tolstoy's educational views.

4. Three editions of translations of Tolstoy's educational writings have been published: Leo Tolstoy, *Tolstoy on Education*, trans. L. Wiener (Chicago: University of Chicago Press, 1967); Tolstoy, *Tolstoy on Education: Tolstoy's Educational Writings 1861–1862*; and Leo Tolstoy, *Tolstoy as Teacher: Leo Tolstoy's Writings on Education*, ed. B. Blaisdell, trans. C. Edgar (New York: Teachers and Writers Collaborative, 2000). All, however, center on the contents of the Yasnaya Polyana journal of the early 1860s.

5. Tolstoy's educational books *Azbuka* (1872), *Novaia azbuka* (1874–75),

and *Russkie knigi dlia chteniia* (1874–75), 21:102–329, were published in 1957 in *The Jubilee*, volumes 21 and 22, overseen by V. S. Spiridonov and V. S. Mishin. See *Azbuka*, 22:6–787; *Novaia azbuka* and *Russkie knigi dlia chteniia*, 21:2–100 and 101–329 respectively.

6. Leo Tolstoy, "On Popular Education" [O Narodnom Obrazovanii] (1874)," in *The Complete Works of Count Tolstoy*, trans. and ed. L. Wiener, 24 vols. (London: Dent, 1904), 12:251–323.

7. Leo Tolstoy's short essay "On Upbringing" [O Vospitanii] (1909) was published in 1936 in *The Jubilee*, volume 38, overseen by A. I. Nikiforov, B. M. Eikhenbaum, and K. S. Shokhor-Trotsky, pages 62–69, respectively.

8. E. H. Crosby, *Tolstoy as Schoolmaster* (London: Fifield, 1904).

9. Tolstoy, *Tolstoy on Education*.

10. Tolstoy, *Tolstoy as Teacher*.

11. This work has been most recently translated as Leo Tolstoy, *A Calendar of Wisdom*, trans. Peter Sekirin (London: Hodder and Stoughton, 1998).

12. R. Edwards, "Tolstoy and John Dewey: Pragmatism and Prosaics," *TSJ* 5 (1992): 15–37.

13. Tolstoy's religion is a vast and complex topic. In addition to Inessa Medzhibovskaya, *Tolstoy and the Religious Culture of His Time: A Biography of a Long Conversion, 1845–1887* (Lanham, Md.: Lexington Books, 2008) and Richard F. Gustafson, *Leo Tolstoy: Resident and Stranger* (Princeton, N.J.: Princeton University Press, 1986), see D. Moulin, "Tolstoy, Universalism and the World Religions," *Journal of Ecclesiastical History* 68, no. 1 (2017): 570–87, for an analysis of the relationship between Tolstoy's religious thought and Anglo-American religious movements.

14. Aylmer Maude renders the title as "The Restoration of Hell" (1903) in one of the volumes of his centennial translations of Tolstoy's works: Leo Tolstoy, *"On Life" and Essays on Religion*, trans. Aylmer Maude (Oxford: Oxford University Press, 1943), 325.

15. Leo Tolstoy, *Anna Karenina*, trans. R. Edmonds (Harmondsworth, U.K.: Penguin Books, 1978), 829.

16. Leo Tolstoy, "Uchenie Khrista, izlozhennoe dlia detei" [The teaching of Christ abridged for children], translated by Aylmer Maude as "The Teaching of Jesus," in *"On Life" and Essays on Religion*, 346–409.

17. Leo Tolstoy, "Komu u kogo uchit'sia pisat', krestianskim rebiatam u nas ili nam u krestianskikh rebiat?" (1862); 8:301–24.

18. Leo Tolstoy, "Devchonki umnee starikov" (1885); 25:62–63.

19. Daniel Moulin, *Leo Tolstoy*, Bloomsbury Library of Educational Thought (London: Bloomsbury, 2014), gives a lengthier introduction to Tolstoy's educational thought.

20. Leo Tolstoy, "Progress and the Definition of Education" [Progress i opredelenie obrazovaniia] (1862–63), in *Tolstoy on Education*, 181.

21. Leo Tolstoy, "On the Education of the People" [O Narodnom Obrazovanii] (1862), in *Tolstoy's Educational Writings 1861–1862*, 77.

22. Tolstoy, "On the Education of the People," 84.

23. G. H. Bantock, "The Non-Interference of the School: Tolstoy," in *The Minds and the Masses, 1760–1980*, vol. 2 of *Studies in the History of Educational Theory* (London: Allen and Unwin, 1984), 280–308.

24. For a consideration of Tolstoy's thought in comparison with more recent trends in spiritual education, see Daniel Moulin, "Leo Tolstoy the Spiritual Educator," in *International Journal of Children's Spirituality*, vol. 13 (2009), no. 4: 345–53.

25. For an analysis of Tolstoy's contribution to religious education, see Daniel Moulin, "Challenging Christianity: Leo Tolstoy and Religious Education," *Journal of Beliefs and Values* 30, no. 2 (2009): 183–91.

26. "Religion is a certain relation established by man between his separate personality and the infinite universe or its source" (Leo Tolstoy, "Religion and Morality" [Religiia i nravstvennost'] [1893], in *"On Life" and Essays on Religion*, 198).

27. Tolstoy, "On the Education of the People," 76.

28. Tolstoy, "On the Education of the People," 85.

29. Tolstoy, "Training and Education," 314.

30. Tolstoy, "On the Education of the People," 85.

31. Tolstoy, *Anna Karenina*, 288.

32. Tolstoy, *A Calendar of Wisdom*, 123.

33. Tolstoy, *Anna Karenina*, 829.

Tolstoy, Opera, and the Problem of Aesthetic Seduction

IN AN IMPORTANT SCENE in book 2 of *War and Peace*, Natasha Rostova, together with her father and her cousin Sonya, goes to the opera in Moscow. The evening becomes the setting for a fateful encounter between Natasha and Anatole Kuragin, an encounter that turns into an act of proleptic seduction on Kuragin's part and stands as a key juncture in the complex narrative structure of the novel. The episode is remarkable for, among other things, a striking feature of its literary and aesthetic construction: the use of an operatic performance as the backdrop (glimpsed in a somewhat oblique and flickering manner) to the social and psychological drama taking place in Natasha's own life.[1] It is crucial to Natasha's experience in the theater that she is unable to give the opera sustained concentration in its own right, despite her intermittent, partially subliminal awareness of a series of dramatic images—of erotic attraction, seduction, danger, but ultimate escape from evil—which the reader can recognize as ironically relevant to Natasha's own unfolding story. The fascination the opera's imagined world appears to hold for most of the audience singularly fails to take hold of Natasha, although she does exhibit an involuntary physical reaction to the music of the overture under way as the family arrives in its box ("her hand opening and closing, obviously unconsciously, in time with the overture" [*W&P*, 560]). She is too nervously excited about her immediate environment—the social drama playing itself out in the auditorium and the psychological drama of her own confused responses to the heady stimulus of the whole occasion—to be able, or even to want, to become absorbed in the work being sung and acted before her. The potential seductiveness of art is displaced by the threat of seduction in the whole environment and atmosphere in which Natasha finds herself. In fact, Natasha's consciousness of the opera seems to diminish in proportion to her growing fixation with Anatole Kuragin, so that during the opera's final act, in a piquantly symbolic contrast, she registers only one thing on the stage (the singing of a devil, who then falls through a trapdoor) while her eyes are constantly drawn to Kuragin himself.

There are several angles from which Tolstoy's handling of this intriguing and memorable section of *War and Peace* might be fruitfully approached. In line with the nature of the present volume of essays, my main aim here is to take this part of the novel as a test case of one of Tolstoy's supreme "problems," indeed one of his obsessions: the (supposed) differences between true and false art and his corresponding conception of the workings of aesthetic experience. This will involve analyzing the opera scene in relation to some of Tolstoy's independently attested views on opera in particular and on the aesthetics of art more generally. But in adopting this approach, which is not unfamiliar, I believe it is imperative to avoid the pitfall of assuming that the operatic backdrop of the scene is little more than a transcription of Tolstoy's own attitudes to the art form, as though the text could adequately be read on this level as a thinly veiled piece of aesthetic autobiography. To read the scene in that way is, I suggest, reductive: it collapses the dynamics of the novel's text into a surrogate for the author beyond the text, treating this element of the fiction in quasi-documentary fashion and thereby failing to do justice to what I shall argue are the intricacies and paradoxes built into the account of Natasha's experience in the opera house. On careful consideration, it will emerge that the relationship between that account and Tolstoy's notoriously trenchant discussion of opera in *What Is Art?* is less straightforward than many have taken it to be. It is part of Tolstoy's greatness and lasting importance, I wish to maintain, that he is capable, even sometimes against the grain of his own character, of making his "problems" serve creative purposes.

It is in a sense an extension of reductive readings of Natasha's evening at the opera in *War and Peace* that some critics have been preoccupied with attempting to establish quasi-historically the identity of the work performed in this episode. The hunt for musical sources may not be entirely without a sort of curiosity appeal, and it has certainly been pursued with some industry; but it continues, inevitably, to prove inconclusive.[2] The opera depicted in Tolstoy's novel is no more a single historically identifiable work, I submit, than is Vinteuil's sonata or Elstir's painting of Carquethuit Harbour in Proust. What matters most, in this regard, about the narrated images of the opera is not that they invite readers to identify the work but that they contain multiple possible echoes of situations, motifs, and typical features found in a range of actual operas: a reader might be struck, for instance, by several thematic similarities to Mozart's *Don Giovanni*, a work we know was of some interest to Tolstoy.[3] But the opera scene in the novel is nonetheless constructed in a way that blocks a consistent, one-to-one parallelism with any particular work. Its dramatic and psychological functions are such that we do not need a specific historical anchorage for its interpretation. On the contrary, Tolstoy has composed the scene in a way that allows it to evoke—and even, in certain respects, to *enact*—problems of art and aesthetics on a larger scale.

As a first step toward positioning the opera episode of *War and Peace* in a more revealing perspective, I would like to advance the claim that the passage serves as a peculiar and ironic variation on one of the oldest literary devices in the Western tradition, ekphrasis, an exercise in vivid, set-piece description. Among the most prominent types of ekphrasis is the description of one work of art (real or imaginary) within the framework of another, especially the evocation of a visual work within a literary medium—the shield of Achilles in the *Iliad* being, of course, the earliest surviving instance of the trope and in many ways the abiding paradigm of its possibilities.[4] The peculiarity of the present Tolstoyan case consists in the manner in which the novel's narrative exploits for its own artistic purposes the (partial and ambiguous) *failure* of another artwork: the failure of the opera to produce any imaginative or emotional seduction over Natasha's mind. The result is a fragmented, intermittent, and distracted focalisation (whose implications I shall return to) of certain parts of the opera, yet one that, paradoxically, helps produce a piece of highly intense and psychologically layered novelistic writing. The failure of one artwork—even, supposedly, the flawed character of a whole art form—is alchemized into the success of another.

That last point, it is worth noticing, is something that significantly distinguishes the scene in question from what has been generally and rightly recognized as an influence on Tolstoy's treatment of opera—namely, one of the letters in Rousseau's epistolary novel of 1761, *Julie, ou la nouvelle Héloïse*, a work that we know made a great impression on the young Tolstoy.[5] Rousseau's novel entails an elaborate correspondence over a period of years between (principally) two characters, Saint-Preux and Julie, who move from being passionate lovers to becoming spiritual friends after marriage between them proves impossible for reasons of social class. The novel's form, together with a narrative trajectory that takes Saint-Preux on extensive travels, enables the inclusion of substantial elements of cultural description and observation that take on, in terms of the work's design, something of a centrifugal force. It is in part 2 of the novel, when Saint-Preux is living in Paris (a world, for him, of empty feelings and social pretense), that he attends the Paris Opera and sends a lengthy report on it to Julie's cousin, Madame d'Orbe. The report contains several details that provide striking parallels to the opera scene in *War and Peace* and that I touch on again later. But there is a critical difference as well. Saint-Preux's scathing critique of the Paris Opera is presented in a voice that, in keeping with the epistolary mode, is both monologic and quasi-anthropological in its aloof observations. Saint-

172

Preux watches with detachment, "assisted by my opera glasses";[6] he admits he is motivated only by curiosity about the mechanics of the art form, as well as about those naive enough to be moved by it, and he remains determinedly uninterested in its musico-dramatic aims. This detachment is far removed in psychological effect from the excited, flustered state of distraction of Natasha, which I shall shortly examine more closely. Nor, equally, does Saint-Preux's report of his visit to the opera have any bearing on the development of the novel's larger narrative: it is a freestanding document in its own right. This is in sharp literary contrast to the images of opera in book 2 of *War and Peace*, which dramatize an event that is integral to the novel's plot structure and whose richness of significance presupposes a reader fully absorbed by the intimate exploration of Natasha's state of mind. Whatever threads of connection there may have been in more general terms between Rousseau's and Tolstoy's views of opera, Tolstoy has made of Natasha's experience something very different from the kind of journalistic review that Saint-Preux's letter represents. It is rather misleading, therefore, to call the two texts "almost identical [*presque identique*]" in this regard.[7] The difference is tied up with the adaptation of an ekphrastic technique to create a complex texture, and an inherent paradox, in the relationship between the operatic background and the novelistic foreground of the scene. Where Rousseau simply gives a scornful voice to aesthetic disengagement, Tolstoy weaves the idea of such disengagement into the dense fabric of his text, thereby making it enhance and deepen the expressive resources of the novel.

To probe further into what I wish to argue is this double-voiced aesthetic effect in the narrative psychology of Natasha's visit to the opera, it makes sense to juxtapose certain aspects of the scene with parts of another, much later, and nonfictional Tolstoyan text, the treatise *What Is Art?* But as I have already indicated, my aim in doing so is not the usual one of simply reaching for evidence that the experience of Natasha in the novel is a mirror to, or transcription of, Tolstoy's own views. It is both possible and desirable to read the combination of texts as standing in a more interesting and intricate counterpoint with each other than that.

The first chapter of the treatise on art notoriously singles out opera for a witheringly satirical critique. The critique is composed around Tolstoy's recollections of attending the rehearsal of an opera (in fact Anton Rubinstein's *Feramors*, though the work is not explicitly identified in the text) on an occasion when he was curiously led through dark backstage passages and a stairwell, and then across the stage itself (with the rehearsal already under way!), into the stalls, where he had a view of the conductor seated between two lamps. Among other resonances of this strange account, it is hard not to detect at least subconscious echoes of the Cave allegory from Plato's *Republic*: Tolstoy's description combines heavy emphasis on dark unreality (both backstage and in the auditorium) with the vignette of the conductor's illuminated music stand and the puppetlike factitiousness of the costumed performers onstage. The passage as a whole is close in several details, including its references to the singers' stilted gestures, tight-fitting costumes, and emotional artificiality, to the flickering images of the operatic performance we are presented with in *War and Peace*. In some of these details as well as its tone of exaggerated sarcasm, it also bears traces of the influence of Rousseau's *Julie*. The account concludes with the claim that opera is so contrived and absurd an art form that no one at all (no one, at any rate, Tolstoy adds belatedly, except perhaps some "depraved artisan") could conceivably be moved by it.[8]

From one point of view, this opening chapter of *What Is Art?*, where Tolstoy constitutes himself as, so to speak, the solitary audience and exclusive judge of the work under rehearsal, can easily be thought to endorse, and to generalize into an aesthetic tenet on the inauthenticity of opera as an art form, young Natasha's disengagement in the opera house. But there are potential complications already lurking here, betrayed in part by the lengths to which Tolstoy has to go—after dwelling on the "enormous labor," the elaborately interlocking set of activities, and the earnest investment of energy on the part of all those involved—to insist that there cannot really be, even though there evidently *is*, any serious interest in such things: "So one is quite at a loss as to whom these things are done for" (79). Complications of a related kind emerge more explicitly in the other part of the treatise where opera is placed in the spotlight, in chapter 13, which contains Tolstoy's most vehement denunciation of the works of Wagner. Here we get an account of a particular occasion (in April 1896) when Tolstoy walked out of the Bolshoi Theatre in Moscow (indeed, "rushed out like a madman," so he told his brother Sergey Tolstoy in a letter the next day, April 19, 1896 [*TL*, 2:538–39]) in the middle of a performance of *Siegfried* that he had gone to see with his wife and the composer Taneyev.[9] He was revolted by what he thought was the spurious nonsense of the whole thing, and he resorted to an extreme rhetoric to register the point: "This is all so stupid . . . that it is surprising that people above seven years of age can witness it seriously." Yet he was equally, if not more, outraged by the fact that his own reactions were so clearly at odds with those of others: "Thousands of quasi-cultured people sit and attentively hear and see it and are delighted." To incorporate this fact into his analysis Tolstoy resorts to the charge against Wagner of "hypnotism," a notion that ironically coincides with Nietzsche's late anti-Wagnerianism.[10]

Contrary to the first chapter's blanket dismissal of opera as lacking any genuine power to enthrall an audience, chapter 13 of *What Is Art?* sets up a stark and perplexing (or perplexed) antithesis, as likewise with the fictional performance in *War and Peace*, between the failure of an operatic work to engage a particular individual's mind and, on the other hand, its ostensibly seductive, "hypnotic" effect on the rest of a large audience. The central issue I am concerned with here is the problem this antithesis represents for Tolstoy's "infectionist" aesthetics of artistic emotion and how he responds to it in these passages from both his fictional and his critical writing. Part of what I want to argue, however, as already indicated and as I shall shortly elaborate further, is that the form that his response takes in the case of the opera episode in *War and Peace* brings with it its own aesthetic complications: it is something more significant and revealing, because filtered through a subtly creative process, than a case of Tolstoy's taking advantage, as it were, of his fictional narrative simply in order to propagate surreptitiously a view of opera he happened to hold and would later proclaim loudly in *What Is Art?* The undoubted connections between Natasha's experience in the opera house and Tolstoy's convictions about the art form do not simply reflect the clear lines of a given aesthetic. They also expose tensions in that aesthetic, tensions to which, for all his dogmatism, Tolstoy was at some level alive both in practice and in his attempts to theorize the psychology of art.

Given my present perspective on how Tolstoy tries to come to terms with those tensions, it is apposite at this point to examine more closely the depiction of Natasha's disengagement or distance from the opera she attends. In doing so I wish to challenge what I think is a misleading claim made about the scene by Viktor Shklovsky in his early essay "Art as Device" (1917) and often repeated unquestioningly by later critics. Shklovsky adduces the scene as an example of what he regards as Tolstoy's characteristic use of "estrangement" or defamiliarization (*ostranenie*), the hallmark, on Shklovsky's understanding, of the poetic and the artistic in general.[11] But the function of estrangement in Shklovsky's poetic-cum-aesthetic theory is to redeem objects from the realm of habituated, automatic, and diluted perception, thereby creatively rendering them freshly available for a special intensity of *re*perception. It is very hard to see how this model of estrangement fits, or helps make sense of, the opera scene in *War and Peace*.[12]

Shklovsky, who simply quotes parts of the scene without any discussion (and alongside what are arguably rather different kinds of Tolstoyan technique), seems to overlook two fundamental and related points. First, the effect of Natasha's disengagement from the performance onstage has a specific psychological matrix within the narrative: if there is "estrangement" here, it is not a direct factor in the communicative relationship between author or text and the reader but a feature of the depicted situation itself, a symptom of Natasha's state of mind and her relationship to the performance before her. Second, and more subtly, the distancing of Natasha from the opera is set within a narrative structure that, from the reader's point of view, does *not* fundamentally defamiliarize its subject. On the contrary, in order to appreciate what is happening to Natasha, we are required to draw implicitly on a sense of what it means to concentrate on and become absorbed in a the-atrical drama, whether musical or otherwise. Without a tacit understanding of the norms of such experience (which is also projected onto the rest of the audience in its at least apparent attentiveness), Tolstoy's reader cannot grasp the contrasting nature of Natasha's situation. But to grasp that situation with all its complications means in turn to care about the fictional world to which it belongs. As I have already emphasized, the "strangeness" of the operatic phenomenon as depicted in this scene is a foil to, and even a component of, the artistic seductiveness of the novel's writing.

What's more, if Shklovsky's suggestion that the scene exemplifies Tol-stoyan estrangement were accepted, it would generate a radical incongruity. According to his larger thesis, estrangement is what, at root, *makes* "art" and gives aesthetic experience the distinctive qualities it possesses; hence his claim that it is something Tolstoy constantly uses in his writing.[13] But in Natasha's case the experience of estrangement is a *barrier* to experience of the opera as art. It is precisely because she cannot help noticing objects and details on the stage for what they "really" are, in their reductive materiality, that she cannot accept them as aesthetically expressive signs. If the scene in its totality enacts a conception of aesthetics, then, it can hardly be a Shklov-skian conception.[14] Tolstoy's narrative implicitly sets up a kind of dialectic between the expectation of rapt absorption and the fact of distracted disen-gagement. It embodies this dialectic in a character whose perceptions of the material conditions onstage are both uncomprehending of the event as art and yet part of a larger state of excitement that will make her vulnerable to personal seduction by Kuragin. Shklovsky's theory of *ostranenie* as outlined in "Art as Device," whatever its other merits may be, cannot cope with the paradoxically layered nature of this section of Tolstoy's text. Above all, it fails to account for the way in which the text uses a particular (imaginary) rupture of artistic and aesthetic experience as a way of drawing in its readers and giving depth to their access to the life and mind of one of the novel's central characters.

But there is more that needs to be said about the narrative focaliza-tion of the episode in the theater, since its interpretation has a bearing on the underlying aesthetic problem of concern here. Prima facie, Natasha's status as focalizer could hardly be any more conspicuous; Tolstoy even uses a chapter break to highlight this formal point with a kind of zooming effect. Chapter 8 concludes with a description of how, as the overture ended, the whole audience fell silent and "with greedy curiosity turned their attention to the stage," followed by the final sentence: "Natasha also began to look" (*W&P*, 560). The perspective we are then given on the opera in chapters 9 and 10 is entirely Natasha's. It is explicitly marked as such periodically ("She was unable to follow . . . she could not even hear . . . she saw only," and so forth [560–61]) and in such a way that the rest of the associated description of what is seen and heard (the perception, above all, of the material properties of the stage sets, the physical attributes of the performers, and the external artificiality of the latter's sounds and movements) can be attached only to her experience. Moreover, the narrative insists on the difference between Natasha's disengagement and the absorption of the audience in general: Natasha observes how "everybody in the theater clapped and shouted" (560), how their faces (including that of Hélène Kuragin in the next box) "were attentive to what was taking place on stage" (561), how their applause broke out several times in mid-act (563–64).[15] Appropriately, of course, the main exception is Kuragin: every time Natasha glances at him during act 2, she sees that he in turn is looking at *her*, not at the stage (563).

In purely formal terms, then, the focalization of the scene could not be clearer. As already mentioned, however, many critics are nonetheless tempted to read the scene in extratextual terms as little more than a convenient opportunity for Tolstoy to project his cynicism about opera onto Natasha. This style of reading is given some intratextual bite by Julie Buckler, who has argued that the account of Natasha's estrangement makes her seem too observant of incidental and circumstantial details onstage to be fully plausible. Natasha's "acuity" in noticing such things as the prompter's box or one of the singers counting the beat before his entry is, according to Buckler, rather "staged" and comes to seem overly directed by the voice of the narrator: far from being a neutral character focalization, on this analysis, the text has its own agenda and "encourages the reader to assume Natasha's narrative perspective as the scene progresses."[16] But it is possible to resist the temptation to read things that way. If we do not do so, we are certainly committed to discerning a flaw in Tolstoy's writing, since the conviction carried by this crucial episode in the novel depends on the plausibility of the picture of Natasha's experience: more particularly, on the way in which a failure (or disinclination) to be drawn imaginatively into the dramatic meaning of what is happening onstage is entwined with Natasha's gradually growing excitement, even "inebriation" (561), over the social occasion in the theater and the encounter with Kuragin.

But the novel's narrative surely does carry such conviction, and in part because of its paradoxically persuasive evocation of the psychological symptoms of a certain kind of failed aesthetic effect. There is, after all, abundant reason to accept that someone who cannot see *beyond* the purely material properties or conventions of an artwork and become absorbed in its aesthetic significance might indeed be arbitrarily sensitive to those properties: someone who "was unable to follow the course" of an opera might well react by "[seeing] only painted cardboard and strangely dressed-up men and women"

(561). In addition, the novel draws attention to the nonaesthetic factors that give rise to Natasha's distraction and disenchantment. We are told, for one thing, that her reaction reflected her recent period of residence in the countryside, implying attunement to urban sophistication as a prerequisite for enjoyment of opera, even though we have been informed earlier in the book that Natasha has taken pleasure in seeing at least one other opera in the past.[17] But her broken concentration above all reflects a swirling mixture of feelings stemming from her recent humiliation at the Bolkonskys and her frustration at the prolonged separation from Andrei: a mixture that includes an initial reluctance to go to the opera at all, "a sweet and amorous sadness" (557), an almost desperate need for love, as well as an underlying agitation (558), and that is compounded, as the evening develops, by an intoxicated impressionability toward the glittering, heady atmosphere of the social scene in the crowded auditorium and, above all, to the seductiveness of Kuragin himself.[18]

Rather than simply transcribing (or, as we might put it, ventriloquizing) his own views of opera in these chapters of the novel, then, Tolstoy has done something creative with those views: he has transmuted them into part of the fabric of an alluring fiction by finding an imaginable equivalent to them in the life of a character completely different from himself. In doing so, however, he has also dramatized what is, in effect, a challenge to his own aesthetics. It is this challenge that I wish to explain in the next part of my argument.

Far from being only, as it were, a consequence of the fictional psychology of the opera scene itself, the elements of this challenge can be detected lurking in Tolstoy's experience of Wagner as described in chapter 13 of *What Is Art?* If we now turn back to that text, what I wish to emphasize is how, despite the overall impression of unmitigated contempt left by the account, there are a series of chinks in its critique of Wagnerism. These emerge from the tripartite movement of thought through which Tolstoy passes in the course of the chapter. He starts and finishes in a mode of purely externalized, detached, and satirically barbed perceptions of both *Siegfried* and the behavior of the audience. This is the mode in which he partly mirrors his own fictional image of opera in *War and Peace*, commenting here repeatedly on the singers' costumes, gestures, faces, and so forth, not so much for the sake of "estrangement," and certainly not in the Shklovskian sense, as in order to *denude* the art form of its expressive and dramatic features by relentlessly reducing it to its bare physicality—performers dressed in wigs and tights, contorted mouths, "stupid" postures, and all the rest.[19]

But if performances of Wagner's operas, or of any other artworks, could be experienced only in this way, in their sheer, reductive materiality, they would not be aesthetic objects at all. It is even possible to invert Tolstoy's terms of reference and to contend, as the painter Eugène Delacroix does in his wonderful diaries, that the use of real objects (statues, columns, rocks, etc.) in operatic stage sets is a contradiction of aesthetic "illusion" and its necessary appeal to the imagination.[20] Clearly, for Delacroix as for many other theorists of art, "illusion" is here not equivalent to straightforwardly taking something for real; it is more like an enabling condition for the imaginative acceptance of aesthetic appearances as expressive vehicles of meaning and emotion. Tolstoy himself believes in such illusion: in *Shakespeare and the Drama* he calls it "the chief condition of art," the powerful sense of conviction that allows an audience to be emotionally engaged by a work.[21] Part of the point of Tolstoy's denial that Wagner's operas are true art at all, only "counterfeit," fake art, is therefore a denial that they are capable of creating an authentic aesthetic illusion. Yet in the middle section of his critique Tolstoy faces up to the question of why, if Wagner is so unendurably sham and so blatantly insincere, many of those present at the same performance of *Siegfried* in 1896, like most of the audience around Natasha in the theater, at least appeared totally seduced by, and absorbed in, the work. In other words, after purporting to strip the art form of a capacity for aesthetic seductiveness, Tolstoy admits that in a perverse way such a capacity is still seemingly at work with audiences that are not equipped, or predisposed, to resist it. His revulsion at *Siegfried* was reinforced by the sight of "three thousand people who not only patiently witnessed all this absurd nonsense but even considered it their duty to be delighted with it" (Tolstoy, *What Is Art?*, 259). There is perhaps a hint of skepticism here about the true state of mind of the audience, just as, in *War and Peace*, Natasha could not help suspecting (though the narrative leaves the suspicion hanging in the air) that the pleasure of those around her was "feigned" (*W&P*, 561). But in *What Is Art?* Tolstoy does not let himself off the hook with such a facile explanation. He accepts that something psychologically potent does take place to make large audiences become absorbed in Wagnerian opera. To account for this he treats Wagner as the most imposing of all practitioners of counterfeit art, the one whose work exhibits an unparalleled skill and power in uniting "all the methods by which art is counterfeited" (214).

In summarizing those methods under four headings (214–17), which in turn pick up chapter 11 of the treatise, Tolstoy lays the basis for his conception of Wagner as a *hypnotist*, but he also makes what could be thought of as partial modifications to his judgments earlier in the chapter. First, he states that Wagner brings into play an entire repertoire of themes and subjects generally considered "poetic." While regarding such things as secondhand and inauthentic, Tolstoy nonetheless allows that the operas' nature motifs, mythology, and so forth have a status rooted in older traditions of cultural imagination—something at any rate more respectable than the ludicrous "nonsense" of which he had earlier accused them. Second, Tolstoy observes that Wagner uses both dramaturgy and music "imitatively" to give a strongly evocative embodiment to his materials: in making this point, he actually describes Wagner as "not destitute of musical talent," even though he had earlier mocked his music as lacking all form, coherence, and significance. Third, Tolstoy says that in Wagner's work "everything is in the highest degree striking in its effects and peculiarities," which is hard to square with his earlier claim that nothing in Wagner could possibly engage the attention of anyone but a small child. And finally, Tolstoy makes the similarly broad concession that everything in the operas is "interesting" both dramatically and musically, as well as in the relationship between those two things: a perception that comes perilously close to undermining the earlier insistence that it is precisely in the attempt to combine separate art forms that opera is doomed to failure.

The points I have just paraphrased very curtly all have tangled ramifications in Tolstoy's aesthetics.[22] It goes without saying that they do not amount to anything like admiration for or legitimization of Wagner's work. But intervening as they do between the uncompromising belittlement with which the critique of Wagnerism in chapter 13 begins and ends, they are designed to try to explain the gross disparity between Tolstoy's alienation from the operas and the power they have over some people's minds. In this respect, they betray Tolstoy's awareness of a threat to his aesthetic philosophy from "counterfeit" art like Wagner's. If genuine art is certified by the emotional "infection" it produces, how can one distinguish between infection and hypnotism? If the latter, as Tolstoy recorded in his diary, requires "belief in the importance of what is being suggested,"[23] why is that different from infection? Moreover, since there is no such thing as a work of art that can be shown to infect in the same way everyone who experiences it—no such thing, then, as art's *auto*-certification—Tolstoy's theory requires an appeal to some sort of normative authority. How, though, can such authority distinguish between different yet similar-looking kinds of psychological response without at least implicit recourse to the testimony of experience? And whose testimony is that to be? May not even a given individual testify to fluctuations in their experience of the same objects of aesthetic experience, as the narrator of *War and Peace* happens to observe at one point?[24] The requirements of theory, as so often, come up against a recalcitrant multiplicity of evaluative points of view, an objection raised with devastating directness, as it happens, in a diary entry of Sophia Tolstaya's in June 1897 while *What Is Art?* was in preparation: "One has only to ask *who* is supposed to be 'infected' for his entire argument to be destroyed."[25]

But this is a deep problem to which Tolstoy was not simply blind, however much he proclaimed a definitive and universal solution to it in *What*

Is Art? He can be shown to have wrestled with it repeatedly in his own experience (not least of music), in his theoretical reflections, and in his fictional imagination. The interest of opera for the purposes I have pursued here is that it manifests the "artifice" in "art" in a conspicuous and magnified manner, even though, for its lovers, it can also be a source of aesthetic "ecstasy."[26] As such it brought to Tolstoy's notice with special force a feature intrinsic to many kinds of aesthetic experience and one that is paradoxical in the strict sense of "contrary to appearances." The capacity of certain kinds of object or performance to elicit imaginative absorption and emotional investment in the worlds they symbolize is a form of seduction that cannot be reduced to or equated directly with appearances: if it could, it would indeed operate (or fail) automatically, as opposed to producing the clashing responses of different individuals by which Tolstoy was so troubled. Instead, aesthetic seduction requires some kind of cooperative, dialectical interplay between work and audience. It requires the mind to open willingly to a plane of meaning that lies beyond the bare appearances—something that Natasha cannot do at the opera, and a process that Tolstoy deliberately reverses in the opera chapters of *What Is Art?*

The paradox of aesthetic seduction, together with radically conflicting inferences about its status (celebration of art's need for illusion, on the one side, condemnation of its falsehood and deception on the other), lies at the root of many of the arguments that have defined the history of Western aesthetics.[27] Tolstoy ultimately wanted himself inscribed in that history as the advocate of an unequivocally austere verdict on these issues. But there were always two sides to the story. The author of *What Is Art?* could call his treatise "negative and evil" (July 24, 1889; *TL*, 1:256–57). The person who wrote that letter to his brother condemning Wagner's *Siegfried* could say at the end of it, "I meant to destroy this letter, I dislike it so much" (April 19, 1896; *TL*, 2:538–39). And even in the midst of his dogmatic onslaught on Wagner in chapter 13 of *What Is Art?* he could feel impelled to assert, almost involuntarily against the grain of his own argument, that "one of the chief conditions of artistic creation is the complete freedom of the artist from every kind of preconceived demand" (205). In these and other ways Tolstoy left evidence that with what might be called his larger, more intuitive self he never ceased to agonize over what is at stake—what might be gained or lost—in how a particular mind responds to the offer of aesthetic seduction. Since he was always acutely, and sometimes almost pathologically, aware of both the creative and the receptive dynamics of such seduction, its status as a fundamental problem of aesthetics was ultimately one he discovered within himself as well as all around him. Here as much as anywhere, "Tolstoy's problems" become the problem of Tolstoy. But that is itself one of the reasons why, in all his complexity, he remains indispensable to us.

NOTES

1. Tolstoy was neither the first nor the last to use opera this way within the novel. See, for a variety of other examples, Cormac Newark, *Opera in the Novel from Balzac to Proust* (Cambridge: Cambridge University Press, 2011).

2. A range of views on the subject can be traced in the following articles: David Lowe, "Natasha Rostova Goes to the Opera," *Opera Quarterly* 7 (1990): 74–81; Margo Rosen, "Natasha Rostova at Meyerbeer's *Robert le Diable*," *TSJ* 17 (2005): 71–90; Joel Hewett, "An Overlooked Source for the Opera Scene in Tolstoy's *War and Peace*," *Notes and Queries* 57 (2010): 223–24. Julie Buckler, *The Literary Lorgnette: Attending Opera in Imperial Russia* (Stanford, Calif.: Stanford University Press, 2000), 97, calls the opera a "hash" of motifs from various sources.

3. Motifs in common with *Don Giovanni* include a seduction scene (with the lover stroking the girl's hand: compare the famous duet "Là ci darem la mano"), a nighttime graveyard setting, and a character falling down into hell.

4. For other Tolstoyan cases of ekphrasis, including the opera chapter in *Anna Karenina*, see Amy Mandelker, *Framing Anna Karenina: Tolstoy, the Woman Question, and the Victorian Novel* (Columbus: Ohio State University Press, 1993), 101–21. On ekphrasis more generally, see James Heffernan, *The Museum of Words: The Poetics of Ekphrasis from Homer to Ashbery* (Chicago: University of Chicago Press, 1993), and Stephen Cheeke, *Writing for Art: The Poetics of Ekphrasis* (Manchester, U.K.: Manchester University Press, 2010). For ancient usage of the term, see Ruth Webb, *Ekphrasis, Imagination and Persuasion in Ancient Rhetorical Theory and Practice* (Farnham, U.K.: Ashgate, 2009).

5. Tolstoy had read the novel by the age of twenty; see the list he drew up in October 1891 of works that had influenced him, where *La nouvelle Héloïse* is ranked in the category of "very great" influence and listed under "age 14–20" (*TL*, 2:485). We know from his diaries and letters that he reread at least parts of the novel on several occasions.

6. Jean-Jacques Rousseau, *Oeuvres complètes*, ed. B. Gagnebin and M. Raymond, 5 vols. (Paris: Gallimard, 1959–95), 2:284; English translation in Jean-Jacques Rousseau, *Julie, or the New Heloise*, trans. P. Stewart and J. Vaché (Hanover, N.H.: University Press of New England / Dartmouth College, 1997), 232.

7. Milan Markovitch, *Jean-Jacques Rousseau et Tolstoï* (Paris: Champion, 1928), 305.

8. Leo Tolstoy, *What Is Art? And Essays on Art*, trans. Aylmer Maude (London: Oxford University Press, 1930), 74–79. Subsequent citations to this work appear in the main text as parenthetical page numbers.

9. Tolstoy, *What Is Art?*, 203–17; for Wagner's "hypnotism," see 215–16. Sophia was present, too (and stayed to the end); see S. A. Tolstaya, *My Life*, ed. Andrew Donskov, trans. John Woodsworth and Arkadi Klioutchanski (Ottawa: Uni-

versity of Ottawa Press, 2010), 877–78. On the production in question, see Rosamund Bartlett, *Wagner and Russia* (Cambridge: Cambridge University Press, 2007), 49–50, 53.

10. See especially Nietzsche's "The Case of Wagner" ("Der Fall Wagner," 1888), §§ 5–7: Friedrich Nietzsche, *Sämtliche Werke: Kritische Studienausgabe* [Collected Works: A Critical Edition], ed. G. Colli and M. Montinari, 2nd ed., 15 vols. (Munich: de Gruyter, 1988), 6:21–29; English translation in *Basic Writings of Nietzsche*, trans. and ed. Walter Kaufmann (New York: Random House, 1968), 620–28. See also Stephen Halliwell, "'And Then They Began to Sing': Reflections on Tolstoy and Music," *COLLeGIUM* 9 (2010): 45–64, quoted text 55–57; online at https://helda.helsinki.fi/bitstream/handle/10138/25827/009_05 _Halliwelll.pdf?sequence=1.

11. Viktor Shklovsky, *Theory of Prose*, trans. Benjamin Sher (Elmwood Park, Ill.: Dalkey Archive Press, 1990), 8–9, where the translator uses the spelling "enstrangement."

12. For acceptance of Shklovsky's view, see, for example, Lowe, "Natasha Rostova Goes to the Opera," 74. See also Victor Erlich, *Russian Formalism*, 4th ed. (The Hague: Mouton, 1980), 177–78; Rimvydas Šilbajoris, *Tolstoy's Aesthetics and His Art* (Columbus, Ohio: Slavica, 1991), 141; and Justin Weir, *Leo Tolstoy and the Alibi of Narrative* (New Haven, Conn.: Yale University Press, 2011), 98. Weir's reading as a whole makes a number of more nuanced claims (98–102).

13. Shklovsky, *Theory of Prose*, 7.

14. For extensive, probing treatment of the tangled relationship between Shklovskian "estrangement" and Tolstoy, see Douglas Robinson, *Estrangement and the Somatics of Literature: Tolstoy, Shklovsky, Brecht* (Baltimore: Johns Hopkins University Press, 2008).

15. On the further detail that Natasha nonetheless feels that the absorption of others is "feigned" (*W&P*, 561), see page 179.

16. Buckler, *The Literary Lorgnette*, 95–96, 234n6.

17. "A phrase [Natasha] remembered from an opera she had heard in Petersburg with Prince Andrei," then identified for Sonya by Natasha as "a chorus from [Cherubini's] *The Water-Carrier*" (*W&P*, 518–19). See later in book 2 where Natasha sings "her favorite musical phrase from Cherubini's opera" (452).

18. In the course of the evening Natasha eventually ceases to find things "strange" (*W&P*, 564) but instead "perfectly natural" (566). This is best taken as a general assimilation to the social world she is in, not to the opera as such, contra, for example, Šilbajoris, *Tolstoy's Aesthetics*, 141. See also George Steiner, *Tolstoy or Dostoevsky*, 2nd ed. (New Haven, Conn.: Yale University Press, 1996), 118, and Ian Bostridge, *A Singer's Notebook* (London: Faber, 2011), 55. Nicholas Till, ed., *The Cambridge Companion to Opera Studies* (Cambridge: Cambridge University Press, 2012), 316, likewise misreads the scene by suggesting that Tolstoy builds into it "condemnation of Natasha . . . for succumbing to . . . the

operatic." Edward Wasioliek, *Tolstoy's Major Fiction* (Chicago: University of Chicago Press, 1978), 108, wilfully imagines that by the end "Natasha will be applauding as wildly as the others." For one reading of Natasha's psychology in the theater, see Richard F. Gustafson, *Leo Tolstoy: Resident and Stranger* (Princeton, N.J.: Princeton University Press, 1986), 349–52.

19. Though I cannot here pursue Tolstoy's accompanying critique of the music, it is worth noting, for a certain ironic attentiveness, that his observations on "beginnings which . . . never get finished" (Tolstoy, *What Is Art?*, 208), "as if a musical thought were commenced only to be broken off" (212), might actually be taken, once the attached sneers are discounted, as thought-provoking formulations of certain traits of Wagner's mature style. Note also: "not a single melody . . . but merely intertwinings of the *leit-motivs*," an awareness of what Wagner himself counted as "endless melody" (210).

20. Entry for April 9, 1856, in Eugène Delacroix, *Journal*, ed. M. Hannoosh, 2 vols. (Paris: Corti, 2009), 1:1009. For an English translation, see Eugène Delacroix, *The Journal of Eugène Delacroix: A Selection*, ed. Hubert Wellington, trans. Lucy Norton, 3rd ed. (London: Phaidon, 1995), 334–35. In the same context Delacroix criticizes long descriptive passages in nineteenth-century novels for their emphasis on outward appearances ("l'extérieur des choses") at the expense of character and emotion.

21. Leo Tolstoy, *Recollections and Essays*, trans. Aylmer Maude (Oxford: Oxford University Press, 1937), 336, 354.

22. Caryl Emerson perceptively traces some of the ramifications, "Tolstoy's Aesthetics," in *The Cambridge Companion to Tolstoy*, ed. Donna Tussing Orwin (Cambridge: Cambridge University Press, 2002), 237–51; see also Caryl Emerson, "Tolstoy and Music," in Donna Tussing Orwin, ed., *Anniversary Essays on Tolstoy* (Cambridge: Cambridge University Press, 2010), 8–32.

23. The diary entry for November 17, 1897, refers in those terms to "the hypnotization of all artistic delusions" (*TD*, 2:450).

24. Note the remark on Natasha's singing: "sounds . . . which leave one cold a thousand times . . . , then for the thousand and first time make one tremble and weep" (*W&P*, 342).

25. See the entry for June 15, 1897, in Sophia Andreevna Tolstaya, *The Diaries of Sophia Tolstoy*, trans. Cathy Porter (New York: Random House, 1985), 200. On the circularity of Tolstoy's "universalist" attempt to negate the implications of such differences in *What Is Art?*, see Halliwell, "Tolstoy and Music," 52–53; for further problems in the theory, see Robinson, *Estrangement and the Somatics of Literature*, 62–67.

26. Bernard Williams, *On Opera* (New Haven, Conn.: Yale University Press, 2006), 99–106, esp. 102, offers some telling reflections on operatic artifice. From a performer's viewpoint, see Bostridge, *A Singer's Notebook*, 55. For opera as inducer of ecstasy, see Susan Sontag, "The Art of Fiction No. 143: Interview

with Edward Hirsch," *Paris Review* 137 (1995), http://www.theparisreview.org/interviews/1505/the-art-of-fiction-no-143-susan-sontag.

27. For one approach to these issues, see Stephen Halliwell, *The Aesthetics of Mimesis: Ancient Texts and Modern Problems* (Princeton, N.J.: Princeton University Press, 2002).

Caryl Emerson

Tolstoy against Shakespeare (A Theatrical Feud Featuring George Bernard Shaw)

AMONG THE PASSIONATE eccentricities of great artists, Tolstoy's disgust with Shakespeare looms large and curious. Intuitively, it does not convince. His own great midlife novels have often been called Shakespearean—in their scope, psychological subtlety, empathetic grasp of the most varied human motivations, in their command of inner monologue (the novel's equivalent to onstage soliloquy) and masterful pacing of scenes. Yet this was no "postconversion" denunciation. It preceded by several decades the categorical no that would thunder forth from Yasnaya Polyana against Church, state, military, private property, tobacco, alcohol, sexual relations, and the idle frivolities of a landed noble class. Nor did it appear abruptly at the end of the 1890s alongside Tolstoy's other celebrated aesthetic bans (of Beethoven, Wagner, Baudelaire, and his own most famous novels) in his treatise *What Is Art?* Tolstoy's Shakespearophobia was of long duration, deeply rooted in his sense of the tasks of drama, and, more broadly, the purpose of art.

Nothing in Tolstoy's well-documented life suggests at any time a passion for theater. But as a young man of letters in the 1850s he was surely literate in it, valuing especially Gogol's *Inspector General* and comedies of social exposure by Alexander Ostrovsky and Molière.[1]

Regarding Shakespeare, it appears that Tolstoy never read through the plays systematically while growing up, although his plans for mastering world culture were ambitious and his English excellent from childhood. What he knew of the plays, he didn't like. This initial disdain might have been Tolstoy's impulse—which began early and lasted until the end—to reject any cultural icon worshipped by European fashion and adopted uncritically by his own circle. But with only the briefest relapses, his nonacceptance of the Bard steadily deepened and darkened, for reasons that strike us as cruder and more personal than the familiar eighteenth-century complaints of excess or shapelessness. A survey of his scattered judgments in diaries, letters, and memoirs reveals an impressive consistency.[2] Early on, Tolstoy had spoken his mind to the more aristocratic "noncivic critics" among his acquaintances. The liberal journalist and art-for-art's-sake traditionalist Alexander Druzhinin recalls Tolstoy, age twenty-seven in 1855, remarking, "Only a man saturated with stock phrases can admire Shakespeare and Homer." One year later, in his diary entry for November 16, 1856, Tolstoy wrote, "Finished reading *Henry IV*. No!" (*TD*, 1:125, 47:100). To the noncivic critic and naturalist Ivan Panaev he was more specific: "*Henry IV*. The work of a run-of-the-mill scribbler . . . Our wonder and ecstasy over Shakespeare is merely the desire not to fall behind others and a habit of repeating the opinions of others" (35:680).[3] That year, Druzhinin had published his translation of *King Lear*, which Ivan Turgenev begged Tolstoy to approach with an open mind: "Don't be put off by external incongruities," he beseeched the younger writer in a letter of January 3, 1857; "penetrate to the heart of the work, you'll be surprised by the harmony and profound truth!" Tolstoy may or may not have done so, but by the 1880s, his references to Shakespeare had hardened still further. To Sophia Andreevna he wrote, on January 28–29, 1884, "Just read *Coriolanus*. Beautiful German translation, reads smoothly, but is absolute nonsense, which only actors could like." The next day Tolstoy remarked in another letter to his wife, "This morning I read through *Macbeth* with great attention. Playhouse plays, written by an actor with a good memory who has read his fill of clever books" (35:681).[4]

Why "plays written by an actor for the playhouse" should be an insult rather than a professional achievement is worth pondering. One peculiarity of Tolstoy's dislike of Shakespeare is his indifference to the plays as *theatrical* experience. To be sure, judging the Bard by the book rather than by the stage has a long history. But for Tolstoy, who assessed all the goods and bads of the world by the psychosensual effect they made on his own body, very possibly another factor was nearsightedness (his poor vision did not compromise his intense experiencing of music, for example). Tolstoy's standard for Shakespeare was a line of print. If a play read badly, it was a bad work of art. When Tolstoy did test his views in an actual theater, the cultural outing (exacerbated, of course, by its urban context) was usually a setup to reinforce the findings of his inner ear and eye. As the sixty-eight-year-old Tolstoy wrote to Nikolai Strakhov in January 1896, "The other day, in order to verify my opinion about Shakespeare, I went to see *King Lear* and *Hamlet*, and if I had any doubts at all about the justice of my disgust at Shakespeare, that doubt vanished completely. What a crude, immoral, trashy, and senseless work *Hamlet* is . . ." (*TL*, 2:533; 69:28).

Drama cut close to the bone during these years, and Tolstoy's judgments were grim. His own tragedy, *The Power of Darkness*, premiered in Moscow at the Maly Theatre in 1895.[5] Throughout the fall, Tolstoy had attended rehearsals. On December 7, 1895, he wrote despairingly in his diary that "art began as play and continues to be a plaything, and a criminal plaything, of adults; even music has no influence and can only distract, while realism weakens meaning" (*TD*, 2:420–21; 53:72). The ethical mission that Tolstoy expected of performance art seemed impossible to meet, in any of its modes. In 1894 he had written in his diary, "Just read *Julius Caesar*. Amazingly foul. If I were young and naughty, I'd write an article about it, to rid people of the necessity of pretending they like it" (84:223).[6] Surely this private quip to himself was cast in part as affectionate self-parody. But however cavalierly Tolstoy might dismiss other people's feelings as mere "pretense," his own response to Shakespeare remained pure and simple disgust. Tolstoy did not get any younger, and certainly no less naughty. And nine years later, in 1903 at age seventy-five, he finally did "write an article about it"—that is, about all the ways this famous playwright had failed.

AGAINST BARDOLATRY

That treatise, "O Shekspire i o drame" (On Shakespeare and on drama), was poorly received, as Tolstoy knew it would be. To this day it continues to puzzle even Tolstoy's most ardent admirers. Flaws in method, common sense, and elemental accuracy abound in it, which the present essay will not attempt to defend. But there is much to be learned from this passionate, highly subjective document—more, I believe, than the facile, somewhat too-brisk conclusions drawn by George Orwell in his famous essay of 1946, "Tolstoy, Lear, and the Fool." Orwell's essay, far better known than the treatise it critiques, is often and incorrectly taken to be an objective explication of it (or a disinterested refutation of its ideas).[7] Neither is the case. After cursorily surveying Tolstoy's opening chapters, Orwell moves to personal ground: Tolstoy's psyche and family life. Before Orwell's essay captured the readership, reviews of Tolstoy's tract (such as G. Wilson Knight's of 1934) had less trouble integrating Tolstoy into a respectable tradition.[8] For Tolstoy's skepticism toward Shakespeare does not, after all, stand alone in the world of letters. From Samuel Johnson and Alexander Pope in the eighteenth century to Tolstoy's disciple Ludwig Wittgenstein in the twentieth, many fine critical minds have found much in Shakespeare that is "botched and dispensable."[9] As midwife to a more evenhanded inquiry into Tolstoy's views, I draw here on another socially engaged world-class writer from the British Isles, one more contemporary to Tolstoy than Orwell and arguably Tolstoy's closest non-Russian equivalent in productivity, longevity, and outrageousness: George Bernard Shaw (1856–1950).

    Shaw was sympathetic to a great deal in Tolstoy's critique of Western civilization. In one bold stage work after another beginning in 1892, Shaw, too, debunked its cult of doctors and science, the hypocrisy of its established religions, the charade of its parliaments, the smugness of its acquisitive capitalism and aggressive empire building, and the enslavement of its cultures to sexually provocative entertainment at the expense of moral and mental discipline. In 1882, coterminous with Tolstoy's spiritual crisis, Shaw, under the influence of Henry George, concluded that private ownership of land was theft; two years later he joined the Fabian Society. By the 1890s Shaw, like Tolstoy, had become a teetotaler and vegetarian. And although Tolstoy almost certainly did not know about it, Shaw, who married in 1898 at age forty-two, put into practice Tolstoy's ideal of a celibate (indeed, an unconsummated) spousal relationship.[10]

In formal aesthetic matters there was also much mutual sympathy. In 1897, Shaw declared Tolstoy's controversially antimodernist *What Is Art?* to be "beyond all comparison, the best treatise on art that has been done by a literary man (I bar Wagner) in these times."[11] The element of scandal and overstatement in Tolstoy's tract appealed to the showman in Shaw. Shaw also appreciated that this polemic was not the whim of some armchair theorist but the mature opinion of a great practicing artist who insisted on art's being a matter of serious ethical communication rather than a hedonistic appeal to the senses, a mystical symbolist riddle, or an idle game. Shaw wrote with delight in his 1898 review of *What Is Art?*, "He [Tolstoy] has no patience with nonsense, especially drunken nonsense, however laboriously or lusciously it may be rhymed or alliterated."[12] It must be emphasized that Shaw (unlike Tolstoy) had the highest respect for poetic rhyme and alliteration. But these poetic devices, especially in a playwright, had to be subordinated to matters of ethical substance. When they were not—that is, when important ideas became the playthings of sound, which was a failing as intolerable as a silly sexual routine onstage being allowed to outshine a serious object lesson on human progress—Shaw rebelled. The prevalence of both those sins in late Victorian-era productions of Shakespeare was part of Shaw's problem with the British Shakespeare cult, which Shaw dubbed Bardolatry. It was an attitude both idolatrous and dishonest.

A few words about that Shavian concept will set the scene for Tolstoy's qualified endorsement of it. Shaw invented the term "Bardolatry" in 1901, in the preface to *Three Plays for Puritans*.[13] He had been shaping the idea for a decade, however, most insistently in theater reviews and feuilletons for the *Saturday Review* between 1895 and 1897.[14] In contrast to Tolstoy, Shaw was a man thoroughly of the theater. An insider to the industry and devoted to its flourishing, he had coined the word partly in jest.[15] Publicity stunt or no, the sins of Bardolatry were held not against Shakespeare the playwright, whom Shaw had revered since childhood and knew almost by heart, but against a vacuous British public and opportunistic, mercantile adapters of the plays—that is, against those who, in Shaw's view, liked the Bard for the wrong reasons. For there were right reasons for adoring Shakespeare, and right reasons for disliking him. Bardolatry was an adoration of the Bard for the wrong reasons.

Shaw identified three wrong reasons for adoring Shakespeare, aspects of which Tolstoy would strongly endorse. First came the fallacy of considering the Bard a great thinker or philosopher. Shaw insisted that he was neither. Shakespeare had absorbed the morality of his time, expressed it with incomparable genius, but nowhere challenges it. Shaw believed that true artists were obliged to do more than absorb and express: they must move the collective mind of humanity forward with new and sounder ideas, thereby fostering its "creative evolution." By this standard, Shaw considered the postconversion Tolstoy a true artist, however his ideas might be hissed down (or perhaps because they were hissed down), whereas Shakespeare's genius was limited to insights into human psychology, a mastery of dramatic pacing, and "word-music."[16]

The second "wrong reason" was a cheapening and coarsening of Shakespeare's plays, facilitated by theater managers or virtuosic actors who cut, rewrote, or supplemented lines and scenes to please the popular appetite for melodrama or tragic "stage sensuousness."[17] This exaggeration of sentimental elements and excision of intellectual content had a further bad effect: it belittled the courage, vision, and hard work of history's progressive heroes. For Shaw (again in contrast to Tolstoy) admired charismatic political and military figures: the ancient empire-building Roman emperors, the genius of Napoléon, and in world theaters contemporary with him, Mussolini and Stalin. Shaw considered many of Shakespeare's plays slanderously deficient in the heroic virtues: hope, courage, discipline, civic mission. The Bard was at his best with *Macbeth, Hamlet, Lear*, all tragedies of "disillusion and doubt"—but for the confident, sober-headed Caesars, Shaw insisted, the Elizabethan era offered no models, and Shakespeare himself was at a loss. He either fell back on chivalric cliché or replaced empire builders with Antonys tied up in a bogus-tragic love plot.[18] And when a gullible theatergoing public is stupefied with sex made too romantic or despair made too sublime, that public can only be miseducated about the nature of human greatness.

A third fallacy is discussed in the preface to Shaw's one-act fund-raiser *The Dark Lady of the Sonnets* (1910)—the mistake of depicting the Bard as a mournful, sentimental, suffering artist. Shaw preferred to imagine Shakespeare more like himself, optimistic and resilient. In his theater reviews Shaw delighted in actors who brought out these "classical" traits in heroes like Hamlet, so often made melancholy or traumatized.[19] Shakespeare was a practical man of the theater, Shaw averred, but also a poetic titan full of dramatic irony, intellectual toughness, a writer whose "impish rejoicing in pessimism" and "exultation in what breaks the hearts of common men" were proof of his genius.[20] Shakespeare the man as a fearless, clear-eyed epic hero was another one of Shaw's "great man" constructs. Tolstoy's confessional route to self-knowledge—the writer as penitent, sunk in continual self-analysis—cut against Shaw's grain. Shakespeare's reactions to the world were strongest when they resembled Shaw's own. And where they did not, Shaw would call him out. In his final year, 1949, Shaw wrote what would become his last play, the nine-minute puppet show *Shakes versus Shav*, in which the Shaw-surrogate marionette challenges the Bard to fisticuffs.

The Shavian campaign against Bardolatry, shot through with farce and full of long-familiar complaints against Shakespeare, caused a scandal. Shaw had hoped for that. "I have made him popular," he wrote in 1908, "by knocking him off his pedestal and kicking him around the place, and making people realize that he's not a demigod but a dramatist."[21] Such was Shaw's goal: to harness the health of the stage to the health of the human race. Tolstoy shared that goal. He would also knock Shakespeare off his pedestal. But Tolstoy had no desire to improve the Bard's image in the theaters. In its humorless negativity, therefore, Tolstoy's critique is the more original.

Over Shakespeare's corpus of plays, these two modern titans warily courted each other's approval. Each was a man of enormous and confident ego, tireless in his efforts to reform Western civilization, shamelessly selective in his reading, and willing to deploy any shock tactic to serve his cause. They had high respect for each other as moral crusaders and artists. (Aylmer Maude recalled how Tolstoy, during his last year, noted the current dearth of good writers everywhere: "There are none now," Tolstoy remarked, "unless, perhaps, Shaw.")[22] But courtship only sharpened the differences. Certain aspects of Tolstoy could only have mystified, or perhaps appalled, the fin-de-siècle Shaw. The titled Russian aristocrat, nurtured by an authoritarian state that worshipped and feared the literary word, could get away with a great deal more than could the self-made writer from Dublin in a skeptical, pluralistic bourgeois democracy with a free press but a robust stage censorship.[23] The two men exchanged half a dozen letters and several dramas during these final, increasingly stressful five years of Tolstoy's life. For this exchange, Shakespeare was both immediate prompt and enduring subtext. I now turn to the Tolstoy-Shakespeare-Shaw triangle between 1903 and 1910, to complicate a famous feud in which Tolstoy—perhaps fairly, but too hastily and shallowly—is almost always declared the loser.

WHAT IS SHAKESPEARE? WHAT IS DRAMA?

Tolstoy's treatise started modestly: as his preface to a pamphlet, *Shakespeare's Attitude toward the Working Classes*, by the American reformer and educator Ernest Howard Crosby (1856–1907). A New York City native with close ties to American socialists, Crosby had converted to Tolstoyanism after a visit to Yasnaya Polyana in the 1890s. His case against the Bard consisted largely of a string of quotations from those plays in which the English commons is either insulted or cheerfully insults itself, laced with Crosby's offended protests. But Tolstoy's preface soon outgrew Crosby's pamphlet. The crude defense that Crosby offered the working class could not satisfy Tolstoy's irritation, for the issue transcended mere representation of persons or ranks (whether kings or commoners). "It's not a question of Shakespeare's aristocratism but of the perversion of artistic taste owing to the praising of inartistic works," Tolstoy wrote the art critic Vladimir Stasov on October 9, 1903. "Let them abuse me if they like. Perhaps you will, too. But I had to express what has been cooped up in me for half a century. Forgive me" (*TL*, 2:633; 35:680; translation modified). The final treatise, with Crosby's text appearing as its appendix, contains no trace of this tentative apologetic tone.[24] It opens on a note of personal combat, a Tolstoyan variant on Shaw's *Shakes versus Shav*. "Before writing this essay, I, an old man of seventy-five . . . again reread all of Shakespeare," Tolstoy confides to his reader. "Not only did I not receive any pleasure, but I felt an irresistible repulsion, weariness, bewilderment" (35:217).

What precisely repelled and bewildered Tolstoy? Some irritants are obvious. In his 1896 letter to Strakhov, Tolstoy had attributed the "trashy senselessness" of *Hamlet* to its "pagan vengeance" and "supernatural effects." Those features of plot construction were certain to offend Tolstoy, a prose writer in the realist mode. Moved into theater, realist strategies produce illusionism of the sort championed by Stanislavsky's Moscow Art Theatre, founded in 1898, whose teaching staff included disciples of Tolstoy.[25] In 1902, the theater mounted Tolstoy's peasant drama *The Power of Darkness*. For the outdoor scenes, the stage was covered with squelching mud.[26] This "naturalist-realist" aesthetic, so exceptional in the history of world theater, was profoundly alien to the minimalist, stylized Elizabethan stage, full of convention and sensational effects.[27] It is often noted, however, that Tolstoy's anti-Shakespearism was triggered most deeply and savagely not by the violence, implausibility, or silliness of stage events but by extravagant metaphorical uses of language.[28] Thus we are not surprised to find this remark by Tolstoy about a scene in *Othello* (incidentally considered by him to be one of Shakespeare's "least bad, least encumbered" plays): "Othello's monologue over the sleeping Desdemona is utterly impossible. A man who is preparing for the murder of a beloved being does not utter such phrases" (*TonSh*, 65–66; 35:245). Such polemical naïveté is wholly within the Tolstoyan zone. "To understand Shakespeare," G. Wilson Knight wrote in his 1934 review of Tolstoy's treatise, "one must make this original acceptance: to believe, first, in people who speak poetry; thence in human actions which subserve a poetic purpose" (15). Unsurprisingly, Tolstoy does not make this acceptance. But other judgments of his do surprise us.

The welcome surprises include everything that makes Tolstoy a genuine revolutionary. He sees keenly the stupefying power of received opinion. His fury at narrow Eurocentric values that pretend to speak for all cultures and ages rings out in this treatise, a century before its time. In pointing to the weak, bad, lazy, and animal habitual in human nature, Tolstoy is as good as ever. But in explaining why intelligent people of discernment and sobriety might assess the same aesthetic phenomenon in entirely different ways, Tolstoy is at a disadvantage. His universal and timeless standard for measuring honesty of response remains his own fickle organism. Following the model of *What Is Art?*, the Shakespeare treatise opens in the high subjective mode, with a personal encounter over the artwork that Tolstoy intends to ridicule and discredit. In *What Is Art?* this target is an opera rehearsal. In the later treatise, it is *King Lear*. Tolstoy pledges to "describe the contents of the drama" as "impartially as possible" (*TonSh*, 9; 35:219). "Contents" here is the sequence of plot action. Although the result can only be a caricature, several details deserve highlighting.

First, Tolstoy knows that no temporal narrative, verbal or musical, can be stripped down to a move-by-move description of its "plot" and survive. He proceeds in this atomizing fashion because it permits him to estrange the text, to comment on formal aspects freed from their larger context, conventions, or aura. The first aspect that offends him is "the pompous, characterless language of King Lear"—the way all Shakespearean kings speak—which underlies the larger lie of the opening scene (*TonSh*, 14; 35:221). No one watching the play could possibly be persuaded that "a King, however old and stupid he may be," after a life lived in the bosom of family, would believe his vicious daughters and not his favorite daughter. Thus the reader, or spectator, "cannot share the feelings of the persons participating in this unnatural scene." Tolstoy admits that the subtle and contrary "play of emotion" within a single character can at times be "expressed correctly and powerfully in some of Shakespeare's scenes" (*TonSh*, 75; 35:249). But given the fake language these people must speak, our sympathy for them is fleeting. Overall, the psychology of characters is governed not by a flow of organic feeling but by "that special Shakespearean language, the main trait of which is that thoughts are born out of the consonance of words, or out of their contrast" (*TonSh*, 29; 35:228). According to the psychic economy of *What Is Art?* such drama cannot infect.

Kings all sound alike, trapped by their power in grandiloquent formulas, surrounded by flatterers and thus constantly furious at being deceived. But what about that universal favorite, Sir John Falstaff, that "natural man" who flatters only himself, who sees through all poses of honor and courage and serves nothing but his own appetites? Tolstoy admits that Falstaff is "perhaps the only natural character . . ." that Shakespeare ever depicted, that "he alone speaks a language proper to himself." Of course, Falstaff, too, is a verbal show-off. He also speaks in "Shakespearean language," defined by Tolstoy as language filled to the brim with "bad puns and unfunny jokes"— but in Falstaff, this sort of talk is more acceptable because it is in harmony with that drunkard's "boastful, distorted, depraved character." Wordplay and deed play honestly match up. But the "artistic effect of the character is spoilt" by its repulsive gluttony, debauchery, and cowardice; no reader can share the playwright's cheerful good humor toward this figure (*TonSh*, 69–70; 35:246–47).

In addition to unnaturalness of situation, excessive verbal cleverness, and unsuccessful attempts to redeem bad habits through humor and wit, Tolstoy's keen ear picks up and rejects all utterances that do not fit the competencies of their speakers. Everyone in a Shakespeare play sounds alike, monarchs and fools, and all are as smart as their creator. Thus the listener cannot tell if an uttered idea originates inside the consciousness of a character or outside it. A novelist can afford this luxury through free indirect discourse, slipping in and out of the mind of created persons, but the stage, conventionally denied a third-person narrator, must not indulge in it.

What is more, Tolstoy argues, Shakespeare takes ancient plots and ruins them. Because he borrows (one of the giveaway signs of counterfeit art), his *King Lear* is crammed with anachronisms; because his dramatic characters are not individualized, they appear to speak at random, "pretentious unnatural" phrases uncoordinated with their gestures. Shakespeare lovers praise this "intemperance of language" as proof of a character's multisidedness, whereas it is, Tolstoy assures us, simply contradictory (*TonSh*, 52–54; 35:238–39). Such is not the case with Shakespeare's far older source, the anonymous *King Leir*. That earlier play ends at the right moment, at the point when the wronged daughter forgives her father, the moment of repentance, self-knowledge, and potential for growth (not as in Shakespeare, who adds that terrible and gratuitous final death). "In the older drama," Tolstoy writes, "there are no tempests nor tearing out of gray hairs, but there is the weakened and humbled old man, Leir, overpowered with grief" (*TonSh*, 60; 35:242). Since the objective of drama is to "elicit sympathy with what is represented," *what* is represented must be given a persuasive acting face and a base in believable experience; more abstract authorial thoughts are appropriate only in a prose treatise (*TonSh*, 77; 35:250). Here, too, we see a criticism that Shaw, with some reservations, shared. Melodramatic bombast, the stuff of spectacle, gets in the way of an idea, an impulse, an enlightening lesson to be grasped for life's betterment. Shaw's way around this problem was to provide vast prefaces to his plays, at times exceeding the length of the drama. For Shaw, of course, what infects an audience is an idea (and preferably *his* idea); it can be developed narratively in words. Tolstoy was not keen on dramatic prefaces because, in his view, one can be infected only by a feeling. If feelings on the stage—and from the stage—are sincere, they are transmitted instantaneously and can be watched. They are spectacular.

The family strife depicted so spectacularly in *King Lear* is real enough. But it is not, in Tolstoy's opinion, sincere. He concludes that this action "does not flow from the natural course of events nor from their characters, but is quite arbitrarily established by the author, and thus cannot produce on the reader the illusion which represents the essential condition of art" (*TonSh*, 48; 35:237). Tolstoy will not grant us infection by the symbolic order. The dramatic stage must mimic our moral obligations in familiar forms. Perhaps for that reason, in recounting Shakespeare's plot Tolstoy "Russifies" words to bring them home: Lear's heath is rendered as "steppe," Shakespeare's madmen are often referred to as *yurodivye*, Russian holy fools (*TonSh*, 29–30; 35:228–29). This estrangement of *Lear* from itself takes up four full chapters. So unforgiving is its tone that we are dissuaded from seeking in later chapters any sensible argument.

One reader who was so dissuaded was George Orwell, in his celebrated 1946 essay.[29] Orwell dismisses most of Tolstoy's arguments against Shakespeare as either "weak or dishonest" (36–37). But he is curious as to why Tolstoy attacks *King Lear* with such ferocity and why he so adamantly prefers the earlier *Leir*—thereby turning tragedy into comedy, or perhaps into melodrama (40). He does so, Orwell surmises, because the whole plot of Shakespeare's *Lear* cuts altogether too close to home. Tolstoy sensed in this regal tragedy his own autobiographical saga: the aging patriarch who wanted to purify his life by giving everything away, and who legally did give everything away, yet who still expected to be treated like a king (43). When the Fool—that "trickle of sanity running through the play" (40)—comments briskly on the situation, Lear winces. Tolstoy, reading the scene, falls into a rage.

Orwell has a point. There might be parallels. But overall he is unfair, for Tolstoy's reasons for renunciation were completely different from King Lear's. Tolstoy was not bidding for family love. His were not the ravings of a very old man "who hath ever but slenderly known himself," as Lear's evil daughter Regan put it to her sister Goneril in the first act (1.1:292–93). Tolstoy knew himself extremely well, indeed far too well—and his desire to renounce, simplify, and cleanse his life had begun thirty years earlier. Tolstoy's wife of forty-five years, Sophia Andreevna, was no Regan or Goneril. She was desperate, proud, aging poorly, and she felt betrayed. Far more productive than a focus on this painful family saga, although not without problems of its own, is Orwell's remark that although "Tolstoy was not capable of tolerance or humility . . . his quarrel with Shakespeare goes further. It is the quarrel between the religious and the humanist attitudes toward life" (42). The Christian attitude, Orwell brazenly asserts, is "self-interested and hedonistic," eager to renounce, convert, attain eternal peace. The humanist, in contrast, is a fighter who insists that the "struggle must continue and that death is the price of life" (48). Shakespeare, Orwell implies, is such a fighter; Tolstoy is pious and thus passive. Even if we ignore all the shallow foolishness in Orwell's definition of "religious attitude," this is harsh criticism of Tolstoy's warrior-like stance against the world. But it is over this Orwellian image of "Shakespeare the fearless humanist" that the Christian anarchist Tolstoy and the agnostic, intellectualizing Fabian-socialist Shaw will refine their respective worldviews on the tasks of drama. Because they begin on shared ground, their ultimate duel ends up all the more fiercely eye to eye.

Tolstoy concurs with Shaw that Shakespeare, despite flimsy nineteenth-century defenses mounted by Gervinus and Georg Brandes, cannot be called a moral or progressive force. What principles run his plays? "Action at all costs," says Tolstoy: "the absence of all ideals, moderation in everything, the conservation of the forms of life once established, and the end justifying the means" (*TonSh*, 92; 35:257). In such a theater, audiences are not transformed but only amused, aroused, distracted, or cravenly reassured of life's will to exist. Tolstoy declines to sanction those appetites in any normal, healthy, or undrugged audience. This permits him to devote the second, post-*Lear* portion of his treatise to demystification. Why, being so bad, is Shakespeare considered so good? His massive popularity can only be because of hypnosis imposed by German professors on public opinion through a gullible commercial press. "There is only one explanation of this wondrous fame," Tolstoy reasons. "It is one of those epidemic 'suggestions' [*vnushenie*, literally "infiltration"] to which people are constantly subject . . . such as faith in witches, the usefulness of torture for uncovering the truth, the search for the elixir of life or the philosopher's stone, the passion for tulips that suddenly seized Holland" (*TonSh*, 97–98; 35:260). Irrational fashion, not conscious choice, runs these events. As George Sand gives way to Zola, so Fourier gives way to Karl Marx: such is the behavior of all fads and crazes.

To explain the force of "suggestion," Tolstoy's examples appear to draw on history. But in fact, historical context has no explanatory power for Tolstoy. Moral value is not a historical category. It is timeless, because ethically we have at our disposal only the present. Just as Tolstoy does not believe in progress, he does not believe in "news." It was the public journalism of the early nineteenth century that had created the Shakespeare boom, in the same irrational way that a sensationalizing press created a world scandal around the Dreyfus case, a botched bureaucratic nightmare of natural interest to very few (*TonSh*, 99–101; 35:261). It follows for Tolstoy that if the current Shakespeare craze, or "infiltration," now seems a permanent fixture in European culture, this can only be the result of a continuing pernicious harmony between Shakespearean values and the worldviews of those who now award him fame (*TonSh*, 103; 35:262). Earlier periods (say, the eighteenth century) did not fall for it; other mental habits were in place. With this argument, too, Shaw partially concurred. But Shaw protested vehemently against Tolstoy's supposition that only individual human beings can move forward morally, that humanity as a whole had no drive to perfect the species. "Creative evolution" was Shaw's cherished alternative to the blind, arbitrary mindlessness of social Darwinism. In Shaw's opinion, the mind of Shakespeare had not earned for itself a place on that creatively evolved path.

In his concluding chapters, Tolstoy reiterates the argument of *What Is Art?* as it applies to the failings of Shakespeare. Art (and especially drama, a costly public art) has always fulfilled a religious function. It begins to serve worldly aims (the amusement of the mob, the interests of the powerful) when religious forms become coarse and unpersuasive. Such decay in Christian culture began during the Renaissance. The essence of authentic drama, however, is neither didactic allegory nor "the inculcation of any religious truths in artistic guise." It is the embodiment of a culture's most serious spiritual goals—"its relation to God, the world, the Universe, the Eternal" (*TonSh*, 112–13; 35:267). Shakespeare's world does not have a moral goal or center. For this reason, blind imitation of that world perverts our natural taste, which Tolstoy, following his beloved Rousseau, must believe always hungers toward the good. "Drama in our time is a person once great and now fallen to the last degree of degradation, who continues to pride himself on his past" (*TonSh*, 121; 35:270). And—Tolstoy adds in a footnote to his main Russian text, perhaps recalling his anxiety at the *Power of Darkness* rehearsals—may the reader not think that I exempt "the theatrical pieces that incidentally [or by chance—*sluchaino*] I wrote myself" (35:270).

This final self-reflexive turn is significant, Tolstoy's rooting out the "Shakespeare in himself." According to a conversation Tolstoy allegedly held with Isaak Feinerman, Tolstoy believed that lengthy self-presentation—monologues of self-searching—were inappropriate for the stage.[30] Such psychology was the task of novels. Drama is sculptural and external, presenting souls in bas-relief. The playwright works with a scalpel. "Do not force [characters] to think onstage . . . or to illuminate their natures through digressions into the past. All of that is boring, tedious, unnatural." Yet in his peasant drama *The Power of Darkness*, even knowing it was wrong, Tolstoy had packed in several such monologues. "It's difficult for an old novelist to restrain from doing that, as it's often hard for an old coachman to hold back his horses," Feinerman records Tolstoy saying. Hearing that his novel *Resurrection* had been adapted for the stage, he was irritated. Prince Nekhliudov is entirely "inside, there's no bas-relief to him"; moved into a play, his inner drama would become "a flat face, as the moon is a flat representation on a decorative canvas."

For Tolstoy, successful theater was physical, spatial, gestural. For him, drama rose or fell on performance practice. It is thus doubly paradoxical that Tolstoy did not feel obliged to seek out productions of Shakespeare's plays, to weigh their relative scenic and somatic merits with the same care that he brought to comparing translations into German or French. Tolstoy was comfortable passing judgment on plays that had not been composed to be read as written texts. But even this bookish approach to Shakespeare's theatrical art gives the lie to the idea that the postconversion Tolstoy cared only for ideology and Truth, not for art.

And it does more. Tolstoy's focus on form also helps explain why he ignored those splendid passages in Shakespeare that parallel or duplicate his own moral seeking on matters of power, morality, and war. Dozens of examples come to mind: the bastard Edmund on the cowardice of blaming astrology for vices we freely choose to indulge; Isabella to Angelo in *Measure for Measure* on the vanities and vice of all political power; Williams and Bates to their incognito king in *Henry the Fifth*, condemning battlefield atrocities on the eve of Agincourt (wisdom echoed by Prince Andrei in *War and Peace*, on the eve of the Battle of Borodino); the straight-talking Hubert to King John against the murder of princes; the cautionary by Ulysses in *Troilus and Cressida* on the "universal wolf" of power, will, and appetite. Such moments are loud and prominent in Shakespeare, ringing out at all levels of the social hierarchy. But Tolstoy does not listen to them. He appears indifferent to the moral content of these famous speeches. Instead, he is taken up by their mode of utterance.

This priority is key for grasping Tolstoy's curious obsession with *King Lear* in his 1903 treatise. In his early drafts, Tolstoy had considered using *Hamlet*, too, as a negative example.[31] He disliked the play in performance. Of the seventy marginal markings in Tolstoy's edition of *Hamlet*, only three are positive. But on closer inspection, Tolstoy might have concluded that the Prince of Denmark (unlike Lear) was an inappropriate target, too difficult to ridicule.[32] Hamlet is no tyrant. He is a soul searcher, a doubter in the efficacy of words, a lucid skeptic who advises the Players to "hold a mirror up to nature"—exactly as Tolstoy would have done to an acting troupe. Safest and best would be to discredit the Bard through an old man's folly and then to concentrate on flaws in formal presentation, which (as Tolstoy saw it) all the plays share. In the treatise as published, Lear takes the full brunt of the blow—and what irritates Tolstoy most is the stage monologue itself: introspective, pretentious, privileged.

Such privileged speech was never a problem for Shaw, artist of the political moment. In addition to his dazzling and polemical prefaces, he routinely embeds a character in his comedies who speaks Shavian truths: John Tanner in *Man and Superman*, Britannicus (and at times Caesar himself) in

Caesar and Cleopatra, Richard Dudgeon in *The Devil's Disciple*, the commonsensical Eve from the Garden of Eden in part 1 of *Back to Methuselah*. These figures do not need to function dialogically on the stage. And indeed they cannot if there is no one smart enough inside the story to take their arguments on. Their utterances can be anachronistic, floating above the time and space of the plot. In analogy with operatic arias, a Shaw stand-in can "sing" a truth directly to the hall, and no one else onstage need hear it or respond to it.

Tolstoy, a realist to the end, resists this device. He insists that all communications in drama occur in a unified time and space through rationally motivated dialogue and gesture within the story space. In an early draft of "On Shakespeare and on Drama," he expressed dismay that Turgenev, a writer so "gifted by aesthetic feeling," could recommend to young playwrights a few strikingly successful but isolated lines in *Macbeth* without commenting on the fake monologue that surrounds and pollutes them.[33] The Bakhtinian image of Tolstoy as patron of the "monolithically monologic" narrator must be adjusted when it comes to the staged arts. Drama is a narrator-free zone. But Tolstoy's stage habits, dialogic as they were, did not equip him to appreciate the buoyant comedy of ideas practiced so brilliantly by Shaw. When Tolstoy desired laughter in the hall, he did satire or farce—not the two-way joyous laughter of comedy. He was highly adept at the dramatized parable, which he modeled on medieval miracle or mystery plays using folk material. He dreamed of writing instructive scenarios for fairs and peasant show booths and in 1909–10 completed some dramatic vignettes under the title "The Wisdom of Children." For psychologically more complex dramas, it was the gravitas of tragedy that appealed to him.

SHAW MEETS TOLSTOY: ENTER CHERTKOV

Between 1905 and 1910, Shaw exchanged half a dozen letters with Tolstoy, mediated by Vladimir Chertkov. Chertkov had left Russia in 1897 and spent more than a decade in England, financing a Tolstoyan publishing house (Free Age Press) out of his family savings. Sensing a kindred spirit, Chertkov sent Shaw, in the spring of 1905, his just-completed English translation of "On Shakespeare and on Drama." Shaw skimmed it and in August wrote back a note of thanks: "As you know," Shaw wrote Chertkov, "I have striven hard to open English eyes to the emptiness of Shakespeare's philosophy, to the superficiality and second-handedness of his morality, to his snobbery, his vulgar prejudices . . . and I, for one, shall value Tolstoy's criticism all the more because it is the criticism of a foreigner who can not possibly be enchanted by the mere word-music which makes Shakespeare so irresistible in England."[34]

Chertkov lost no time stitching these opinions into the cause. He edited Shaw's epistle and attached it (without permission) as an appendix to his 1906 English edition of Tolstoy's treatise, presenting it as "extracts" from a letter and obscuring the fact that it was addressed to him and not to Tolstoy.[35] Meanwhile, Shaw read Tolstoy's tract more carefully, and he was shocked by Tolstoy's errors, irresponsible critical strategies, and faulty logic, confiding to Chertkov in a follow-up letter (November 3, 1905) that "overall, the essay is very bad."[36] "Have you verified the accuracy of [your] translation?" he asked in dismay. "It's full of utterly inexplicable mistakes." If published, Shaw feared that such mistakes would distract readers from taking seriously the sensible arguments and damage Tolstoy's reputation. (Again we must marvel how the Anglo-Saxon Shaw, accustomed to answering for the accuracy of his statements to an alert civic readership, underestimates the license that Tolstoy and his followers enjoyed; their reputation, fame, and integrity were sustained precisely through radical, uncompromising statements.) Shaw now reproached Tolstoy for his dishonest paraphrase of *King Lear*, indifference to Renaissance stage conventions, inability to appreciate Shakespearean humor, and insistence that the world, in loving the Bard these past three hundred years, had been hypnotized against its will rather than responding consciously to the associative, rhythmic richness of Shakespeare's language. One comment of Shaw's would have caused the music-loving, piano-playing Tolstoy to wince: "Tolstoy can prove that Chopin's music is only the jingling of strings in a wooden box, but will those people who have experienced the effect of Chopin's music heed this proof?" Shaw concluded his letter to Chertkov with a defense of artistic imagination. "Life isn't logical, and it is not for Tolstoy, who writes his works like a poet, to condemn Shakespeare because he does not write his works like a lawyer."

Chertkov handled this second, far harsher letter very shrewdly. It was neither copied nor circulated. He delayed sending both letters to Tolstoy. And then he betrayed Shaw, who had requested that any publication of the first, carelessly and casually positive letter be accompanied by the criticisms detailed in the second, especially of Tolstoy's caricature of *King Lear*. But the story does not stop there. Shaw rethought his own strategies and priorities. Several days later (November 19) he sent Chertkov a third letter softening the harsh tones of the second. In it Shaw reaffirmed his disagreements with Tolstoy over Shakespeare's art but implored Chertkov to "make it absolutely clear to the public that I'm on Tolstoy's side, and that I attribute huge significance to the authority of all his opinions." Shaw respected righteous scandal. He categorically stated that he counted Tolstoy among "humanity's prophets"—and "even at the price of a few misunderstandings of minor significance," he preferred to be "on the side of the prophets rather than the journalists."

From that point on, the wrap-up was risk-free. Chertkov decided against burdening Tolstoy with the originals—he hinted to Tolstoy that Shaw's reaction had been the result of personal envy—and paraphrased their content in a letter to Tolstoy (on November 21): "Having read your article, he [Shaw] wrote a rather stupid letter, and then, after several days, another little letter [*pis'metso*], from which it is clear that he was ashamed of the preceding one." Herein lay Chertkov's shrewdness. On the Shakespeare question, both Shaw and Tolstoy were strong critics. They welcomed allies but not really interlocutors, and they certainly did not welcome being corrected in their moral rhetoric. Chertkov, of course, knew this. When Tolstoy acknowledged receipt of Shaw's feedback and then requested that the Shakespeare essay nevertheless "be printed as it is," he added as an afterthought to Chertkov, "If those 'blunders' that Shaw speaks of really exist, correct them yourself."[37] Surely both men, master and disciple, took it for granted that there would be no corrections whatsoever.

There matters rested on the Shakespeare treatise. Before moving from theater theory to playwriting practice—the final portion of this essay—let me highlight one aspect of the argument so far. Shaw eventually produced a body of some sixty plays, most of them in the genre of a "comedy of ideas." All are committed to the Shakespearean notion that poetic wit not only makes for efficient, fast-paced theater but can also be cognitively enriching, even conducive to an epiphany. Tolstoy trusted ideas far less. In his view, ideas were slaves to feeling (and often cover-ups for despicable feelings), incompetent to infect on their own. An overly pliable wit worked against wisdom.

One who grasped this Tolstoyan dynamic perfectly was the Russian formalist critic Viktor Shklovsky. His essay on Tolstoy's struggle against the Bard opens on this note: "Shakespeare's language, as Tolstoy observed, is based not only on metaphor but on the metaphor-pun."[38] In keeping with his activist agenda for art and his passion for estrangement and for "waking up" life, Shklovsky understood Tolstoy's preference for working models over mere metaphoric images. The resonant example he brings forward is the remark of Lear's Fool that the two evil daughters are the "parings" of an egg. Why did Tolstoy, upon encountering such utterances, feel the same heavy discomfort he experienced upon "hearing a bad joke"? In Shklovsky's view, poets like Shakespeare and Mayakovsky know that "puns are often supported by rhyme, which imparts to them a special profundity." But for the prose-writing Tolstoy this collaboration is unnatural, immoral, its crispness fraudulent. Tolstoy's metaphors are never merely aural or juxtapositional. They involve not fleeting "music" but the slow building up of visible worldviews (of an oak, a beehive, a game of chess, peasants pulling a log). On this issue, too, Shaw sided with the poets. He heard in the art of Shakespeare's "word-music" (its harmonies, rhythms, and intricate wordplay) the stuff of absolute inspiration. It could create worlds of its own. In the mid-1890s Shaw had cautioned young actors to "leave blank verse alone" until they had "experienced emotion deep enough to crave for poetic expression, at which point verse will seem an absolutely natural and real form of speech to you."[39]

Over this conceptual and linguistic divide we move from theory to practice. It takes us outside the Shakespeare controversy strictly defined to larger questions of dramatic integrity and the potential of staged art to enlighten conscience, as Tolstoy and Shaw understood it. In December 1906, perhaps hoping to smooth out any residual tension caused by the Shakespeare squabble (and this time through Aylmer Maude), Shaw sent Tolstoy a copy of his recently completed play *Man and Superman*, including its appendix, *A Revolutionist's Handbook*. Shaw marked several places in act 3 of the play that he hoped Tolstoy would appreciate.

A TALE OF TWO—OR PERHAPS THREE—PLAYS

On its first reading, in January 1907, Tolstoy didn't like Shaw's play at all.[40] But a year and a half later he reread the work, took notes, and on August 17, 1908, wrote Shaw a long letter. *Man and Superman* is most famous for its third act, a dream set in Hell with a cast of characters (and snatches of music) from Mozart's opera *Don Giovanni*. Its purpose is to provide a forum for Shaw to rewrite the Don Juan myth. The dream is full of monologues (by Juan, Mephistopheles, the statuesque Commendatore; only Dona Anna is dialogic). Shaw turns Hell into a trivial, decadent, boring place filled with erotic pursuits, and Heaven into a difficult site of intellectual inquiry. In this dream space Don Juan—who in the larger-frame play is John Tanner, a Shaw stand-in—becomes a new sort of hero, one who finally escapes (unlike Tanner in the larger play) the hungry women who, on behalf of the Life Force, relentlessly seduce and trap him.

In his August 17, 1908, brief response to Shaw, Tolstoy praised the serious moral argument of *Man and Superman* and the boldness of Shaw's "Don Juan (John Tanner) in Hell." This sober, cerebral, robustly "postsexual" being must have struck Tolstoy as a vigorous moral improvement on the eponymous libertines of Molière, Mozart, Lord Byron, and Pushkin. That John Tanner shared Tolstoy's own horrific awe before (and disillusionment with) the female Life Force must have increased the appeal. But then Tolstoy reproached Shaw for what we recognize as Shakespearean failings: an excess pleasure in wit and wordplay, a "desire to surprise and astonish the reader by [his] great erudition, talent, and intelligence." "Dear Mr. Shaw," Tolstoy implored, "life is a great and serious matter. One should not speak jokingly about such a subject as the purpose of human life, or the causes of its perversion." The matter of life, death, and moral progress would have benefited from "a more serious approach to it, rather than its being a casual insertion in a comedy." And indeed (Tolstoy continues) since ideas—rather than infectious feelings or graphic gestures—seem to be the paramount commodity in this play, why bother with the pretext of fiction at all? "I would prefer the speeches of Don Juan to be not the speeches of an apparition but the speeches of Shaw," Tolstoy reasons. The *Handbook* should not have been presented as the work of some nonexistent Tanner but of "the living Bernard Shaw, responsible for his own words" (78:201–2).

Tolstoy's reading of *Man and Superman*—like his naive wonder at Othello's premurder monologue—is so odd from any conventional theatrical perspective and so consistent from within Tolstoy's own worldview that one hardly knows how to gloss it. His reluctance to credit Shavian humor as a possible path to Truth is grounded in the same disgust he shows toward Shakespeare's jesters, door porters, and gravediggers. Tolstoy never concealed his belief that staged art was fraudulent when built up out of abstract ideas mechanically exchanged rather than from human actions and emotions. But more positive reasons for Tolstoy's problems with *Man and Superman* emerged two years later, in a final epistolary exchange between these two formidable writers. Featured in this ultimate exchange was a little-known play of Shaw's and a very famous play of Tolstoy's. Both dramas deal with the risk and bliss of personal revelation, and both revolve around initially failed, and then ultimately successful, spiritual mentoring.

In 1909 Shaw was fifty-three years old, an experienced theater critic, and the author of twenty-two innovative works for the stage. Tolstoy, the most famous writer in the world, was eighty-one. Shaw had seen a performance of *The Power of Darkness* in London (it premiered at the Stage Society in December 1904). Impressed by the production, Shaw sent Tolstoy, on February 14, 1909, a copy of his own just-finished one-act play, *The Shewing-Up of Blanco Posnet*.[41] Shaw's playlet was not typical for him in topic, locale, or genre—a morality play (or perhaps a mock morality play) that involved horse stealing, blasphemy, and guilt and redemption on the colonial American frontier. Subtitled *A Sermon in Crude Melodrama*, it was preceded by a massive preface on the evils of British stage censorship quite unrelated to the content of the play.[42] In that preface, Shaw referred to his one-act drama as a "religious tract in dramatic form." To Tolstoy, he wrote ingratiatingly, "If I may say so, it is the sort of play that you do extraordinarily well."[43]

The "sort of play" Shaw had in mind was Tolstoy's *The Power of Darkness*. Its naturalistic plot is indeed melodramatic and crude. The handsome hired hand, Nikita, poisons his master, Pyotr, so that he can marry Pyotr's wife, Anisya, and take over the farm. Tiring of Anisya, Nikita begins to eye the late master's weak-minded elder daughter, Akulina (his own stepdaughter); they slip into sin, and the horror of the play peaks with Nikita's crushing of their newborn child under the floorboards of the stage. Arguably the real villain is not Nikita, however, but his mother, Matryona, an amoral schemer armed with self-serving folk proverbs who panders for her son against the will of her husband, the righteous Akim. Into this ghastly tale, during Akulina's cover-up wedding, wanders a drunken ex-soldier named Mitrich, who starts boasting of his misbehavior in the army: "Just go your own way, even if they flog you," he mutters. "Don't be afraid of people." Nikita overhears this bit of drunken babble—and suddenly, overcome by the weight of his sins, drops to his knees. To the horror of Matryona and to the ecstasy of Akim, he confesses his guilt and begs forgiveness of all he has wronged.

Watching that play in London, Shaw had been struck not by the clichéd figures standard for such melodramas (Don Juan, faithless wife, deceived husband, seduced maiden, illegitimate child violently disposed of) but by the babbling tramp Mitrich. Wholly by accident, this worthless walkthrough figure Mitrich had triggered spiritual transformation in Nikita, who suddenly "went his own way," the way of repentance. And Shaw intimated to Tolstoy that his own little play had a similar structure and lesson.

The Shewing-Up of Blanco Posnet is a detective drama (or perhaps a mystery play) set in the courtroom of a small town on the American frontier.[44] Its hero, Blanco, is an outcast, drinker, brawler, hooligan—a theatrical type and something of a dandy, not unlike Nikita in Tolstoy's play. Blanco has an older brother, a sanctimonious born-again minister who never misses a chance to lecture his younger brother about sin. Blanco has been arrested for stealing the Sheriff's horse. If a witness can be found, the Vigilance Committee will hang him for it. Strapper Kemp, the Sheriff's bullying brother, persuades his girlfriend, Feemy, the village slut, to testify that she saw Blanco on horseback at dawn. Blanco, meanwhile, is in a strange and excited state: he insists that he does not have the horse. God, he says, "has done me out of it." Although Blanco wants to be a strong bad man, God, it seems, sneaked up on him in the form of a vision of a woman with a child. Slowly the truth emerges. Blanco had indeed stolen the horse but then had given it to a stranger whose child was dying. With a horse she could make it to a doctor. Blanco sees God's words written on a rainbow, hands over the animal, and is pinned to the spot. Strapper seizes him alone in the field. Then the "rainbow woman" is found not far from town, wandering aimlessly with the Sheriff's horse, and is summoned as a witness. "I was desperate," the woman tells the court. "I saw the horse, the man, and thought it was a miracle; I put the child in his arms . . . the man cursed me, cursed the child, called him a little Judas and said that he would hang for it." Then suddenly "he gave me the horse, and went away." The child died anyway, she said. "Don't touch the man, hang me instead." The woman's story inspires Feemy to confess her false testimony and persuades the Sheriff to dismiss all charges of horse theft. But it infuriates Blanco. "Just what He would do," Blanco says: "God and His tricks, getting back at me because I lived my own life in my own way."

At the end, however, Blanco jumps up on the table and delivers a sermon. The sermon is partly in jest—it is often interrupted with laughter—but there is also anguish and ecstasy in it. "Why did the child die?" Blanco asks the court. "Why did He make me go soft on the child if He was going hard on it Himself? Why should he go hard on the innocent kid and go soft on a rotten thing like me? . . . There's two games being played . . . I played the rotten game; but the great game was played on me." Over the dead body of this innocent child, a rowdy crowd identified by Shaw only as "the Boys" cries, "Hurrah!" and heads out to the saloon to celebrate. Drinks are on Blanco. The ending of Shaw's odd little play might seem more Dostoevskian than Tolstoyan, more resonant with Alyosha Karamazov promising pancakes to a band of schoolboys after Ilyusha's burial than with the shock and awe caused by Nikita's confession of his crimes at Akulina's wedding. But Shaw was convinced that the play would please Tolstoy.

Shaw's letter to Tolstoy about his *Blanco Posnet* and Tolstoy's answer a half year before his death return us to their watershed disagreements over Shakespeare and the tasks of drama. I address here only one detail in that final correspondence, relating to Tolstoy's saintly Akim and Nikita's confessional moment. In his lengthy letter to Tolstoy of February 14, 1910, Shaw reiterated the philosophy of his *Man and Superman*: "God does not yet exist, but there is a creative force constantly struggling to evolve an executive organ of godlike knowledge and power." In the fullness of our creative evolution, the death of the little boy in *Blanco Posnet* would be seen as an evil that humanity would overcome. But most interesting to Shaw is the episodic character central to the "conversion moment" in *The Power of Darkness*, act 5, scene 10: Mitrich. Around that "old rascal of a soldier" Mitrich, the whole moral lesson of Tolstoy's peasant drama revolved. What was that lesson? Shaw made bold to explain it to Tolstoy: "The preaching of the pious old father, right as he was, could never be of any use—it could only anger his son and rub the last grains of self-respect out of him. But what the pious and good father could not do, the old rascal of a soldier did as if he was the voice of God." It was Mitrich, a sinner with the "voice of God," who gave Nikita the strength to confess.

"To me," Shaw wrote, "that scene where the two drunkards [Nikita and Mitrich] are wallowing in the straw, and the older rascal lifts the younger one above his cowardice and his selfishness, has an intensity of effect that no merely romantic scene could possibly attain." Shaw then thanks Tolstoy for this moment: "In *Blanco Posnet* I have exploited in my own fashion this mine of dramatic material which you were the first to open up to modern playwrights." Akim is ineffectual. In *The Power of Darkness*, only the fallen Mitrich can raise up the fallen Nikita—just as only the blaspheming sinner Blanco can raise up the perjuring Feemy in Shaw's play.[45] And in the same way that "Blanco does not want to be like his [pious] brother," so, Shaw argues, "none of us want to be like our fathers, the intention of the universe being that we shall be like God."

Shaw hastened to add that there was a great deal of humility, tolerance, and humor in such situations. Crude melodrama can be healthily comedic when it respects the ability of individuals to change unexpectedly—and comedy in general was effective for resurrecting the moral sense. Shaw whimsically confronted Tolstoy: "You say my manner is not serious enough . . . But why should humor and laughter be excommunicated? Suppose the world were only one of God's jokes, would you work any the less to make it a good joke instead of a bad one?"

After reading Shaw's February letter, Tolstoy scribbled on the envelope, "From Shaw: clever stupidities [*Ot Shou: umnoe glupoe*]" (81:254–55). When he answered Shaw's letter on May 9, he thanked Shaw for sending *Blanco Posnet* and then, on the subject of God and evil, repeated what he had said two years earlier—that this habit of turning serious matters into jokes left a "very painful impression." Tolstoy agreed that "the preaching of righteousness has generally little influence on people." But then he added, "It does not follow, however, that such preaching is unnecessary. The reason for the failure is that those who preach do not fulfill what they preach, i.e. hypocrisy" (*TL*, 2:700).

There could not be a more Tolstoyan response to the Shavian challenge. On Shaw's side, the world is a carousel of ideas in which good drama explores many different carriers; on Tolstoy's side, a solipsistic personalism remains the most reliable path to truth. Or put another way, for Tolstoy preaching fails not because the sin is difficult, the sinner conflicted, the future uncertain, life and fate unfair, or because the validity of a judgment depends on one's perspective. Such factors prompt a playwright to be objective (i.e., sympathetic to all sides). Those are, we might say, Shakespearean values and virtues. Tolstoy always held it against the Bard, and against Shaw, that one could not tell where they were, which side they were on. Impersonal (or objective) ideas are "nowhere." In Tolstoy's moral system, every value, to be communicated, requires a code of behavior and a face. If preaching fails, then, it is because the preacher has failed—for if the preacher were honest, exemplary, internally consistent, not hypocritical, his message would have "infected" the sinner, just the way a genuine work of art infects its audience. It is not the immensity or complexity of the sin but the behavioral purity of the speaker who exposes it that determines the effectiveness of the cure.

Thus any living subject with genuine moral experience can lift up a sinner. This might happen by bumbling accident, as it did with the drunken Mitrich, whose confused testimony triggered Nikita's confession. Or it could be the steady pressure and presence of a "righteous person," someone (preferably) who did not need to talk at all, because this person had learned a truth by living it and radiating it.[46] Such people don't need to startle others with their clever words, the way Lear's Fool startles that royal household; they are at one with their words. In fact, clever words are usually an evasion or a cover-up. It's the coward who goes on talking. No surprise, then, that Tolstoy's righteous people are almost always inarticulate. They are resolute in action, but in their words they are stutterers, bunglers, ill spoken—exactly like Akim in *The Power of Darkness*.

That Akim is a stutterer was crucial to Tolstoy. But Akim was not a bumbler in any other dimension. In March of 1887, Tolstoy had written to Pavel Svobodin, the actor in Petersburg's Aleksandrinsky Theatre cast in the part of Akim, with the following advice: "Speak with a hesitation, and then suddenly phrases will burst out, and then again a hesitation, and 'y'know' [in Russian *tayeh*] . . . It is not, in my view, necessary to mumble. [Akim] walks firmly . . . His gestures, his movements, are earnest [*istovye*]; it's only nimble, smooth speech that God did not grant him."[47]

Perhaps if Shakespeare's jesters and fools were not so nimble and "smooth of speech," if they had stuttered while walking firmly, they could also be for Tolstoy the vehicle for truth that they are for audiences around the world.

Tolstoy and Shaw exchanged no more letters. Later that autumn Tolstoy fled Yasnaya Polyana, and by the end of the year he was no more. In a letter of March of 1907 he had confided to the German Shakespeare scholar Eugen Reichel that he had no hopes of convincing anyone with his treatise against the Bard, written "a long time ago now" (*TL* 2:664–66). Artistic sense among people is "so unevenly distributed" that any press campaign, without resistance, can put over any literary or philosophical fraud. "No one knows Kant now, they know Nietzsche," Tolstoy lamented, and the "same sort of [false] reputation for new Shakespeares" is inevitably on the horizon. Bernard Shaw lived, worked, laughed, and wrote with superhuman energy and wit for another forty years. These years included two decades of supporting Joseph Stalin in his "Great Soviet Experiment." In July 1931, Shaw celebrated his seventy-fifth birthday in Moscow.[48] His venerable figure was greeted by huge bussed-in crowds of workers shouting "Hail Shaw!"—much as Tolstoy had been greeted in his time, although for Tolstoy no one had to be bussed in. Shaw showed little interest in socialist-realist theater (or in any theater) during his trip. But he returned home singing Russia's praises and chiding the greedy, free-market West, sunk in Depression. This birthday trip was an enormous propaganda victory for the Stalinist establishment.

◦ ◦ ◦

What can be said in closing about these two writers in the shadow of Shakespeare? Both Tolstoy and Shaw were very public, didactic, "theatrical" men. But Shaw sought out theater and built his plays on humor. Like Shakespeare, he believed that comedy was at base festive, therapeutic, conciliatory, and instructive. Tolstoy, on some level, always dreaded the theater and never successfully managed a healthy comedy—that is, one where everyone is both laughed at and has the right to laugh back. Shaw never lost his pleasure in the public realm, the pulpit, and fame. His many thousands of personal letters (as a correspondent he rivals Tolstoy) play affectionately with his own image, his own loves and antipathies, providing his interlocutors with glimpses, tantalizing prefaces, into his own soul. Tolstoy's recurring fantasy for his final decade was to be alone and anonymous—to let Truth speak for itself, without his name on it. But by 1910, the most private details of Tolstoy's life had become public melodrama. His death was the most photographed and filmed event of its time, a stage extravaganza that the entire world could witness and replay. For all these differences, however, Tolstoy and Shaw were both "on the side of the prophets" (as Shaw had written to Chertkov in November 1905)—and thus more concerned to jolt and instruct the crowd than to please it, as had their illustrious Elizabethan predecessor. Tolstoy would have agreed with this graphic metaphor from the preface to *The Shewing-Up of Blanco Posnet*:

> It is no more possible for me to do my work honestly as a playwright without giving pain than it is for a dentist. The nation's morals are like its teeth: the more decayed they are the more it hurts to touch them. Prevent dentists and dramatists from giving pain, and not only will our morals become as carious as our teeth, but toothache and the plagues that follow neglected morality will presently cause more agony than all the dentists and dramatists at their worst have caused since the world began.[49]

If Leo Tolstoy and Bernard Shaw, sparring over the didactic utility of Shakespeare, were striving to be "humanity's prophets," they hoped for very different futures. Shaw, a model secular humanist, put his faith in creative evolution. To the twenty-first century, his optimism feels dated, naive, even archaic. Tolstoy was sterner and less starry-eyed. Near the end of "On Shakespeare and on Drama" he insists that drama return to its true vocation, "to serve the clarification of religious consciousness," the "only principle that permanently unites human beings" (*TonSh*, 188; 35:269). This argument has ancient credentials, which in our anxious era is experiencing a renaissance.[50] But happily, as Shakespeare testifies, theater prospers equally well as a laboratory and as a liturgy.

NOTES

1. An evenhanded survey of Tolstoy's dramatic preferences can be found in Aleksei Zverev, "Dramaturgiia Tolstogo" [Tolstoy's Dramaturgy], appendix to Aleksei Zverev and Vladimir Tunimanov, *Lev Tolstoy* (Moscow: Molodaia Gvardiia, 2006), 722–53, esp. 724–26. Zverev suggests that Tolstoy's delight at "exposé satire" presaged his later ideal, "the possibility of uniting people in common spiritual space, in unanimity and the quest for truth" (725). All translations, unless otherwise credited, are mine, and cited translations are in certain instances modified.

2. These judgments were culled chronologically from *The Jubilee* edition by V. S. Mishin to open his commentary to Tolstoy's 1903 essay "On Shakespeare and on Drama," which is my basic source here. See V. S. Mishin, "'O Shekspire i o drame': Istoriia pisaniia i pechataniia" ['On Shakespeare and on drama': The history of its writing and publication], which was published in 1950 in *The Jubilee*, volume 35, overseen by A. P. Sergeenko and V. S. Mishin, pages 680–84, respectively. George Gibian, *Tolstoj and Shakespeare* (The Hague: Mouton, 1957), 12–25, paraphrases *The Jubilee* commentary almost exactly, with some compression, additions, and one curious mistranslation; see note 9 below.

3. Also cited in Gibian, *Tolstoj and Shakespeare*, 16. "Run-of-the-mill" or "dime a dozen" renders the Russian *diuzhenyi*.

4. "Playhouse plays" is a rendering of *balagannye p'esy*, literally show or puppet-booth plays, public-fair spectacles. In citing this letter, Gibian, *Tolstoj and Shakespeare*, 19, translates *pamiatlivyi* (retentive, memory-ful) *akter* as "clever actor," but Tolstoy's criticism would seem to be directed less against cleverness per se than against "pulling strings," against the secondhand knowledge of the actor who reads about, and then imitates, an emotion rather than lives through it as a personal event.

5. *The Power of Darkness* was published in 1887. Tsar Alexander III read it, liked it, approved it for the stage but then rescinded his approval at the request of the Holy Synod. Meanwhile, European premieres took place in Paris (with the encouragement of Émile Zola) and in Berlin; by the time of the Moscow and Petersburg premieres, therefore, the play had a performance history as well as in-print fame. See Justin Weir, "Violence and the Role of Drama in the Late Tolstoy: *The Realm of Darkness*," in Donna Tussing Orwin, ed., *Anniversary Essays on Tolstoy* (Cambridge University Press, 2010), 183–98, esp. 185.

6. Gibian, citing this diary entry, renders *Vot esli by byl molod i zadoren* (If I were young and naughty) as "If I were young and healthy," apparently confusing *zadornyi* (naughty, fervent. provocative. quick-tempered) with *zdravyi* (healthy) (Gibian, *Tolstoj and Shakespeare*, 19).

7. All attempts to understand Tolstoy's assessment of Shakespeare must grapple with the authority of Orwell's canonized essay, a provocative piece of journalism but weak as a refutation of Tolstoy's argument. For a defense of Tolstoy that begins with a severe critique of Orwell, see H. O. Mounce, "Shakespeare," in *Tolstoy on Aesthetics: What Is Art?* (Farnham, U.K.: Ashgate, 2001), 94–98.

8. G. Wilson Knight, *Shakespeare and Tolstoy* (Oxford: Oxford University Press and London: English Association, 1934), 29. (This was Pamphlet no. 88 released by English Association in April 1934.) Subsequent citations to this work appear in the main text as parenthetical page numbers. Knight's two major arguments—that the German Romantics deified Shakespeare by applying criteria more appropriate to great novelists than to great poets and that Tolstoy's trenchant resistance to "poetic grandeur" in language or in character contributed to his unfair assumption that Shakespeare lacked moral or religious subtlety—are a valuable supplement to the revisionism of the present essay.

9. The phrase is George Steiner's. See George Steiner, "A Reading against Shakespeare," in *No Passion Spent: Essays 1978–1995*, 108–28 (New Haven, Conn.: Yale University Press, 1996), 112. Steiner's sympathies are with Wittgenstein.

10. Shaw married Charlotte Payne-Townshend, an Irish heiress and fellow Fabian. For an account of this mutual decision (insisted on by the wife), see Arnold Silver, *Bernard Shaw: The Darker Side* (Stanford, Calif.: Stanford University Press, 1982), 131–42. Silver cites Shaw's explanation from 1930: "As man and wife we found a new relation in which sex had no part. It ended the old gallantries, flirtations, and philanderings for both of us. Even of these it was the ones that were never consummated that left the longest and kindliest memories. Do not forget that all marriages are different, and that marriages between young people, followed by parentage, must not be lumped in with childless partnerships between middle-aged people who have passed the age at which the bride can safely bear a first child" (134). Biographers dispute Shaw's assertion that his philanderings were in fact abandoned.

11. Shaw to the English dramatist Henry Arthur Jones (1851–1921), May 20, 1898, in Bernard Shaw, *Collected Letters 1898–1910*, ed. Dan H. Laurence (London: Reinhardt, 1972), 44. The full discussion is more nuanced, however: "Have you read Tolstoy's 'What Is Art?' . . . His theory is right all through, his examples the silliest obsolete nonsense. Among other things he is very strong on the Universality of good art, and the classiness of bad art—that good art is as intelligible to a peasant as to a gentleman &c."

12. Shaw's review of Aylmer Maude's translation of Tolstoy's *What Is Art*,

Daily Chronicle, September 10, 1898, in Bernard Shaw, *Selected Non-Dramatic Writings of Bernard Shaw*, ed. Dan H. Laurence (New York: Houghton Mifflin, 1965), 428.

13. See the section "Better Than Shakespear?" in the preface to *Three Plays for Puritans* (1901), which addresses the middle play *Caesar and Cleopatra: A History*, written by Shaw in 1898 as a corrective to Shakespeare's *Antony and Cleopatra*: "It is a significant fact that the mutilators of Shakespeare, who never could be persuaded that Shakespear knew his business better than they, have ever been the most fanatical of his worshippers . . . So much for Bardolatry!" (Bernard Shaw, "Better Than Shakespear?," in *Complete Plays with Prefaces*, 6 vols. [New York: Dodd Mead, 1963], 3:lv–lvi).

14. Edwin Wilson, ed., *Shaw on Shakespeare: An Anthology of Bernard Shaw's Writings on the Plays and Productions of Shakespeare* (New York: Dutton, 1961; New York: Applause Theatre and Cinema Books, 2002).

15. Shaw's first biographer suggests the entire Bardolatry vendetta was a publicity stunt to promote the plays of Shaw's own hero, Henrik Ibsen: "Shaw's crusade against Bardolatry . . . is one of the most amusing of his campaigns to attract attention" (Archibald Henderson, "Blaming the Bard," in *George Bernard Shaw: Man of the Century* [New York: Appleton-Century-Crofts, 1956], 689).

16. In 1895, reviewing *All's Well That Ends Well*, Shaw wrote that while Shakespeare's morality was secondhand and commonplace, his magic was in "the turn of the line," the alliteration, rhythm, word-music. "It is the score and not the libretto that keeps the work alive and fresh" (Bernard Shaw, "All's Well That Ends Well," in Wilson, *Shaw on Shakespeare*, 7).

17. Both Tolstoy and Shaw despised the marketing of sexual appetites onstage, but Shaw, in addition, resented Victorian hypocrisy: since the social facts of sexuality could not be openly addressed (as he did in several early plays, especially *Mrs. Warren's Profession*, 1893), theaters were given over to acts of tedious sensuousness "without the courage of their vices." The result was the boring "romantic play"—the "substitution of sensuous ecstasy for intellectual activity and honesty" (Shaw, *Complete Plays*, 3:xlv).

18. "Shakespear, who knew human weakness so well, never knew human strength of the Caesarian type" (Shaw, *Complete Plays*, 3:liv). His strong men all default to wantons, and this was a failure in dramatic genre. Shaw had a "technical objection to making sexual infatuation a tragic theme. Experience proves that it is only effective in the comic spirit." Mrs. Quickly's pawning her plate for love of Falstaff is tolerable and even endearing, he insisted, but not Antony's quitting the Battle of Actium for love of Cleopatra (Shaw, *Complete Plays*, 3:liv).

19. For a fine discussion of Shaw as "performance critic" that bypasses issues of artistic rivalry, intellectual competition, and strategic showmanship, see Robert B. Pierce, "Bernard Shaw as Shakespeare Critic," *Shaw* 31, no. 1 (2011): 118–32, esp. 123.

20. Bernard Show, preface to *The Dark Lady of the Sonnets* (1910), in Shaw, *Complete Plays*, 2:634.

21. Henderson, *George Bernard Shaw*, 715.

22. Aylmer Maude, *The Life of Tolstoy*, 2 vols. (London: Constable, 1908–10; Oxford: Oxford University Press, 1987), 464. Page reference is to the 1987 edition.

23. For an account of Shaw's struggle with puritanical British stage censorship—in certain ways more arduous than restrictions in tsarist Russia, with its thoroughly "French" high culture—see James Woodfield, "The Censorship Saga," in *English Theatre in Transition 1881–1914*, 108–31 (London: Croom Helm, 1984).

24. The first authorized English translation of "O Shekspire i o drame" (35:216–72) contained Crosby's text, as well as portions of Shaw's letter to Chertkov, edited by Chertkov. See Leo Tolstoy, *Tolstoy on Shakespeare: A Critical Essay on Shakespeare, Translated by V. Tchertkoff and I. F. M., Followed by "Shakespeare's Attitude to the Working Classes" by Ernest Crosby and a Letter from G. Bernard Shaw* (New York: Funk and Wagnalls, 1906); subsequent citations to this work appear in the main text as *TonSh*. The "letter from Shaw" was misrepresented (as being addressed to Tolstoy), edited (to remove criticisms of Tolstoy), and included without Shaw's permission.

25. The most famous of these was Leopold Sulerzhitsky (1872–1916), an intimate of the Tolstoy household and a teacher in the Moscow Art Theatre's First Studio. For the influence of Tolstoy's literary technique on Stanislavsky's theories of acting, see Daniel Larlham, "Stanislavsky, Tolstoy, and the 'Life of the Human Spirit,'" in *The Routledge Companion to Stanislavsky*, ed. R. Andrew White, 174–94 (London: Routledge, 2014), 186–88.

26. On this production and "Stanislavsky's proverbial passion for the material richness and realness of the stage event," see Anna Muza, "The Organic and the Political: Stanislavsky's Dilemma (Ibsen, Tolstoy, Gorky)," in White, *Routledge Companion*, 37, 40.

27. In "Leo Tolstoy, Debunker of Shakespeare," Alexander Anikst remarks that all we must do is turn everything Tolstoy rejects into a positive sign, and we have a perfect recipe for Elizabethan theater. See Aleksandr Anikst, "Lev Tolstoi—nisprovergatel' Shekspira," *Teatr* 11 (1960): 42–53.

28. Rimvydas Šilbajoris sees "the relationship between reality and language" as the major battle site between Tolstoy and Shakespeare. See Rimvydas Šilbajoris, *Tolstoy's Aesthetics and His Art* (Columbus, Ohio: Slavica, 1991), 142–43, and the forum on this book in *TSJ* 4 (1991): 105–45.

29. George Orwell, "Tolstoy, Lear, and the Fool," in *Shooting an Elephant and Other Essays* (New York: Harcourt, Brace and World, 1950), 32–52. Subsequent citations to this work appear in the main text as parenthetical page numbers.

30. I. Teneromo, "L. N. Tolstoi o teatre" [Tolstoy on theatre], *Teatr i iskusstvo* 34 (1908): 580–81. Like most of the journalism of Isaak Feinerman (Teneromo) about his famous friend, the "interview" published in 1907, a composite of conversations and memoirs, was not authorized by Tolstoy. On Tolstoy and Feinerman in this volume, see Medzhibovskaya, "Tolstoy's Jewish Question." Roughly the same testimony is provided (also without annotation) by Zverev: "Novel and story are pictorial work, there the master wields a brush and lays down oil paint on a canvas. There, background hues, shadows, transitional tones; but drama is a purely sculptural realm. One must work with a scalpel and not lay down paint but carve out bas-relief . . . I understood the whole difference between novel and drama when I sat down to write my *Power of Darkness*" (Zverev, "Dramaturgiia Tolstogo," 734).

31. S. M. Breitburg, "Tolstoi za chteniem i na predstavlenii 'Gamleta' (po neopublikovannym materialam)" [Tolstoy while reading *Hamlet*, and while watching a performance of it (based on unpublished materials)], *Internatsional'naia literatura* 11/12 (1940): 233–50. It bothers Breitburg (who would like to rehabilitate Shakespeare) that Tolstoy claimed to have reread all of Shakespeare for his treatise but then discusses in detail nothing beyond the single tragedy *Lear*. He notes that in the early drafts, when the tract was still conceived as a "preface" to Crosby's pamphlet, Tolstoy admitted the problem and limited himself to "the impressions made on him by Shakes[peare]'s dramas" (233). In a later draft, Tolstoy anticipated the criticism in his typically sly way: "I know that no matter which Shakespearean play I chose to survey, people would always be found who would say, yes, you took *Lear*, in which there is indeed a great deal that is imperfect; you should have taken *Hamlet*, or *Julius Caesar*, or *Macbeth*. And if I had taken *Macbeth* or *Hamlet*, they'd would have said, why didn't you take *Lear*?" (234).

32. This persuasive thesis belongs to Philip Rogers, who, in "Tolstoy's Hamlet," *TSJ* 5 (1992): 55–65, reexamines all the documents and pushes Breitburg's conclusions further. Rogers notes that "Hamlet has taken the 'words, words, words' out of Tolstoy's mouth . . . and both the tone and content of Hamlet's indignation at the popular success of egregiously false art would not be out of place in *What Is Art?*" (59).

33. In this draft, Tolstoy reprimands Turgenev, who, in his memoirs, had praised as exemplary of compact verbal onstage horror that scene in *Macbeth* (4.3:248–50) where Macduff hears of the slaughter of his family: "My children too? My wife killed too?" "Yes, those words are good, that's true," Tolstoy writes, "but Turgenev forgot to say that [Macduff] does not limit himself to those words, he goes on to speak an entire long, false, pompous monologue." In not sensing and not censoring what was bad, Turgenev, too, had fallen prey to "suggestion," for "this is how Shakespeare is handled even by people who are gifted by aesthetic feeling" (Leo Tolstoy, "Varianty k stat'e 'O Shekspire i o drame' № 17 [ruk. № 11]" [From variants of the essay 'On Shakespeare and on drama.' Variant

no. 17 [manuscript no. 11]; 35:571–72). What hope was there for the ungifted? Throughout his rebuttal, Tolstoy mistakenly calls Macduff "Duncan."

34. Shaw, *Collected Letters*, 551–52.

35. The edited document appears as "Letter from G. Bernard Shaw (Extracts)," in *TonSh*, 166–69.

36. The story of subsequent letters was first told in full in S. Breitburg, "B. Shou v spore s Tolstym o Shekspire (po neizdannym istochnikam)" [B. Shaw's quarrel with Tolstoy over Shakespeare (from unpublished sources)], in *L. N. Tolstoy (Part II)*, vols. 37–38 of *Literaturnoe Nasledstvo* [Literary Heritage], ed. P. I. Lebedev-Polyanskii et al., 617–32 (Moscow: Nauka, 1939); quotes are on 624 and 627. This November 1905 letter from Shaw to Tolstoy was, if not repressed, at least not featured by Soviet-era Tolstoy scholars. Breitburg's jubilee essay in 1939 (Shakespeare's 375th birthday) might have been motivated by an attempt to defend Shakespeare, a heavily sponsored playwright in Stalinist Russia, against Tolstoy's attack—using Shaw's second letter to Chertkov (November 3, 1905, unpublished) as an indirect means of reprimanding one canonized figure (Tolstoy) in the just interests of another. The task was facilitated by Chertkov's death in 1936 at age eighty-two.

37. "Blunders" is in English in the text. This final letter was received by Chertkov on December 19. All excerpts cited from archival correspondence are in Breitburg, "B. Shou v spore s Tolstym," 630–31. The November 1905 letter does not appear in Shaw's published collected correspondence nor in Tolstoy's *Jubilee* collected works.

38. Viktor Shklovsky, "Stat'ia Tolstogo 'O Shekspire i o drame' kak rezul'tat stolknoveniia dvukh poetik" [Tolstoy's essay "On Shakespeare and on drama" as the result of a clash of two (types of) poetics], in *Khudozhestvennaia proza: Razmyshleniia i razbory* [Artistic prose: Reflections and analyses], 124–36 (Moscow: Sovetskii pisatel', 1959), 124, 125, 129.

39. Shaw makes this statement in a review (February 2, 1895) of *All's Well That Ends Well* performed by the Irving Dramatic Club; see Wilson, *Shaw on Shakespeare*, 9.

40. See headnote to letter 557, "To Bernard Shaw" (August 17, 1908), in *TL*, 2:677. The letter itself follows on pages 677–79. It was composed by Tolstoy in Russian (78:201–2) and translated for Shaw by Chertkov. Tolstoy tries hard to recruit Shaw for his own value system—or rather, to define him as already present in it. At several points he unapologetically translates a bit of the Shaw he approves of into his own more theistic framework: for example, Don Juan's desire to "discover the inner will of the world" is, Tolstoy confides to Shaw, "in my language to recognize the will of God."

41. Tolstoy read the play in English, but it was quickly translated, appearing as *Probuzhdeniia Blanko Poznet* in two Russian versions the year of Tolstoy's death: translated by O. Vsevolodskii in volume 6 of V. M. Sablin's 1910 edition

of G. B. Shaw and by L. Nikiforov in a Moscow anthology in 1910. It was first performed in 1921 in the Moscow cabaret Letuchaia Mysh' (The Bat) under the title *Sud lincha* (Lynch court). See commentary in Bernard Shou, *Polnoe sobranie p'es v 6 tomakh* [Complete plays in six volumes] (Leningrad: Iskusstvo, 1979), 3:643.

42. The seventy-page preface to *Blanco Posnet*, written in July 1910, was devoted to the recent censorship scandal (1908–9). Only at the end do we learn that *Posnet* had been denied a license for London theaters (its premiere took place at the Abbey Theatre in Dublin on August 25, 1909). Shaw had long been on the warpath against the Examiner of Plays, part of the Lord Chamberlain's Office and the seat of British licensing. That three of his plays were refused a license was an important reason why Shaw, in the 1890s, spearheaded a drive to publish plays in book form and to found the Stage Society (1899), whose performances were not subject to formal censorship. For this story, see chapters 3 and 5 in Woodfield, *English Theatre in Transition*.

43. Shaw, *Collected Letters*, 900.

44. Bernard Shaw, *The Shewing-Up of Blanco Posnet*, in *Complete Plays*, 5:245–76. The "Preface" and "Rejected Statement" (against the London theatrical censorship and licensing bureau) take up more than twice as many pages as the playlet, 171–243.

45. Tolstoy takes issue with Shaw, but let me do so as well. In my view, it is incorrect to suggest that these "two drunkards wallowing in the straw" raise each other up. In that scene, Mitrich is talking about—or better, bragging about—something different. Nikita did not need his particular story. He did not even grasp what Mitrich was saying except for the bold phrase "Why should I be afraid of them? . . . as soon as you fear men, then the hoofed one just collars you and pushes you where he likes." Nikita did not need Mitrich any more than Prince Nekhliudov from Tolstoy's *Resurrection* needed precisely Katiusha Maslova. Nikita needed the moment. Life had long been preparing him for this spiritual turn—and Tolstoy had been preparing his audience for it. Nikita was on the brink of repentance. He had come to hate his way of life, he wanted to hang himself (as he confesses at the wedding to Marinka, earlier seduced by him), and only accidentally was it Mitrich who "opened up the path." Nikita heard what he needed to hear. This surely is the meaning behind Akim's outburst at the police, "Don't talk, what do you mean, 'dictments [*akhty*]! Here God's work is being done . . . A man is confessing, I mean! And you, what d'ye call it . . . 'ditements!" When the soul is ready, anything will prompt its resurrection, and then we must simply get out of God's way. This truth might be the positive reverse side of the dark epigraph to Tolstoy's play: "If a claw is caught, the whole bird is lost [*Kogotok uviaz, vsei ptichke propast'*]." If the bird is ready to break free, nothing will hinder its flight.

46. Tolstoy's comments to Shaw about "hypocrisy" suggest the difference

between an Anglo-Saxon Protestant "preacher" of the sort often featured by Shaw (Anthony Anderson in *The Devil's Disciple* or James Morrell in *Candida*) and Tolstoy's own deeply religious, noninstitutional Christian model. Shaw's preacher goes to church on Sunday and does good works during the week; Tolstoy's true "preacher" could never be a "man of the cloth" but only a "righteous person" (*pravednik*). Judging from Tolstoy's mature examples of this type (most famously Father Sergius), the more righteous they become, the less they talk.

47. See Tolstoy's letter to P. M. Svobodin (Kozienko) of March 5, 1887 (64:24).

48. For this story, see T. F. Evans, "Myopia or Utopia? Shaw in Russia," in *Shaw Abroad*, ed. Rodelle Weintraub, 135–45 (State College: Pennsylvania State University Press, 1985). For a devastating eightieth-anniversary retrospective of Shaw's fascination with tyrants, see the dean of American Shaw scholars, Stanley Weintraub, "Shaw and the Strongman: GBS's Dealings with Dictators on Stage and in Reality," *Times Literary Supplement*, July 29, 2011, 13–15.

49. *Complete Plays*, 5:236.

50. See Larry D. Bouchard, *Theater and Integrity: Emptying Selves in Drama, Ethics, and Religion* (Evanston, Ill.: Northwestern University Press, 2011).

Epilogue

What Can We, in the Twenty-First Century, Learn from Tolstoy? Ruminations on Reading All Ninety Volumes of *The Jubilee* Edition of Tolstoy's *Complete Works*; . . . and a Bit about Pigeons, Cookies and Milk, and Snails . . .

WHEN I WAS ASKED to contribute to a volume on the topic of Tolstoy in the twenty-first century, I decided that in order to be thorough I would have to first read all ninety volumes of Tolstoy's writings. Given the busyness of life and the capacity—at least *my* capacity—for figuring that I can get inhuman amounts of work done, since the deadline is so far in the future, I, of course, did not come even close to reading all ninety volumes. (By the way, I recently read that those ninety volumes weigh the same as a newborn beluga whale.[1] [I didn't test the hypothesis.])

I could have changed the title of my essay. I did not, because I realized that *not* having attained my goal—to read *all* those volumes—was actually *very* Tolstoyan. How many times do we read in his diary about the tasks he sets himself, the rules he lists to resolve to do something, and then how many times do we read that he has failed to do so? He strives for perfection. He admits that he is imperfect. He tortures himself for his transgressions. We, in the twenty-first century, can learn that it's okay to acknowledge that we are but imperfect human beings. We don't have to torment ourselves. We can accept our all-too-imperfect selves.

The way I chose what to read is also Tolstoyan. I was guided by what he talks about in, for example, *War and Peace*, and in many other places— that to truly understand and depict life, one has to avoid systems. So my journey through those Tolstoy volumes was random, not systematic. I chose what I did by chance. After all, my last name is Chances.

The first part of my title is also not 100 percent accurate, but I left that intact as well. For it is often not only what we in the twenty-first century can learn from Tolstoy but also what we in *any* era can learn.

Still having to do with the title of my essay, I added a subtitle, "A Bit about Pigeons, Cookies and Milk, and Snails." For now, I won't explain.

One more thing before I begin—

In reflecting upon the topic of our volume, I set myself the task of reading Tolstoy with only this theme in mind: Tolstoy's legacy in the twenty-first century. I decided, too, to try to approach the task of reading Tolstoy not as a literary scholar but as one person, one individual reader reading these writings.

First of all, a bit about Tolstoy's legacy, and then I'll turn to what we can learn from Tolstoy. We can think of many people, from the late nineteenth century to the present, who have been powerfully influenced by Tolstoy. I'll name but a very few—for example, Chekhov, from the beginning of his career to the end. For instance, as we know, his short story "Lady with a Dog" has been interpreted as a response to *Anna Karenina*. Solzhenitsyn's *August 1914* has been said to be modeled on *War and Peace*. In Andrei Bitov's novel, *Pushkin House*, the narrator wonders why the third-person so-called objective narration of realist novels like Tolstoy's is called realist: "Where [was —E.C.] the author hiding when he spied on the scene that he describes [? —E.C.]." In the same passage, he writes, "But only Lev Tolstoy has permitted himself to write from God's standpoint, and we won't even discuss here the extent of his competence in those efforts. Especially since our hero was named Lev in his honor, whether by us or by his parents . . ."[2] The character, Lev Nikolaevich, is also the name, of course, of the main character in Dostoevsky's *The Idiot*.

Margaret Mitchell's Pulitzer Prize–winning 1936 novel, *Gone with the Wind*, is said to have been similar to Tolstoy's *War and Peace* in its intertwining of personal fates with the momentous events of war and dislocation. Pablo Neruda wrote that Russian writers Dostoevsky, Tolstoy, and Chekhov were important to him throughout his life.[3] We can see that same vitality of *this* world that we see in Tolstoy's descriptions in, for example, Neruda's "Ode to Things." Here are a few lines from the beginning of the poem:

> I have a crazy,
> crazy love of things.
> I like pliers,
> and scissors.
> I love
> cups,
> rings,

and bowls—
not to speak, of course,
of hats.
I love all things,
not just
the grandest,
also
the infinite-
ly
small—
thimbles,
spurs,
plates,
and flower vases.[4]

Nobel Prize laureate Romain Rolland, author of *Jean-Christophe*, was inspired by Tolstoy, as was Proust, as was Irène Némirovsky. Her recently discovered novel *Suite française* documents the fates of individuals against the backdrop of occupied France in World War II. Cuban-American playwright Nilo Cruz, in his 2002 play, *Anna in the Tropics*, bases his characters on those in *Anna Karenina*. Through that technique, he offers commentary on the novel and commentary on the importance of books in the present age.[5]

Some of Woody Allen's works bear the imprint of Russian literature. There is the film *Love and Death* (1975), an obvious takeoff on Tolstoy's *War and Peace*, the novel, and on Sergey Bondarchuk's film, *War and Peace* (1966–67). Not so obvious is Woody Allen's indebtedness to Tolstoy in the film *Hannah and Her Sisters* (1986), which focuses on Manhattan life. Allen has acknowledged that the structure of *Anna Karenina* influenced the structure of his film, with one line exploring a man's search for meaning and one line dealing with adultery.[6]

Oprah Winfrey chose *Anna Karenina* as a selection for her Book Club. Millions of people read the novel, and at the time *Anna Karenina* was on the *New York Times* best-seller list. During the autumn of 2010, Oprah Winfrey announced that a novel that had just come out, Jonathan Franzen's *Freedom*, would be a selection of her Book Club. That novel, too, has connections to Tolstoy. One character, Patty, reads *War and Peace* and thinks about *its* characters in relation to the people in her life. The structure of Franzen's novel as a whole, in certain ways, resembles that of *War and Peace*—the fates of personal lives against the canvas of societal dislocation. Like Tolstoy, Franzen shows the discrepancy between the false surface glitter of people's lives and the reality beyond and beneath the surface. Like Tolstoy, he exposes the lies that live behind the veneer of convention.[7] Reviews of the Franzen book have pointed out similarities to *War and Peace*. In fact, the review in the *New York Times Book Review* was titled "Peace and War."[8]

But there is something more, in Franzen's book, that both points out certain roots in *War and Peace* and starkly highlights the differences between the two books. In Tolstoy's novel, no matter how devastating the life events—the mortal wounds and the blood and violence on the battle-field; the collapse of Natasha's happiness after her ill-fated infatuation with Anatole Kuragin; the necessity of people to flee from their Moscow homes when the French enter the city in 1812; Pierre's time as a prisoner of war—no matter how devastating all these things and many more, there is very often, intertwined, a sense of the beauty and wonder of life, even during some of those most horrible and horrific moments. (I'll return to this point a bit later.)

Life, for Tolstoy, is whole. It includes everything, ugliness and beauty, death and birth, despair and hope. This is not true in the Franzen novel. Contemporary American society is described primarily with a focus on the crass and ugly. Faulty plumbing causes a bathtub to fill with sewage. Cats vomit.

Here are two more examples of Tolstoy's legacy. One is the 1996 Russian novel by Vasilii Staroi, *P'er i Natasha* (*Pierre and Natasha*), which carries Tolstoy's major characters' fates to 1828, when, on August 28 (that, of course, is when Tolstoy was born), Nicholas Rostov's wife, Marya, gives birth to a son, Lev Nikolaevich. (This is, of course, Tolstoy's name.)[9] And in an instance of the interweaving of influences, it is said that the author of *Pierre and Natasha* got the idea of writing his book from the novel *Scarlett*, which had been written as a sequel to *Gone with the Wind*.[10] Mitchell's novel was very popular in the Soviet Union.

And finally, there is the example of a twenty-first-century Russian work, *Anna Karenina*, a comic book created by Katya Metelitsa, a script-writer, and Valery Kachaev and Igor Sapozhkov, who are illustrators.[11] The captions, in the original, are in Russian and in English. Following are a few of those captions (with their page numbers in brackets):

1. "For Levin, it was as easy to recognize Kitty in this crowd as if she was a rose among nettles" [14]. This is the scene of the skating rink near the beginning of Tolstoy's novel. In the twenty-first-century comic-book version, ads bedeck the walls of the skating rink.

2. In one frame, Vronsky is reading *Cosmopolitan* magazine [23].

3. Vronsky arrives at the racetrack in a fancy car, with the license plate including the letters FR-FR, a reference, of course, to his horse, Frou-Frou [29].

4. In another frame, Anna has texted Vronsky, "I'm pregnant. See you after the races [Ia beremenna. Uvidimsia posle skachek]" [34].

5. Anna arrives at the station with her little red bag. The steam engine is called *Lev Tolstoy* [75].

6. In one of the frames, one sees empty soda cans on the track. One also sees a reference to *Trainspotting*, a 1990s book and movie about Edinburgh heroin addicts [85].[12]

The examples of Tolstoy's legacy that I have mentioned are only a very few responses. There are, of course, many more, in many fields—Gandhi, Thomas Mann, the Dukhobors, and so forth. But what about the response of the individual reader? In the rest of my essay, I shall focus on the experience of one reader—me—as I pondered the question of what we can learn from Tolstoy.

I'll start with something that we all know we *shouldn't* learn from him, and that is his attitude toward women. In his very earliest writings—his diary entries of 1847, when he was nineteen years old, while he was in the hospital being treated for venereal disease—he disparaged women. Still intending to become a lawyer, he was writing a critique of Catherine the Great's *Instruction*. About Catherine the Great, he writes (on March 18 of that year), "However great a woman's mind may be, you will always find in its manifestations a certain pettiness and inconsistency" (*TD*, 1:4). On June 14 he wrote, "Who is to blame for the fact that we lose our innate feelings of boldness, resolution, judiciousness, justice, etc., if not women? A woman is more receptive than a man, and therefore women were better than us in virtuous ages; but in the present depraved and corrupt age they are worse than us" (*TD*, 1:12). As we know, Tolstoy's ideal woman, in *War and Peace* and *Anna Karenina*, is the devoted wife and mother, whose only aspirations are to be a devoted wife and mother. And of course, Tolstoy kills off the beautiful, passionate Anna Karenina, and in his later years he speaks of women as the devil.

Paradoxically, it is equally important to remember that in his fiction, Tolstoy created magnificent, vibrant, sensitive portraits of women. Think, for example, of Anna Karenina and Dolly Oblonsky in *Anna Karenina*, and of Natasha Rostova and Princess Marya in *War and Peace*. Think of Tolstoy's nuanced portrayals of women's interrelationships with their children, such as Dolly's involvement with her children, or Natasha's and Kitty's concern for their children, or Anna's visit to Seriozha on his birthday.

What we *can* learn from him, here, as in so many aspects of his life and works, is the contradictory nature of human life. This is brought out, for example, in his constant striving for perfection, his constant striving to be a good and moral person, and his constant acknowledgments that he has fallen short. We see this, for example, in his diaries, again, from his earliest entries.

He makes rules for himself, and he breaks them. The first (March 24, 1847) is, "What is required to be carried out without fail, carry out in spite of everything" (*TD*, 1:7). Three weeks later (April 18), he writes, "I wrote down a list of rules . . . and wanted to follow them all, but I wasn't strong enough to do so" (*TD*, 1:11). This pattern continued throughout his life.

Yet the admirable thing is that Tolstoy did not give up. And that, too, is something that we can learn. Even near the end of his life, he continued to try to improve himself. Thus, in 1903, as a seventy-five-year-old man, he compiled a book of moral sayings, *Sayings by Wise People for Every Day, Compiled by L. N. Tolstoy*, with teachings for helping people, and himself, to live a moral life. Tolstoy had been thinking of compiling such a book for the previous thirty years.[13]

He included sayings from ancient times on, from many different cultures. We read, for example, Laozi, Confucius, the Buddhist *Dhammapada*, Arabic proverbs, the Gospel of Saint Matthew, John Ruskin, Epictetus, Marcus Aurelius, Dostoevsky, Goncharov, and even an occasional saying written by Tolstoy. He included one—or sometimes two or three—sayings per day for an entire year. He said that he hoped that people would find these pieces of wisdom edifying. He also said that he himself found that by reading them, he, too, was helped in improving his life. One example is from Epictetus: if you find yourself getting upset about some worldly matter, think about the fact that you will die, and the thing that was upsetting you will no longer seem important.[14]

What else can we learn by reading Tolstoy? One thing, among the many, many others, struck me as I reread *War and Peace* in preparation for writing this essay, and that is Tolstoy's attention to the aging process. In contemporary American society, older people are all but invisible. Visually, one has only to think of TV, where, with the exception of reruns of *The Golden Girls* and, more recently, *Hot in Cleveland* (2010–15), starring the then eighty-eight to ninety-three-year-old Betty White as Elka Ostrovsky, about the only people above forty-five whom one sees (and I only slightly exaggerate) are in ads for sexual-performance-enhancing drugs.

As a person, Tolstoy maintained his intellectual vitality, even as he was physically failing. Until the end of his life, he kept growing intellectually, kept up his spiritual searches, continued offering his views on morality, science, the arts, and politics. Even in his pre-1880 fiction, he includes older people. Just as he presents many perspectives on other aspects of life, so, too, does he do so in his passages about older people. As we know, he gives us all of life, from the very young—the newborn baby, Levin's son, and the newborn calf of Pava the cow, in *Anna Karenina*—to children (Nikolai, in *Childhood*; Anna's and Karenin's son, Seriozha), to the old.

In *War and Peace*, we see all of life—the very young, the very old, and everyone in between. In that novel, we see different aspects of old age, and we see different attitudes, on the part of the young, toward old age. Thus, as we know, Tolstoy respects the wisdom and experience that come with age. We see this, of course, in his depiction of Kutuzov, who understands, from long life experience, when it makes sense *not* to take action. For example, in the case of Austerlitz, he knows that the battle will be lost. In the case of the French retreat from Moscow, he understands the wisdom of *not* attacking the French army, even though by not doing so, he incurs the wrath of many of the Russian political and military authorities. Yet Tolstoy also presents Kutuzov's last days, when he was no longer needed, for, Tolstoy writes, he had played his role.

We read about the attitude of the young toward the elderly in the scene of the dinner for Bagration in the English Club. Tolstoy writes,

> Most of those present were elderly, respected men with broad, self-confident faces, fat fingers, and resolute gestures and voices. This class of guests and members sat in certain habitual places and met in certain habitual groups. A minority of those present were casual guests—chiefly young men, among whom were Denisov, Rostov, and Dolokhov. The faces of these young people . . . bore that expression of condescending respect for their elders which seems to say to the older generation, "We are prepared to respect and honor you, but all the same remember that the future belongs to us."[15]

About the old Count Bolkonsky, Tolstoy writes that when he bent over Marya, "she felt herself surrounded on all sides by the acrid smell of old age and tobacco" (93). After the death of Count Rostov and Petya, Countess Rostova is described as merely going through the motions of life. She circumscribes her life more and more. Tolstoy describes the younger family members' response to her moving ever closer to death. He comments that the very young and very old are similar in the lack of

> external aims—only a need to exercise her various functions and inclinations was apparent . . . The old lady's condition was understood by the whole household though no one ever spoke of it . . . Only by a rare glance between Nicholas, Pierre, Natasha, and Countess Mary was the common understanding of her condition expressed. But those glances expressed something more: they said that she had played her part in life, that what they now saw was not her whole self, that we must all become like her, and that they were glad to yield to her, to restrain themselves for this once precious being formerly as full of life as themselves, but now so much to be pitied . . . Only the really heartless, the stupid ones of that household, and the little children failed to understand this and avoided her. (1291–92)

Tolstoy gives us different perspectives on the young, too. We glimpse the twenty-year-old Nicholas Rostov as he is returning home, in 1806, after having been at war. He is very much an adult. He has grown from his experience, yet the minute he gets near home, he is moved by memories of his childhood—seeing the familiar shop where he bought gingerbread. He is moved by seeing the familiar door handle and the familiar chipped cornice of the entrance door to his family's house (320). And once home, he sometimes slips into the familiar patterns of his prewar child life.

In terms of a young person's responding to an older person, near the beginning of the novel, we see the thirteen-year-old Natasha react not to the words of an adult, but to that visitor's tone of condescension toward a child. She asks Natasha whether her doll, Mimi, is "a relation of yours? A daughter, I suppose?" "Natasha did not like the visitor's tone of condescension to childish things. She did not reply, but looked at her seriously" (40).

We see the tragic foolhardiness—the lack of wisdom—of the puppy-like energy of the young Petya that leads to his death in battle. We see the positive effect of the young on others when Natasha's young energy has a positive effect on Andrei, in that famous scene where he overhears her as she is sitting in the window on a moonlit night.

And in the first epilogue to the novel, there is Andrei's son Nicholas's admiring attitude toward Pierre, his father's adult friend, precisely because Pierre had been his father's close friend.

The young horses in Tolstoy's short story, "Strider," make fun of the decrepit old horse "Strider" partly because of his old age and infirmity and partly because of what they think is his less-than-sterling pedigree. After he tells them the interesting story of his life, they begin to respect him. One of Tolstoy's short stories, in one of his *ABC Books* for children, is called "The Old Poplar Tree."[16] He tells the tale of looking out over a field and seeing a large old poplar tree that he thinks is stifling the growth of the young poplars that are in that same area. He starts to chop down the old tree in order, he believes, to allow the young trees to flourish. It turns out that when he examines the roots of the trees, after he has chopped down the old tree, he realizes that his assumptions had been wrong. It wasn't the old tree that had been sucking the life juices out of the young trees, but the other way around. The old tree had been nurturing, nourishing, and giving life to the young trees.[17]

What else can we, in the twenty-first century, learn from reading Tolstoy? Here is where pigeons come in. Have you ever noticed that pigeons are not what we call pigeon-toed—that is, with their feet pointed inward? Pigeons don't walk that way. All of us who have read Tolstoy are aware of his profound commitment to authenticity. Don't take things at face value, even if the entire world does so, we read in his works and in his pronouncements on religion and on war. See things as they really are. See for yourself what is really true. In other words, if pigeons aren't pigeon-toed, say so.

We all know about the Tolstoyan literary technique "defamiliariza-tion" (*ostranenie*), of making the world look strange by describing things in a fresh, new way rather than in a conventional, stereotypical way. We all know that we can think of entire characters, like Pierre and Levin, as being "defamiliarized," as breaking through the surface veils of conventionality to see and live the simple, spiritual truths of a life of authenticity. It therefore makes perfect sense to me that one of the stories that Tolstoy included in his 1872 *ABC Book* for children was Hans Christian Andersen's "The Emperor's New Clothes."[18] In 1907, he again paraphrased that story and planned to include it in a book, *Children's Cycle of Reading.*[19]

Tolstoy's attitude toward historians and toward history in *War and Peace* can also be seen as an example of "the emperor's new clothes," as de-familiarization. As we know, he writes that we shouldn't look at theories, we shouldn't look at the conventional views of war as constructed by historians. Instead, he says, look at the reality of all the little pieces of all people's ac-tions that go into any human endeavor.

In so many ways, Tolstoy reduces things to their essence. He strips away superfluous layers. In education, he urges teachers to teach students not on the basis of abstractions, in science or history, for instance, but on the basis of the teachers' experience. He writes that the most important thing is the teachers' love for what they are doing.[20] Tolstoy wanted to live according to the essence of Christianity rather than according to what the Church hier-archies taught. He was interested in the most basic questions—what is the meaning of life? Why are we here? His compilations of wise sayings attest to that same search for essence. (Were Tolstoy alive today, I wonder whether he would post these distilled bits and bytes of wisdom on a Tolstoy Twitter.)

What can we, in the twenty-first century, learn from his "emperor's new clothes" attitude toward life, and from his reduction of things to their essence? Or, in the following example, what *might* we have learned from Tolstoy (and, by the way, from Dostoevsky, too)? We now know that one of the major reasons for the 2008 financial crisis was that financiers relied too much on computer models—that is, on theories. As Paul Krugman and other economists have pointed out, the financiers didn't take into account the irrationality of human behavior. They didn't take the limitations of theory into account. Psychologist Daniel Kahneman and others have explored behavioral economics—that is, psychological factors in people's decision-making process. Had the financiers who were paying attention to computer models instead been reading Tolstoy, they might not have gotten us into our 2008 economic mess. (It is puzzling, isn't it, that some people question the role of the humanities. One might answer to the skeptics—one role of the humanities is to preserve common sense and wisdom.)

What else can we learn from Tolstoy? We know that Gandhi was profoundly influenced by his ideas of nonresistance to evil, of pacifism. As we know, Tolstoy believed in the connection of and the universality of different cultures and different religions.[21] In our world of people's intolerance toward the ideas of those whose beliefs differ from their own, in this world where human beings often ignore the needs of other forms of life—animals, plants—we can learn about the ties that bind one religion to another, one person to another, one species to another, one form of life to another. We can learn lessons from Tolstoy's reverence for life. We know that Tolstoy found commonalities in—was as interested in—the wisdom of ancient Greek philosophers, the ancient religious teachings of Confucius, the teachings of Zoroaster, Islam, the Talmud, Buddhism, Taoism, and Hinduism, as in Christianity. His way toward "Truth," of course, as his writings show, was through Christianity, through living the lessons of the Gospel.[22]

He was interested in searching for the Truth, with a capital *T*, in expressing truth in a way that could be understood by children and that could be reduced to the most basic terms. Thus, we have the peasant schools that he created; the *ABC* books that he compiled and wrote for children; and the simple truths about living, every day, a moral, good life in the sayings that he compiled and wrote.

In connection with that Tolstoyan principle of the universality of simple truths, I leave you with a couple of examples. I don't want to use railroad imagery, but these examples, I believe, *are* on parallel tracks with Tolstoy. The first is a 1989 book by the writer and former Unitarian minister Robert Fulghum that has been read by millions: *All I Really Need to Know I Learned in Kindergarten*. Fulghum considers himself a philosopher who, in his books, wants to make "elemental" truths accessible to the general public. In seminary, Tolstoy's teachings were part of the curriculum. Fulghum credits Tolstoy with his involvement in the civil rights movement and the anti–Vietnam War movement. It's not enough to have belief. One has a moral obligation to contribute.[23]

At the beginning of his book, Fulghum writes that all his life he was searching for Truth. He offers readers a credo—which he learned in kindergarten—for leading the good life at any age, young and old:

> Share everything.
> Play fair.
> Don't hit people.
> Put things back where you found them.
> Clean up your own mess.
> Don't take things that aren't yours.
> Say you're sorry when you hurt somebody.
> Wash your hands before you eat.
> . . .

Flush.

Warm cookies and cold milk are good for you.

Live a balanced life—learn some and think some and draw and paint
and sing and dance and play and work every day some.

Take a nap every afternoon.

When you go out into the world, watch out for traffic, hold hands,
and stick together.

Be aware of wonder. Remember the little seed in the Styrofoam cup:
The roots go down and the plant goes up and nobody really knows
how or why, but we are all like that.

Goldfish and hamsters and white mice and even the little seed in the
Styrofoam cup—they all die. So do we.

And then remember the Dick-and-Jane books and the first word you
learned—the biggest word of all—LOOK.[24]

The last thing in his credo is "Look." This means to pay attention, to be aware. This leads to my second example of being on parallel tracks with Tolstoy. As we know, in Tolstoy's writings there is so much life energy, awe at the wonder of life that comes from paying attention. There is a nonfiction book that came out in 2010, *The Sound of a Wild Snail Eating*,[25] by Elisabeth Tova Bailey. Bailey is a writer from Maine with a debilitating chronic illness of the autonomic nervous system (autoimmune dysautonomia). She was so sick that she could do nothing but lie in bed. A friend gave her a vase of violets with a woodland snail. Little by little, when she was too sick to do anything else, Bailey started observing and listening to the movements of the snail as it slowly climbed out of the vase, as it ate tiny holes in an envelope on Bailey's night table, as it munched a violet leaf, as it extended its tiny tentacles to make its nocturnal explorations farther and farther away from the vase, as by day it slept under a violet blossom.

The snail became Bailey's companion during sleepless nights. She shared, with the snail, a journey toward healing. Each helped the other. From Bailey, the tiny snail, torn away from its forest habitat, received sustenance—leaves, mushroom slices, and a terrarium with moss. From the snail, Bailey derived the comfort of knowing that she was not the only slow being, and that healing can take place at a snail's place.

Bailey's insights and her appreciation of life, of the bond between her and her snail companion, came from her capacity to look, to observe, to pay attention, to be aware of life in this moment.

What reading Tolstoy gave me is a heightened sense of appreciation for life, in all its multifarious, miraculous shapes and forms. It gave me a heightened sense of appreciating what is important in life. It gave me a heightened sense of the divinity—however each individual may define that word—encapsulated in every moment of life. It gave me a renewed sense of awe at life.

I think, for example, of a passage in *Anna Karenina*, a few pages after Kitty has made clear to Levin that she loves him. Tolstoy writes,

And what he then saw he never saw again. Two children going to school, some pigeons that flew down from the roof [Pigeons again! —E.C.], and a few loaves put outside a baker's window by an invisible hand touched him particularly. These loaves, the pigeons, and the two boys seemed creatures not of this earth. It all happened at the same time; one of the boys ran after a pigeon and looked smilingly up at Levin; the pigeon flapped its wings and fluttered up, glittering in the sunshine amid the snow-dust that trembled in the air; from the window came the scent of fresh-baked bread and the loaves were put out. All these things were so unusually beautiful that Levin laughed and cried with joy.[26]

And remember, Levin, in that novel, comes to the conclusion that the meaning of life is life itself. Tolstoy lived life *fully*, . . . and so should we . . .

NOTES

1. Elif Batuman, *The Possessed: Adventures with Russian Books and the People Who Read Them* (New York: Farrar, Straus and Giroux, 2010), 27. Batuman writes, "I brought my bathroom scale to the library and weighed it [the Tolstoy volumes —E.C.], ten volumes at a time."

2. Andrei Bitov, *Pushkin House*, trans. Susan Brownsberger (Ann Arbor, Mich.: Ardis, 1990), 56–57.

3. Neruda wrote, "I can say that Gabriela [Mistral —E.C.] introduced me to the dark and terrifying vision of the Russian novelists and that Tolstoy, Dostoevsky, and Chekhov soon occupied a special place deep within me. They are with me still" (Pablo Neruda, *Memoirs*, trans. Hardie St. Martin [New York: Farrar, Straus and Giroux, 2001], 210).

4. Pablo Neruda, "Ode to Things" [Oda a las cosas], in *Odes to Common Things*, trans. Ken Krabbenhoft (Boston: Little, Brown, 1994), 10–11.

5. Ellen Chances, "Tolstoy in the Tropics: The Importance of Nineteenth-Century Russian Literature in Twenty-First-Century Cuban-American Drama," in *Word, Music, History: A Festschrift for Caryl Emerson*, ed. Lazar Fleishman, Gabriella Safran, and Michael Wachtel, 2 vols. (Oakland, Calif.: Stanford Slavic Studies, 2005), 2:742–51.

6. Ellen Chances, "Moscow Meets Manhattan: The Russian Soul of Woody Allen's Films," *American Studies International* 30, no. 1 (April 1992): 65–77.

7. Jonathan Franzen, *Freedom* (New York: Farrar, Straus and Giroux, 2010).

8. Sam Tanenhaus, "Peace and War," *New York Times Book Review*, August 29, 2010, 9–11.

9. Vasilii Staroi, *P'er i Natasha: Prodolzhenie romana L. N. Tolstogo "Voina i mir"* [Pierre and Natasha: The continuation of L. N. Tolstoy's novel *War and Peace*] (Moscow: Vagrius, 1996).

10. Alexandra Ripley, *Scarlett* (New York: Warner Books, 1991).

11. Katya Metelitsa (script), Valery Kachaev and Igor Sapozhkov (illustrations), *Anna Karenina L'va Tolstogo* (Moscow: Mir novykh russkikh, 2000).

12. All citations are to *Anna Karenina L'va Tolstogo*.

13. S. M. Breitburg, "Predislovie k tridtsat' deviatomu-sorok vtorumu tomam" [Preface to volumes thirty-nine through forty-two]. The preface was placed at the beginning of volume 39 of *The Jubilee*, which was published in 1956 and overseen by V. S. Mishin, 39: v–xxxviii. See especially Breitburg, "Predislovie," xx, xxvii, xxviii.

14. Leo Tolstoy, "Mysli mudrykh liudei na kazhdyi den': Sobrany L. N. Tolstym" [Sayings by wise people for every day, compiled by L. N. Tolstoy] (1903). The work was published in 1956 in *The Jubilee*, volume 40, overseen by N. N. Gusev and V. S. Mishin, pages 67–216.

15. Leo Tolstoy, *War and Peace*, trans. Louise Maude and Aylmer Maude, ed. George Gibian (New York: Norton, 1966), 331. In the text of my chapter, subsequent citations of page numbers to this work appear in parentheses immediately following the quotation.

16. Tolstoy compiled many different versions of literacy manuals and readers, for children in general, and in addition, specifically, for peasant children. The most well-known ones were collected in *Azbuka* [The ABC] (1871–72), which consisted of four separate books with many additional subdivisions; *Novaia azbuka* [The New ABC] (1874–75), which was one volume of about a hundred pages; and *Russkie knigi dlia chteniia* [Russian books for reading], four books compiled in 1875, with the fourth revised by Tolstoy in 1885. There are also extremely interesting plans, drafts, and variants of the above ABCs and readers, all collected and published in 1957 in *The Jubilee*, volumes 21 and 22, overseen by V. S. Spiridonov and V. S. Mishin. Subsequent citations will be to these volumes, with the title of the specific Tolstoy fable, story, or educational work under discussion. For *Azbuka*, see 22:6–787; for *Novaia azbuka* and *Russkie knigi dlia chteniia*, 21:2–100 and 102–329, respectively. For plans and variants, see 21: 427–43.

17. Leo Tolstoy, "Staryi topol'," (in book 4 of *Azbuka*), published in volume 22 of *The Jubilee*, pages 69–70. For V. S. Spiridonov's and V. S. Mishin's editorial commentary, see pages 629 and 630, respectively. Quite interestingly for us, in recent research, Peter Wohlleben, a contemporary German specialist on trees,

writes about the fact that trees live in social communities and nurture one another. See Peter Wohlleben, *The Hidden Life of Trees*, trans. Jane Billinghurst (Vancouver, Can.: Greystone Books, 2016).

18. Leo Tolstoy, "Tsarskoe novoe plat'e," in book 4 of *Azbuka*, 22:15–16, 575–76.

19. Leo Tolstoy, "Tsarskoe novoe plat'e," in *Rasskazy dlia 'Detskogo Kruga chteniia'* [Stories for 'The Cycle of Reading for Children']; 40:403. On the history of the writing of this and other stories, see 40:507–13.

20. Leo Tolstoy, "Obshchie zamechaniia dlia uchitelia" [General observations for the teacher], in book 1 of *Azbuka*, 22:180–85.

21. D. Moulin, "Tolstoy, Universalism and the World Religions," *Journal of Ecclesiastical History* 68, no. 1 (2017): 570–87.

22. On Tolstoy's religiosity, see, for example, Richard F. Gustafson, *Leo Tolstoy: Resident and Stranger* (Princeton, N.J.: Princeton University Press, 1986), and Inessa Medzhibovskaya, *Tolstoy and the Religious Culture of His Time: A Biography of a Long Conversion, 1845–1887* (Lanham, Md.: Lexington Books, 2008).

23. Ellen Chances and Robert Fulghum telephone conversation, New York, Utah, October 9, 2010.

24. Robert Fulghum, *All I Really Need to Know I Learned in Kindergarten: Uncommon Thoughts and Common Things* (New York: Villard Books, 1989), 6–7.

Fulghum's relationship to Tolstoy is more than a case of parallel tracks, as Fulghum pointed out, in both the October 9, 2010, telephone conversation and in an October 8, 2010, email letter to Chances. In his email letter, he stated that he had "read the great Tolstoy novels at least twice." Fulghum also wrote, in the same email, that Tolstoy was part of the curriculum when he was in the seminary. Fulghum remarked, "It never occurred to me that the kindergarten piece was directly influenced by Tolstoy, but surely my experience with his thought affected my own in subtle ways."

25. Elisabeth Tova Bailey, *The Sound of a Wild Snail Eating* (Chapel Hill, N.C.: Algonquin Books, 2010).

26. Leo Tolstoy, *Anna Karenina*, trans. Louise Maude and Aylmer Maude, ed. and trans. George Gibian (New York: Norton, 1995), 367.

Contributors

Jeffrey Brooks is a professor of history at Johns Hopkins University. He is the author of *When Russia Learned to Read: Literacy and Popular Literature, 1861–1917*, which was awarded the Wayne S. Vucinich Book Prize of the American Association for the Advancement of Slavic Studies in 1985; *Thank You, Comrade Stalin! Soviet Public Culture from Revolution to Cold War*; and, with Georgiy Chernyavskiy, *Lenin and the Making of the Soviet State: A Brief History with Documents*; as well as many essays on Russian history, culture, and politics. His current research and writing focus on Russian culture, high and low, from 1850 to 1950.

Ellen Chances is a professor of Russian literature at Princeton University. She is the author of the first book on Bitov's works, *Andrei Bitov: The Ecology of Inspiration*, which was translated into Russian in 2007. Her other publications include *Conformity's Children: An Approach to the Superfluous Man in Russian Literature* and dozens of articles. She is currently at work on a book on Bitov's most recent writings. Chances's scholarly interests include the nineteenth-, twentieth-, and twenty-first-century Russian novel; Chekhov; Dostoevsky; Kharms; journalism; the ethical dimensions of contemporary Russian cinema; and comparative Russian and American literature and culture. She also writes essays, memoir, fiction, and poetry.

Michael A. Denner is a professor of Russian, East European, and Eurasian studies and director of the University Honors Program at Stetson University. He has been the editor of *Tolstoy Studies Journal* and is the coeditor of *Tolstoy on Screen* (Northwestern, 2014). He is also the cotranslator of Tolstoy's *On Life* (Northwestern, 2019) and author of numerous essays and chapters on Tolstoy.

Caryl Emerson is A. Watson Armour III University Professor Emeritus of Slavic Languages and Literatures at Princeton University. Her work focuses on the Russian classics (Pushkin, Tolstoy, and Dostoevsky), Mikhail Bakhtin,

Russian music (especially opera), Soviet-era theater, and the Russian modernist Sigizmund Krzhizhanovsky.

Stephen Halliwell is a professor of Greek and Wardlaw Professor of Classics at the University of St Andrews in Scotland. His intellectual interests center on ancient Greek philosophical theories of poetry and art, especially those of Plato and Aristotle, and their relationship to the later history of aesthetics. His books include *The Aesthetics of Mimesis: Ancient Texts and Modern Problems*, winner of the Premio Europeo d'Estetica (2008); *Greek Laughter: A Study of Cultural Psychology from Homer to Early Christianity*, winner of the Criticos Prize (2008); and *Between Ecstasy and Truth: Interpretations of Greek Poetics from Homer to Longinus*. He is a fellow of both the British Academy and the Royal Society of Edinburgh.

Jeff Love is Research Professor of German and Russian at Clemson University. He has published two books on Tolstoy, *The Overcoming of History in "War and Peace"* and *Tolstoy: A Guide for the Perplexed*. He is also the cotranslator of *Schelling's Philosophical Investigations into the Essence of Human Freedom*, coeditor of *Nietzsche and Dostoevsky: Philosophy, Morality, Tragedy*, and editor of *Heidegger in Russian and Eastern Europe*. His most recent book is *The Black Circle: A Life of Alexandre Kojève* (2018).

Inessa Medzhibovskaya is an associate professor of liberal studies and literature at Eugene Lang College of Liberal Arts and at The New School for Social Research in New York City. She is the author of *Tolstoy and the Religious Culture of His Time*, a study in the genre of a long intellectual biography, and has published more than fifty journal essays and book chapters on Russian authors and philosophers, ideology and education, and the interplay of philosophy, religion, politics, and literary aesthetics. She is the editor and cotranslator of Tolstoy's *On Life: A Critical Edition* (Northwestern, 2019), an editor of the volume *A Critical Guide to Tolstoy's "On Life"* (book imprint of the North American Tolstoy Society, 2018), and is completing a new monograph, *Tolstoy and the Fates of the Twentieth Century*. She is also at work preparing the first multivolume anthology of Tolstoy's thought in English.

Daniel Moulin-Stożek is a research fellow at the Jubilee Centre for Character and Virtues at the University of Birmingham, England. He is the author of *Leo Tolstoy* in the Bloomsbury Library of Educational Thought series and has written many essays in the fields of education and religion.

Vladimir M. Paperni is a representative of the renowned Tartu school of semiotics. Since 1991, he has taught Russian literature and literary theory at the University of Haifa in Israel. Paperni is the author of more than one hundred scholarly works on the history and poetics of Russian literature, Russian religious thought (especially the philosophy of Tolstoy and Lev Shestov), and Russian-Jewish cultural interactions. He recently edited *Philosophical Writings of Lev Tolstoy* in Hebrew.